SEA ROUTES (THICKNESS OF LINE INDICATES
COMPARATIVE WEIGHT OF TRAFFIC)

U-BOATS

SURFACE RAIDERS

WARSHIPS · AT DATES SHOWN

AUXILIARY CRUISERS

GERMAN AIR ATTACKS

ALLIED AIR COVER ZONES BY 1944

AXIS AND AXIS OCCUPIED TERRITORIES

CALCUTTA

BOMBAY

COLOMBO

Battle of Midway,
✕ 4 June 1942

Area of Japanese expansion

Japanese
attacks from
Dec 1941

✕ Battle of the Coral Sea,
7-8 May 1942

PERTH

SYDNEY

AUCKLAND

1939-44

MERCATOR PROJECTION

THE BATTLE OF THE ATLANTIC

U124: Rendezvousing with the battleship
Gneisenau off the Azores on 10 March 1941

Terry Hughes and John Costello

THE BATTLE OF THE ATLANTIC

The Dial Press/James Wade New York

The authors would like to thank the following photographers and organisations who have supplied photographs for this book:

Bundesarchiv, Koblenz, Germany, Page 2, 6 (top), 43, 50–51, 62, 64–65, 72–73, 82, 83, 88–89, 92–93 (bottom), 96 (left & right), 97–98, 97 (left & right), 102–103, 106–107 (top, centre & bottom), 104, 111, 114–115, 124–125 (top & bottom), 134, 146, 150 (top), 158–159 (bottom), 166, 167 (top & bottom), 170–171 (top), 178–179 (bottom), 190–191, 191 (both), 194 (bottom), 195, 202–203, 204, 205, 222–223, 228–229 (top), 242, 254–255, 256, 263, 270–271 (top), 290–291 (bottom), 293.
Imperial War Museum, London, 8–9, 17, 44, 46, 68–69, 81, 92 (top), 99, 100–101, 101, 105, 108, 112, 126 (inset), 132–133 (top), 136, 149 (top & centre), 150 (inset), 152, 156 (inset), 160–161, 172–173, 180–181, 192 (bottom), 212–213 (top), 224–225, 226–227, 232–233, 236, 240–241, 244–245, 250, 252–253, 258–259, 266, 270–271 (bottom), 273 (bottom), 278–279, 279, 280–281, 294–295 (bottom), 302–303.
Public Records Office, London, 109, 128, 132–133 (bottom), 137, 150 (bottom), 151 (bottom), 154 (inset), 164–165, 165, 168, 182–183, 219, 220–221 (top & centre), 246–247, 256–257, 260–261, 262–263, 266, 272, 285, 287, 288–289 (top), 290–291 (top), 292, 296, 297, 298–299.
Radio Times Hulton Picture Library, London, 28 (both), 32 (top), 37, 48–49, 54–55 (both), 61, 66–67, 86 (top), 118 (top right, centre & bottom left), 122 (top), 127 (inset), 129 (top), 131 (top), 156–157.
W. P. Trotter Collection, London, 19, 27, 34–35 (top & bottom), 41 (top), 57 (top & bottom), 62–63, 78–79, 116–117 (top), 135 (top), 136–137, 144–145 (top & bottom), 148–149, 182–183 (bottom), 264.
US National Archives, Washington, DC, 4, 32 (top), 54–55 (both), 61, 162–163, 172–173, 176–177, 185, 189, 194, 196, 198, 200–201, 208, 209, 210, 211, 235, 238, 250–251, 256, 262–263, 276–277, 278, 279, 295 (top), 302–303.
US Navy, Washington, DC, 118 (top right, centre bottom, 138–139, 164–165, 165, 178–179 (top & bottom), 186–187, 188–189, 201, 202–203, 204, 205, 215, 228–229 (bottom), 275 (both), 276–277, 288–289 (bottom).
US Air Force, 232–233. *US Coast Guard,* 284–285. *US Office of War Information,* 219. *US Information Service,* 208, 217 (top). *Foto Drüppel, Wilhelmshaven, Germany,* 30 (top), 222–223. *Bapty & Co,* 92–93, 158–159. *Syndication International,* 41 (top), 118 (top left), 127, 131 (top), 216–217, 238. *Associated Press, London,* 78–79, 121 (right), 132–133 (top). *J. G. Moore Collection,* 136, 246. *Suddeutscher Verlag, Munich,* 37. *Ullstein Verlag, Berlin,* 30. *Interdisciplinary Science Review, London,* 72–73 (left). *Lockheed Corporation, California,* 144–145. *Private Collection,* 124–125, 146, 224, 244, 268–269, 273, 284–285, 286. *John Frost Newspaper Collection, London,* 76–77. *New York Herald Tribune, New York,* 17.

Published by
The Dial Press/James Wade
1 Dag Hammarskjold Plaza
New York, New York 10017

Originally published in Great Britain by Wm. Collins Sons & Co., Ltd.

Manufactured in the United States of America

Library of Congress Catalog Card Number 77-087580

ISBN 0-8037-6454-2

First U.S.A. printing

Designed by Colin E. Reed

Drawings by Pierre-Andre Tilley/Blitz

Contents

THE BATTLE OF THE ATLANTIC

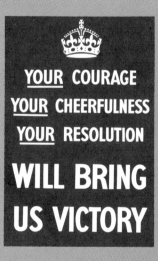

Foreword

In the course of our researches for this book, a leading American naval authority asked 'Which Battle of the Atlantic are you concerned with? The one we had 30 years ago or the one that's coming up?' His comment crystallised the importance of this crucial sea campaign of the Second World War. The Atlantic lifeline was then, as it still is today, the foundation of Western security and defence.

In this book, the Battle of the Atlantic has been reassessed in the light of hitherto secret documentation and set in a contemporary perspective. Underlying the bitter campaign at sea was an intense political struggle which had begun long before the outbreak of hostilities, when the British government appreciated that there would be no chance of winning a long war against a German dominated continent without the economic, financial and industrial support of the United States. This was clearly perceived by President Roosevelt, whose Administration went much farther in aiding Britain than American public opinion would have tolerated. His actions in support of Churchill laid the foundation for the Anglo-American 'special relationship' and the post-war strategic alliances. At the same time, in their creation of the Atlantic Charter, these two towering personalities raised the battle to the level of crusade which in its turn ultimately led to the United Nations.

Fortunately for the Allies, Hitler at first under-rated the importance of the Atlantic campaign, even though his naval advisers pressed for the immediate adoption of a total siege and a thrust to drive the British from the Mediterranean. Intuitively, he recognised the danger of involving the United States in a sea war for which Germany was ill-prepared. Even so, the U-boats, under the brilliant direction of Karl Dönitz, one of the war's leading strategists, came very close to bringing Britain to her knees in 1940, but it was not until 1943, when the U-boats were again on the brink of victory that Hitler finally appreciated the importance of the campaign. Huge quantities of steel and an important part of the Reich's production were then diverted to the construction of a new generation of U-boats. Had this fleet come into operation, it could have turned the tide against the Allies at the critical time when they were assailing the German armies on the European mainland.

But as Dönitz recognised, by 1942 it was too late to win the war and a year later the tide had turned decisively against Germany. The Allied technological and production effort had moved into top gear and, apart from the attrition of the convoy battles, the Germans had lost the tonnage war through the American industrial miracle of large-scale ship construction.

In the final analysis, the Battle was won as much in the shipyards and on the farms, as on the stormy waters of the Atlantic, but above everything else, the longest campaign of the war depended on the courage and determination of the seamen of not just the British and American merchant marine, but those of many other belligerent and neutral nations. It is to their memory and to those thousands of other men and women who perished in the Battle of the Atlantic that this book is dedicated.

CLEVELAND

98TH YEAR—NO. 247

CLEVELAND, MONDAY

BRITISH SHIP ABOARD IS AS EUROPE

BRITAIN, FRANCE ACT; BLOCKADE OF BALTIC ON

Liner Athenia Struck by Torpe

BULLETIN

LONDON, Sept. 3—(UP)—The Admiralty announced tonight that the British Navy has started a blockade of Germany, presumably blocking the entrance to the Baltic at Skagerrak. The British home and reserve fleets are in the North Sea, stretched across to the Scandinavian Peninsula.

By J. C. STARK

LONDON, Sept. 3 — (AP) — Great Britain and France went to war against Germany today.

Prime Minister Chamberlain's announcement of the momentous decision was followed quickly by a

Two full pages of pictures on Pages 10 and 32
War news on Pages 1, 2, 3, 4, 5, 6, 7, 8, 9, 11, 12

series of fast-moving acts to place the nation on a war-time basis.

The announcement came fifteen minutes after the expiration of an 11 a. m. (5 a. m. Cleveland time) ultimatum to the Nazi government to withdraw from invaded Poland.

France joined her old ally just five minutes after her own 5 p. m. (11 a. m. Cleveland time) deadline passed without a reply from Hitler.

In a weary voice that sometimes faltered, Chamberlain announced Britain's fateful decision in a broadcast to the empire. He was followed by King George, who broadcast an appeal to his subject to stand fast in the hour of con...

Prime Minister Ch...

Poles Say Army Enters East Prussia

BY EDWARD W. BEATTIE, JR.

WARSAW, Sept. 3—(UP)—Polish troops, cheered by news that Britain and France have entered the war on their side tonight were reported to have smashed across the border...

ROOSEVELT GIVES U. PLEDGE TO KEEP

BY WALKER S. BUEL

Plain Dealer Bureau, 611 Albee Bld...

President R...

1 Total Germany

MORNING, SEPTEMBER 4, 1939

32 PAGES

FINAL EXTRA

THREE CENTS

WITH 1,400 TORPEDOED GOES TO WAR

West of the Hebrides

246 · AMERICANS ON BOAT WHICH RADIOS 'SINKING'

BULLETIN

WASHINGTON, Sept. 4—(Monday)—(AP)— United States Ambassador Kennedy at London reported today that the British admiralty had so far been unable to determine whether the steamer Athenia had sunk or whether rescue arrangements were being made.

LONDON, Sept. 4—(Monday)—Germany struck the first blow at England as the 13,581-ton British liner Athenia, with at least 101 Americans among her 1,400 passengers, was torpedoed early today 200 miles off the Hebrides, west of Northern Scotland.

The last official information received by the Admiralty from the ship was that she was sinking "rapidly." Since there were no further advices, it was assumed she had gone down.

There was no h......

Partial List of Americans Liner Carrie...

Sunday 3 September 1939 dawned clear and bright but the warm sunshine did little to relieve the grim mood of Britain as thousands flocked to early service in churches all over the country. The BBC bulletins and the Sunday newspapers carried headlines about a final ultimatum to Germany. National prayers were being offered for peace, but by now most people had resigned themselves to the inevitability of war. This change in the public mood was detected by *New Yorker* correspondent, Mollie Panter-Downes, who wrote on 3 September: 'For a week everybody in London had been saying that if there wasn't a war tomorrow there wouldn't be a war. Yesterday people were saying if there wasn't a war today it would be a bloody shame.'

This same eagerness to be in action was shared by the men in the German submarines which were already patrolling at their war stations. The most westerly of the thirty U-boats ringing the British Isles was U-30 which pitched into a heavy Atlantic swell on the surface some 250 miles off the Hebrides. A stiffening breeze increased the rolling motion of her narrow cigar shaped hull making it unpleasant for the crew as they busied themselves with the usual morning routine of cleaning their cramped messdecks and checking the torpedoes. Up in the conning tower her commander, 26 year old Kapitänleutnant zur See Fritz Julius Lemp, had joined the lookouts scouring the horizon. Every man aboard knew from the radio traffic that they could expect the signal sending them racing into action to arrive at any minute.

Less than a hundred miles separated U-30 that fateful Sunday morning from the passenger liner *Athenia* which had rounded the northern tip of Ireland and was steaming westwards into the Atlantic swell at a steady ten knots. The stiff northwesterly breeze was whipping the smoke haze from her single funnel astern of the black painted hull as her captain set course for Canada. The 14,000 ton *Athenia*, built sixteen years previously for the Glasgow based Donaldson Line, was not rated amongst the glamorous liners on the Atlantic run but this hardly mattered to the 316 Americans aboard. They counted themselves lucky to have found a berth at all, as the threat of war in Europe had sent thousands rushing to book passages to home and safety. Their relief had been even greater at 4 o'clock the previous afternoon when *Athenia* finally sailed from Liverpool with a full complement of 1,418 passengers and crew. The latest news had been black indeed. German troops supported by tanks and aircraft were smashing their way deep into Poland. A British declaration of war seemed only hours away.

Fighting had begun at dawn on 1 September when a stage-managed SS raid on the German frontier radio station at Gleiwitz was made the pretext for Hitler's carefully planned 'Blitzkrieg . . . 'to crush Poland and annex the whole country'. Britain's Prime Minister, Neville Chamberlain, whose government had given guarantees to Poland, now faced an agonising choice between declaring war on Nazi Germany or accepting a humiliating political defeat more disastrous than Munich. It was a dilemma shared by Edouard Daladier, the French Premier, who was painfully aware that his own countrymen were wavering at the prospect of a second war with Germany in a generation.

Appeals to the German Government to suspend 'all aggressive action' had no effect. For a day, Chamberlain had clung to the vain hope of finding a

Poised to strike: On 3 September 1939: 49 of Germany's 57 U-boats were on station ready to open War Orders as their Commander, Karl Dönitz reported, 'The focal point of the war against England and the one possibility of bringing her to her knees lies in attacking sea communications in the Atlantic.'

diplomatic solution, but the following afternoon his temporising statement in the House of Commons brought Arthur Greenwood, the Deputy Leader of the Labour Opposition, rising to cries of 'Speak for England', angrily to demand: 'I wonder how long we are prepared to vacillate at a time when Britain and all that Britain stands for and human civilisation are at a peril . . . every minute's delay now means the loss of life'.

Faced with a rebellious House and a threatened split in his own Cabinet, the Prime Minister called an emergency meeting at 10 Downing Street. Shortly before midnight, they decided to issue a final ultimatum to Germany the next morning. The British telegram demanding cessation of the German invasion of Poland was delivered by the Ambassador in Berlin at 9 am on 3 September. Dr Schmidt, the German Foreign Ministry's official translator, took the telegram into the Führer's huge study in the Chancellery building and read it out aloud:

> Hitler sat immobile gazing before him . . . After an interval which seemed like an age, he turned to Ribbentrop who had remained standing by the window. 'What now?', asked Hitler, with a savage look, as though implying that his Foreign Minister had misled him about England's probable reaction.
>
> Ribbentrop answered quietly: 'I assume that the French will hand in a similar ultimatum within the hour.'

Already, the BBC had announced that the Prime Minister would address the nation at 11.15 am. Preparations for war were already under way, an Emergency Committee of the Cabinet was in session, and in surburban gardens people were busy piling earth over corrugated-iron Anderson air raid shelters. Overhead fat barrage balloons floated lazily to deter the Luftwaffe. London railway stations were crowded with reservists and volunteers on their way to join their units. Heavily equipped soldiers mingled with groups of mothers waving goodbye to tearful children who were being evacuated to escape the expected terror bombing.

As the hand of Big Ben reached eleven, the order went out to Britain's forces, 'TOTAL GERMANY'. Minutes later the BBC announced the Prime Minister and from the Cabinet room in 10 Downing Street, the flat voice of Chamberlain, told the nation:

> This morning, the British Ambassador in Berlin handed the German Government a final note stating that unless the British Government heard from them by 11 o'clock that they were prepared at once to withdraw their troops from Poland, a state of war would exist between us. I have to tell you now that no such assurance has been received, and that consequently this country is at war with Germany.

The Prime Minister had hardly finished speaking when the air-raid sirens wailed over London. The false alarm sent thousands running for their nearest shelter. In Berlin there had been no dramatic aftermath to the war announcement and German civilians had listened in attentive silence, unaware that Hermann Goering's immediate reaction had been 'God help us if we lose this time!'

Aboard the *Athenia* steaming out into the Atlantic, Captain James Cook reassured his passengers that the ship was immune from enemy submarine

'I know you will all play your part' a tired Neville Chamberlain told the nation as the last streams of evacuees left London.

3

'We were assembled aft and the *Emden*'s Executive Officer told us that England had declared war on Germany. It was not a happy moment. We recalled that our fathers had told us how they cheered on the declaration of war, but nobody knew now what to say. We all thought "now we're in a mess" '.

Werner Schuenemann
Wilhelmshaven,
3 September 1939

attack under international law. As an added precaution he told them that he was increasing speed and commencing to zig-zag. Lifeboat drill that day was practised in deadly seriousness.

Aboard U-30, shortly after 11 am, Lemp was passed a signal:

> To Commanders in Chief and Commanders afloat, Great Britain and France have declared war on Germany. Battle-stations immediate in accordance with instructions already promulgated for the Navy.

Within minutes of the expiry of the British ultimatum the Kriegsmarine's powerful Goliath wireless station at Frankfurt-an-der-Oder, deep in the heart of the Reich, began sending out orders to German vessels all over the world. The U-boat commanders like Lemp were disappointed to find that their War Orders did not allow them total freedom to attack. Not only were they ordered to spare *all* French ships, but they had to operate strictly in accordance with the Prize Laws. Germany had signed the 1936 Submarine Protocol accepting a code of conduct adopted by the world's navies, drawn up as a result of British pressure. This aimed at neutralising the submarine by forcing it to operate against merchant ships under the Hague Convention Prize Laws as they applied to surface warships. These made it illegal to sink a ship,

> without having first placed passengers, crew and ship's papers in a place of safety. For this purpose the ship's boats are not regarded as a place of safety unless the safety of the passengers and crew is assured in existing seas and weather conditions by the proximity of land or the presence of another merchant vessel which is in a position to take them on board.

The strict code removed the submarine's greatest advantage – its ability to strike suddenly and invisibly from beneath the surface. The German Naval War Staff was determined to restore this freedom of action as soon as possible, but the Führer had insisted that the Kriegsmarine observe the Prize Laws to the letter as a measure of his intention to avoid any provocative clash at sea that might upset his plans 'to hold a great peace conference with the Western Powers'.

Hitler was convinced that Britain and France would accept a political solution once he had dealt with Poland. To this end he was particularly concerned to allay neutral fears that Germany was about to resort to the unrestricted U-boat warfare that had been instrumental in bringing the United States into the war in 1917. Above all, he had no wish to begin a sustained naval campaign against Britain which would be a diversion from his European heartland strategy aimed at winning for the Reich *Lebensraum* in the east. The German Foreign Ministry buttressed Hitler's attitude, insisting that U-boat Command signal their captains that afternoon:

> Troop ships and merchant ships carrying military equipment are to be attacked in accordance with the Prize Regulations of the Hague Convention. Enemy convoys are to be attacked without warning on condition that all passenger liners carrying passengers are allowed to proceed in safety. These vessels are immune from attack even in convoy.

Neither the warning signal nor his strict orders made a deep impression on

U-30's young commander as he and his lookouts searched the horizon, determined to achieve the honour of striking the first blow at sea.

As the U-boats lay in wait astride the British shipping lanes, the Royal Navy was already deploying its superior strength across the world in a tight blockade of German shipping. Cruiser patrols were already on station in the North Sea searching for the enemy and stopping neutral ships to search for war contraband. The Channel was being mined and the Home Fleet was already at sea, hoping to intercept the German liner *Bremen* known to be making a dash for home across the North Atlantic. In the Skaggerak and off the Kriegsmarine's bases in the North Sea, British submarines and aircraft kept a constant vigil.

Hitler's hopes of avoiding a major clash at sea had already been diminished by the appointment of Winston Churchill to take over the Admiralty. After years of lonely warnings against the Nazi menace, Churchill was determined to prosecute the sea war against Germany as vigorously as he had done as First Lord in the First World War. The signal *WINSTON'S BACK* had gone out to the Fleet as Churchill hurried to take over his old office, delighted to discover behind a panel in the First Lord's Room the very map on which he had directed the sea war against the Kaiser 25 years earlier. Wasting no time he summoned the Board and then began a personal tour of all departments. He was still at his desk that evening when the news was brought to him from the Admiralty Operations Room of the incident that opened the long and bitter war against the U-boats. He was later to write of the Battle of the Atlantic:

> Battles might be won or lost, enterprises succeed or miscarry, territories might be gained or quitted, but dominating all our power to carry on the war, or even keep ourselves alive, was our mastery of the ocean routes and the free approach and entry to our ports . . . the only thing that ever really frightened me during the war was the U-boat peril.

Arrival and Departure: Winston Churchill arriving to take over the Admiralty on the first afternoon of the war. In another part of London the Führer's effigy was making an undignified exit from Madame Tussaud's waxworks.

FIRST BLOOD

Shortly after 7.30 pm, U-30's lookout reported a large steamer approaching in the gathering dusk. Lemp made out the shape of a liner, which he assumed from her lone zig-zag course must be an auxiliary cruiser. Without taking further steps to confirm whether or not the ship was armed, he dived to attack. At 7.43 pm, with the *Athenia* large in his attack periscope, Lemp gave the order to fire a salvo of torpedoes.

> 'I was standing on the upper deck when suddenly there was a terrific explosion,' recalled Mrs Elizabeth Turner, from Toronto. 'I reckon I must be a very lucky woman because when I recovered from the shock I saw several men lying dead on the deck.'

Down below Mr and Mrs Tom Connally of New York were just putting their three sons to bed.

'We were all in our state room, but the youngest child was in bed, when without warning the explosion occurred. Without being told, we realised what had happened. We only waited to throw some clothes on the child and then made a dash for the lifeboats. One of the hatches had been blown right up on deck and many passengers had been badly injured by flying splinters.'

One of U-30's torpedoes struck *Athenia*'s port side. Most of the force of the explosion was absorbed in shattering the bulkhead between the boiler rooms and the liner started settling as water flooded into the damaged compartments. The ship took on a six degree list to port, making it difficult for those struggling to reach the lifeboats on the upper deck. Passengers in the tourist and third class dining rooms found that they were trapped as the explosion had wrecked the stairways to the upper deck.

As darkness fell, Lemp judged that it would be safe to inspect his work and surfaced about half an hour after the explosion. He called some of the crew, including Adolf Schmidt, up to the conning tower to see the torpedoed ship. Observing the commotion on board from half a mile away, Schmidt later recalled: 'I did not think the ship could see our U-boat at that time on account of the position of the moon'. He was wrong, the U-boat was spotted by about a dozen people, including John McEwan of Glasgow, who was stunned when 'to our amazement and horror we saw them turn their gun upon us and fire two shots'.

Lemp had tried to shoot away her wireless aerials to prevent the *Athenia* transmitting warning signals, and as he watched the doomed liner he realised that he had sunk a passenger ship in violation of both international law and his strict instructions. Then U-30 submerged without attempting to offer the assistance demanded by the Submarine Protocol. Ten days later, after Adolf Schmidt had been badly wounded in an attack on U-30 by carrier borne aircraft, Lemp swore him to secrecy before putting him ashore in Iceland on 19 September.

The *Athenia*'s urgent SSS (attacked by submarine) signals sent Royal Navy destroyers and merchant ships racing to her aid, but it was not until the early hours of the following morning that they were able to reach the scene to find *Athenia* still afloat, surrounded by bobbing lifeboats. The first to arrive was the Norwegian freighter *Knute Nelson* which began rescuing the survivors, a difficult operation in the dark and heavy swell. A seaman and three other members of the *Athenia*'s crew were in charge of a boat full of 52 women; he recalled

> We made for the Norwegian ship, but as we drew alongside our boat was drawn under the stern of the ship. The propeller struck us and ripped the bottom out of the boat, only about 8 or 9 of the occupants survived.

Two destroyers, the US steamer *City of Flint* and the motor yacht *Southern Cross* joined in rescuing 1300 survivors before the *Athenia* finally sank stern first later that morning. Her destruction cost the lives of 118 persons, the first casualties of the Battle of the Atlantic. Even before shocked survivors were landed at Galway in Ireland, the news of the torpedoing had sent a wave of horror around the world. In America, public opinion was deeply outraged to find that 22 United States citizens had perished.

The Tragic Mistake: By Torpedoing the liner *Athenia*, Fritz Julius Lemp (above) the 26 year old commander of U-30, exceeded the strict orders of U-boat Command, whose War Diary noted 'It is inconceivable that they could have been misinterpreted.'
The first victim in the Battle of the Atlantic (below) photographed as she sank by an American survivor rescued by the *Knute Nelson.*
The horrors of unrestricted submarine warfare were reported by the world's newspapers as soon as the survivors landed in Ireland (right)

'Children ran screaming for their mothers. Women raced for their children. I saw one girl standing by her mother, who lay on the floor with a deep gash in her head. The child placed a towel on the gash. 'Mummy sick' she said, 'This will keep her warm'.

'We saw the bodies of children on the deck and in the water. Other little ones had lost their parents and ran around screaming. The Terror increased as the shells hit the ship'.

William Dawson, Glasgow

The Hunger Blockade: Germany's seaborne trade was blocked by the Royal Navy which seized all enemy merchant shipping and instituted an elaborate system of patrols to stop and search all neutral shipping. Manifests and cargoes were examined for 'contraband' goods which might be on their way to the Third Reich. The British Government soon extended the long list of contraband cargoes to include German exports and food imports as well as strategic raw materials and arms. This resulted in Nazi charges accusing Britain of 'piracy on the high seas' and that a 'hunger blockade' was being set up against civilians.

CHALLENGE TO ISOLATION

The Admiralty reacted immediately to this first U-boat sinking, which was taken as a timely warning of German intentions to lay siege to Britain's trade routes with unrestricted submarine war. The survival of the United Kingdom depended on the fleet of 3000 ocean-going merchant ships which brought into the country every gallon of oil, half its food and most of industry's raw materials. The nation's economy also depended on ships to export manufactured goods to world markets. If the U-boats succeeded in cutting these lifelines, Britain would starve – physically and financially.

The bitter lessons of the First War had demonstrated just how vulnerable Britain was to a siege. In the spring of 1917, the nation had been brought to the brink of a defeat by unrestricted U-boat warfare. Over 800,000 tons of shipping had been destroyed in the black month of April when one out of every four ships leaving her ports failed to reach its destination. Only the belated introduction of the convoy system had beaten the U-boats.

After the torpedoing of the *Athenia* Churchill, taking no chances, ordered the immediate institution of a full convoy system. He told the War Cabinet the next morning that the evasive routing of merchant vessels was not likely to be sufficient to counter the U-boats if, as appeared certain, they ignored the Submarine Protocol. He also announced an offensive campaign based on the Admiralty's current but mistaken policy, that the most effective way of killing submarines was by sending out hunting groups of destroyers and aircraft carriers. These tactics suited the Navy's desire for aggressive action, but they flew in the face of First War experience which had shown how unsuccessful it was to hunt submarines all over the ocean. Far better results could be obtained by forcing them to attack escorted convoys.

Aware that the Germans might attempt to repeat their previous strategy by striking at the ocean life lines, the Admiralty had set up a special Shipping Defence Advisory Committee in 1937 to examine the problem. The Committee had seen the major threat being directed at the Atlantic routes, the main line for much of the 55 m. tons of food and raw materials annually imported. The principal danger areas were the Western approaches to the British Isles into which all the shipping lanes converged.

The decisive importance of the North Atlantic was emphasised in the spring of 1939 in an Anglo-French Staff report that, in the event of war, 'There seems no doubt that we shall be obliged to rely upon the United States of America for supplies of a large range of raw materials and manufactured articles.' Britain would also depend heavily on Canada particularly for wheat and many 'manufactured articles' had already been ordered from North America by both Britain and France in the race to re-equip their armed forces after the Munich crisis. The French had taken the lead in sending the energetic Jean Monnet to head a French Purchasing Mission, which had placed a contract for 555 aircraft and begun to finance the expansion of American aircraft output. Britain depended on US supplies of phosphates, sulphur and cotton as well as large quantities of machine tools. Deprived of these vital imports, neither country would be able to survive for long the superior military and industrial power of Nazi Germany.

The sinking of the *Athenia* was immediately seen by the British as a useful opportunity to condemn Germany for ruthless disregard of American rights. As Churchill reminded the War Cabinet: 'The occurrence should have a helpful effect on public opinion in the United States' and the British government encouraged the indignant international outcry by raising the spectre of the *Lusitania* which caused the death of 128 Americans in 1915 and had been instrumental in bringing the United States into the war two years later. The latest German outrage was a warning that a U-boat offensive in the Atlantic would again present a threat to their lives and interests.

In 1939 America was committed to a policy of strict isolation, although President Roosevelt and his Secretary of State, Cordell Hull, had long ago realised that it was impossible for the United States to quarantine itself from world events. Hull had already advised 'that it would be to our own international interest to assist Britain and France, first in the effort to keep the war from coming and, second, to win the war if it came'.

American public opinion, however, did not see the war in these terms and many leading political figures were determined to preserve a strict neutrality which was deeply rooted in the traditional attitudes of the Republic. George Washington had warned against 'entangling alliances' and a return to isolationism had followed a deep revulsion after the sacrifice made by American soldiers in the First War. This had been reinforced by suspicion in Congress that the Eastern financial establishment had a vested interest in supporting United States involvement in the war.

Strong support for isolationism was to be found in the ethnic groups, such as the 12 m. US citizens of German descent, and the 15 m. Irish Americans. Even if they did not support the Nazi's they were against aid for Britain. As one commentator put it: 'they do not want Communism, Nazism or fascism and they do not want British Imperialism. They want Americanism.' As the European crisis boiled up that summer these feelings had manifested themselves in expressions of pacifist sentiment.

Many politicians on Capitol Hill in Washington were equally determined to stop the President manouvering the United States into war and a body of complex neutrality legislation had been built up by Congress with the intention of putting the United States into international purdah. The 1936 Neutrality Act laid down that, in the event of a war, the President must declare an arms embargo, making it unlawful for any American to supply arms to a belligerent state. It was made illegal for US citizens to travel on vessels of warring states and loans were forbidden to countries which had not cleared their First War debts.

This was particularly embarrassing for Britain who still owed the United States $2000 m. from World War I. Just how serious a block this lack of US credit would be was pointed out by Sir John Simon, Chancellor of the Exchequer, who told the Cabinet, 'our total resources are vastly inferior to that at the start of the last war'. With total reserves at a little more than £1000 m. he warned on 8 September 1939:

The Vital Supply Line: Armaments worth billions of francs ordered by Jean Monnet's (top) French Purchasing Mission in the United States were blocked by the Neutrality Laws. For Britain, also critically dependent on American supplies, the position was even more serious. Chancellor of the Exchequer, Sir John Simon (above) warned that even if the embargo were lifted, a monthly balance-of-payments deficit of £80m meant that the British government could not afford the massive US deliveries required for a long war.

'the door is doubly barred in the United States by the Johnson Act against War Defaulters, and by the Neutrality legislation. . . . . it is obvious that we are in grave danger of our gold reserves being exhausted at a rate that will render us incapable of waging war if war is prolonged.'

Yet Britain and France knew that they depended on American supplies and the Chiefs of Staff had optimistically made their war plans on the assumption that 'the President can be counted upon to do everything in his power to lend support to Great Britain and France'. They knew that though Congress might be hostile, Roosevelt was profoundly conscious of the degree to which America's industrial and financial strength was needed. He had already given notice in January 1939 that 'there are many methods short of war but stronger than mere words of bringing home to aggressor nations the aggregate sentiments of our own people.' His determined effort to get the Neutrality Laws scrapped soon after was frustrated by intransigent Congressional isolationism. Now war had broken out, Roosevelt knew that he would soon be forced to deny Britain and France the precious armaments they had on order with American industry. Before this disastrous situation came about, the President decided to persuade Congress to accept a limited modification of the laws by removing the arms embargo.

In a 'fireside chat', broadcast to the nation hours after Chamberlain's declaration of war, Roosevelt recognised the deep national sentiment for neutrality. At the same time, however, he revealed his intention of keeping a close watch on the Atlantic. American security was 'bound up with the safety of the Western Hemisphere and the seas adjacent thereto. We seek to keep war from our firesides by keeping war from coming to the Americas.'

Significantly this first wartime broadcast gave a clear indication of the President's readiness to stand by the democracies:

> This nation will remain a neutral nation, but I cannot ask that every American remains neutral in thought as well. Even a neutral has a right to take account of the facts. Even a neutral cannot close his mind or his conscience.

His audience did not yet know that Roosevelt was planning to take more practical steps to ensure that the United States did not remain neutral solely in conscience. He had already determined to recall Congress so that his Administration could face isolationist opposition and seek a repeal of the arms embargo. The President had decided that the United States could not afford to remain a mere spectator of the war between the democracies and the Nazi dictatorship.

The possibility of American involvement was precisely what Hitler feared and the broadcast, followed by the news of the sinking of the *Athenia*, made him extremely apprehensive. Such incidents would only drive American public opinion behind Rossevelt's scheme to aid Germany's opponents. Accordingly on 4 September, after Naval High Command had been unable to confirm or deny that one of the U-boats was responsible because of the strict radio silence, Hitler ordered the transmission of a special signal:

BY ORDERS OF THE FUHRER: PASSENGER SHIPS UNTIL FURTHER NOTICE WILL NOT BE ATTACKED *EVEN IF ESCORTED*.

The American Connection: In declaring a State of Limited Emergency on 8 September 1939 President Roosevelt (below) broadcast 'There is no thought in any shape, manner or form of putting the nation, either its defences or its internal economy, on a war basis'. Yet many months before the outbreak of war the President and Secretary of State, Cordell Hull, (bottom) had decided that it would be in America's interest to assist Britain and France.

At the same time, German press and radio were instructed to deny any responsibility for the sinking. This was taken to extreme lengths by the Nazi Party organ *Volkischer Beobachter* which came up with the astonishing claim: 'if the *Athenia* has actually been torpedoed, this could only have been done by an English submarine . . . there is also the possibility that Churchill had a little bomb blown up inside her.'

Such scurrilous propaganda, aimed at confusing American public opinion, was countered by a vigorous British campaign to brand the U-boats as merciless destroyers of ships and murderers of defenceless women and children. In Britain, anti-German feeling was whipped up to such ridiculous levels that *The Times* had to warn about ill treatment of Dachshund dogs which were being 'singled out for contumely as being symbolically teutonic'.

Most U-boat commanders, anxious to avoid behaving like 'the beastly Hun', at first went out of their way to carry out their duty in as chivalrous a manner as possible. Often submarines were put at a disadvantage by the truculent attitude of their intended victims, as Kapitänleutnant Herbert Schultze found out when he fired a warning shot across the bows of the British steamer *Royal Sceptre* in the approaches to the Bay of Biscay the day after the *Athenia* had been sunk. The steamer had promptly increased speed and sent out a stream of SSS signals so that Schultze was left with no choice but to stop her with a well placed shot amidships. Alongside him, on the conning tower of U-48, was his executive officer Reinhard Suhren:

We let the people get off into their lifeboats and then torpedoed the ship. Minutes later another vessel had been spotted, the British steamer *Browning*. Schultze asked me what we ought to do: 'Let the people get off and then sink this ship?' It was a difficult decision, for *Royal Sceptre*'s lifeboats were many hundreds of miles out in the Atlantic with little hope of rescue. The *Browning*'s crew were abandoning ship and people were already in the lifeboats. Amongst them was a Brazilian woman who held her baby up towards us. We couldn't bring ourselves to torpedo the ship after that. We told the officers to take their boats back to the *Browning*, then to pick up the survivors from the *Royal Sceptre*. We made one condition: they were not to use their wireless.'

Six days later, the British steamer *Blairlogie*, became the first ship to be intercepted by U-30 since she had sunk the *Athenia*. This time Lemp was careful to observe the Prize Laws, even supplying a bottle of schnapps and cigarettes to the lifeboats. This was the fourteenth ship sunk, bringing the total tonnage lost after one week of war to over 80,000 tons. It was a good start for the U-boats, but after introducing the convoys and stepping up air and sea patrols, Churchill confidently reported: 'the position from our point of view was probably past its worst, and would now improve.'

The War Cabinet had overestimated the success of their own aggressive initiative when, on the second afternoon of the war, the RAF had struck the first blow against the Kriegsmarine. Strictly observing international law which forbade the bombing of civilian targets, 29 Blenheim bombers swept in to attack the naval anchorage at Wilhelmshaven. The only damage was caused when one pilot desperately crashed his flaming bomber into the bows of the light cruiser *Emden*, killing twelve sailors. 'Is that war? – asked the

Sticking to the Rules:
Following the *Athenia* sinking, U-boats scrupulously observed the Prize Laws and on 11 September, after sinking the steamer *Firby*, U-48 boldly radioed Churchill the position of the lifeboats. A week later when the thirtieth ship the SS *Kensington Court* (above) was stopped and sunk by U-32 off Lands End – the survivors were lucky to be soon picked up by Coastal Command flying boats. Britain also observed the strict rules of warfare by dropping leaflets rather than bombs 'to rouse the Germans to a higher morality'. A newspaper cartoonist suggested (below) that this would be about as effective as dropping leaflets on the U-boats.

German press, but the British public were delighted, although they were not told that seven of the aircraft were shot down, nor that the bombs which hit the pocket battleship *Scheer* failed to explode. A simultaneous high level raid on the *Scharnhorst* and *Gneisenau* anchored off Brunsbüttel on the Elbe was also abortive.

The bombing attacks, made shortly after the *Emden* returned to base following a foray into the North Sea, increased the general apprehension in the Kriegsmarine that they were 'up against it', outnumbered nearly ten to one by the Royal Navy. However, it was soon apparent that German fears of the imminent destruction of their small fleet were premature. Apart from the Wilhelmshaven raid, the British and French pursued a cautious policy, believing that a rigidly enforced maritime blockade would bring Hitler to heel without risking retaliation by the vastly superior forces of the Luftwaffe.

Aggressive action against the Reich was restricted to bombarding the Germans with leaflets. The playwright Noel Coward, who was at the time in the British Bureau of Propaganda in Paris, commented sarcastically: 'If it is the policy of His Majesty's Government to bore the Germans to death, I don't believe we have quite enough time'. But the British and the French had agreed to respect Roosevelt's appeal to all belligerents to avoid bombardment from the air of civilian property or of unfortified cities. Hitler had also cabled his acceptance – as the Luftwaffe continued to blitz Polish cities.

The Kriegsmarine's Commander-in-Chief, Grossadmiral Erich Raeder, accepted the need for restraint during the first weeks of the war at sea and resisted the Naval Staff's arguments that the U-boats should strike a ruthless blow before the British could organise their convoy system effectively. He was confident that the Führer would be able to contain hostilities to the 'Polish incident' and instructed that, 'an attack should not be forced and our strength should be saved for the time being.'

This was in accordance with German policy because although the American Neutrality Laws had compelled the President to put an arms embargo on supplies to Britain and France, Hitler could have been under no illusions about Roosevelt's ultimate intentions after he had received a report

13

from the German Chargé d'affaires in Washington, Hans Thomsen on 12 September:

> For the time being, Roosevelt believes himself able to keep the United States out of the war by strengthening the Allies chance of winning the war through unlimited exportation of arms, military equipment and raw materials. But if defeat should threaten the Allies, Roosevelt is determined to go to war against Germany, even in the face of the resistance of his own country.

Roosevelt was well aware of the dangers of the situation by which the Neutrality Laws forced him indirectly to aid Hitler by denying the Allies weapons to resist. But the most favourable amendment which the isolationist Congress could be expected to pass was the replacement of the embargo by a 'cash and carry' requirement. Arms would be supplied, provided the Allies could pay cash for them and transport them to Europe in their own ships. On 11 September, the President wrote to reassure Chamberlain: 'I hope and believe that we shall repeal the arms embargo within the month and this is definitely part of Administration policy'. In his reply Chamberlain pinned great hopes on the moral effect of the President's action: 'My own belief is that we shall not win by a complete spectacular military victory, which is most unlikely in modern conditions, but by convincing the Germans that they cannot win.' The Prime Minister's wishful thinking worried the President, who detected a lack of resolve. He was already half-suspicious that Chamberlain might succumb to French pressure and be tempted to seek a negotiated peace.

At the same time as the President had written to the Prime Minister he had also taken care to open links with the one man in the British government who could be counted on to stop another Munich, Winston Churchill. Roosevelt had long admired his lonely campaign against Hitler, but now he took the highly unorthodox step of offering him a 'private line' to the White House, bypassing official channels. The two men had met only briefly once before, in 1918 when Roosevelt was Assistant Secretary of the Navy. Churchill was delighted to receive the letter and adopting the *nom de plume* 'Former Naval Person', he began the long series of communications, including more than a thousand personal letters and cables. It was to last until the President's death five years later and was to prove one of the most remarkable correspondences in history, enabling both men to keep the Atlantic alliance on a firm personal footing.

In the early months of the war, this 'private line' between the Admiralty and the White House countered the pessimistic reports of Ambassador Kennedy. The Irish-American millionaire banker had been convinced that Britain and France would not be able to hold out against Hitler, ever since his son John had visited Germany and presented him with a glowing report of the Reich's immense industrial and military strength. Prominent American industrialists like Henry Ford, who had seen German industry at first hand, were equally convinced that Britain was no match for Hitler. Another powerful voice urging Americans not to get involved in the war was national hero Colonel Charles Lindbergh, who had become a personal friend of fellow pilot

Presidential Intervention: After the 'cash and carry' amendments had been placed before a specially recalled Congress on 21 September, the public debate – encapsulated by the pro-Allied *New York Herald Tribune* (right) – became fast and furious. Ten days earlier, Roosevelt had expressed his confidence in a message to Chamberlain that the proposals would be carried. At the same time he had privately written to Churchill (below) offering him an unprecedented personal access to the Presidency laying the foundations of the 'special relationship' that became the corner-stone of the Atlantic Alliance.

THE WHITE HOUSE
WASHINGTON

Private

September 11, 1939.

My dear Churchill:-

It is because you and I occupied similar positions in the World War that I want you to know how glad I am that you are back again in the Admiralty. Your problems are, I realize, complicated by new factors but the essential is not very different. What I want you and the Prime Minister to know is that I shall at all times welcome it if you will keep me in touch personally with anything you want me to know about. You can always send sealed letters through your pouch or my pouch.

I am glad you did the Marlboro volumes before this thing started -- and I much enjoyed reading them.

With my sincere regards,

Faithfully yours,

Franklin D. Roosevelt

The Right Honorable
Winston Churchill, P.C., C.H.,
First Lord of the Admiralty,
London,
England.

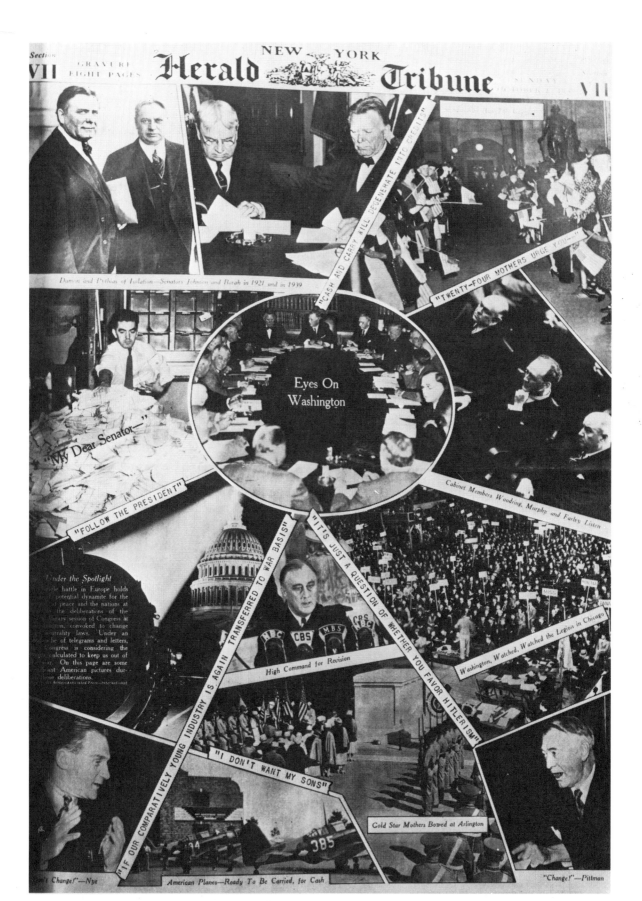

Damon and Pythias of Isolation—Senators Johnson and Borah in 1921 and in 1939

"CASH AND CARRY WILL DEGENERATE INTO CREDIT!"

"TWENTY-FOUR MOTHERS URGE YOU—"

Eyes On Washington

"My Dear Senator—"

Cabinet Members Wooding, Murphy and Farley Listen

"FOLLOW THE PRESIDENT"

Under the Spotlight

...he battle in Europe holds ...potential dynamite for the ...t peace and the nations at ...the deliberations of the ...nary session of Congress at ...ton, convoked to change ...trality laws. Under an ...r of telegrams and letters, ...ongress is considering the ...alculated to keep us out of ...ar. On this page are some ...ant American pictures dur-...ese deliberations.

"IT IS JUST A QUESTION OF WHETHER YOU FAVOR HITLERISM"

"INDUSTRY IS AGAIN TRANSFERRED TO WAR BASIS"

High Command for Revision

CBS MBS

Washington Watched, Watched the Legion in Chicago

"IF OUR COMPARATIVELY YOUNG

"I DON'T WANT MY SONS"

Gold Star Mothers Bowed at Arlington

...n't Change!"—Nye

American Planes—Ready To Be Carried, for Cash

"Change!"—Pittman

Hermann Goering and an admirer of the Luftwaffe.

When the special session of Congress opened on 21 September 1939, the fight over "cash and carry" became furious. Isolationist Senator McNary argued 'the world might conclude if we repealed the whole Neutrality Act, that we were repealing our neutrality'. Senators and Representatives were bombarded with letters, telegrams and petitions. The campaign against the President's proposals found support in high places as well as with the raucous fascist fringe of Fritz Kuhn's *Amerika – Deutsche Volksbund*.

Roosevelt, a disciple of Admiral Mahan's philosophy of seapower, had a very clear appreciation of the strategic issues at stake. He realised that a defeated Britain would give the Wehrmacht control of the Atlantic coastline and the ocean itself could be dominated by Nazi seapower which could then reach across to South America, where German commercial and political influence was already making itself felt.

Yet the President was worried that the United States could not deploy sufficient maritime forces to counter a Nazi threat in the Atlantic and at the same time deal with the growing menace of Japanese expansion in the Pacific. Steps had been put in hand by the Administration after the Munich crisis in 1938 to build up the strength of the US Fleet, but it was still essentially only a 'one ocean Navy' and Roosevelt depended on the Royal Navy to exercise the principal burden of seapower in the Atlantic. However, he was prepared to provide whatever help he could and top secret joint Anglo-American staff talks in Washington in May had agreed that in the event of war 'command of the western and southern Atlantic, as well as the Pacific, would have to be assured by the US Fleet.' During private discussions with King George VI during his State Visit in July, the President had made it clear that his intention was for the US Navy to patrol up to a thousand miles out into the Atlantic.

These secret proposals had been welcomed by the British who were nevertheless sceptical about how the President was going to affix this 'chastity belt' without openly prejudicing the United States' strict neutrality. Roosevelt's solution was characteristically ingenious. On 14 September, he had called a special conference of all 21 American Republics at Panama to agree on a bold re-assertion of the traditional Monroe doctrine to protect them from being drawn into the European war. The most important practical step contained in the Act of Panama on 2 October was the declaration of a Neutrality Zone. This quarantined a large belt of the western Atlantic from Canada to the tip of South America, reaching out from 300 to a thousand miles, into which belligerent warships were forbidden to enter. These waters were to be patrolled by the newly formed US Navy Atlantic Squadron, which consisted of five battleships, nine cruisers and a powerful force of destroyers operating with the ships of the US Coastguard Service.

This intervention by the US Navy disturbed the German Naval War Staff, who were increasingly frustrated by the diplomatic restrictions on the U-boats. The British were stepping up their anti-submarine countermeasures; convoys were being rapidly organised and on 14 September the Royal Navy had sunk its first U-boat. When U-39 had missed

16

the aircraft carrier *Ark Royal*, her torpedoes had exploded in the carrier's wake alerting two screening destroyers which soon located the U-boat on their Asdic before launching a successful depth-charge attack. Three days later, U-39 was dramatically avenged when the carrier *Courageous*, carrying out anti-submarine patrols in the Western Approaches, was sighted by Kapitänleutnant Otto Schuhart in U-29 who,

> decided to intercept the carrier. At the time it looked a hopeless operation. Because of the aircraft I could not surface and my underwater speed was less than 8 knots while the carrier could do 26. But we were told during our training to always stay close and that is exactly what I did, following him submerged until I was close enough to fire. After firing our torpedoes there was a tense silence in the boat until we were sure that we had been successful. Then without being able to see, we could hear the explosions.

Fifteen minutes after being hit, the 22,500 ton carrier sank, with the loss of 518 officers and men. Schuhart escaped the heavy depth-charging and after he had radioed the news of his success, the German propaganda machine exploited this spectacular blow against the world's strongest naval power.

The British public were as shocked as the War Cabinet, which insisted that the *Ark Royal* was to be recalled from her anti-submarine operations immediately. The ease with which Schuhart had penetrated the destroyers' Asdic screen raised the first serious doubts about its effectiveness. It called into question too, the Royal Navy's policy of aggressive U-boat hunting because the withdrawal of the carriers and their aircraft left a huge gap in the convoy defences in the dangerous waters of the Western Approaches. The removal of the carrier hunting groups also accentuated the dire shortage of warships available for covering the convoys. To improve the utilisation of their escort forces, the Admiralty urged that the Irish government be asked to restore base facilities at Berehaven and Lough Swilly which would have

'A Wonderful Success' was how U-boat Command's War Diary noted the sinking of the aircraft carrier HMS *Courageous* (below) on 17 September. When the Führer visited Wilhelmshaven on 28 September to greet the victorious crew of U-29 (inset) Dönitz was able to report 'It is not true that England has the technical means to neutralise the U-boats. Their experience so far confirms that the English anti-submarine apparatus is not as effective as they claim it to be.'

added more than 200 miles to the range of escorts operating in the Western approaches. These ports which Churchill described as the 'sentinel towers of the Western Approaches' had been returned to Eire in 1938 as a gesture of goodwill and now the question of their use by the British became deeply entwined with the problem of Irish unity. Gentle persuasion and reasoned argument failed to persuade Eammon de Valera, Ireland's Prime Minister, to restore them without some concession by Britain towards the ending of partition.

Churchill was indignant at de Valera's intransigence, urging seizure of the Irish ports by force. But the War Cabinet was more cautious. With the United States Congress now debating the crucial Neutrality Amendments, it was no time to offend the influential Irish-American lobby. The outcome was so evenly balanced that Roosevelt had to put off a visit by the Governor General of Canada, writing to him: 'I am almost literally walking on eggs, and having delivered my message to Congress and having good prospects of the bill going through, I am at the moment, saying nothing, seeing nothing and hearing nothing'.

President Roosevelt's friendly attitude towards the Allies and the prospect that Congress would amend the Neutrality Law and scrap the arms embargo, persuaded Churchill to take a sanguine view of the war at sea when he rose to make an anxiously awaited statement in the House of Commons on 26 September. Pointing out the last weeks' decline in the sinking rate he guardedly predicted: 'the failure of the first German U-boat attack on our trade'.

PARTIAL VICTORY

That same afternoon Naval High Command in Berlin was signalling the two pocket battleships, *Graf Spee* and *Deutschland*, lurking in remote areas of the Atlantic, to begin their offensive against the distant shipping lanes. This decision to launch the surface war against British trade had been taken three days earlier after Admiral Raeder had confronted Hitler with the declining effectiveness of the U-boats as a result of the 'political restrictions' imposed following the *Athenia* incident. The Führer's cautious directions for 'no attacks on passenger vessels and no action against French naval and merchant shipping' had contributed to a rapid falling off in the number of sinkings and prevented the U-boats disrupting the troop convoys carrying the British Expeditionary Force to France.

The Führer objected that an escalation of the naval war would threaten his strategy 'to drive a wedge between England and France', but he accepted that French warships could be attacked and that the U-boats could start sinking, without warning, enemy merchant ships 'since it may be assumed that they are armed'. Passenger vessels were however still to be excepted and he instructed that 'a neutral ship should occasionally be treated especially well in order to show that the situation had not been altered'. The pocket battleship attacks on the Atlantic trade routes were to be co-ordinated with

Raiders Are Out! On 26 September the two pocket battleships which had slipped out into the Atlantic before the outbreak of war were signalled to begin 'The disruption and destruction of enemy merchant shipping by all possible means'. Four days later the *Admiral Graf Spee* (right) sank the steamer *Clement* (top inset) and by the time she had claimed her third victim the SS *Ashlea* (bottom inset) half the Royal Navy's capital ships were trying to hunt her down.

the new wave of U-boats putting to sea. Refuelling from her supply tanker off Greenland, the *Deutschland* headed south into the North Atlantic shipping lanes off Bermuda. Three thousand miles away in the mid Atlantic, *Graf Spee* set course for the shipping routes off the Brazilian coast. On 30 September Captain Langsdorff intercepted the steamer *Clement* off Pernambuco. The war had not yet become too savage for the chivalrous Langsdorff to pick up all the British crew before he invited the *Clement*'s Master to watch the destruction of his ship from the *Graf Spee*'s bridge, 'I am sorry, Captain, but I've got to sink your ship. We are, you see, at war.' He had maintained his friendly politeness even though, in defiance of his signals, the *Clement*'s radio operator had managed to transmit a RRR warning (attacked by raider). Langsdorff soon turned this to his advantage by sending out a rescue message ostensibly from the *Scheer*.

At first confused that the bomb damaged *Scheer* was out, the news that a pocket battleship was in the Atlantic electrified the Admiralty. All available carriers, battleships, battlecruisers and cruisers were formed into 8 powerful hunting groups to search the whole Atlantic from Greenland to the Falklands. The simultaneous American announcement of the Neutrality Zone was seen by Churchill, who was actively supervising the Atlantic hunt from the special map room in the Library of Admiralty House, as an immense advantage. He made immediate use of his privileged access to President Roosevelt to cable his endorsement of the Zone, at the same time encouraging the US Navy to assist in the chase informing the President, 'the more American ships cruising along the South American coast the better, as you, Sir, would no doubt hear what they saw or did not see'.

The German warships proved as elusive to the American Atlantic Squadrons as to the British. It was nearly a week before there was any news of their whereabouts, then on 6 October, RRR distress signals were picked up from the steamer *Newton Beach* off the African coast. On the same day the *Deutschland* made her first kill, sinking the SS *Stonegate* in Bermudan waters. No distress signals were sent, and it was not until the arrival of the seized US *City of Flint* in Norway two weeks later that the Admiralty realised that a second raider was loose. The unpredictable appearances of the pocket battleships forced the British to scatter their naval forces all over the Atlantic. As part of this carefully orchestrated deployment of the Kriegsmarine's small fleet to disperse the Royal Navy's superior strength, Raeder sent out the fast new battleship *Gneisenau*, accompanied by the cruiser *Köln*, to make a feint thrust off Norway on 8 October with the objective of distracting the attention from the pocket battleships in the Atlantic.

The German Fleet Commander, Admiral Boehm, succeeded in luring out the British Home Fleet and then escaping being boxed in. But the plan failed in its second objective, which was to lure the enemy heavy units into range of the Luftwaffe's 'ship busting' bomber squadrons. To the fury of the German Naval Staff, this first exercise in interservice co-operation proved a miserable failure. Goering's vaunted bomber pilots failed to score a single hit on the two cruisers, *Southampton* and *Glasgow*.

As the Kriegsmarine's surface warships began implementing the plan to

Hostages to Fortune: The alarming news that a second pocket battleship was loose in the Atlantic broke with the seizure of the US cargo ship *City of Flint* (above). She had been captured by the *Deutschland* four days after the raider had sunk the British freighter *Stonegate* and Captain Wennecker had presented a signed souvenir to her Master. (centre) The *City of Flint*'s crew were forced to sail their ship to Murmansk at gunpoint because the Germans held her cargo of tractors, fruit and grain bound for Britain to be

r City of Flint,
l Her to Russia;
st Plot Reported

**German Cruiser Captures
American Ship, Puts
Prize Crew on Board**

**Inquiries Are Begun
By Maritime Board**

**Its Vessel, an Athenia
Rescuer, Is Reported
Interned by Soviets**

By Joseph Driscoll

WASHINGTON, Oct. 24—The United States Maritime Commission announced tonight that the 4,963-ton American freighter City of Flint had been captured by a German cruiser and taken last Saturday to a German prize crew into the neutral port of Tromsø, Norway, from which she soon sailed for an unknown destination.

Press dispatches from Moscow to-night reported that the American ship, flying a German flag, had been taken by a German prize crew of eighteen men into Soviet Russia's Kola Bay, north of Murmansk, where the German trans-Atlantic Bremen laid up following her successful dash from New York through the British blockade.

[Tass, the Soviet news agency, re-ported that the Murmansk port au-thorities had detained the City of

*llled Unneutral
r British Victory*

ate, Assert President Lent
ords; Barkley Threatens
argo Vote Likely Friday

ld Tribune Bureau

esident Roosevelt was criticized in the afternoon for being unneutral in lend-

contraband. This caused a souring of diplomatic relations between Berlin and Washington in the final stages of the Neutrality debate in Congress. To counter this, the Reich Foreign Ministry sent urgent instructions to sympathisers in the United States to 'ask all our American friends to appeal by telegram for the full maintenance of the Neutrality Laws . . . and in particular remind them that there is no real difference between the American and German people.'

disperse the Royal Navy's strength, the propaganda offensive to use the *Athenia* incident to cloud the Neutrality Amendment debate gained a new impetus after a Gallup poll had revealed that no fewer than 40 per cent of Americans were prepared to accept the German version. Yet by this time Naval High Command knew the truth. On 26 September, U-30 had returned to Wilhelmshaven and, on her arrival, the 'regrettable mistake' of her commander in assuming that the liner was an armed merchant cruiser had been communicated to the Führer's headquarters. Immediately, strict orders were received that the true facts were to be covered up. Instead of being courtmartialled for disobeying orders, Lemp was obliged, along with his crew, to take an oath of absolute secrecy and his log for that day was torn out and replaced by a forgery.

To lend credibility to their claim that the British had engineered the sinking of the liner, Raeder's officers in Berlin issued warnings about other bombs on US ships. Then ten days before the vital vote was due to take place on the Neutrality Amendments in Congress, the fantastic claims of an Illinois travel agent, Gustav Anderson hit the headlines.

Anderson, a survivor, claimed that he had been told by an officer on board the liner that the *Athenia* was carrying guns for Canadian harbour defences. To add credibility to his story, he maintained that the ship had already been fitted-out as an armed merchantman and that 'passengers had been warned not to strike matches on board and that the officers were nervous'. In spite of denials from other passengers, which clearly disproved the story, the Nazi press and radio stations broadcast the news, 'Churchill sinks the *Athenia*'. Pamphlets were sent through the US Mail to prominent people, accusing Churchill of putting a bomb aboard the liner in order to engineer another *Lusitania* incident and drag America into the war.

On 26 October, the day before the Senate voted on the Neutrality Amendments the President decided to put matters in proportion in a fireside chat:

> In and out of Congress we have heard orators and commentators and others beating their breasts proclaiming against sending the boys of American mothers to fight on the battlefields of Europe. That I do not hesitate to label as one of the worst fakes in current history. It is a deliberate set-up of an imaginary bogy.

Next day, it was clear that the isolationists and the German Foreign Ministry had overplayed their hands. The Senate approved Roosevelt's amendments by 63 votes to 31. The House of Representatives followed with a 61 vote majority a week later. The arms embargo was lifted on Britain and France and they could now draw on American industrial capacity. The British Ambassador in Washington cabled London: 'Both the President and Isolationists have had a partial victory and the present neutrality act represents very fairly the compromise between the two'.

The first important political battle in the Atlantic war had been won.

2. The Power of Audacity

'On land I am a hero, at sea I am a coward'.
ADOLF HITLER

The launch of the Reich's first big battleship, *Scharnhorst*, on 3 October 1936 was a moment of great satisfaction for the Commander-in-Chief of the Kriegsmarine, Admiral Erich Raeder (left of Hitler). Yet even before the ship entered service early in 1939 the Führer's megalomania had plunged Germany into a great naval construction race to match Britain's navy. Hitler was attracted by the prestige and glamour of the big ships and the details of their guns and armour, but never grasped the principles of naval strategy. He also failed to appreciate that his great 'Z Plan Fleet' of aircraft carriers and super-battleships would take more than five years to complete.

On 10 October, two weeks after the fall of Warsaw, Admiral Raeder had a decisive conference with Hitler. Poland was defeated and with the Soviet Union sharing the spoils under the terms of her non-aggression treaty with Germany, the Führer was free to concentrate against the West. It seemed an ideal moment for the Naval War Staff to press their plan for stepping up the sea war against Britain. Raeder urged Hitler to embark upon a total siege of British Isles 'at once and of the greatest intensity'. He outlined plans to strike at her sea communications with a fleet of auxiliary cruisers which would support the operations of the pocket battleships in distant waters. The decisive spearhead of the offensive would be the U-boat arm and he advised the Führer to increase submarine construction and to lift all restrictions on U-boat warfare. Hitler appeared to agree with Raeder's analysis, but little was done to set the scheme in motion. There was no acceleration of U-boat construction; no stream of directives tightening the blockade. Gloomily the Naval Staff reflected on the missed opportunity for striking at Britain's vulnerable life-lines before her defences were strengthened. At Naval Headquarters on Berlin's Tirpitz-Ufer, the atmosphere of frustration concealed deep anxieties about Germany's ability to wage a long naval campaign.

The Kriegsmarine had been thrust into war long before it could boast a surface Fleet strong enough to challenge the Royal Navy. The knowledge of this handicap had led Raeder to try to dissuade Hitler from a premature declaration of war. When hostilities finally broke out, such was his disillusionment and frustration that the elderly Admiral had locked himself away in private to commit his forebodings to paper:

> Today the war against England and France broke out, the war which according to the Führer's previous assertions we had no need to expect before 1944 . . . as far as the Navy is concerned obviously it is in no way equipped for the struggle with Great Britain. The submarine arm is still much too weak to have a decisive effect on the war. The surface forces are so inferior in number and strength to those of the British Fleet that even at full strength they can do no more than show how to die gallantly . . .

For Admiral Raeder the war had come seven years too soon. He was still struggling to build up the German Navy to its full strength after the years of restriction imposed by the Treaty of Versailles. Since his appointment as C-in-C in 1928 at the age of 52, Raeder's aim had been to create a fleet capable of holding its own against any other European power but his overriding aim was to avoid a clash with the Royal Navy which he believed would be *Finis Germaniae*. The son of a Hamburg teacher, Raeder had risen rapidly in the Kaiser's navy; he had served with distinction at the Battle of Jutland and was a first class strategist who thought in global terms. Hitler showed great respect for his stern judgement and he was allowed a large measure of independence in his control of the Navy. Yet according to one observer the stiff Admiral was 'neither a good psychologist nor a master of the art of handling men. To enter into close personal relations with him was difficult.' He was always cold and reserved but he possessed a degree of political skill acquired from his days as a young officer aboard the Kaiser's yacht which had been the scene of endless intrigues and cabals.

The Tiger's Smile: Hitler showed his keen interest in naval affairs by visiting Kiel in the summer of 1933 soon after he had become the Reichs Chancellor. Watched closely by Dr Joseph Goebbels, Germany's new leader admires a cruiser's mascot. Already Germany had made preparations for a global naval campaign with the establishment of a world wide secret supply organisation, the *Etappendienst* directed by Captain Canaris (below) later head of German Counter-Intelligence, the *Abwehr*.

This experience had helped Raeder in his first task as C-in-C of piloting through the Weimar Assembly a scheme for the first new capital ship permitted Germany under the Treaty of Versailles. The Navy's plans had faced a bitter socialist campaign of 'Battleships or Child Welfare', but the durable Raeder had won the day by skilful lobbying. When the 10,000 ton *Deutschland* was launched on 1 April 1933 her revolutionary design attracted close attention in Britain and France. Her remarkable 21,500 mile cruising range and formidable 11″ guns in two triple turrets put her into a new class of warship, capable of outgunning any cruiser and fast enough to out-run a battleship. Half admiringly, the major naval powers had coined the term 'pocket battleship' to describe this new type of warship which clearly presented a menace to their shipping.

The new direction of German naval strategy aimed at the ocean trade routes was reflected in a pamphlet published at the time by Rear Admiral Wolfgang Wegener. In *The Naval Strategy in the World War* he had criticised Tirpitz's pre-First War policy of building a large Imperial battle fleet whose role was limited to challenging the Royal Navy in the North Sea. In Wegener's view Germany needed a balanced fleet powerful enough to break out of the 'wet triangle' of the North Sea and capable of operating in the Atlantic. This approach was eagerly taken up by other officers like Captain Waldemeyer Hartz, who wrote that 'future operations are no longer going to be directed upon the enemy's armed forces but against his economic resources . . . Attack upon the enemy's trade and protection for our own trade are the decisive tasks to which everything else is going to be subordinated.'

THE SECRET CHALLENGE

Raeder and his older staff officers did not totally accept the trenchant arguments of the 'Control of Communications' school but the decision to build a fleet of the pocket battleships was heavily influenced by the new theories. The world-wide role of the *Deutschlands* against enemy commerce was carefully thought out and accompanied by the development of a secret supply organisation, the *Etappendienst*. Originally set up to overcome the Imperial Navy's lack of bases, it was revived under the direction of Captain Canaris, later to become head of the Abwehr – Military Counter-Intelligence. *Etappen* agents were set up in ports all over the world, communicating with Canaris' Berlin headquarters through the cables and mails of the German shipping lines like Norddeutscher Lloyd, whose bank accounts were also used to channel funds to set up the global naval supply system. The *Etappendienst* by 1939 had become a highly efficient intelligence network for reporting on the worldwide disposition of merchant ships, whilst its agents made plans to supply German warships and blockade runners in time of war.

When the Nazis came to power in 1933, Raeder at once realised that Hitler would back his dream for a powerful German Navy. The two men, although very different personalities, soon established a bond of mutual respect. Hitler, in spite of his suspicion of Prussian officers, admired and accepted the Admiral's professionalism in an area where he lacked any understanding or

DEUTSCHLAND

ADMIRAL GRAF SPEE

ADMIRAL SCHEER

LEIPZIG

KÖLN

EMDEN

SCHLESIEN

SCHLESWIG-HOLSTEIN

confidence. Raeder, although he never overcame his distaste for the former army corporal, saw in Hitler 'a great and very skilful politician' who would provide the means and then leave him to run the Navy in his own way.

At first Raeder had been impressed by Hitler's ability to master technical details and flattered by the apparent attention he paid to naval affairs. The latest edition of *Jane's Fighting Ships* was always in the Führer's study and like Kaiser Wilhelm II, Hitler found an outlet for his artistic talent in sketching grandiose designs for battleships. At conferences and launchings he delighted in showing off his encyclopaedic knowledge to the professional naval officers, who soon came to realise, however, that Hitler's pre-occupation with tonnages, armour plate and gun calibre concealed a profound failure to grasp sound naval strategy.

It was a romantic vision of seapower which was inspired by 100,000 ton battleships. The glamour of big ships appealed to the Führer and he always took care to be present when these symbols of the Reich's increasing might were launched. Hitler's state yacht *Aviso Grille* led the Fleet out of Kiel to its annual manoeuvres, but usually the Führer was not aboard; he suffered from seasickness. First and foremost Hitler was a landsman who told Raeder: 'The war on land is my affair, you must run it at sea'. Although he never trusted his Army generals, by 1939 Hitler had come to rely so heavily on Raeder that he prevailed upon him not to retire and promoted him to the rank of Gröss-admiral. By then the Kriegsmarine had achieved a great deal more independence and was largely insulated from the worst excesses of the Nazi regime. Interference by the SS was not tolerated and the Navy kept itself strictly apart from politics by rejecting large numbers of Hitler Youth Candidates as being 'psychologically unstable'. Raeder, a staunchly religious man, managed to retain a strong naval chaplaincy and his insistence on religious toleration protected many naval officers of Jewish origins.

Hitler's rise to power did not at first result in as rapid a programme of naval expansion as Raeder hoped. The two years delay before the Nazis felt strong enough to throw off the rearmament restrictions imposed by the Versailles Treaty proved a serious handicap. Hitler also never appreciated that battle-ships, unlike aircraft and tanks, took many years to design and build. However, during this time the Navy made rapid progress with its clandestine preparations to rebuild a U-boat arm which was strictly forbidden by the Versailles 'diktat'. Since the end of the First War the Navy had been covertly supporting the work of a thirty man submarine design and engineering team through intermediaries like the ubiquitous Captain Canaris. Since early 1922 the U-boat work had been carried out under cover of a Dutch registered firm called *Ingenieourskaantoor voor Scheepsbouw* (IvS) of the Hague. From 1928, operations were supervised by a Berlin cover company, *Ingewit*, and under conditions of the greatest security, work began in preparation for constructing 16 U-boats in Germany. The designs were based on the IvS submarine contracts for Turkey, Spain, Finland and Russia. German 'civilian' crews and engineers had clandestinely participated in submarine trials in Spain and the Soviet Union. Inside Germany secret programmes were carried out under the guise of 'Anti-Submarine' operations with former

Joining the Race: In 1935 when Hitler renounced the Versailles Treaty he assured Admiral Raeder that 'he had no intention of challenging Britain's position at sea.' At that time the Kriegsmarine's fleet of capital ships (left) was tiny compared to the world's biggest navy whose most modern battleship was the 35,000 ton HMS *Nelson* (right). Her unique design, with the three triple 16″ turrets for'ard, was the result of the 1921 Washington Naval Treaty. By 1935, attempts to limit the international naval arms race with such agreements were crumbling and Germany seized the opportunity to lay down the two battleships *Scharnhorst* and *Gneisenau* in defiance of Versailles. Although it was announced that the two ships would not exceed 20,000 tons their true displacement was 35,000 tons.

U-boat officers supervising courses in specially made trainers constructed with mock-up control rooms tracking over seascapes on long gantries.

By March 1935, when Hitler finally renounced the Versailles Treaty limitations, the prefabricated parts of six U-boats were already being secretly assembled in the heavily guarded black sheds at the *Germania* and *Deutsche Werft* at Kiel. The new U-boats were carefully omitted when the Navy immediately announced plans for two big, fast battleships, which were officially designated as 25,000 tons to conform to the Washington Naval Treaty limits. The *Scharnhorst* and *Gneisenau* were intended to be over 30,000 tons displacement, yet Hitler still felt it prudent to restrict their armament to 11" guns rather than the 15" that the Navy wanted. As a result, the first big German battleships were under-gunned by contemporary standards.

The Reich's unilateral abrogation of the Versailles Treaty, which was marked by the setting up of the Luftwaffe, the introduction of conscription and the new battleships, provoked no more than a mild rebuke from the League of Nations. The Führer was even more delighted to find the British keen to discuss a naval treaty. Germany had been excluded from the post-war naval conferences in Washington and London that had sought to prevent a future naval arms race by limiting the navies of Britain, the United States and Japan to a 5:5:3 ratio; with France and Italy accepting a still smaller proportion of 1.75

Raeder seized this opportunity to restore Germany's status by proposing to build a Fleet one third the size of Britain's. The hard-fought naval agreements were, by 1935, crumbling under a determined Japanese bid for parity and the British government wanted to contain any future German threat. When Joachim Ribbentrop was sent to London at the head of special mission that summer to demand that Britain 'must' recognise a 35 per cent ratio, he found his proposals were favourably accepted. In return, Ribbentrop agreed that Germany would sign the Submarine Protocol and offered to support Britain's attempt to get the submarine outlawed.

The Admiralty's readiness to accept the German terms was outlined in a secret brief advising, 'it would be greatly to our advantage to recognise the decision of the German government before the demand should be increased'. They hoped to limit the German surface Fleet by 1942 to five battleships, two carriers and the supporting squadrons and destroyers. To achieve this they were prepared to overlook the threat of a revived U-boat arm by agreeing that the Germans could build up to 45 per cent of the British submarine tonnage – with an escape clause allowing construction up to 100 per cent 'on due notification'.

The Anglo-German Naval Agreement was signed on 18 June 1935, a day which Hitler confessed to Raeder was 'the happiest of my life'.

The French, furious at the unilateral British action, told London that 'Germany would violate the Agreement as soon as it suited her'. This cynical, if realistic, view of Nazi integrity was confirmed eleven days later when, U-1, the first new U-boat took to the water at Kiel. But the British Government sent only the mildest of protests to Berlin, preferring to officially ignore the fact that not even Teutonic efficiency could produce a 250 ton submarine in a

First Round to Germany: On 2 June 1935 Joachim Ribbentrop (above) and his delegation arrived in London to seek British recognition of Germany's demands to build a surface and submarine fleet, up to 35% of the Royal Navy's strength. The Anglo-German Naval Treaty was signed on 17 July and the British government announced 'Germany has agreed never again to resort to what was known during the war as unrestricted submarine warfare.' Yet U-boats were already being rapidly completed and in August the Führer was inspecting them at Kiel (below).

week and a half. Naval intelligence had been warned by their agents about the secret U-boat construction programme, but the Admiralty Board believed, as fervently as ever, that future naval wars would be decided by gun power and battleships, not submarines. They were confident that, even if Germany broke her agreement 'never again to resort to unrestricted U-boat warfare,' the Royal Navy's secret Asdic underwater detection device had made the submarine an obsolete weapon.

The German Naval Staff were under no such illusions. They set about turning out U-boats to the limits of the London Agreement as fast as possible. Most important of all, they selected a man to master-mind the rebuilding and training of the U-boat arm who would prove himself one of the most capable naval tacticians of the century.

FORGING THE WEAPON

In 1935 Captain Karl Dönitz was preparing to set off on a world cruise in command of the cruiser *Emden*. At 44, he was one of the most promising senior officers in the Kriegsmarine. A Berliner, he was the son of an engineer in the Zeiss works and had joined the Imperial Navy as a cadet in 1910. Promoted to Lieutenant in 1916, he had transferred to the U-boat arm and as commander of U-25, and later U-68, he had shown cool determination and fine leadership in action. After U-68 had been sunk in the Mediterranean in 1918, Dönitz spent a year in an English prisoner-of-war camp before getting himself repatriated by feigning sickness. He commanded a torpedo boat in the tiny postwar German Fleet before becoming Commander, then Captain of the *Emden*. At first, Dönitz was inclined to turn down his chance to lead the new U-boat arm, because he believed: 'in the new and balanced fleet which we were planning, the U-boat arm would represent only a small and comparatively unimportant part'. But he was a submariner at heart and this finally overcame his reservations about the appointment.

On 28 September 1935, Dönitz arrived to take command of the first flotilla of nine new U-boats. These 250 ton craft were so small and cramped that their eager young crews referred to them as 'dugout canoes', but Dönitz soon plunged them into a training programme so rigorous that the small size of the submarines became unimportant in their new-found enthusiasm to rebuild Germany's elite naval force. The Weddigen Flotilla, called like all the later flotillas after First War U-boat aces, became the floating classroom in which Dönitz could experiment with his theories of submarine warfare as well as providing training for the new officers and men.

In little over a year Dönitz had built up the nucleus of a highly trained and steadily growing force. He had devised and directed a thorough training programme lasting six months, frequently going to sea with his young commanders or directing operations from his command vessel *Saar*. Each new crew and their commander were required to complete 66 surface, and 66 submerged, practice attacks before being allowed to go to torpedo firing practice.

The mystique of an elite force soon enabled Dönitz to draw on the best

'**Der Löwe**': Karl Dönitz, Officer Commanding U-boats, on spring naval manoeuvres in 1939 which saw the first large scale test of his *Rudeltaktik*. It was the culmination of four years' intensive effort for his fifty strong force: 'In which the crews were trained as far as possible for war conditions. I wanted to confront my U-boat crews in peace with every situation with which they might be confronted in war . . .'

young officer and rating talent in the German Navy. There was already fierce competition to get into the Kriegsmarine and standards were very high. 40,000 men would volunteer annually at Kiel for the 2,000 or so lower-deck vacancies and competition to become an officer was even greater – in 1932 618 applied for only 45 places. Selection was rigorous and officer candidates especially had to score high marks in a battery of written, physical and psychological tests including the "Mutprobe" (Courage Test) in which they would be filmed by hidden cameras as an increasing electric voltage was applied to metal bars held in each hand. Successful cadets, usually those that held on longest defying the pain, then faced many months hard life on square rigged sailing ships before commencing their academic training to University level at the Murwik Naval Academy.

This gruelling first year 'tested the crews to the very limit of human endeavour' according to one commander; but it laid a firm foundation of morale, leadership and efficiency on which the U-boat arm would grow and survive even in the blackest periods of the war. The first full-scale exercises with the Flotilla at the end of the year tested Dönitz's ideas for the concerted surface attacks – the so-called *Rudeltaktik* ('Pack Attacks') – which were later to be perfected in full scale Atlantic exercises in the Spring of 1939. Dönitz was convinced that the *Rudeltaktik* was the U-boats' answer to the defensive convoy system which had been instrumental in defeating it in the First War.

The training exercises were often made so realistic that U-boats suffered serious damage and many had to be repaired before even becoming operational. On several occasions U-boats were actually rammed and one was accidentally sunk but these risks were accepted in Dönitz's scheme to produce alert efficient crews.

Training the Wolf Packs: The 1st U-boat Flotilla – at Kiel (top) in the summer of 1937. Tactical exercises were carried out in the Baltic with Dönitz supervising operations from the tender 'Saar' (background) which stood in for convoys. Two years later, in April 1939, realistic operations were devised on an Atlantic scale (map above). These were envisaged as a full scale test of the assault on Britain's lifelines.

THE ASDIC MYTH

Whilst Dönitz was forging the U-boat arm into an effective weapon to attack merchant shipping, the British Admiralty never doubted that Asdic* had ended the submarine threat. Carefully rehearsed 'shows' were put on to demonstrate the effectiveness of the 'underwater eye' that 'removes from the submarine that cloak of invisibility which was its principal weapon'. Winston Churchill had attended one of these demonstrations by the Anti-Submarine Training Squadron in Weymouth Bay in 1936. 'The faithful effort has relieved us of our great danger', he wrote afterwards to the then-First Sea Lord, who had arranged the display to show 'that our methods are now so efficient that we will need fewer destroyers in the North Sea and the Mediterranean'.

The Admiralty's confidence in Asdic was underlined in a memorandum of that year which stated: 'So important is the development of Asdic that the submarine should never again be able to present us with the problem we were faced with in 1917'. It was comforting news to the British Government, besieged by financial stringency in the Depression years, to know that 'one destroyer could do the work of a whole flotilla'. They happily axed destroyers and new convoy escorts from the naval estimates.

Even when the first real test of Asdic came in the Spanish Civil War, the disappointing results failed to shake the Royal Navy's belief that it had increased the chance of detecting U-boats by 80 per cent. The fallacy of this should have been clear from incidents like that of 31 August 1939 when the destroyer HMS *Havoc* was narrowly missed by a torpedo from a trigger-happy Italian commander. Asdic contact was soon lost and chaotic depth-charge attacks failed to damage the culprit, the *Iride*, which made an easy escape. But the Admiralty maintained its confidence in the efficiency of Asdic and, in the wardrooms of the Fleet, wild stories circulated of Neapolitan dentists being kept busy repairing Italian submariners' teeth broken in the depth-charge explosions.

The comparative inefficiency of Asdic apparatus under operational conditions did not surprise those officers who had to manage the delicate equipment on those few ships that were fitted with it. Far from proving to be the all-seeing 'underwater eye' it was effectively limited to searching with a narrow beam at a fixed angle and at ranges of often less than a mile. The high energy sound pulses radiated from the transmitter on the vessel's keel were only capable of operating at low speeds and were seriously disturbed by rough water and speeds above eight knots. The echoes reflected back by an object caught in the beam were received as a characteristic 'PING-ping' and it needed a skilled operator with the highly sensitive ears of a piano tuner to distinguish between the different pitches in echoes caused by a submarine and those coming from shoals of fish, whales, wrecks, the sea bed or even different layers of water.

'As compared with the situation in 1915–1917 the problem of dealing with the submarine is more than simplified by the invention of Asdic. This instrument takes the place of the 'eye' and removes from the submarine that cloak of invisibility which was its principal source of strength in the late war. . . . and in fact it is considered that war experience will show that with adequate defences, the operation of submarines against merchant vessels in convoy can be made unprofitable.'

Report of
The Defence of Trade
Committee 1936.'

---

*Asdic was the name given to the device for locating submerged submarines by using sound waves. It took its name from the Anti-Submarine Detection Investigation Committee which had initiated its development in 1917.

The Anti-Submarine Branch – derisorily known as 'Pingers' in the Service – suffered from the disadvantage that the rest of their brother officers regarded them as the 'lowest of God's creatures'. They had the reputation of being 'third choice specialists' who had failed the more glamorous Torpedo or Gunnery specialisations and were regarded as 'not being very clever'.

The most striking error made by the Admiralty Plans Division in the interwar years was their total refusal to acknowledge that the submarine could or would operate by night. To the fury of many submarine officers, in all the exercises they were ordered to 'surface at dusk, switch on their navigation lights and take no further part in operations until dawn the next day'. This blinkered attitude ignored all the experience gained during the final stages of the First War when the U-boats made many of their attacks during the night on the surface, taking advantage of their low silhouettes and high surface speed to get inside convoys undetected. This attitude was even more incomprehensible because it was known that Asdic was ineffective against surfaced U-boats.

The Admirals who ran the Royal Navy were largely gunnery officers and it was perhaps not surprising to find that their attention was directed principally to ensure the survival of their precious battleships. They were obsessed with the idea of preparing for another Jutland-style confrontation of battlefleets, and it was convenient for them to accept the illusion that the U-boat had been mastered and that the other modern weapon of war at sea – the aircraft – presented no real threat to their battleships. As one naval officer of that generation resolutely maintained, 'The bloody gunnery officers came to the top between the wars so that we had to spend the first two years losing the next one whilst we got rid of them!'

The Admiralty's complacent attitude to the threat of aircraft was fortunately made so embarrassingly plain that action was taken before it was too late. In one pre-war demonstration a radio-controlled *Queen Bee* target plane

Guns NOT Torpedoes: This was the philosophy which the Admiralty believed would be decisive since it was believed that Asdic had neutralised the submarine's attacking potential. The Royal Navy's ten to one capital ship superiority was demonstrated in Home Fleet exercises in April 1939 (below). The battleships *Nelson*, *Rodney*, *Royal Sovereign* and *Resolution* in line abreast with part of their destroyer screen. Yet the British Submarine Service taking part in manoeuvres had shown:

'In Fleet exercise after Fleet exercise we (the submarines)

had circled unscathed for over two hours whilst every gun in the Fleet blazed away. A series of enquiries eventually resulted in an alarming report that 'many warships were virtually defenceless against air attack'. After this damning indictment of the inadequate British *Multiple Pom-Pom* anti-aircraft guns, Swedish designed *Bofors* and Swiss *Oerlikon* guns were being rushed into production as the war began.

Unfortunately, there was no similar failure of Asdic to jolt the Admiralty, so with incredible disregard for all the lessons of naval history from the age of Elizabeth I to the black spring of 1917, it was firmly believed unnecessary to put merchant shipping into convoys. In 1933, the Parliamentary Secretary of the Navy, Lord Stanley, had announced, 'the convoy system would not be introduced at once on the outbreak of war' and successive parsimonious Governments used this as a reason to block funds for convoy escorts.

In March 1938, by which time the Admiralty Plans Division had reversed their earlier views and called for the 'institution of a convoy system', the Government, were still cutting escort construction from naval expenditure and only the imminence of war in the spring of 1939 finally panicked the Government into authorising funds for 56 'special escort vessels'. The decision had been left so late that the Admiralty had to settle for a compromise, 'off-the-shelf', escort design that could be rapidly adapted and built. The whalecatcher *Southern Pride*, from the Middlesbrough firm of Smith's Docks Ltd was selected as being closest to requirements. Its maximum speed was known to be a good three knots less than the surface speed of German U-boats but there was no time for major modifications. The sturdy whalecatcher was transformed overnight into a warship and a crash programme for the 'Flower Class Corvettes' began just before the war.

The Admiralty had for so long neglected to provide adequate numbers of convoy escorts, that it was hardly surprising when it completely ignored the potential anti-submarine role of aircraft, where preparations were almost

would invariably penetrate the destroyer screen and torpedo the target. But our claims were often dismissed as "only knocking two knots off the speed of a battleship".'
Admiral Sir Hugh Mackenzie

Britain's overconfidence that she could deal with the underwater menace is summed up by the *Picture Post* cover of 10 October 1939 (above left) 'The right way to treat a submarine'. In the same month a German magazine *Simplicissimus* cartoon (above right) emphasised her isolation and the dangers she faced from the Luftwaffe and U-boats.

non-existent. This was because for most of the inter-war years the Naval and Air Staffs had been locked in bitter battle over control of aircraft at sea which had resulted in the Navy finally winning command over the Fleet Air Arm and the RAF jealously preserving its authority over Coastal Command.

Moreover aircraft by themselves had not sunk any U-boats during the First War but there was ample evidence in the records to show that they played a useful role in forcing the U-boats to submerge, thereby drastically reducing their efficiency. The dramatic increase in protection which this afforded would have been immediately clear from any statistical study which would have shown that in the final year of the war, those convoys that had been escorted by both sea and air had lost only two ships.

This prejudice led to an ignorance of the true anti-submarine potential of aircraft. As a result, not only did Coastal Command start the war with 300 fewer aircraft than it had had in 1918, but most of them were totally unsuited for patrolling long distances over sea and the crews were untrained in anti-submarine operations. When they were eventually deployed against the U-boats it was found that their land bombs often bounced back off the water, to do more damage to the plane than to the U-boat.

THE Z PLAN

In 1939, the Admiralty was fortunate that the German Navy, because of its own internal divisions, was so short of U-boats that it would not be able to launch a full-scale offensive against Britain for two years. The U-boat arm had steadily pressed for more submarines and Dönitz, in the spring of 1939 after his big Atlantic exercises, sent a detailed memorandum to the Naval Staff setting out the need for at least 300. With that number he believed he could win a naval war against England, warning that with his present force of 57 boats he could accomplish no more 'than a series of pinpricks'.

Many of the senior officers on the German Naval Staff, like their British counterparts, were gunnery officers, whose thinking was dominated by Jutland. This had become clear in 1937 when they had backed plans to build two great battleships – *Bismarck* and *Tirpitz* – as the foundation of a powerful battlefleet. At this stage Raeder and the other German Admirals were not contemplating a challenge to British naval supremacy but hopes of avoiding

H44 (length 345 m)

The Z Plan Challenge: In 1938 Hitler's modest naval plan for a fleet (top) of 4 battleships, 2 aircraft carriers, 8 cruisers, and 46 U-boats was tripled. 6 super-battleships, 2 more carriers, 25 cruisers and an additional 221 U-boats as well as a large number of destroyers, were to be built by 1947. After the launching of Germany's first carrier *Graf Zeppelin* (above) in December, the first of the Z Plan 60,000 ton super battleships was laid down (left).

another clash with their old enemy were finally shattered on 5 November 1937 when Hitler assembled his service chiefs in a secret session at the Chancellery for a four-hour lecture on his political objectives. This made it plain he intended to go to war and Raeder was alarmed to hear Hitler single out England as 'the hateful enemy to whom a strong German colossus in the centre of Europe would be intolerable'. The Kriegsmarine was ordered to plan accordingly a Fleet powerful enough to take on the world's greatest naval power.

It seemed an impossible task, but Raeder set up a special committee under a brilliant young staff Commander, Helmuth Heye, to produce a plan. After six months of study, during which it rejected a plan for a vast U-boat fleet, the Heye Committee finally presented the Naval Staff with a choice between a fleet of pocket battleships and U-boats that could be built quickly for mercantile warfare, or a balanced force of battleships and carriers capable of matching the Royal Navy but requiring many years to complete.

Raeder and Hitler both accepted the Naval Staff's recommendation for the big ship strategy. This called for a powerful 'Z Plan Fleet' to operate in four main forces. First would be a *Home Fleet* strong enough to take on the British Home Fleet, which would consist of four super battleships, two heavy cruisers and flotillas of destroyers. Second, *Raiding Forces* for attacking commerce, which would be made up of the three pocket battleships, five armoured cruisers, five light cruisers and 190 U-boats and finally two strong *Attack Forces* each consisting of an aircraft carrier and three fast battleships, two cruisers and destroyers.

The Z Plan Fleet was a skilful attempt to operate two naval strategies: 'the fleet in being' and 'the control of communications'. The main fleet would tie down the British Home Fleet whilst the raiding forces would attack her trade. Any attempt to hunt down the raiders by dispersing British Fleet units would result in the two fast attack forces being sent to trap them.

The Z Plan was given priority over all other projects in January 1939 after Raeder had warned Hitler that such an ambitious naval construction programme could not be completed before 1946. But as Hitler's determination to force a decision on Poland brought the international situation to crisis point, it soon became clear to Raeder that building the Z Plan Fleet was a hopeless race against time. In September 1939, the Kriegsmarine found itself in the appalling situation of having to fight a war it was not ready to face for another seven years with a paper Fleet. The *Bismarck* and *Tirpitz* were still a year from completion; the Reich was outnumbered by the British 7:1 in battleships, 6:1 in cruisers, and 9:1 in destroyers, whilst only two carriers were being built against Britain's six. The U-boat arm was only one sixth the strength estimated as necessary for a war against British trade. After his first grim reaction that it was 'like sending a soldier into battle without his arms', Raeder resolved to apply Tirpitz's old maxim of using 'the power of audacity' to make bold and cunning strikes against the Royal Navy's defences. It was essential for the U-boats to begin ruthless attacks on British shipping as soon as possible.

TOTAL WAR

The British government was now organising for total war and, remembering the chastening experience of 1917, top priority was given to organising the country to counter the threat of a U-boat siege. Apart from the anti-submarine and trade defence activities of the Admiralty, elaborate systems for the control of imports, licensing of commodities and organisation of merchant shipping were put in hand. Docks, harbours, inland transport and storage facilities were all included in the comprehensive defence plans which had been worked out in peacetime, on the assumption that Britain would be subjected to an immediate air bombardment and a long siege.

The government's measures also affected people's lives as the state assumed increasing responsibility for everyday needs. On 29 September, National Registration Day, every man, woman and child's name was listed and identity cards were issued. This National Register formed the basis of the food-rationing scheme which had been drawn up before the war. Although the public expected immediate rationing, there was muddle and delay in setting up the system. The Cabinet was uncertain how much rationing was necessary in view of conflicting estimates of food reserves by their experts.

The Post Office struggled to deliver 45 m. ration books, which would allow each citizen a regular and equal supply of bacon, butter and sugar. The day on which rationing was due to commence was pushed back repeatedly and when the threatened air bombardment failed to materialise and the Admiralty felt confident of controlling the U-boat menace, the War Cabinet debated whether rationing should be introduced at all. It was believed to be politically unpopular and damaging to morale, but this consideration had to be weighed against the danger that 'rationing by the purse', could lead to inflation and serious social pressures. With the reduction in the U-boat attacks during early October, Churchill sent a strong memorandum to the Home Secretary:

'**Cheap & Nasties**': Churchill gave top priority to an emergency programme for the mass production of new Flower Class escorts. Based on a whalecatcher design of Smith's Dock Co. Ltd, Middlesbrough, the ships were simple to build, and cost only £90,000 apiece. Churchill immediately added another 30 to the 56 already on order and a further batch were ordered from Canada. Eventually 288 were built and their destruction of 50 U-boats proved they were very 'nasty'.

By all means have rations but I am told the meat ration for instance is very little better than that of Germany. Is there any need of this when the seas are still open? If we have a heavy set-back from air attack or surface attack it might be necessary to inflict these severities. Up to the present there is no reason to suppose that the Navy has failed in bringing in the supplies, or that it will fail.

The First Lord had embarked upon a hectic round of inspections, visits and conferences throughout the fleet, and to the frustration of senior officers ventured opinions and instructions on subjects well within their professional sphere. As soon as Churchill had taken over the Admiralty he wanted to cut battleship construction, seeing it as his 'duty to readjust our programme to the need of the hour and to enforce the largest possible expansion of the anti-U-boat vessels'. He ran into fierce opposition from some Admirals when he proposed putting everything into the escort programme and stopping work on new battleships that could not be completed by 1941. In a memorandum, dated 12 September, Churchill called for one hundred of the new corvettes: 'These will be deemed the "Cheap and Nasties" (cheap to us, nasty to the U-boats). These ships, being built for a particular but urgent job, will no doubt be of little value to the Navy when that job is done – but let us get the job done.'

The difficult task of dealing with both Churchill and the Kriegsmarine fell on the shoulders of the First Sea Lord, Admiral Sir Dudley Pound, whose character was a contrast to that of his political master. A quiet and humourless man, Pound kept his emotions under firm control and rarely lost his temper, but his professional skill and keen analytical mind were deeply respected. It was both his strength and weakness that he lacked the political flair of his First Lord. There were many in the Admiralty who felt that his predecessor, Admiral Lord Chatfield, ought to have been recalled when war broke out but there is little doubt that Churchill would have clashed with such a strong personality.

The close working relationship with Pound was to endure after Churchill became Prime Minister, allowing him to continue to feel that he was directly involved in the Admiralty's decisions. Pound's death, in 1943, from a brain tumour was deeply felt by Churchill. He had continued working to the last, apparently unaffected according to those who worked with him daily, although Churchill had noted that Pound had a tendency to sleep at War Cabinet meetings until the Navy was mentioned; then he mysteriously awoke. The fact that his temperament was so different to Churchill's probably helped Pound evolve a very effective relationship with his volatile political master. Avoiding head-on clashes with Churchill, Pound used the calm logic of staff papers to dissuade the First Lord from some of his more ambitious and risky schemes. According to one staff officer, the first Sea Lord's approach, 'calm and deaf as required – never getting into heated argument', made for peace.

This formidable team was soon to be tested by Raeder's 'power of audacity' when the Reich renewed its naval offensive in the second week of October.

Churchill's 'Man at the Admiralty' The First Sea Lord, Admiral Sir Dudley Pound (above) was a determined and taciturn leader who soon established a close working relationship with Churchill. The partnership was to take the Royal Navy through the most critical years of the Battle of the Atlantic. For Pound, Churchill was a difficult master. According to one of his senior Admirals the First Lord's 'battery of weapons included: persuasion, real or simulated anger, mockery, vituperation, tantrums, ridicule, derision, abuse and tears which he would aim at anyone who opposed him or who expressed a view contrary to the one he had already formed, sometimes on quite trivial questions.'

3. The Acme of Villainy

'Driven from the gun to the torpedo and from the torpedo to the mine,
U-boats have now reached the acme of villainy.'

WINSTON CHURCHILL, November 1939

'**Abandon Ship!**' The crew of a steamer scrambling into the lifeboats after their ship had been mined. Scenes like this became alarmingly frequent during the last months of 1939 as the Germans stepped up their mining operations of English ports.

After the fall of Poland and the lull in the war at sea following the return of the first wave of U-boats to refuel, Hitler launched his planned 'Peace Offensive' with the announcement that 'it would serve the interests of all people to put an end to the state of war between Germany, Britain and France.' In a long harangue to the Reichstag on 6 October he cast himself as the man of peace, declaring 'it would be more sensible to find a solution before millions of men and milliards of riches are destroyed.' But neither the British nor the United States government saw any future in dealing with the Nazis. Six days after the Reichstag olive branch, in an uncharacteristically tough speech, Chamberlain rejected the peace proposals when he told the House of Commons, 'it is no longer possible to rely on the unsupported word of the German Government. We must persevere to the end.'

Germany's reply to the rejection of Hitler's peace terms was rapid and stunning. In the early hours of 14 October a U-boat penetrated the Home Fleet anchorage at Scapa Flow in the Orkneys and sank a battleship.

This 'boldest of bold enterprises' had been meticulously planned by Dönitz after a study of intelligence photographs of the base's extensive anti-submarine nets, barriers and minefields, had revealed what appeared to be an unprotected fifty foot channel between the three blockships in Holm Sound which might just allow a U-boat to slip past 'on the surface at the turn of the tide'. He selected 31-year-old Kapitänleutnant Günther Prien, a stocky, former merchant navy officer of the Norddeutscher Lloyd Line, for a briefing. As commander of the U-47, Prien had proved one of the most determined of the new U-boat captains, with a reputation for being a strong disciplinarian. It was not unknown for him to return from patrol with a third of his crew on a charge. But so dangerous did Dönitz regard the operation that he gave Prien 48 hours to consider whether he would take on the mission. The young commander accepted without hesitation.

Total secrecy was preserved when U-47 sailed, and by 12 October Prien approached the heavily-guarded Orkney base. After an anxious day spent on the bottom whilst his engineers struggled to repair defective machinery, Prien surfaced late on the evening of the 13 October. He made the difficult approach during slack water after high tide which gave him the best chance of navigating the narrow channel. If he had arrived twenty four hours later he would have found the channel barred by a new block-ship which arrived the next morning, but shortly after midnight his luck was in, as his log recorded:

It is disgustingly light. The whole bay is lit up . . .

South of Cava there is no shipping; now staking everything on success, all possible precautions must be taken. Therefore, turn to port is made. We proceed north by coast. Two battleships are lying at anchor, and, further inshore, destroyers. Cruisers not visible, therefore attack on the big fellows. Distance apart 3,000 metres. Estimated depth 7.5 metres. Impact firing.

0116: One torpedo fired on the northern ship, two on southern. After a good 3½ minutes a torpedo detonates on the northern ship; of the other two nothing is to be seen.

0121: Torpedo fired from stern; in the bow both tubes are loaded; *three torpedoes from the bow*. After three tense minutes come the detonations on the nearer ship. There is a loud explosion, roar and rumbling. Then come columns of water,

'The Dove Appears': This American newspaper cartoon summed up the sceptical reception of Hitler's 'Peace Offensive'. On 6 October he declared: 'At no time and no place have I ever acted contrary to the British interests . . . why should this war in the West be fought?' Within three days he was ordering his military chiefs to prepare plans to attack France, Belgium and Britain telling them that Germany's war aim 'is and remains the destruction of our western enemies'.

followed by columns of fire and splinters flying through the air. The harbour springs to life. Destroyers are lit up, signalling starts on every side, and on land 200 metres away from me, cars roar along the roads. A battleship has been sunk, a second damaged and the other three torpedoes have gone to blazes. All the tubes are empty.

What Prien had taken to be a second warship was a seaplane carrier but he had sunk the battleship *Royal Oak*. 786 officers and men from her crew were lost. The rest of the Home Fleet had been dispersed after hunting the *Gneisenau* across the North Sea and the destruction of the old battleship was less of a disaster than it might have been, nevertheless for the Royal Navy it was a humiliating revelation of the vulnerability of their principal naval base.

To the British public a battleship was still a battleship – whatever its age – and the loss of the *Royal Oak* was a keenly felt disaster. There were angry press reactions against the triumphant German propaganda which told the world how Britannia was being 'driven from the North Sea.' To show that this was no hollow boast, three days later the Luftwaffe penetrated the British defences to bomb ships of the Home Fleet now at anchor under the shadow of the Forth Railway Bridge and, next day Scapa Flow was raided. With some embarrassment the Admiralty ordered the Home Fleet to disperse to the Clyde and Loch Ewe on the West Coast of Scotland beyond the range of the Luftwaffe but they were not beyond the reach of Dönitz's U-boats which were sent to mine the approaches of the Scottish anchorages. On 31 October 1939, the brand-new cruiser *Belfast* had her back broken by a mine laid by U-31 in the Forth, and serious damage was caused five weeks later to the battleship *Nelson*, the flagship of the Home Fleet, which detonated another magnetic mine laid by U-33 off Loch Ewe.

'A Magnificent Feat of Arms': This was Churchill's comment on the destruction of the battleship *Royal Oak* (top) which was a severe blow to the prestige of the Royal Navy. To Kapitänleutnant Günther Prien (above) it brought a hero's welcome in Berlin and his Commander in Chief, Karl Dönitz was promoted for conceiving the 'boldest of bold' enterprises.

41

ECONOMIC WARFARE

Admiral Raeder wasted no time in using Prien's triumph and Hitler's improved opinion of the Navy to press for an intensification of the U-boat war. On 16 October he presented a Naval Memorandum which argued for immediate, unrestricted U-boat warfare since Germany was now in a fight to the finish with Britain which demanded the subordination of neutral interests and international law to 'military requirements'. Advising the 'most ruthless form of economic warfare', Raeder concluded:

> no threat by other countries, especially the United States, to come into the war – which can certainly be expected if the conflict continues for a long time – must lead to a relaxation of economic warfare once it is begun. The more ruthlessly economic warfare is waged, the earlier it will show results and the sooner the war will end.

In spite of this warning the Führer was still not prepared to risk the political repercussions of 'a ruthless siege of England', but he lifted his previous restrictions on attacking French merchant shipping, although insisting that passenger ships should be given notice.

A week later, when it was plain that the Führer's hopes for a negotiated peace had collapsed, Raeder renewed his pressure for the adoption of the Naval Staff's 'Economic Warfare Plan'. This called for a co-ordinated offensive to bring Britain to her knees with massive bombing of British ports and industrial centres by the Luftwaffe to support the Kriegsmarine's operations against Britain's sea communications. This ambitious plan at first received Hitler's enthusiastic backing. General Keitel, Chief of the *Oberkommando der Wehrmacht* (OKW) – the High Command of the German Armed Forces – was ordered to set up a staff specifically to direct 'the war against merchant shipping and all other measures for attacking the economic installations, resources and trade of the enemy'.

Fortunately for Britain, inter-service planning was alien to the German High Command so that the committee broke up soon after its preliminary meetings. The Army staff was totally absorbed in planning a great western offensive and Goering boasted that his airfleets could eliminate England without assistance from the Navy. This rivalry between the services extended to industrial production and the Economic Ministry refused to give the Kriegsmarine the priority needed to increase U-boat construction. After three weeks Raeder was bitterly complaining to Hitler about the lack of progress in the U-boat programme, pointing out that the half dozen losses sustained by the U-boat fleet already exceeded current output.

Absorbed by his plans to attack France, Hitler soon cooled towards the Naval War Plan and informed Raeder that the Navy would have to wait for the essential allocations of steel and labour until the conclusion of the land campaign in the west. The German economy had been geared to a short Blitzkrieg war aimed at limited objectives and there was insufficient steel and industrial capacity available for making all the tanks and guns required by the army, as well as increasing U-boat production for the Navy. Raeder was told that he could expect no more than seventeen new U-boats in the coming

MARITIME REQUIRE-MENTS FOR THE DECISIVE STRUGGLE AGAINST BRITAIN
'Germany's principal enemy in this war is Britain. Her most vulnerable spot is her maritime trade . . . The principal target of our naval strategy is the merchant ship, not only the enemy's but every merchantman which sails the seas in order to supply the enemy's war interests. Military success can most confidently be expected if we attack British sea communications where they are most accessible to us with the greatest ruthlessness. The final aim of such attacks is to cut off all imports into and exports from Britain.'
    Naval War Staff
    Memorandum
    Berlin 15 October 1939

Crisis in U-Boat Construction:
The promised priorities for steel and labour were not given to the Navy and output from the yards such as the main Krupp Germania Werft (above) at Kiel was falling off. In November, Raeder warned Hitler that with only 3 new boats by January and with the anticipated 8 losses, only 15 U-boats were currently operational. This number would fall to 11 or less early in 1940.

twelve months, insufficient even to replace the anticipated 10 per cent loss rate. This was totally inadequate to run an all-out campaign and during the first winter of the war, Dönitz was never able to maintain more than ten U-boats in the operational areas, and sometimes only two.

Faced with this lack of U-boats Dönitz resolved: 'that they could achieve results only if they took the bull by the horns and attacked, as far as possible, the concentration point of traffic in or near harbours'. This tactic achieved results out of all proportion to their numbers. In October they had torpedoed 27 ships which, together with the 19 destroyed by U-boat laid mines, brought the total sunk since the beginning of the war to nearly 200,000 tons.

The high losses and the accelerating pace of attacks pointed to a steady escalation towards unrestricted U-boat warfare. This had been anticipated as early as 11 September when Churchill had announced to the Shipping Defence Committee his decision to arm 'a thousand merchant ships' to force the enemy to operate under water. This, he believed, would act to Britain's advantage, as he explained to the shipowners:

> they will not be successful with the underwater attacks; there is nothing like the free play on the surface. So although the war will become more brutal, nevertheless it will be to our advantage . . . they will have the ignomity of adopting a method of warfare which is condemned by the whole of world opinion.

QUARTERLY SCORE CHART
See Key p. 308

Sep-Dec 1939

MERCHANTMEN AT WAR

The decision to arm merchant ships was at once seized upon by Germany as a justification for attacking all armed ships without warning. Some owners resisted the arming of their ships for fear of inviting attacks, but most ships' Masters and crews welcomed the chance to fight back and the U-boats soon found some of their intended victims capable of surprising things. Captain Ernest Coultas of the SS *Clan MacBean* had seen two ships of the 27 strong convoy HG 3 sunk before it scattered for safety across the Bay of Biscay. On 18 October he reached the bridge minutes after a torpedo had missed his own vessel 'by inches'.

> I manoeuvred the ship, which is very responsive to her helm, so as to continually point at the submarine, following each of her turns – or rather anticipating them – with the net result that, although the submarine was feinting, I constantly managed to close her. When we were about 200 feet apart the submarine opened fire with her gun, firing three rounds but registering no hits . . . When we had closed to within 100 feet of the U-boat she realised the danger of being rammed and dived. She apparently left the gun crew in the water, for almost immediately after we heard loud cries of distress. We passed right over the top of her, but apparently she had gone deep enough to avoid us. We saw her later astern trying to rescue the gun crew. This delayed her and allowed us to escape.

Accounts of similar incidents were circulated to shipping companies to encourage their captains to fight the U-boats. The courage and skill displayed was typical of the resolute way in which the merchant seamen accepted that from now on they were now going to be in the front line of the war at sea. The

Arming the Merchantmen: At the outbreak of hostilities work began on rapidly equipping a thousand ships with 12 pounders from the large stock of First War guns (above) which were installed on specially constructed stern platforms. It was believed that this measure would force the U-boats to attack submerged, making them more vulnerable to Asdic patrols. However, these proved ineffective and it served to provide the Germans with an excuse for sinking armed merchant ships without warning.

men of the Merchant Navy were a fiercely independent body of civilians who were inclined to refer to their uniformed colleagues as 'the pansy Royal Navy with its perishing gas and gaiters'.

Nowhere was the gulf more obvious between the Red and the White Ensign than at the top. Merchant ships' Captains attended the pre-sailing conferences 'nearly all clasping bowlers and wearing fawn raincoats over civilian suits (the Merchant Navy Captain's usual visiting-the-owners rig)' as Rear Admiral Kenelm Creighton noted at his first convoy conference. His reaction was shared by many of the retired and often very senior naval officers, whose average age was over sixty. They had answered the call to active service to become Commodores in charge of the merchant convoys. As Kenelm Creighton remarked,

> The masters struck me on first acquaintance as being ordinary, unpretentious people, but I soon found that there was something which set them apart from their contemporaries ashore, a compact self-contained confident and calm simplicity . . . Their small talk is generally nil, their speech usually abrupt, confined to essentials and very much to the point . . . They uphold discipline by sheer character and personality – for their powers of punishment under Board of Trade Regulations are almost non-existent.

When war broke out, there were some 4,500 masters in command of the ships of the world's largest merchant marine that employed 120,000 men. They were backed up by about 13,000 deck officers and 20,000 engineers. The bulk of the service, was made up of 36,000 deck ratings, 30,000 engine room ratings and 17,000 stewards. This traditionally independent and hardy service numbered less than eight army divisions, but every uniformed serviceman as well as every man, woman and child in the British Isles, depended on them for ultimate survival.

The men who sailed under the Red Ensign had little regard for rank. They were either officers or donkeymen, greasers, deck hands, stokers, trimmers or stewards drawn from all the races and creeds of the British Empire. A third were Lascars – indentured coloured seamen – three quarters of whom were Indians. Many stewards came from Bombay and the Chittagong waterfronts, with Sikhs from the Punjab traditionally recruited as stokers in the boiler rooms of the many coal-burning ships. In most engine rooms could be found African greasers and some ships were crewed with Arab seamen from the Gulf ports, or Malays and Chinese from Hong Kong.

In peace time these multi-racial crews had been hired for service by those lines sailing between their home ports on the tropical routes, but with the introduction of war routine they frequently found themselves serving on the northern waters of the Atlantic where many of the Lascars would become the first to succumb in open lifeboats. Most engine room staff, in any case, lived closer to death than those on deck. Their chances of survival were slight in the steam-filled inferno of a torpedoed ship's engine room.

Britain's merchant marine could ill afford serious losses. Although it was the world's largest mercantile fleet with some 6,000 ships over 500 tons, the pre-war recession had hit the industry hard. There had been heavy unemployment and Britain's share of world shipping had declined. The slump had

IN THE FRONT LINE

A Convoy Commodore: Rear Admiral Kenelm Creighton.

A Master: Captain A. L. Davis of the SS *Cyclops*.

A Fireman: Patrick O'Neill, a Dubliner with 30 years service.

A Lascar Seaman: An African greaser, one of the 50,000 coloured men in the British Merchant service.

45

also been disastrous for the shipyards which, in the decade before the war, were working at only half the rate of 1918. The industry had contracted so much that Britain started the war with 2,000 fewer merchant ships than she possessed at the end of the First War, a shortage made more serious because the population of the country had increased by nearly four million. Furthermore, transport and industry were consuming ten times more petroleum products than in 1918, but pre-war governments had neglected building up a large tanker fleet, with the result that Britain relied heavily on American and Norwegian tonnage.

In an effort to get every available cargo ship back on to the trade routes the Government offered generous insurance cover, so that many ageing vessels which would otherwise have been broken up were sent back to sea. Owners quickly saw a chance of making a profit from old ships that had been rusting for years in creeks and rivers and many of the crews found conditions aboard

Harnessing the Merchant Navy: To make the most efficient use of shipping, the Admiralty Trade Division plot in Whitehall (above) controlled the route and position of every British vessel throughout the world. The expansion of the Merchant service to meet war demands and the high casualty rate brought many to sea for the first time. Volunteers were exempted from call-up into the armed services and some passed through special training courses (above). Most of the young men who were attracted by the sense of adventure and freedom from discipline joined their first ship with no previous training or experience. John Harrison of Liverpool was 16 and left school:

'I joined the tramp steamer SS *Bathna* as a cabin boy after being turned down by the army who told me "come back when you start shaving". On my first trip my mother made me take a huge box of sandwiches telling me "They'll last you until you get home".'

some of these old boats unbearable. Urban Peters, who signed on the passenger ship SS *Oropesa*, 'probably the tallest funnel out of Liverpool', recalled 'She was a dirty ship and even after laying up for years the bugs came out in force, attacking all and sundry. It was so bad that we were given the passenger accommodation'.

After sailing from the Mersey in one of the early convoys escorted by 'a couple of destroyers to a point several hundred miles out in the Atlantic', Peters, who had signed on as a storekeeper, was kept busy catering for troops on their way to Bermuda.

> You just didn't mention being torpedoed. It always happened to the other fellow, not you, and the further afield you got the less you worried about submarines. We had boat drills every day and the boats swung out ready. We had a gun mounted aft which was just about the most antiquated thing I had seen up to then. It was a Japanese 4.7″ which was laid and trained by hand. Directly underneath the mounting was the crew galley and about six cabins accommodating the quartermaster and the gunners. When they had practice firing the galley funnel would get blocked and all the coal smoke would come back into the galley and force the cook to evacuate. At the first round of firing my mate, the storekeeper, would head for the lifeboat.

Once through the Panama canal 'the whole routine changed' and Peters recalled many occasions when the war seemed far away. In the South American ports, when the *Oropesa* tied up alongside German vessels trapped by the blockade:

> The amazing thing was that, instead of clashes between the two rival seamen, we all used to go aboard each other's ships, sampling the beer and having a good time. Valparaiso was full of Germans, including the crew of a training ship manned by cadets. These were all working ashore as waiters in the bars and cabarets, so once again we were in amicable conflict with the enemy. The whole thing seemed ludicrous at the time.

Drawing on its experience of the First War, the Admiralty Trade Division was soon organising the movements of British ships with Naval Control Officers stationed in ports all over the world. This vital work was of great personal interest to Churchill, who had minuted the First Sea Lord in October: 'Ought we not to have a daily report of every convoy as regularly worked out as a signal system on the railway?' Admiral Pound was able to point out that Captain Mansergh, then Director of the Trade Division, had almost perfected just such a scheme. The main outward-bound Atlantic convoys sailing from the Thames were designated 'OA'. They assembled at Southend and moved down Channel, picking up ships from the South Coast ports. In the North, 'OB' convoys left Liverpool and sailed through the Irish Sea, where they were joined by ships from Bristol and the West Coast. Homeward-bound convoys from Halifax, Nova Scotia, the main departure point for the western end of the North Atlantic run, were coded 'HX' and 'KJ'. Mediterranean and South Atlantic convoys had their own codification, when they passed Gibraltar, outward-bound convoys were named 'OG' (Outward Gibraltar), whilst those which were homeward-bound were labelled 'HG' (Homeward Gibraltar) and 'SL' (Sierra Leone).

The convoys were kept to a maximum of seventy ships sailing in a compact formation covering about twenty square miles of sea, each vessel 3½ cables apart. At first, because of pressure from the shipping companies and the shortage of escorts, faster ships were allowed to sail independently in the hope that their speed would beat the enemy. The escorts, usually two destroyers in the first months of the war, only accompanied the outward-bound ships to a point a hundred miles out into the Western Approaches. Their role was then taken over by a single Ocean Escort, usually an armed Merchant liner. The destroyers then picked up a homeward-bound convoy, escorting it as far as the South Western Approaches of Ireland where it split into two streams, heading for the Irish Sea and the Channel.

Coastal Command aircraft flew air patrols over the convoys whenever possible, but the inexperienced pilots often made appalling navigational errors. One aircraft radio fix placed a convoy in the middle of the Place de la Concorde, and another convoy was plotted for two days before it was discovered still at anchor off the Liverpool Bar Light Vessel!

Station keeping was at first chaotic as engineers and masters struggled to keep in their appointed colums with fine adjustments of propeller revolutions to maintain a constant speed. There were often uneasy moments of tension between the captains of Royal Navy escorts and the independent-minded merchant skippers who believed that they knew as much about seamanship as the 'Grey Funnel Line'. The difficult task of controlling the merchantmen fell to the Convoy Commodore who, although a highly experienced Royal Navy Reserve officer such as a retired Admiral or the ex-commander of an ocean liner, had to exercise his authority tactfully since he would usually be in a merchant ship. He had to depend on his Navy-trained Yeoman of Signals who was kept busy warning the more wayward vessels to keep their position. Ships, particularly the coal-burners that betrayed the convoy by emitting black clouds of smoke, were a major problem. Merchant skippers puzzled over the detailed station-keeping orders, and voluminous instructions on what to do in an attack. They also had to take care not to make smoke by day or show lights at night. They were warned not to dump rubbish overboard or pump the bilges during the daytime so that floating waste or oily slicks would not betray the convoy's route.

The complex procedures for zigzagging a convoy were carefully set out, but the rehearsals of a first-time convoy were a hair-raising experience for all concerned – particularly at night without lights. Keeping a convoy together in heavy weather or when a thick fog necessitated each ship following a buoy streamed from the one in front was a nightmare that both Commodores and Masters prayed to avoid.

Nevertheless, after a few weeks shake-down the convoys were soon proving their practical value. The Admiralty could easily divert them around reported U-boat positions and the small number of enemy submarines ensured that there was plenty of empty searoom in the Western Approaches through which the convoys could be safely diverted.

Assault on the Shipping Lanes: As the Allied convoy system got into full swing in October, with one in every four ships being escorted through Western Approaches by French destroyers (below) the first *Rudeltaktik* operations proved a failure because there were too few U-boats. To counter the convoys the Germans stepped up the mining of Britain's ports (right). The first of the new magnetic mines were laid on 18 November and it was to be many months before successful countermeasures were introduced to deal with the devastating new weapon.

THE MINE OFFENSIVE

In answer to the improving British defences and evasive tactics, Dönitz prepared to switch his attack to the convoys themselves, using the 'Pack' tactics (*Rudeltaktik*) which had been so thoroughly rehearsed in the pre-war exercises. Nine boats, heading out to operations in October, were detailed to operate in a pack against the Gibraltar-routed convoys. The first attempts at *Rudeltaktik* under war conditions, however, proved a disappointment. Only three of the nine boats were ready on station when the group received the signal on 13 October to strike against HG 3 south west of Ireland. A couple of ships were sunk and the convoy dispersed, but torpedo failures and the difficulties experienced by Kapitänleutnant Hartmann of U-37 in directing the operations of the pack were considerable. The same problems dogged other attempts at pack operations during late October, leading Dönitz to conclude:

> On each occasion the number of U-boats available was not big enough to enable them to locate the convoys on the high seas and deliver joint attacks against them. This to my mind seemed clearly to prove that the number of U-boats available was still too small for us to be able profitably to build up the sort of concentration of force I had envisaged.

After this, Dönitz was forced to postpone an all-out pack offensive for a year. He also took a decision that was profoundly to influence the development of the Battle of the Atlantic when he decided; 'I myself could quite easily direct the whole tactical operation against a convoy from my headquarters ashore.'

A new offensive against shipping was launched in mid-October as mining operations were carried out in the approaches to British ports. So while sinkings by U-boats fell in November to half the previous month's total, no fewer than 27 ships, amounting to 121,000 tons, were sunk by mines in what the Admiralty interpreted as, 'an attempt to prove to neutral countries that it was suicidally dangerous to trade with Britain'.

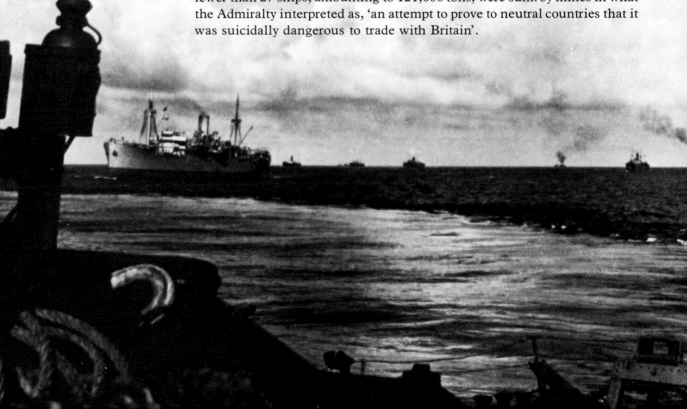

Since the outbreak of war, U-boats had been sprinkling mines at the entrance to ports and they were proving so successful that early in November, operations were stepped up when fast destroyer forces were sent out at night to lay extensive minefields off the East Coast and in the approaches to the Thames Estuary. The mining offensive of the late autumn had a devastating effect because the Germans had started to use the first of their secret weapons – the magnetic mine, triggered by the magnetic effect when a ship passed over them. The idea was not new. In 1917 the Royal Navy had tried their own experimental models but the device had not been taken seriously, so that the Navy possessed only one towed magnetic sweep. For months the only certain way of establishing the presence of a magnetic minefield was to wait until it claimed its first victim. The Admiralty for a long time refused to accept that these extensive minefields were the work of surface forces, and it was not until the New Year that destroyers were sent out on nightly patrols off the East Coast. Matters became serious when a big minefield was laid astride the main channel in the Thames Estuary, destroying two ships and a large tanker. Shipping was disrupted, and for weeks the Port of London was faced with a shutdown. Churchill fumed and accused the Germans of committing: 'an outrage upon the accepted international law. Driven from the gun to the torpedo and from the torpedo to the mine, U-boats have now reached the acme of villainy.'

Fortunately for Britain, the German Naval Staff's plan to lay their remaining stock of 22,000 magnetic mines before the British could produce counter-measures was frustrated by Goering, who refused to release aircraft for minelaying, so that the Kriegsmarine had to do its best with the handful of sea-planes at its disposal. On 23 November the German offensive suffered a major setback when a Navy pilot dropped two magnetic mines on the mudflats of Shoeburyness. They were immediately spotted and a Royal Navy mine disposal team succeeded in defusing a mine and dismantling its firing device. Their courageous efforts contributed to the development of the highly effective 'LL' electrical sweep and a system for 'degaussing' a ship's magnetism by passing a current through cables wrapped around its hull. Small vessels were degaussed at special stations where their magnetism was 'wiped', allowing them to pass over the mines.

Putting these elaborate counter-measures into full operation took many months and the German magnetic and contact minefields in home waters added considerably to the dangers faced by the merchant fleet during the first winter of the war. At the same time, in distant waters, the pocket battleships *Graf Spee* and *Deutschland* were preying on the shipping lanes. The speed and unpredictability of their attacks had thwarted the Admiralty's attempts to hunt them down with the eight powerful hunting groups.

On 22 October the *Graf Spee* had sunk the steamer SS *Trevarion* off the coast of South West Africa before heading into the Indian Ocean to shake off her pursuers. Nothing more was heard of her by the Admiralty, although on 15 November she had sunk the small tanker *Africa Shell* in the Mozambique Channel before she could send an RRR signal. The *Deutschland* was equally elusive and succeeded in reaching Germany undetected after sinking three ships. Hitler had ordered her home because he did not want the embarrassment of risking the loss of a ship bearing her name. On 15 November she reached her Gotenhafen base in East Prussia where she was renamed *Lützow*.

This successful penetration of the British blockade encouraged Raeder to send out his newly completed fast battleships, *Scharnhorst* and *Gneisenau*, a week later with orders to 'roll up the enemy control of the sea passage between the Faroes and Iceland'. The operation, designed to distract the Royal Navy from the *Graf Spee*, was made possible because the Kriegsmarine's *Beobachtungs-Dienst* (B Dienst Intelligence Service) had broken the British codes and could accurately forecast the movements of the enemy air and sea units.

The two battleships had almost succeeded in breaking out into the Atlantic undetected, when, late on the afternoon of 23 November, they ran into the armed merchant cruiser *Rawalpindi* on Northern Patrol midway between Iceland and the Faroes. In the gathering dusk Captain E. C. Kennedy had barely time to send off the urgent signal 'ENEMY BATTLECRUISERS SIGHTED' before his converted liner was surrounded by waterspouts from the two battleships' 11″ broadsides. Ordering his eight 6″ guns to reply, Kennedy took on his mighty opponents in a heroic action that lasted just sixteen minutes. The *Rawalpindi*'s shells caused slight damage to the *Scharnhorst* before flames engulfed the former liner, lighting up the dark sea.

The Germans chivalrously decided to rescue their gallant opponents, an effort that nearly ended in disaster when the cruiser HMS *Newcastle* arrived at the scene, alerted by the Admiralty's urgent signals to intercept what they assumed was the *Deutschland*'s attempted break-back. The battleships abandoned their rescue mission and slipped away. For three days they were unsuccessfully hunted by every unit in the Home Fleet but the German squadron escaped, aided by very accurate intelligence about British movements and a skilful use of the thick weather to cover their movements down the Norwegian coast and into the Skaggerak. The 'power of audacity' was proving that the small German surface Fleet could be as big a menace to Britain's sea supremacy as the U-boats.

23 November 1939: Royal Navy experts succeeded in recovering their first German magnetic mine intact (left, King George VI inspecting it after it had yielded up its secrets). That day also saw the heroic stand by the armed merchant cruiser HMS *Rawalpindi* commanded by Captain E. C. Kennedy (top) against the two battleships *Scharnhorst* and *Gneisenau* (below) which thwarted their attempted breakout into the Atlantic.

4. The Sinister Trap

'The news which has come from Montevideo has been received
with the greatest thankfulness in our island, and with
unconcealed satisfaction throughout the greater part of the world'
WINSTON CHURCHILL World Broadcast, 18 December 19⎯

An Inglorious Fate: The shattered hulk of the *Graf Spee*
settling into the mud of the
River Plate six weeks after the
epic battle had ended her career
as a commerce raider (map).

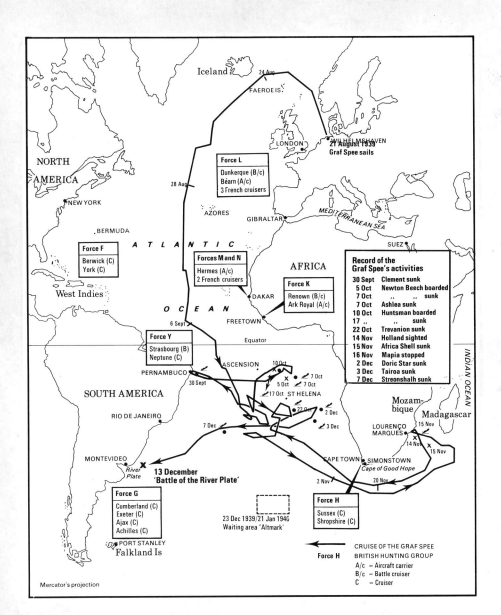

Iceland

NORTH
AMERICA

NEW YORK

BERMUDA

West Indies

FAEROE IS.

24 Aug

WILHELMSHAVEN
21 August 1939
Graf Spee sails

28 Aug

LONDON

AZORES

GIBRALTAR

MEDITERRANEAN SEA

SUEZ

Force L

Dunkerque (B/c)
Béarn (A/c)
3 French cruisers

Force F

Berwick (C)
York (C)

Forces M and N

Hermes (A/c)
2 French cruisers

A T L A N T I C

AFRICA

**Record of the
Graf Spee's activities**

30 Sept   Clement sunk
5 Oct   Newton Beech boarded
7 Oct   „   „   sunk
7 Oct   Ashlea sunk
10 Oct   Huntsman boarded
17 „   „   „   sunk
22 Oct   Trevanion sunk
14 Nov   Holland sighted
15 Nov   Africa Shell sunk
16 Nov   Mapia stopped
2 Dec   Doric Star sunk
3 Dec   Tairoa sunk
7 Dec   Streonshalh sunk

Force K

Renown (B/c)
Ark Royal (A/c)

DAKAR

O C E A N

FREETOWN

6 Sept

Equator

Force Y

Strasbourg (B)
Neptune (C)

PERNAMBUCO

ASCENSION

10 Oct

5 Oct   7 Oct

7 Oct

17 Oct   ST HELENA

22 Oct

2 Dec

INDIAN OCEAN

SOUTH AMERICA

30 Sept

RIO DE JANEIRO

3 Dec

Mozam-
bique

Madagascar

7 Dec

LOURENÇO
MARQUES

15 Nov

14 Nov

15 Nov

MONTEVIDEO

CAPE TOWN   SIMONSTOWN

*River
Plate*

**13 December
'Battle of the River Plate'**

2 Nov

Cape of Good Hope

20 Nov

Force G

Cumberland (C)
Exeter (C)
Ajax (C)
Achilles (C)

23 Dec 1939/21 Jan 1940
Waiting area 'Altmark'

Force H

Sussex (C)
Shropshire (C)

PORT STANLEY

Falkland Is

⟵   CRUISE OF THE GRAF SPEE
Force H   BRITISH HUNTING GROUP
            A/c = Aircraft carrier
            B/c = Battle cruiser
            C   = Cruiser

Mercator's projection

By December 1939, in the absence of any land fighting after the fall of Poland, both sides had settled into the uneasy routine of the 'Phoney War'. In France, the opposing armies faced one another across the great defensive barrier of the Maginot line and the Commander in Chief of the British Expeditionary Force, General Ironside, confidently asserted 'Hitler has missed the bus'. The German soldiers, dug into their prepared positions, joked about *Sitzkrieg* as the Army planners made preparations for *Fall Gelb* – the code name for the spring offensive in the West. But there was no let-up in the war at sea, which was becoming more bitter every day. Britain had already suffered the loss of 150 merchant ships to the U-boats as well as a battleship and aircraft carrier. The half million tons of merchant shipping destroyed represented over 2 per cent of the Merchant Navy's total pre-war strength. After initial optimism that Asdic hunting and the convoy system had mastered the U-boat menace, the Admiralty's confidence was badly shaken. Losses continued to climb throughout October and November as the Germans moved towards unrestricted mining and U-boat warfare, in fulfillment of Hitler's decision that 'a concentrated attempt must be made to cut Britain off.'

To bring home the serious threat to Britain's lifelines, Goebbels began a new propaganda offensive using Rudyard Kipling's *Big Steamer*. The final verse of this poem, written during the U-boat crisis of the First War, was familiar to many English listeners and it was repeated with a taunting monotony in the final weeks of 1939:

> For the bread that you eat and the biscuits you nibble,
> The sweets that you suck and the joints that you carve.
> They are brought to you daily by all us big steamers,
> And if anyone hinders our way then you'll starve!

The radio broadcasts followed hard on the War Cabinet's unnerving discovery that wheat stocks were running out. Flour mills were on short time and for a few weeks it looked as though bread might have to be rationed.

It was the closest Britain came to bread rationing during the whole war and the November crisis was less attributable to losses of cargo ships than to bureaucratic muddle, resulting from a late harvest and lack of foresight by the Government in ensuring sufficient reserves the previous year.

The Government's complacency over laying in adequate stockpiles was revealed in a Ministry of Food warning that less than three weeks' supply of wheat remained whilst a number of other commodities, including sugar, had fallen to less than a month's supply. Raw-material reserves were even more alarming. Although there was six months' reserve of oil, supplies of other essentials were critically low, and there was only a couple of weeks' stock of iron ore. To aggravate the crisis, the newly set up Ministry of Shipping warned that previous estimates of sufficient shipping capacity to carry the 50–60 m. tons of annual imports were wrong, and calculations now showed that imports would have to be slashed by nearly 20%.

The first shipping crisis of the war soon produced a bitter row between the Ministries of Food and Supply over which one should concede the biggest

Better Off than the Germans?
During the 'Phoney War' rationing was the only manifestation of the conflict for most civilians. Petrol had been allocated by coupons (left) from the outset but food rationing was introduced gradually. By January 1940 only ham, bacon, butter, eggs and sugar had been restricted (below) to 4 ozs per adult per week. The Home Secretary confidently told the nation 'this is only a precautionary measure as there is no real shortage of either. Whereas in Germany weekly rations are: meat 1½ lbs, fats 8 ozs, sugar 8 oz, milk 2 pints, tea ¾ oz a month. Coffee, tapioca, clothes, soap, boots, shoes and lighting are all rationed.'

cuts. The War Cabinet was told, 'we have reached conditions of dangerous scarcity', by the Minister of Food, who also claimed that he needed at least 15 m. tons of the new total of 40 m. tons of cargo-carrying capacity to ensure 'a minimum requirement of food necessary to maintain the population'. The War Cabinet decided to place 'butter before guns', and in December ordered every available ship to North America to collect wheat supplies before the Ministry of Supply got their turn with the ships to overcome the iron ore shortage. It was a delicate juggling act that the War Cabinet had to repeat many times during the first year of the war.

POCKET BATTLESHIP SIGHTED!

The Nelson Touch: Commodore Henry Harwood (above) whose brilliant tactical plan of using his three faster cruisers to harry the much more powerful pocket-battleship and divide her gunfire brought the Royal Navy a spectacular triumph. HMS *Exeter* (top) was badly damaged and knocked out of the 90 minute battle (diagram) but the *Graf Spee* made the tactical error of fleeing from her two weaker opponents, HMS *Achilles* (middle) photographed during the action and HMS *Ajax* (bottom). Had the *Graf Spee* risked damage from their tenacious gunfire the *Exeter* would have been finished off.

By the end of December 1939 the Germans were far closer than they might have realised to achieving the grim threats contained in their broadcasts of Kipling's poem. Ironically, within hours of the poem's first reading on 2 December the *Graf Spee* had sunk the *Doric Star* with her cargo of meat, dairy produce and wool *en route* from New Zealand. The victim's frantic 'RRR' distress signals were the first news of the warship's whereabouts in three weeks. Next morning, in the same waters, the *Taiora* was stopped by a large warship apparently flying a grubby French ensign. It was another of Captain Langsdorff's ruses and, after picking up the crew, the *Graf Spee* sank her eighth 'big steamer' with her cargo of meat, wool and lead from Australia.

The *Taiora*'s signals, transmitted in spite of *Graf Spee*'s warning 'Do not use your wireless or you will be fired upon', interrupted a series of urgent conferences between Churchill and his Naval Staff. Orders went out to the eight hunting squadrons to ensure that this time the raider did not escape. In the South Atlantic the commander of Force G, Commodore Harwood, made a shrewd guess that the *Graf Spee* would now be heading for the River Plate 'with its large number of ships and its very valuable grain and wheat trade'. Deciding that 'this was the vital area to be defended', he ordered his cruiser squadron to patrol off the broad estuary between Uruguay and Argentina.

Early on the morning of 12 December Harwood's two 6″ gun light cruisers, *Ajax* and *Achilles*, were joined 150 miles from the mouth of the Plate by the 8″ gun cruiser *Exeter*. The next morning the *Graf Spee* was to arrive in the same area, hunting for a final triumph to round off her cruise before returning to Germany in time for Christmas. Captain Langsdorff was planning to intercept the large freighter *Highland Princess*, whose sailing from Buenos Aires had been announced in a newspaper taken from his last victim, *Streonshalh*, sunk on 7 December off the Brazilian coast.

December 13 dawned clear and sunny as the three cruisers of Force G patrolled in line ahead through the flat calm. Visibility was near perfect when at 6.14 am a look out in *Ajax* sighted a smudge far away on the North Western horizon. *Exeter* raced ahead to investigate and two minutes later her signal light flashed back to *Ajax*, 'I think it is a pocket battleship'. Harwood immediately ordered full speed and his ships deployed quickly into their pre-arranged positions as gun crews rushed headlong to their turrets.

56

HITS ON EXETER
SMOKE SCREEN

0   NAUTICAL MILES   6

Graf Spee retires to
Montevideo.
Arrives there midnight
13/14 December

0730

Ajax hit, two turrets
knocked out

0708

Ajax fires
torpedoes

17,000 yds

0722

11,000 yds

0700

0700

0730

0646

Graf Spee

0614

0636

0800

0644

Opens fire on
Ajax and Exeter

0615

Ajax and Achilles in pursuit

Achilles damaged

Ajax flies off
aircraft

Exeter retires badly
damaged and
firing one turret in
local control

Fires
torpedoes

2

0630

Fires
torpedoes

Range
19,200 yds

2

19,400 yds

Ajax opens fire

Achilles opens fire

To Falkland Islands

Exeter opens fire

0614

Smoke sighted to N West

Exeter, Ajax and Achilles

There was much less sense of urgency aboard the *Graf Spee*. Her spotter plane was out of action and the look-outs had made out the *Exeter*; the four tiny masts coming up behind her were believed to be screening destroyers. Confident that his radar-controlled main armament could make short work of a single cruiser, Langsdorff decided to close rapidly for a quick kill. This misjudgement cost Langsdorff his principal advantage of being able to out-range, as well as out-gun, the enemy cruiser. This would have frustrated Commodore Harwood's tactical plan to use his weaker squadron's superior speed to divide the pocket battleship's fire.

At 6.18 am the first salvo thundered from *Graf Spee*'s forward turret, as Langsdorf concentrated his fire on the bigger cruiser with occasional shots at the lighter ships. Two minutes later HMS *Exeter* fired back, soon followed by *Ajax* and *Achilles*. Six minutes after opening fire, one of *Graf Spee*'s 11″ shells had wrecked *Exeter*'s 'B' turret and swept the bridge with a murderous hail of splinters. Everyone was killed or badly injured except Captain Bell who made his way through the wreckage and fires to con the ship from the emergency steering position aft. To gain some relief from the severe hammering his ship was taking, he ordered the firing of the starboard torpedoes which forced the pocket battleship to temporarily turn away.

Just before Harwood's flagship, *Ajax*, had joined the action, she had catapulted her light aircraft to spot for gunnery control but the action soon became so confused that differentiating between the fall of shot from the three British ships became impossible and gunnery accuracy worsened as the range opened up. Now Langsdorff saw his chance to concentrate all his firepower on the *Exeter* and he closed for the kill. But Harwood's two light cruisers racing in with every gun blazing away, put up such a spirited attack that the pocket battleship turned to deal with her new assailants. This bold stratagem gave Captain Bell enough time to haul *Exeter* away as his last turret was put out of action. Blazing furiously amidships, the badly battered cruiser withdrew from the action.

With *Graf Spee* now turning every gun onto the light cruisers, the captains of *Ajax* and *Achilles* found their shiphandling tested to its limit as they weaved at high speed to dodge the German salvos which surrounded them with giant waterspouts. Luck was on their side, until two of *Ajax*'s turrets were knocked out in quick succession and her mast was brought down by another well-placed salvo. The action had now become too hot and Harwood, knowing that his lightly-armoured cruisers would not take much more punishment, ordered torpedoes to be fired and the range to be opened under cover of a smokescreen.

When the *Graf Spee* turned away to avoid their torpedoes, the action, which had lasted for a furious ninety minutes, subsided shortly after 7.30 am.

Casualties had been heavy in the crippled *Exeter*, with 64 of her officers and men killed. She was now heading towards the Falkland Islands naval base as damage control parties battled with the fires that threatened to overwhelm her. *Ajax*, with two of her turrets out of action and seven men dead, together with the less badly damaged *Achilles*, had taken up station astern of the pocket battleship, just beyond gun range. The *Graf Spee*'s fighting ability

Requiem for a Pocket Battle-ship: Captain Hans Langsdorff at a burial service in a Montevideo cemetery for the 36 Germans killed in the action. British newspapers made much of the fact that he deliberately refrained from giving the Nazi salute at the graveside. When he found himself interned with his crew in Buenos Aires two days after the scuttling, Langsdorff shot himself after writing in a final letter, 'I am still convinced that under the circumstances this decision was the only one left, once I had taken my ship into the trap of Montevideo. For "with the ammunition remaining" any attempt to fight my way back to open and deep water was bound to fail . . . For a Captain with a sense of honour, it goes without saying that his personal fate cannot be separated from that of his ship'.

was still unimpared although she had suffered 20 hits and 36 men were dead. Most of the light cruisers 6″ shells had bounced off her armoured sides but her superstructure was battered, her bakery was wrecked and an 8″ shell from *Exeter* had torn a six foot hole above the waterline. Instead of turning on his pursuers, Langsdorff decided to make for the shelter of Montevideo the nearest neutral port, to patch up the damage.

The *Graf Spee* anchored just before midnight in the harbour and for the next four days the Uruguayan capital was the scene of intense diplomatic activity. The German Ambassador argued, and was granted, an extension to the 24 hours for repairs allowed under international law whilst the British sought to delay her sailing so that the battlecruiser *Renown* and carrier *Ark Royal*, then refuelling north of Rio de Janeiro, could join up with the two light cruisers off the Plate. A succession of British cargo ships sailed daily to prevent the warship leaving until the regulatory 24 hours which had to elapse after every such departure. All light aircraft that could have flown reconnaissance missions became 'unavailable' to the Germans and the BBC overseas broadcasts reinforced the carefully laid rumours that a battleship and aircraft carriers had arrived off the Plate. All these developments were anxiously watched by the United States Government, fearing that another naval battle would make a nonsense of their Neutrality Zone warnings.

On 16 December with the 72 hour extension running out, Langsdorf telegraphed Raeder for instructions, reporting that strong British forces made 'a break-through to home waters hopeless'. He proposed battling his way across the muddy river to the sympathetic neutrality of Buenos Aires. If this proved impossible, he asked for a decision on whether the ship should be scuttled or interned. The Führer was consulted, and making clear his displeasure over the whole situation, instructed Raeder to signal back: '*NO* internment in Uruguay. Attempt effective destruction if ship is scuttled'.

At 6.15 pm on 17 December 1939, the *Graf Spee* moved slowly out of Montevideo harbour with her battle ensigns flying. Further down the wide Plate estuary the *Ajax* and *Achilles*, which had been reinforced by the heavy cruiser *Cumberland*, closed up to action stations. Crowds lined the waterfront expecting the opening shots in a dramatic battle. Then, to everybody's astonishment, the pocket battleship stopped just outside the three mile limit and through binoculars they saw her skeleton crew being transferred to the German freighter alongside. Minutes later, just as the first red glow of sunset began to stain the muddy water, explosions erupted throughout the warship. The Wagnerian spectacle brought to an end the *Graf Spee*'s career in which she had sunk 50,000 tons of merchant shipping and tied down half of the British Fleet. Throughout the night sheets of flame licked round her blackened hulk as she settled on the river bed. Langsdorff, after reaching the safety of pro-German Argentina, wrote a final testament two days later. It concluded: 'I am quite happy to pay with my life for any possible reflection on the honour of the flag'. That night he shot himself, after he had carefully wrapped himself in the Imperial Navy Ensign under which he had fought at Jutland.

RAISING THE STAKES

News of the destruction of the *Graf Spee* set off a great outburst of rejoicing in Britain. It was the first victory of the war and Churchill summed up the national mood: 'In a cold winter it warmed the very cockles of the British nation's heart.' This spectacular feat of naval arms won wide admiration in America, although Washington was obliged to proffer a frosty official protest at the blatant violation of the Pan-American Neutrality Zone. On Christmas Eve, the First Lord sent the President a long cable expressing his irritation at the official United States reaction and the difficulties faced by the Royal Navy in policing the world trade routes:

> Much of world duty is being thrown on Admiralty. Even a single raider loose in North Atlantic requires employment of half a battle Fleet to give sure protection. Now unlimited mining campaign adds to strain on our flotillas and small craft. We are at full extension . . .

Coming after less than three months of war, this confession of 'considerable strain' was a measure of the success of Germany's disruptive naval strategy. As Churchill had reported to the War Cabinet in a memorandum of late November, 'almost the whole of the British Fleet is on the defensive, in order that the essential flow of trade may be maintained'. To deal with the dual threat to trade from U-boats and raiders, the memorandum urged an Admiralty plan for a gigantic 'Northern Barrage' of mines to seal off the North Sea from Scapa Flow to the Norwegian coast. It was to be a double barrier; the deep mines would prevent U-boats getting through submerged and surface mines would stop the surface raiders getting out into the Atlantic.

The very scale of this 'huge project' appealed to Churchill but the War Cabinet were sceptical when they learned that it would take a year to complete, and would require 200,000 mines costing a staggering £20 m. He had pointed out that 'a modern 15 knots meat ship with its cargo is worth in round figures £3/4 million and that 12 knot tanker carrying 10,000 tons of petrol £330,000, the additional expenditure of normal estimates incurred by laying the Northern Barrage is not unreasonable insurance'.

The Ministers not only found the cost excessive but also feared the international repercussions from neutral nations. To Churchill's dismay, the decision to go ahead with the Northern Barrage was deferred. No such scruples restrained the Germans from increasing their mining operations off the British East Coast during the first months of 1940. The arctic weather conditions of the worst winter for forty years gave German destroyers and minelayers, disguised as merchant ships, the necessary cover to carry out clandestine operations off the East Coast and the approaches to the Thames Estuary. For months the Admiralty failed to appreciate the extent of the German mining operations, assuming that sporadic mines had been dropped by aircraft or U-boats. It was mid-February 1940, after a hundred merchant ships had been claimed, by the now very extensive, minefields, that the full extent of the danger was recognised and nightly destroyer patrols were organised as countermeasures.

Arms and Diplomacy from America: January 1940 and the first Lockheed Hudsons purchased for Coastal Command anti-U-boat patrols arrive in Liverpool (right). The following month Roosevelt's Assistant Secretary of State, Sumner Welles (above with the German Foreign Minister Ribbentrop) was sent to visit European leaders on a peace mission. This American initiative disturbed the British and French, but after encountering Berlin's intransigent demands this first attempt at 'shuttle diplomacy' collapsed.

The huge, undeclared minefields off Britain's coasts gave the German High Command the cover it needed to begin unrestricted U-boat warfare. On 17 January, Dönitz received authority 'to sink by U-boats without warning all ships in those waters near the enemy coasts in which the use of mines is possible'. Sudden sinkings could now be blamed on mines and losses increased dramatically, with a large number of neutral ships being torpedoed without warning. The Admiralty's monthly Anti-Submarine Warfare bulletin concluded: 'There appear to be two objects to this policy, to frighten neutrals away from English ports, and to decrease the total world tonnage since this will work to the allied disadvantage'.

In less than six months the face of the U-boat war had undergone a profound change. The humanitarian element had vanished and U-boats no longer stopped and searched merchant ships. At first there was some reluctance by the commanders to intensify the war and Dönitz had to order:

> Do not rescue any men, do not take them along, and do not take care of any boats from the ship. Weather conditions and the proximity of land are of no consequence. Concern yourself only with the safety of your own boat and with the efforts to achieve additional successes as soon as possible. We must be hard in this war. The enemy started the war in order to destroy us, and thus nothing else matters.

The Kriegsmarine soon recovered from the blow to its prestige caused by the sinking of the *Graf Spee*. By the end of January 1940 the U-boats and mines together disposed of another 200,000 tons of merchant shipping and German Admirals made regular radio broadcasts about the success of 'the third attempt by the Continent to defeat Britain'. Admiral Lützow explained in his broadcast of 17 January how Nazi Germany would win where Napoleon and the Kaiser had failed:

> War is not won with gold but iron ... We do not consider it most important to damage the enemy's financial power, but aim at decimating the Fleet which carries on trade with England and especially at destroying all cargo ships with vital supplies destined for Britain.

In spite of the terrible weather, the Kriegsmarine was proving remarkably successful at destroying cargo ships and Raeder hoped to use the current wave of enthusiasm to persuade the Führer to let him send U-boats to the

Taking on the Convoys: In March 1940 Dönitz planned a new assault on the convoys. The U-boats were equipped with new magnetically triggered electric-powered torpedoes (top U-37 at Kiel with the battleship *Gneisenau* in the background).
The offensive was cancelled before the invasion of Norway. This saved the convoys because the Royal Navy was still desperately short of Asdic escorts and had available less than 24 old First War destroyers, a handful of sloops

American side of the Atlantic to operate against the other end of the convoy system but Hitler vetoed the idea, 'in view of the psychological effect on the USA'.

In February, Allied shipping losses for the month were approaching a quarter of a million tons, two thirds of which had been sunk by only ten operational U-boats. Statistics prepared by the Department of Anti-Submarine Warfare made it plain that the offensive against the U-boats had been a disappointing failure. The best estimates showed that only about a dozen had been destroyed since the beginning of the war and of these, probably no more than three had been sunk by the hunting patrols; most had been accounted for by convoy escorts or the mines laid in the Channel and off the approaches to the German bases.

Realising the damage this might do to morale, Churchill had already ordered that these statistics should be 'kept to the smallest circle' and that 'encouraging messages' should be sent to the Commands engaged in anti-submarine patrols. He left little doubt that he, too, put little faith in such pessimistic reports, minuting: 'Personally I think we are inclined to underestimate the successes obtained. The U-boats have been practically cut out of business, especially on the Western approaches, and it is evident that they must have suffered from very heavy losses.'

It was now abundantly clear from the statistics that the Admiralty strategy for dealing with the U-boats by aggressive hunting had failed but Western Approaches Command still believed that the anti-submarine patrols were the best way of containing the U-boats until the planned Northern Barrage could be laid. This official view was endorsed by the Director of Planning. 'The convoy system . . . will not in itself defeat the U-boat Campaign.' So the Admiralty continued the policy of committing more and more destroyers to the anti-submarine patrols, squandering their limited escort resources.

At the outbreak of war, the Royal Navy had only 180 Asdic-fitted warships capable of anti-submarine operations – and 150 of these were destroyers, many of which were allocated to protecting the Fleet. This left less than two dozen of the older First War destroyers, a handful of sloops and a few anti-submarine trawlers for convoy duties. In the winter of 1940 there were insufficient escorts to provide two for each convoy and the Admiralty had to requisition 70 trawlers from the fishing fleets.

However by the end of February the Admiralty was at last beginning to acknowledge that their hunting policy was not producing results. Whatever the problems caused by too few escorts and aircraft, it was becoming clear that the best means of defense against the U-boats was the convoy; only three convoyed ships were sunk in February as against 33 sailing independently.

This important fact was not lost on U-boat Command. Operational orders had already been prepared for a new assault by the Wolf-Packs on the convoys, when orders came from Berlin on 4 March, 1940: 'All further sailings of U-boats to be stopped forthwith. U-boats already at sea will refrain from any operations in the vicinity of the Norwegian coast. All ships will be made ready for action as soon as possible.' The next day, Hitler issued directives for the invasion of Norway.

and 70 trawlers requisitioned from the fishing fleets. In April the first of the new Flower class corvettes were ready for service HMS *Periwinkle* (above) which was known as 'Winkle' after an exchange of signals on joining her first convoy off Plymouth:
'What are you?' signalled the escorting destroyer
'Periwinkle'
'Can I stick a pin in you?'
'No I am a pale blue flower – not a shellfish'
'Then I will come over and fertilise you!'

OBJECTIVE NORWAY

The strategic significance of Norway had for long concerned Grossadmiral Raeder. Much of the Reich's vital iron ore from Sweden came down the Norwegian coastal shipping lanes during the winter months when the Baltic was frozen. This 'covered way' was vulnerable to British attacks should the War Cabinet decide to interfere with Norwegian neutrality and since October 1939, Admiral Raeder had been urging Hitler to consider forcing the Norwegians to accept the stationing of German naval forces in Trondheim. The threat of a pre-emptive British move had increased at the beginning of December when Russian troops moved against Finland and Hitler began seriously to consider intervention after Raeder had engineered a visit to Berlin by Vidkund Quisling, the leader of the Norwegian Nazi party. It was agreed that funds and agents should be channelled into Norway to assist in Quisling's promised Nazi coup. At the same time contingency planning began for a full scale military takeover code-named *Fall Weserübung* in case the plot collapsed.

The strategic importance of Norway was also appreciated by Churchill who was attracted to the idea of launching a full-scale naval operation against the German iron ore traffic. The British Chiefs of Staff had accepted the need for such an operation in December and 1940 began with each side tentatively planning to move against Norway. What finally persuaded the German High Command to act was the '*Altmark* incident'. On 15 February Captain Vian, on Churchill's direct instructions, had taken his destroyer HMS *Cossack* into Jössing Fjord to board the *Graf Spee*'s supply ship *Altmark*. 299 British seamen were rescued and five Germans were killed in a clear British violation of territorial waters that indicated to Berlin a breakdown in Norwegian neutrality.

The rescue was turned into a major propaganda victory in England and the cry 'The Navy's here', which had echoed round the dark waters of the snow-swept Fjord, was more than enough to convince Hitler that, if he failed to act, the Royal Navy might move first. The Führer finally decided to invade Norway after the spring offensive in the west, *Fall Gelb*, had to be postponed when plans fell into Allied hands with the capture of a Wehrmacht staff officer.

9 April 1940 was set as the date for the combined operation and the directive on *Weserübung* declared that the operation was to have the character of 'A peaceful occupation', designed to protect by force of arms 'the neutrality of the Northern countries'. This exercise in 'friendly protection' was to be carried out by six army divisions, transported and covered by every available warship, to take over the Norwegian ports from Narvik to Oslo. Denmark was to be seized at the same time and both occupations were to take place under a massive umbrella of air cover provided by the Luftwaffe.

Everything depended on surprise and the biggest fear was that the British might strike first. But in spite of Churchill's passionate pleas, no firm decision had yet been taken over the scheme to mine the 'covered way'. What Chamberlain referred to as 'the sinister trance' had paralysed Allied action.

'Where was the British Fleet?
On 8 April 1940 the heavy-cruiser *Hipper* the spearhead of the invasion force sank the British destroyer *Glowworm* which was covering minelaying operations off the Norwegian coast. The rapidity of the German invasion of Norway (right) took the Allies by complete surprise and overwhelmed their attempts to counter it. Roosevelt was 'hopping mad' and complained 'It is the most outrageous thing I have ever heard of'.

GERMAN

→ SEABORNE LANDINGS AND ATTACKS

PARATROOP LANDINGS

Group I NAVAL GROUPS

ALLIES

1 Div NORWEGIAN DISPOSITIONS

LANDINGS AND ATTACKS

WITHDRAWALS

0 — 150 MILES

0 — 200 KILOMETRES

9 April
Gneisenau damaged by Renown

Narvik: 8 April
2 British destroyers sunk by German troop-ferrying destroyers.
10/13 April, 10 German destroyers sunk

✗ 8 June
Glorious sunk, Scharnhorst damaged in naval action

9 April 1940
German forces land simultaneously at Oslo, Kristiansand, Stavanger, Bergen, Trondheim & Narvik

8 April
Hipper sinks destroyer Glowworm

Group II

18 April
Br 148 Inf Bde

1 May
ÅLESUND

10 April
Light cruiser
Königsberg bombed
& sunk

Group III

16 February 1940
Altmark boarded

9 April
Cruiser Karlsruhe
torpedoed & sunk

TROMSÖ

15 April
British, French, Polish

Br 24 Gds Bde

8 June

Bardufoss

HARSTAD

BJERKVIK

NARVIK
6 Div

28 May
French & Norwegian forces take Narvik

Lofoten Islands

Group I

15 May

30 May

BODÖ
Saltfjord

Germans advance to relieve their force at Narvik

31 May

MO-I-RANA
14 May

MOSJÖEN
10 May

NORWEGIAN SEA

16/17 April
Br 146 Inf Bde

2/3 May

NAMSOS

STEINKJER
19 Apr

SWEDEN

Trondheim fjord

Vaernes
HEGRA

TRONDHEIM
5 Div

DRAGSET
29 Apr

MOLDE

ÅNDALSNES
2 May

30 Apr

TYNSET

DOMBÅS

RENDAL
24 Apr

KVAM

RENA
19 Apr

ELVERUM

25 May

LILLEHAMMER
21 Apr

HAMAR

L. Mjösa

N O R W A Y

GOL

2 Div

1 May

Randsfjord

HÖNEFOSS

Fornebu

9 April
Heavy cruiser
Blücher sunk
by shore batteries

OSLO
1 Div

KONGSBERG

HALDEN
12 Apr

4 Div

BERGEN

Oslofjord

Group V

11 April
Heavy cruiser
Lützow damaged
by torpedo

27 Apr

ARENDAL

STAVANGER

Sola

3 Div
KRISTIANSAND

Jösenfjord

SKAGERRAK

Then on 28 March, after seven months of argument, the Anglo-French Supreme War Council agreed to the mining of Norwegian waters. At once, the Admiralty issued its operational orders, which Churchill cynically dubbed '*Wilfred*' – 'because by itself it was so small and innocent'. At the same time plans were made for a limited Allied Expeditionary Force to be landed to counter any resultant German reactions in Southern Norway. By a curious chance the minelayers taking part in 'Operation Wilfred' were already heading for the Norwegian coast on Sunday 7 April at the same time as the German heavy warships, escorting the destroyers packed with seasick German troops, were heading north to Narvik. The Admiralty was alerted to enemy movements in the North Sea by Coastal Command aircraft but a full appreciation of the scale of the enemy operations was not made until too late.

The first clash came during the early hours of 8 April, when the destroyer *Glowworm*, blundered into German invasion Group 2 on its way to Trondheim covered by the heavy cruiser *Hipper*. Hopelessly outgunned, with desperate courage, Lt Cdr Gerard Roope ordered full speed to ram. HMS *Glowworm* ripped into the *Hipper*'s bow, tearing a 120 ft long gash before rolling over and sinking, leaving 38 survivors to be rescued from the raging seas.

Incredibly, it was not until the dawn the next day that the Admiralty became aware that a full-scale German invasion of Norway was well under way. Muddle and confusion dogged attempts to intervene and the troops who had been standing by to support 'Wilfred' had actually been disembarked the day before. The Home Fleet was still at Scapa Flow and the only warships near enough to prevent the invasion were the battlecruiser *Renown* and a flotilla of destroyers covering the minelayers. The battlecruiser sighted the German ships and a brief gunnery duel was fought in driving snow with the *Scharnhorst* and *Gneisenau*. Admiral Lütjens, whose battleships were covering the Narvik force, successfully drew the British away to the north west, but not before *Gneisenau* suffered a hit from *Renown*'s 15″ guns.

In the south, although British submarines and aircraft knocked out two German light cruisers and the Norwegians sank the new heavy cruiser *Blücher* as she was entering Oslo fjord, the Wehrmacht completely overwhelmed the weak defences. Within hours of paratroops landing in Oslo the Germans had a strong grip on most of Norway. The only serious threat to their operations came at Narvik where a destroyer attack by Captain Warburton Lee's flotilla and a second foray backed by the *Warspite* eliminated the German destroyer force and a number of supply ships.

The invasion of Norway had been a remarkable military success but at the cost of heavy losses to the Kriegsmarine. For Hitler the price was well justified. He told Raeder: 'even if the whole German Fleet is sunk in getting me to Norway it will have fulfilled its purpose'. But the Führer could scarcely have foreseen the totally unexpected failure of the U-boat arm to have any impact on the campaign. Morale among the highly-trained crews sagged, and the U-boats' loss of operational efficiency was to have a major effect on the sea war for many months.

The failure of the new electric torpedoes, with their magnetic firing pistols, supposed to be the most advanced in the world, had been the main cause of the fiasco. It was, as Prien bitterly complained on his return after missing several important British ships, like having to fight 'with a dummy rifle'. Dönitz recorded in his war log: 'It is my belief that never before in military history has a force been sent into battle with such a useless weapon'. On 20 April Raeder set up a special Torpedo Commission which soon unearthed a scandalous failure of design and testing. At the same time he made a morale-boosting tour, and bluntly told the crews the facts, promising that something would be done. But the magnetic firing pistol was not finally perfected until 1942; so for two of the most critical years of the Battle of the Atlantic, the U-boats were forced to operate with faulty weapons.

CHURCHILL TAKES OVER

The outcome of the Norwegian operations with their muddle and confusion, exposed Chamberlain's inadequacy as a war leader. On 9 May, during a bitter no confidence debate in the House of Commons, the Government majority fell dramatically from 231 to 81. Next day Chamberlain resigned, to be replaced by Churchill on 10 May.

Winston Churchill had barely time to take the first steps to form a new coalition Government before Hitler launched *Fall Gelb* on 13 May 1940. As the German Panzers crashed through the 'impenetrable' Ardennes, the Norwegian exercise became a sideshow. All that remained was to rescue the army of 25,000 men stranded in the north of Norway. But the disastrous ill luck of that ill-starred campaign continued when the carrier *Glorious* and two destroyers were sunk on 7 June by the *Scharnhorst* and *Gneisenau*. The Scandinavian campaign ended with Germany in an immeasurably stronger strategic position. The Kriegsmarine's strength had been drastically reduced as a result of *Weserübung*, with almost every major ship under repair, but the Reich now had Atlantic bases.

The Allies were desperately anxious about the threat to the Atlantic islands and realised that Hitler might try to seize the Danish dependencies of the Faroes, Iceland and even Greenland. Far the most serious and likely development would be the German occupation of Iceland because this island dominated a large part of the North Atlantic convoy route, which was beyond the range of British air and sea patrols. The Allies decided to act fast. The invasion of Norway and Denmark removed all their inhibitions about the integrity of Danish possessions. On 13 April the Faroes were seized and on 6 May the decision was taken to base a strong garrison of British troops on Iceland which eventually numbered 25,000 men. The anchorage at Hvalfiord and Reykjavik airfield were soon to assume a crucial importance in the Battle of the Atlantic. Already the American Administration could see itself being drawn into the defence of the Atlantic against the Nazi menace now entrenching itself on the Norwegian coast. The speed and daring of the invasion had been breathtaking. In one day Hitler had seized key strategic points over a thousand mile front and if Norway with an army of 200,000 men and the support of the Royal Navy could be rapidly overwhelmed, why not other strategic areas far closer to the United States?

In May 1940 the launching of
Hitler's long-planned offensive
against the West brought
150,000 tons of Allied shipping
losses from heavy air attacks in
the Channel. But the convoy
system had proved its worth in
the first phase of the Battle of
the Atlantic (left). In nine
months 215 merchantmen and
two warships had been sunk at
a cost of only 23 U-boats, yet
only 21 of these ships had been
in escorted convoys.

HALIFAX

GIBRALTAR

Pan-American Neutrality Zone

SIERRA
LEONE

• ALLIED AND NEUTRAL MERCHANT SHIPS SUNK
○ U-BOATS SUNK
CONVOY ROUTES, ESCORTED
   "   "   , UNESCORTED
GERMANY, 3 SEPT. 1939
GERMANY AND GERMAN OCCUPIED
TERRITORY, 31 MAY 1940

ALLIED SHIPPING LOSSES 3RD SEPTEMBER
1939–31ST MAY 1940

MERCATOR PROJECTION

5. A Certain Eventuality

At 7.30 on the morning of 15 May Winston Churchill was awakened by his bedside telephone. He had been Prime Minister for only five days, during which time events had moved at lightning speed as 134 German divisions, including ten panzer formations, had attacked on a front extending from the Dutch border to the Ardennes. The telephone call was from the French Premier, Paul Reynaud, who 'spoke in English, and evidently under stress. "We have been defeated". As Churchill did not immediately respond he said again, "We are beaten; we have lost the battle".'

In a remarkable display of co-ordination between army and airforce, the Wehrmacht was pressing forward in two main thrusts. Army Group B had overrun Holland to push back the main Allied armies in Belgium and Army Group A had outflanked the Maginot Line defences to achieve a spectacular breakthrough in the Ardennes. Paris was threatened as well as the Channel ports north of Boulogne.

The success of the German offensive presaged a strategic catastrophe for the Allies with the prospect of Nazi occupation of the entire European coastline from Norway to Spain. If France fell there would be a danger that England would herself face invasion, thereby allowing Germany to dominate the Atlantic. There was alarm in Washington after William Bullitt, the shrewd U.S. Ambassador to France, frankly warned the President: ' . . . if Hitler should be able to conquer France and England he would turn his attention at once to South America and eventually attempt to install a Nazi Government in the United States'.

These dramatic victories in the West were accomplished without the support of the Kriegsmarine, whose few undamaged units were kept busy ferrying supplies and troops to Norway. Even the U-boats were pressed into service which reduced still further the numbers available to Dönitz to resume his offensive. He complained that 'three months had passed since we had withdrawn our boats from the Atlantic in order to concentrate them for the Norwegian operations . . .' In this time his commanders had sunk less than a hundred thousand tons of merchant shipping and although mines and aircraft brought the combined total close to a quarter of a million tons, the Admiralty took this improvement as proof that it was at last containing the German threat. But the Director of Anti-Submarine Warfare disagreed and reported on 24 April that only 19 U-boats had been sunk since the beginning of the war. This displeased Churchill who was convinced that at least 50 had been destroyed. 'This conclusion leads me to think that it might be a good thing if Captain Talbot went to sea as soon as possible' he angrily minuted to the First Sea Lord when the pessimistic report was received. In fact Talbot's estimate that 43 U-boats were still operational was soon seen to be correct as sinkings began to rocket again, but this did not save him being replaced by Captain Creasy a few months later.

After the war, captured German records would prove the accuracy of the Admiralty Assessment Committee's analysis of anti-U-boat operations. They would also confirm the part played by the Operational Intelligence Centre which had been built up since 1938 to co-ordinate naval intelligence by the brilliant efforts of Paymaster Commander Norman Denning. The Submarine Tracking Room, established under Captain Tring, a veteran of the famous First War naval intelligence team known as Room 40, recruited an up-and-coming barrister, Roger Winn. As Paymaster Commander he would later take over the Tracking Room and his small team's ability to provide an accurate picture of U-boat operations played a crucial role in the Battle of the Atlantic. Rear Admiral John Godfrey was the energetic Director of Naval Intelligence who completed its pre-war re-organisation by bringing in some of the best civilian talent from the City, law and journalism. His own personal assistant, Lieutenant Commander Ian Fleming RNVR came from Reuter's News agency and would draw on his wartime experience in creating the James Bond novels.

Admiral Godfrey and his staff, known as the 'Zoo' to their regular service colleagues, directed the multi-farious operations of Naval Intelligence Division from Room 39 in the Admiralty Building overlooking Horseguards Parade. Many feet underground was the bomb-proof complex completed just before the war. It housed the Operation Intelligence Centre's plot, the Operations Division, Trade Plot and the communications registry. This was the nerve centre of the war at sea, connected to naval bases and ships by radio links, telephone lines and teleprinters. It was to the Citadel that Churchill and the naval staff came during moments of crisis. As Admiral Godfrey wrote:

> When any 'naval occasion' took place, or showed signs of breezing up, everyone concerned crowded into the small conference room in the underground OIC, with the First Lord and other Sea Lords coming and going. There we used to wait for news to come in during such episodes as the Battle of the Plate and the sinking of the *Rawalpindi*. The hours spent during the night, sometimes for long periods in complete silence in the fuggy, thickening, gloomy atmosphere, were not the best precursor to a fruitful day's work.

The Operational Intelligence Centre's principal handicap during the first two years of the war was its inability to penetrate the Kriegsmarine's codes. The German war machine, uniquely dependent on radio for its communications had taken elaborate precautions to create a cypher system which would defy all attempts at penetration by a listening enemy. The Wehrmacht's communications network was not only the most sophisticated but, because it relied on Enigma machines, it was also the most secure.

The Enigma machines were electromechanical encoding devices, which were easily operated in the field and resembled a portable typewriter. Their ingenious secret lay in providing a constantly varying electrical path for the circuit, completed whenever the letter to be coded was typed in on the keyboard. The signal passed back and forth through the internal wiring of three rotors and, to complicate the process, a plugboard was also set up which together with the combinations and starting positions of the rotors determined the code. The resulting meaningless jumble of letters in the coded message in theory could only be sorted out by reversing the process through an exactly similar Enigma machine, set up with its plugboard and rotors in the same starting positions.

The system offered the choice of an astronomic six million million million

Blitzkrieg in the West: On 10 May 1940 German land and air forces launched an overpowering offensive in the West. The devastating success of this lightning warfare was made possible by a sophisticated and secure system of wireless communications. At its heart was the portable *Enigma* coding machine believed to provide an unbreakable cypher system, but, thanks to pre-war Polish efforts, British Intelligence had begun to penetrate the German army codes. (Left an *Enigma* machine adapted by the Poles to try and crack the system). This warned the War Cabinet of the desperate situation in France and was vital for the planning of the Dunkirk evacuation.

possible permutations for every letter. Sorting out this code was the seemingly impossible task confronting the brilliant team of cryptanalysts, mathematicians and engineers who had been assembled in a Victorian mansion at Bletchley Park some 40 miles north of London. The objective of this aptly named 'Government Codes and Cypher School' was to penetrate the German cyphers. Fortunately they had been given a head start by the mathematical analysis and early Enigma device built by Polish military intelligence. With the aid of a primitive computer called 'Bombe', by the spring of 1940 the Bletchley Park team was just beginning to piece together small portions of army and Luftwaffe Enigma traffic. Each service had its own model of the Enigma machine and there were some 80 different cyphers in use. Unfortunately for the Admiralty's operational intelligence centres staff, the Kriegsmarine had introduced one of the most sophisticated – and therefore the most difficult to crack.

The Convoy Code-breakers

Whilst the Kriegsmarine's Enigma defied all the British attempts at penetration, the Germans had the great advantage of being able to read much of their opponent's signal traffic. Pre-war muddle and the conservatism of Britain's top military command had rejected the new coding machines in favour of traditional hand cyphers which relied on code books. This system was known to be far from secure. A breakthrough into the British codes had been made by the *B Dienst* which, since 1936, had been carefully monitoring and interpreting Royal Navy signals. Headed by Kapitän Kupfer, its fifty man staff, after four years of experience, had become so adept at their task that during the Norway campaign they had been able to intercept and read 50% of British naval signal traffic within hours of its transmission. The remarkable efficiency was demonstrated when the Royal Navy changed its codes after losing several destroyers in the Battle of Narvik. Fearing that their codebooks might have been captured, the Admiralty had to undertake the huge task of reprinting thousands of new manuals in secret at the Oxford University Press, and then having each one delivered by courier to the ships. Yet within a matter of weeks the *B Dienst* had broken the new codes and were once again reading the British naval traffic.

More than 2,000 signals a month were being decoded by the *B Dienst* office in the Kriegsmarine's Tirpitz-Ufer headquarters in Berlin. A large part of the messages were convoy signals giving the details, including course and escort rendezvous, for Atlantic convoys and independently routed merchant ships. These were immediately passed by wire to the headquarters of U-boat Command at Wilhelmshaven. Dönitz more often than not had precise advance information about where to concentrate his forces and his ability to read the enemy convoy traffic compensated for the lack of German air reconnaissance in the Western Approaches. For a year U-boat Command was to hold the advantage in the intelligence war.

Ruthless Attack: On 24 May 1940 the U-boats were ordered to begin unrestricted attacks on shipping in a War Zone which extended up to 100 miles into the Atlantic. The all-out offensive against merchant shipping began with Dönitz's operational orders: 'Carry through the attack with a tenacious will until the *aim of complete destruction is attained* . . . Keep your nerve. Remain on the surface where you will stay in command of the situation . . .'

The new German offensive began on the morning of May 16, when Kapitänleutnant Öhrn in U-37 attacked the shipping routes off Cape Finisterre. Equipped with the new contact firing pistols as well as the old magnetic ones, it was hoped his early successes would raise U-boat morale after the torpedo failures in the Norwegian campaign, but the first radio reports were ominous; Öhrn suffered four torpedo failures. Dönitz immediately suspected the magnetic pistols and ordered that they be abandoned. He was soon proved correct when, using a new contact pistol, U-37 sank 11 ships in 26 days and returned with a tally of 43,000 tons sunk.

'The spell of bad luck' for the U-boat arm was broken but the misfortunes of the merchantmen were just beginning. On 24 May Hitler finally gave Raeder permission to lift all restrictions on U-boat operations around Britain and France. The only exceptions were US ships and those of 'friendly neutrals' – Italy, Japan and Russia. As the war against shipping had re-started in deadly earnest, Kapitänleutnant Öhrn showed a particularly ruthless dedication to his new orders when, through U-37's slim attack periscope, he sighted a British freighter on the afternoon of 27 May. His log chronicled in dispassionate detail the new ruthlessness at sea.

The distance apart is narrowing. The steamship draws in quickly, but the position is still 40-50. I cannot see the stern yet. Tube ready. Shall I or not? The gunnery crews are also prepared. On the ship's side a yellow cross in a small square, dark blue ground. Swedish? Presumably not. I raise the periscope a little. Hurrah, a gun at the stern, an A/A gun or something similar. Fire! It cannot miss.

Surface. Stern is under water. Bows rise higher. The boats are now on the water. Lucky for them. A picture of complete order. They lie at some distance. The bows rear up quite high. Two men appear from somewhere in the forward part of the ship. They leap and rush with great bounds along the deck down the stern. The stern disappears. A boat capsizes. Then a boiler explosion. Two men fly through the air, limbs outstretched. Bursting and crushing. Then all is over. A large heap of wreckage floats up. We approach it to identify the name. The crew have saved themselves on wreckage and capsized boats. We fish out a buoy. No name on it. I ask a man on the raft. He says, hardly turning his head, 'Nix Name'. A young boy in the water called, 'Help, help, please!' The others are very composed. They look damp and somewhat tired. An expression of cold hatred on their faces. On to the old course. After washing the paint off the buoy, the name comes to light: *Greatafield* Glasgow, 5,000 gross registered tons.

Before the end of May 60,000 tons of shipping were sunk by U-boats; with losses from mines and increasing Luftwaffe bombing attacks, the month's total approached 300,000 tons – the highest to date. The pressure was clearly building up on the Royal Navy. The ill-fated Narvik campaign dragged into June, and even more serious was Mussolini's threatening attitude in the Mediterranean, bringing the need for naval reinforcements. But the most urgent priority was the need to protect the Atlantic convoy routes from the rapidly escalating U-boat offensive and the renewed threat by surface raider.

With one pocket battleship sunk and the other three undergoing repairs or refitting, the German surface threat was continued by warships, disguised as merchantmen which roamed the oceans preying on enemy shipping. The

KOMET

WOOD PULP 38%
TIMBER
ALUMINIUM
PAPER 7%

WOOD PULP 38%
PAPER 34%
TIMBER 20%

FLAX 20%
BUTTER 14%
TIMBER 12%

FLAX 30%
TIMBER 17%
BARLEY 8%
WHEAT 8%

PAPER 0.7%
ZINC 15%

BUTTER 39%
MEAT 10%

ALUMINIUM 34%
FLAX 29%
PAPER 25%
ZINC 17%
TIN 8%
CHEESE 8%
BUTTER 8%
IRON 7%

WESTERN EUROPEAN
PORTS 5%

JUTE 100%
MANGANESE
TEA
RICE
OIL NUTS
COTTON
LEAD
WHEAT
WOOL

IRON 27%

WIDDER
THOR
ORION

FERTILIZERS 60%
IRON 28%
ESPARTO 15%

NORTHERN
PORTS 4%

BARLEY 29%
PETROLEUM 19%

COTTON 18%
OILS & FATS 14%

SUGAR 27%

COFFEE 37%

OILS & FATS 57%

INDIAN
PORTS 6%

TEA 5%
RUBBER 8%

SUGAR 14%

PETROLEUM 30%

COCOA 30%
TIN 23%
OILS & FATS 15%
IRON 8%

AFRICAN
PORTS 3%

COFFEE 68%
HEMP 27%
OILS & FATS 5%

RUBBER 66%
TIN 8%

OILS & FATS 8%
MEAT 6%
COTTON 6%

SUGAR 11%

RUBBER 17%
TEA 1%

TIN 40%
COPPER 28%
COTTON 5%

PINGUIN
THOR
KORMORAN
ATLANTIS

COPPER 27%

WOOL 12%
MAIZE 10%
SUGAR 7%

PINGUIN
ORION
ATLANTIS
KOMET

ORION

MAIZE 83%
MEAT 34%
WHEAT 16%
WOOL 9%
BARLEY 5%

SCHIFF OHN

'Ghost Cruisers', were converted merchant ships of some 7,000 tons capable of long endurance. They were fitted out with dummy funnels, telescopic masts, false derricks and deck houses all of which could give the appearance of a peaceful merchantman, but concealed behind hydraulically-operated flaps were batteries of guns and torpedo tubes. Some of the auxiliary cruisers carried aircraft to increase their hunting range as they lived like pirates, roaming from ocean to ocean avoiding British warships and living off the cargoes of captured ships. Rendez-vous were also kept whenever possible with U-boats and the *Etappendienst* blockade runners for repairs or revictualling.

Six raiders had sailed in the Spring of 1940. The *Atlantis* put out from Kiel on 31 March for the South Atlantic, followed by the *Orion* which eventually reached New Zealand, where she laid mines at the entrance to Auckland harbour before operating in the Pacific. The *Widder* sailed in May for the Central Atlantic, where she operated for five months, sinking ten ships before returning safely to base in October. By the end of June more auxiliary cruisers were ready to leave for the distant trade routes; *Thor* for the South Atlantic, *Pinguin* for the Indian and Antarctic Ocean whilst the *Komet* made her voyage to the Pacific via the Northeast Passage – along the pack-ice of the North Russian coast with the aid of Soviet icebreakers. The sudden appearance of these warships on the trade routes presented a new menace to merchant ships. It was an impossible task for the Royal Navy to find these raiders in distant seas, especially when the worsening situation in France called for a concentration of every available warship in home waters placing very great pressure on the destroyer flotillas, which were being put out of action at an alarming rate as the Luftwaffe stepped up their dive-bomber attacks. Already hard-pressed in hunting U-boats and protecting convoys, destroyers were now having to be sent to support the Allied armies driven back on the Channel ports.

A DESPERATE REQUEST

On 15 May Churchill had discussed this serious decline in Britain's naval strength with Ambassador Joseph Kennedy, who had immediately telephoned the President, warning him to anticipate an urgent message.

As the Ambassador had forecast, Churchill's appeal for immediate aid arrived the same day:

> I trust you realise, Mr President, that the voice and force of the United States may count for nothing if they are withheld too long. You may have a completely subjugated Nazified Europe established with astounding swiftness, and the weight may be more than we can bear. All I ask you now is that you proclaim non-belligerency, which would mean that you would help us with everything short of actually engaging armed forces. Immediate needs are; first of all the loan of forty or fifty of your older destroyers to bridge the gap . . .

This cable clearly indicated that Churchill had every intention of calling on American resources for massive support. In addition to the destroyers, the British also wanted 'several hundred of the latest types of aircraft', and

Ships without Harbours: German propaganda about the auxiliary cruiser *Orion* and her Captain (below) underlined the remarkable success achieved against Britain's worldwide shipping (left, map from captured German archives showing the vulnerability of Britain's lifelines to attack with over 1,500 ships at sea in any one day). Armed with concealed guns, the 'Ghost Cruisers' that set out in the Spring of 1940 sank or captured nearly half a million tons by the end of 1941:

Atlantis: 145,697 tons sunk by HMS *Devonshire* 22/11/41

Orion: 57,744 tons returned to Brest 21/8/41

Widder: 58,645 tons returned to Brest 31/10/41

Thor: 83,000 tons including 3 British armed merchant cruisers

Pinguin: 13,550 tons sunk by HMS *Cornwall* 8/5/41

Komet: 42,959 tons

Kormoran: 68,274 tons lost after sinking the cruiser HMAS *Sydney* 19/11/41

75

'anti-aircraft equipment and ammunition of which again there will be plenty next year, if we are alive to see it'. In characteristic style he brushed aside financial considerations. 'We shall go on paying in dollars for as long as we can but I should like to feel reasonably sure that when we can pay no more you will give us the stuff all the same.'

Apart from military supplies, the Prime Minister wanted Roosevelt to use American diplomatic strength to dissuade Mussolini from siding with Hitler and to persuade De Valera to let Britain use her former bases.

These detailed requests came at a time when public opinion in the United States, stunned at the lightning speed of the German advance, began to register alarm. Jokes about *Sitzkrieg* vanished as the German armies approached the Channel and Roosevelt's speechwriter, Robert Sherwood, wrote: 'A sense of terror swept through the civilised world as a result of these bewildering events, these incredible achievements of mechanized barbarism'. Many Americans were prepared to write off Britain and France and a *Fortune* Magazine poll showed that only 30% still believed in the chance of an Allied victory, whilst, even more disturbingly, 63% thought Hitler might attempt to seize territory in the Americas.

The United States was poorly equipped to meet such a threat with an army able to put only five divisions in the field with scarcely any armoured formations. The US Navy was in better shape and undergoing a major expansion programme to transform it into a 'two ocean' navy capable of operating at strength in the Atlantic and Pacific. Nevertheless, it was not yet equal to the Japanese, whose Fleet had the strongest and most efficient naval air arm in the world. Even in aviation, where the United States boasted a strong industry, her own services had been starved of new aircraft.

The day after he had received Churchill's urgent cable, President Roosevelt set in motion the first of a series of massive efforts to transform the American armed forces. The war industries, which so far had been struggling to fulfil the modest orders of Britain and France, were now to be rapidly expanded to supply the United States services. In a message to Congress the American people were asked to 'recast their thinking about national protection' and to support a staggering billion dollar rearmament plan and an additional fund of 200m. dollars. 50,000 fighters and bombers were to be built to make America the strongest airpower in the world. The President, mindful of the pressing needs of Britain, advised Congress 'not to take any action which would in any way hamper or delay the delivery of American-made planes to foreign nations.'

Isolationists and Nazi sympathisers were already being answered by a new and powerful organisation, William Allen White's 'Committee to Defend America by Aiding the Allies'. Encouraged privately by Roosevelt, its objective was 'to fill the radio and the newspapers and the Congressional mail with the voice of prominent citizens urging America to become the non-belligerent ally of France and England'. Nevertheless, isolationist sentiment was still sufficiently strong to prevent Roosevelt from feeling able to meet Churchill's desperate request for destroyers.

On 16 May his reply was non-commital. 'As you know,' Roosevelt

e Reconditioned

reminded Churchill, 'a step of that kind could not be taken except with the specific authorization of the Congress and I am not certain that it would be so wise for that suggestion to be made to the Congress at this moment.' It was a bitter, yet not unexpected refusal which left the Admiralty facing a critical shortage of destroyers for escort duties, but Churchill remained resolute. On 20 May, in answer to Roosevelt's anxious enquiries about the future of the British fleet, the Prime Minister cabled back his stubborn resolve to face the worst – with or without outside help:

> Our intention is, whatever happens, to fight on to the end in this Island and, provided we can get the help for which we ask, we hope to run them very close in the air battles in view of individual superiority. Members of the present administration would likely go down during this process should it result adversely but in no conceivable circumstances will we consent to surrender.

British and French troops were already beginning an orderly withdrawal into the Dunkirk perimeter under constant attack by the Luftwaffe, the Admiralty became increasingly concerned about the attrition suffered by its destroyer forces. To replace the losses an urgent message was sent to Canada and four Royal Canadian Navy destroyers were ordered across to Britain, leaving the Western Atlantic without any anti-submarine escorts.

The destroyers were now to play a crucial role as the backbone of the 861 small craft of all shapes and sizes which flocked across the Channel to Dunkirk. This 'fleet of little ships' began its heroic effort on 26 May 1940. At first the progress of 'Operation Dynamo' was slow and only 7,669 men had been lifted from the burning mole when the Admiralty ordered all available destroyers to Dunkirk. On 31 May Churchill once more cabled:

> The situation here as regards destroyers is getting rather desperate. They have lost three outright in this withdrawal from Dunkirk and thirteen have been damaged. If it were practical or possible to get any legislation that would give them destroyers or some aircraft immediately, the psychological effect could be of even more value than the actual help.

Next day two more destroyers were lost and many more seriously damaged in the unceasing air attack, but they had played a major part in evacuating over 180,000 men, with crews who were 'approaching a condition of complete exhaustion'. When Operation Dynamo ended on 4 June, 330,000 Allied fighting men had been miraculously saved. But the cost to the Royal Navy had been high. Of the 39 destroyers taking part in Dynamo, 6 had been sunk and 19 damaged. This had so seriously weakened British seaborne defences that Captain Kirk, US Naval Attache in London, reported to Washington, that of a total strength of 94 destroyers in home waters after Dunkirk, only 43 remained ready for action.

But Roosevelt's power to come to Britain's aid was limited and opinion was now polarising dangerously in the United States between those who wanted to retreat into a 'Fortress America' and those who could see that the democracies had to be supported. If some Americans wondered whether any effort

Roosevelt's Dilemma: In spite of desperate appeals, the President was at first reluctant to release any of the First War destroyers (above) that the US Navy was taking out of its 'mothball fleet'. He needed the support of the pro-Allied lobby to counter the vocal isolationists and their attempts to block the arms deal in the Senate. William Allen White (left), Editor of the *Kansas Star* was urged by the White House to step up the campaign of his 'Committee to Defend America by Aiding the Allies'.

could now save England and France, the British Chiefs of Staff, in a significant strategic reassessment for the War Cabinet, were in no doubt that survival depended almost entirely on the United States. Titled enigmatically 'British Strategy in a Certain Eventuality' their report investigated 'the means whereby we could continue to fight single-handed if French resistance were to collapse completely.' This key memorandum was based on two assumptions, first that Italy would intervene with her strong navy, threatening to overturn Britain's strategic position in the Mediterranean. Second, that 'the United States of America is willing to give us full economic and financial support without which we do not think we could continue the war with any chance of success'.

Future prospects were not bright. Britain now faced all-out air attack, a U-boat siege and invasion.

> As time goes on – over a period of some months – our enemies will be able to extend their economic and military control to Spain, Portugal and North Africa in the West and to the Balkans except Turkey in the East. This will somewhat improve their economic situation, will provide additional bases for attack on British trade in the Atlantic . . . *we have assumed that we can count on the full economic and financial support of the United States possibly extending to active participation.*

The Chiefs of Staff believed that air defence was 'the crux of the problem'. Fighter command was to take top priority, and the report went on to propose that the country must be organised as 'a fortress on totalitarian lines'. Apart from the R.A.F., the main defence of the country would be in the hands of the

Fighting on Single-Handed: On 4 June 1940, with the completion of Operation Dynamo (below, HMS *Havant* arriving back with her decks crowded with troops) the British Chiefs of Staff were already making plans to withstand a long German siege. But it was clear that Britain would need American help and 50 US destroyers were badly needed to replace the 25 lost and badly damaged in the Channel.

Navy. 'With Germany in possession of ports in Norway, Holland, Belgium and France our Naval dispositions must be planned to meet the threat of seaborne invasion on either the East or South Coasts of the United Kingdom.'

The Navy still had to perform the vital task of protecting seaborne supplies and be the first line of defence against the invasion threat. British trade could also be threatened by air attack on ports in the South and East which might force their abandonment, and the report concluded that.

> Even if our imports were reduced to a mere trickle we should be able to tide over a critical period of a few weeks by drawing on our reserve stocks which have been accumulated to meet a crisis of this nature. Strict rationing and careful distribution of stocks would have to be maintained: Nevertheless our ability to carry on the war is absolutely dependent upon the eventual maintenance of supplies through the West Coast ports.

The report understandably concentrated on the defence of Britain in the totally changed strategic situation but the Chiefs of Staff still held out a glimmer of hope that Germany could be defeated, although this would depend on American economic and military aid.

The 'grave and grim' report was of such import that it was signed by the Chiefs of Staff, Admiral Pound, Air Marshal Newall and Field Marshal Lord Ironside, as well as their deputies. More than any other single document it spelt out the underlying shift in the balance of world power away from Western Europe to the United States.

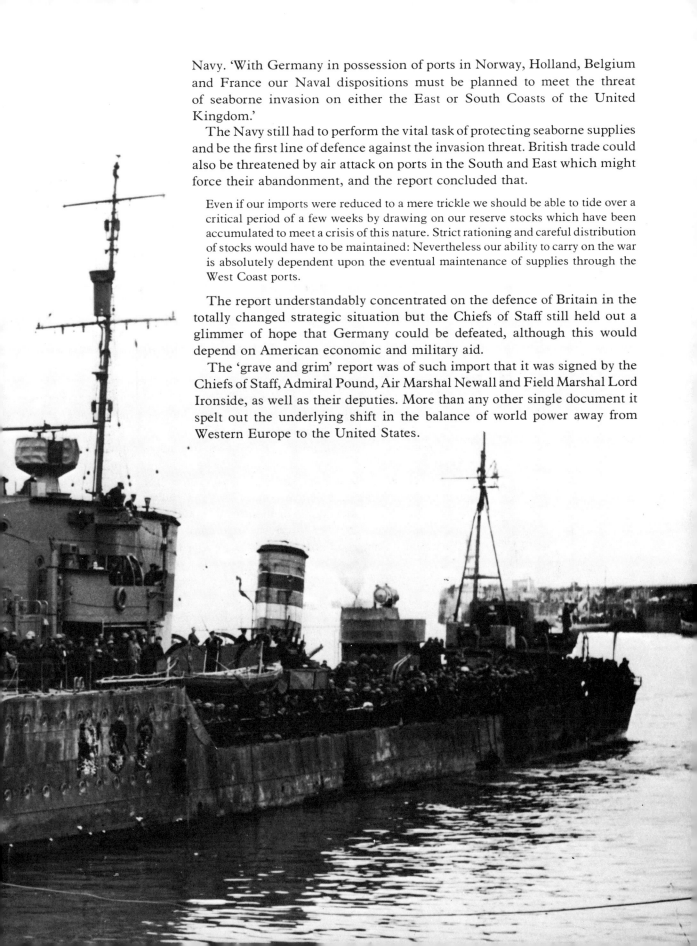

WE SHALL NEVER SURRENDER

Allied chances of survival appeared bleak as the panzer divisions rolled on toward Paris. In London the fleeting mood of relief after the 'miracle of Dunkirk' gave way to a firm determination to resist a Nazi siege 'We must be very careful not to assign to this deliverance the attributes of a victory. Wars are not won by evacuations' Churchill told the House of Commons on 4 June before declaring defiantly:

> We shall fight in France. We shall fight on the seas and oceans. We shall fight with growing confidence and growing strength in the air. We shall defend our island whatever the cost may be. We shall fight on the landing grounds. We shall fight in the fields and in the streets. We shall fight in the hills. We shall never surrender!

The Prime Minister's stirring speech roused the nation to face its darkest hour. But the Army would need more than ringing words to repel an invasion. Most of its tanks and guns had been abandoned on the beaches of Dunkirk, and the troops desperately needed replacements from American stocks, yet the politics of deliverance ground painfully slowly in Washington.

Now that Britain's survival was utterly dependent on the flow of arms and supplies across the Atlantic the Germans warned all shipping on 29 May that unrestricted U-boat warfare was about to begin in the waters around the British Isles. It was a severe challenge for the Royal Navy, whose destroyer forces were so drastically reduced, that convoy defence had to take second priority to the threat of imminent invasion.

In the first weeks of June the U-boats headed out into the Western Approaches for their most concerted offensive so far. Their attacks heralded what Dönitz and his commanders called the 'Happy Time . . . As the U-boats encountered large numbers of vessels sailing independently and weakly escorted convoys and not all of them were escorted by aircraft'. The main brunt of the offensive fell on the merchant shipping in the Western Approaches which had only forty escorts and a handful of armed merchant cruisers to protect it. It was during these black weeks that sixteen year old John Harrison found himself looking for a new ship in Liverpool docks:

> There was a vacancy chalked up on the blackboard for a scullery man on an armed merchant cruiser, so I went over and applied for the job.
> I was shown to a Chief Petty Officer in navy uniform. He looked at my discharge book and said 'Sorry' when he saw my date of birth. 'You have only just turned 17, you have to be 18.' So I walked away and stood waiting for another vacancy. There was a group of seamen standing next to me and one of them said: 'You didn't apply for that job, did you?'
> I said yes and he said to me, 'Don't go in one of those ships, they are Death Traps!'
> No one would take the job, so I just hung around until the Petty Officer shouted out, 'Isn't there one man amongst you that will take the job?' One of the men shouted, 'You can stick it, mate!'
> The Petty Officer called me over and said 'Are you still interested in taking the job?' and I said 'Yes'. Then he told me he could sign me on as a boy, so I agreed and signed on. I was paid two weeks pay in advance and went home to collect my gear. When I arrived home I told my mother I was going on a Navy ship, and she cried. The articles I had signed were for two years, my pay was £2 10/-.

80

After the sinking of the *Rawalpindi*, the armed merchant cruisers had
acquired a reputation for being bad risks, but most merchantmen were
equally vulnerable to torpedo and air attack. Except for the fastest ocean
liners, there was no protection against surprise U-boat attack and few ships
could be fitted with anti-aircraft guns in the face of the desperate shortage.
Once a ship had been badly hit by a torpedo or bomb its survival was often
measured in minutes. Ore carriers would sink rapidly like a stone in seconds
and oil tankers would blow sky high even more quickly. It was a danger well
appreciated by Chief Officer John H. Drew of the 12,000 ton tanker *Saranac*
which had two lucky escapes from bombs before she was sighted in U-31's
periscope 350 miles west of Bantry Bay, Eire.

At approximately 3 pm on 25 June, a day or so after dispersing from the convoy and
proceeding independently towards a US port, *Saranac* was torpedoed in the main
engine room at the stern of the ship. The ship was rapidly losing buoyancy aft, and
within a few minutes *Saranac* settled with the main poopdeck a few inches above
sea level and the bow high out of the water. Our gunlayer, a colour sergeant of the
Royal Marines, stood by our 4.7″ gun aft in readiness to retaliate if the U-boat
surfaced. *Saranac* was completely immobilised and a sitting duck for further attack.
We experienced a premonition that our movements on the deck of *Saranac* were
being watched from the U-boat's periscope. At about 4.30 pm Captain Alcock and
myself mutually agreed to abandon ship with our volunteers in the least damaged of

the two remaining lifeboats, and to lay off *Saranac* until darkness, intending to reboard the ship if rescue vessels or tugs arrived to assist us in response to our earlier radio message.

At about 4.45 the U-boat suddenly surfaced between us and *Saranac* and immediately opened fire with her deck gun. Two shells exploded in the sea adjacent to our boat – obviously a warning – the next round scored a direct hit on *Saranac*'s defensive armament and the ammunition magazine, which exploded. The U-boat then circled the ship, firing round after round into the hull along the waterline and the officer's midship accommodation. She sank almost vertically by the stern about 3 hours after the initial attack. It took about 50 rounds of shell and two torpedoes to sink her . . .

We agreed that our only chance of survival in our damaged and leaking boat was to attempt to sail the 350 miles to Bantry Bay, since we had no motor to assist us and it was impracticable to row the waterlogged boat any distance with only seven of us. The only provisions comprised ship's biscuits, a case of condensed milk, a few tins of sardines and several thousand cigarettes but few matches. The lifeboat compass had been badly shaken and was unreliable. Nevertheless, by making use of the bearings obtained from the sun by day, the Pole Star by night, we made steady progress for the first two days, helped by a light following Westerly wind, slight sea and swell.

About the 27 June a strong Westerly gale with rough tumbling seas and heavy swell overtook us. Time and again the boat broached to and almost capsized, but with determination and bailing by all seven of us and using our oil bag trailing astern, we managed to keep the boat running before the gale until a sudden heavy squall split the only sail and mast. Then we hove to and re-rigged an improvised sail using the remnants of our sail and our only blanket. The gale petered out and twenty four hours later on 30 June we sighted a trawler bearing down on us close west of Bantry Bay . . .

The destruction of this big tanker contributed to the grim total of 289,000 tons sunk by the U-boats during June 1940. This record monthly loss had

Happy Hunting: As the new U-boat offensive got under way in June 1940, the Germans were able to sink over a quarter of a million tons in four weeks with only six operational boats. The absence of air and sea escorts made the Western Approaches a happy hunting ground for U-boats like Prien's U-47 (below) which sank a record ten ships in a single patrol.

been achieved with a daily average of only six operational U-boats sinking a ship every twenty-four hours.

The spirit of aggression behind the renewed assault on shipping is revealed in the preface to Dönitz's new standing orders issued in June:

> In the first place attack and keep on attacking; do not let yourself be shaken off; if the boat is temporarily forced away or driven under water follow up in the general direction of the convoy, try to get in touch again and once more ATTACK!

Kapitänleutnant Prien, showed what a really ruthless and determined execution of Dönitz's orders could achieve when he made one of the most spectacularly successful patrols of the whole war. Returning to Wilhelmshaven in U-47 on 4 July, he had sunk 66,588 tons to become the first U-boat Ace. Two days later 'The Bull of Scapa Flow', as he was known to listeners all over the Reich, broadcast an account of his latest exploits. The programme was monitored with keen interest by the Anti-Submarine Warfare Division which reported:

> Early on the morning of the 19th Prien opened his operations by attacking convoy HGF 34 NW off Finisterre and torpedoed three ships, *Baron Loudon, British Monarch* and *Tudor*. He followed the convoy northwards until the evening of the 20th. It is possible that an aircraft dropped two bombs near him at 18.35. Two hours later Prien torpedoed *Otterpool*; the *Fellside*, which was in the vicinity and opened fire on the U-boat, claimed to have registered two hits and made her escape. Prien then turned northwestwards and on the morning of the 21st torpedoed the tanker *San Fernando* in convoy HX 49 escorted by two sloops. On the same evening, following up the convoy, he torpedoed and sank the Norwegian *Randsfjord*. Turning westwards again, he met a U-boat which had sunk the *Eli Knudsen*, a Norwegian tanker from the same convoy. Prien and his men then had a quiet period for five days until the afternoon of the 27th when they torpedoed and sank the Greek *F. B. Goulandris*. On the 29th he set out for home.
> When northwest of Ireland, on the morning of 2nd July, the *Arandora Star* crossed his track and she was torpedoed without warning.

The U-boats' growing successes gave a new urgency to the Prime Minister's messages to the President asking for destroyers and aircraft. Urgent lists of arms, equipment and ammunition needed to bolster Britain's home defences against what was believed to be the imminent threat of invasion had poured into the offices of the British Purchasing Mission in New York. This key part of the war materials supply system was under the direction of Scottish-Canadian industrialist Arthur Purvis who was acknowledged to be 'one of our definite bits of good fortune in this war.' His close contacts with the US business world, together with his friendship with Henry Morgenthau Jr, Secretary of the US Treasury and confidante of the President, had done much to move the vital supply operation moving into top gear. Now Purvis, together with the French representative, Bloch Lainé, submitted a six page memorandum listing Allied arms requirements, grouped under the heading 'Supplied from stocks on hand with US Army. *Specially urgent.*' The only hope of procuring arms rapidly was to ask the American armed forces to sacrifice some of their own supplies but though sympathetic to meeting these requests, the President held out little hope of being able to assist with yet more aircraft or the destroyers Churchill was pressing for. For rifles and other arms Roosevelt indicated that the chances were 'quite promising provided the United States Department of State can find a legal way'. A frantic search was organised by Morgenthau for a legal formula which would enable the President to effect the transfer within his own prerogative to avoid Isolationist opposition in Congress.

On 2 June, the Attorney General felt able to declare that, under a law of July 1919, the Administration could legitimately dispose of weapons 'surplus to requirements' without advertising and on terms deemed suitable to any individual or corporation. The door was now open. Within hours Purvis was in Morgenthau's office, agreeing to purchase the weapons for a price of $37,619,556 and 60 cents. He jubilantly cabled London on 4 June: 'Orders tonight have been given for the despatch of the material by railway express from various arsenals throughout the country'.

On 3 June, the first batch of rifles had already begun to move from the US arsenals. Ships and handling teams were on standby at the East Coast ports to get the arms across the Atlantic with the minimum of delay. A week later the British cargo ship *Eastern Prince* left Raritan, New Jersey with 48 field guns, 12,000 rifles, 15,270 machine guns and 37 million rounds of .30 ammunition.

As the first shipload of desperately needed arms began its journey across the Atlantic, the Germans began their final push towards Paris and on 5 June Paul Reynaud sent an urgent telegram to Roosevelt:

> I want to tell you that France will fight to the last man . . . But Mr President, in order to continue the struggle during the coming decisive weeks, in order to intensify it to the point of victory, we need immediately all the planes that you can procure for us. Can you stretch your hand across the sea to help us save civilisation?

Two days later the Panzers had broken through the French lines and Paris stood defenceless. But it was not the Germans who delivered the final blow to French morale. On 10 June, Mussolini decided that he had sat too long on the sidelines and declared war on Britain and France in characteristically grandiose style: 'We have only one watchword – to conquer and we shall conquer to give at last a long period of peace to Europe, to the world.'

Roosevelt was furious that the Italian dictator had ignored all American appeals to stay out of the conflict. Condemning Mussolini's attack, 'the hand that held the dagger has stuck it into the back of its neighbour', the President pledged United States support for the democracies:

> We will extend to the opponents of force the material resources of this nation, and at the same time we will harness and speed up the use of those resources in order that we in the Americas may have the equipment and training equal to the task of any emergency and every defense.

Stirred by the increasingly partisan American position, Berlin instructed the German Minister in Washington to reassure the President that Hitler's view was 'Europe for the Europeans, and America for the Americans'. Indeed, the Führer wanted it known that he had no intention of harming the British Empire or the United States.

Reynaud, facing defeat and evacuation to North Africa, tried to enlarge the American commitment to direct military involvement but the most emotional pleas from the French Premier, aided and abetted by Churchill, could not move Roosevelt beyond his commitment to all aid short of war. Faced by military disintegration, the French government split and decided to open Armistice negotiations.

THE DEADLY STRIKE

The question of the French fleet now became an issue of major importance for Britain and the United States since it could heavily influence the balance of power in the Atlantic. Under the command of Admiral Darlan, France had a fleet of older battleships, with three powerful modern battleships in various stages of completion, as well as an aircraft carrier and two cruisers, two heavy destroyers and a large submarine fleet. The French Navy had provided valuable assistance escorting some of the Atlantic convoys as well as playing a powerful strategic role by holding the balance of Mediterranean seapower for the Allies. The approaching French collapse, together with the entry of Italy into the war, saw the naval balance tilting dangerously against Britain and also the United States. The Duce was now in a position to carry out his boast to turn the Mediterranean into *Mare Nostrum* with Italy's six battleships, strong cruiser and destroyer forces and the biggest submarine fleet in the world.

If the French and Italian fleets joined the Kriegsmarine, a naval power far stronger than the Royal Navy would be pointed like a 'cocked gun' at the Anglo-Saxon powers. An American Naval Intelligence study of 13 June 1940, which tried to estimate Britain's chances of survival, forecast that such a German-Italian-French naval coalition would be one third stronger than the combined British and American strength in the Atlantic – even if the US Pacific fleet were to be brought back from Hawaii.

Specially Urgent: Anxious about Britain's defencelessness against a German invasion, the President sanctioned the release of urgently needed surplus arms on June 2 1940. The deal was engineered by businessman Arthur Purvis, Head of the British Purchasing Mission (top), who worked closely with US Treasury Secretary Henry Morgenthau Jr. (centre). A week later as the first shipload of armaments was on its way across the Atlantic the Italian dictator Benito Mussolini (below) declared war.

The French fleet was bound to become an important pawn in the Armistice negotiations and one that Hitler was to use skilfully. Churchill had hoped that the French would continue the fight, well aware that Britain had already benefited from the arrival of Polish, Dutch and Norwegian warships in her ports volunteering to continue the war against Germany. On 12 June, on a flying visit to the French Cabinet in Briare, the Prime Minister had taken aside the powerful Naval Commander in Chief and told him 'Darlan, I hope you will never surrender the Fleet'. The frosty reply was: 'There is no question of doing so; it would be contrary to our Naval traditions and honour.'

As the Franco-German Armistice discussions began Roosevelt became as concerned as Churchill about the large arms purchases that had been made by France in the United States. The contracts were so interwoven with those of Britain that an almost insuperable legal tangle threatened unless action were taken before the Armistice was signed. Purvis had the good fortune to have the co-operation of Bloch Lainé, and, meeting in Purvis' Washington apartment on the evening of 16 June 1940, the two men coolly transferred to Britain the French contracts valued at $600m. Purvis had now committed a large proportion of Britain's dollar reserves with a few strokes of the pen.

Meanwhile, Churchill increased his pressure on the French Cabinet to send its ships to Britain or friendly ports. Two large battleships were moved beyond Hitler's reach; the *Jean Bart* to Casablanca and the unfinished *Richelieu* to Dakar. Few warships were in French home ports when the terms of the Armistice were announced on 22 June. Its clauses had been astutely drafted and reflected Hitler's deep attachment to a Continental strategy, France would keep 40% of her territory and her own government, although the Northern provinces and the long coastline from the Belgian frontier to the Pyrenees would be garrisoned and controlled by Germany. This semblance of independence was designed to drive a wedge between the French and British and although Raeder would have liked to acquire control of French ships for the Kriegsmarine, Hitler 'wished to refrain from taking any measures that would affect French honour' and left them nominally under the command of the new Vichy Regime.

The suspicion remained that Germany intended to seize the ships when it suited, thus creating a serious situation for the United States and a desperate one for Britain. Churchill decided to act. Taking advantage of the dispersal of the French fleet in ports outside Metropolitan France, orders were given to the Royal Navy Fleet commanders to offer terms directly to their erstwhile allies. The French warships were to be given the choice of continuing to fight their ships alongside Britain in the all-out war against Hitler; of accepting internment or repatriation; or of scuttling their ships. If none of these offers were acceptable, the French Admirals were to be told, 'the Royal Navy should use whatever force may be necessary to prevent your ships falling into German or Italian hands.'

The day of decision for 'Operation Catapult' was set for 3 July. The French ships in British ports either made terms or were rapidly overcome. Resistance aboard the submarine cruiser *Surcouf* resulted in the death of three British

The Deadly Stroke: The intransigence of Admiral Jean Francois Darlan (left), Minister of Marine in the new Vichy Government, prompted Churchill to order 'Operation Catapult' to prevent the French Fleet from falling into German hands as part of the armistice settlement and undermining Britain's sea supremacy. Admiral Sir James Somerville (right) commander of the Royal Navy's *Force H*, was given the difficult task of trying to persuade the main body of the French Fleet at Oran to comply with the British terms. When negotiations broke down on 3 July, Somerville had the distasteful duty of neutralising the naval threat by ordering his ships to fire on their former allies (below).

sailors. In Alexandria, skilful handling of the situation by Admiral Andrew Cunningham persuaded the French Admiral Godfroy to disarm his ships, but, at the main French North African base of Mers el Kebir, it was a different story. Admiral Somerville, with the powerful Force H comprising the *Hood*, *Valiant*, *Resolution* and *Ark Royal* had been sent to offer terms to Admiral Gensoul under whose command were the most powerful units of the French fleet – the two powerful battlecruisers *Strasbourg* and *Dunkerque*, as well as two older battleships, the *Provence* and *Bretagne*, together with a number of large destroyers and a seaplane carrier. After a long tense day of negotiations, however, Gensoul felt bound to reject the British terms. Shortly before 6 pm Admiral Somerville ordered his ships to open fire on the French. In 16 minutes the *Bretagne* blew up after a direct hit by a 15″ salvo from the *Hood*, the *Provence* was damaged and beached whilst the *Dunkerque* and heavy destroyer *Mogador* were disabled. The battlecruiser *Strasbourg* made a spectacular escape to Toulon in company with four heavy destroyers.

The British War Cabinet were immensely relieved and more than ready to accept the hostility of the new Vichy Government. Most important, Churchill's bold and decisive move had won approval in the United States. When Roosevelt replied to the French complaint against Britain's odious aggression, he confessed: 'I would not have acted otherwise. I am a realist.' Public opinion in both Britain and the United States was gratified by the action, which was seen as a ruthless demonstration of Britain's determination to fight on alone and not to compromise her sea supremacy.

The golden horseshoe of U-99
brought its crew the victor's
spoils. The seaman on the right
is wearing British army
battledress after arriving in
Lorient on 8 August following
a record breaking patrol on
which Kretschmer sank 65,137
tons. His success was typical of
the 'Happy Time' from July to
the end of October 1940 when
the U-boats sank over a million
tons of shipping. The Royal
Navy was severely stretched
with the result that no more
than six operational U-boats
managed to sink an average of
over 9,000 tons a day – the
highest success rate of the
whole war.

5. The 'Happy Time'

'We all felt like schoolchildren at Christmas time'
Kapitänleutnant OTTO KRETSCHMER, U-99

ELROSE

'I am instructed by the British Government to purchase 350 long-range heavy bombers, and by my wife to purchase one "O-So-Handy" hair-drier.'

Two days after Paris fell on 14 June 1940, the British Government received a pessimistic assessment of the chances of surviving alone. A report entitled 'Economic Aid from the New World to the Old' prepared by Arthur Greenwood deputy Labour Party leader and Minister without Portfolio in Churchill's Coalition War Cabinet, finally dispelled any remaining illusions:

> However indomitable the spirit of the country, the task of maintaining our resistance until such time as our material resources have so increased as to enable us to attempt to achieve a military decision against the enemy will be well nigh impossible unless we are able to draw assistance on a large scale from the New World.

The Nazi takeover of Norway, Denmark, Belgium, Holland and now France had not only stripped Britain of her Allies but had cut her off from important sources of food and raw materials. Most of Europe's large industrial plant was under German direction, vastly increasing the power of the Reich's war machine and frustrating the British naval blockade. In the face of this ominous economic reverse the Greenwood report set out the ways in which the United States had to be called upon to help. If Britain was to be turned into 'a heavily armoured fortress' to withstand a long siege, the most important and immediate need was for American financial assistance since 'there is no single measure which would afford us more rapid or more important relief than the removal of the present bar on the grant to us of loans and credits'. Shortage of cash reserves meant that the government was being 'forced to all kinds of arts and stratagems' to eke out the dwindling foreign reserves. Without massive American financial aid the only way Britain could continue to earn the money to go on fighting was 'to retain in the export trade large numbers of skilled workers who might otherwise be diverted to the production of war materials'.

To combat the Nazi war machine the full support of American industrial effort was needed, and to harness this war production would require a 'self denying ordinance' on the part of the Americans. The report concluded: 'The United States can only give us effective assistance in the production of aircraft and armoured vehicles if, in certain vital directions, means can be found to reduce the level of consumption in the United States.' It was a formidable demand to make on a nation not yet at war, but the British Government had no alternative.

A long list of supplies was cabled to Washington on 27 June 1940. Cordell Hull, the US Secretary of State, was at first stunned by the scale of the requirements for Britain's survival:

> aircraft, destroyers, light naval craft, military equipment and supplies; also personnel, possibly volunteers to man ships and aircraft. She [Britain] suggested stoppage at source of all supplies to enemy countries and occupied territories and full co-operation in her contraband control with reference to the remaining neutrals, including Asiatic Russia. She requested supplies of food, munitions and raw materials on a credit basis, if necessary, and merchant shipping to ply between the Americas and the United Kingdom.

The US Chiefs of Staff doubted Britain's chances of survival, and submitted their pessimistic conclusions to the President. Britain was thought

Arts & Stratagems: Churchill's decision to stand firm against the German onslaught concealed the harsh truth of Arthur Greenwood's top secret report that Britain desperately needed massive economic and military aid from the United States to survive. The British Ambassador, Lord Lothian (opposite) was told by Churchill: 'Never cease to impress on the President and others that if this country was successfully invaded and occupied after heavy fighting, some Quisling Government would be formed to make peace . . . In this case the British Fleet would be the solid contribution with which this peace government would buy terms'. Roosevelt was now moving to aid Britain. After bringing in Republican allies Frank Knox and Henry Stimson (above), he asked Congress to support his 4 billion dollar re-armament programme.

unlikely to repel an invasion and Army Chief of Staff, General George C Marshall, Roosevelt's principal adviser, was worried that US reserve munition stocks were now running so low that 'if Britain were defeated the Army and the Administration could never justify to the American people the risk they had taken'.

It was proposed that the United States should concentrate her resources on defending her own hemisphere. German influence was strong in some South American States like Argentina, and Washington was concerned at the way in which Dr Goebbels' propaganda was rallying the expatriates to support the Reich. Fears that Nazi agents might be trying to engineer Quisling style takeovers were given credence in May with rumours of agents landing on the coasts of Guiana and Brazil, and in June the US Navy rushed the heavy cruisers *Quincy* and *Wichita* to Montevideo to back up the Uruguayan government's action in outlawing the country's Nazi party. The Americans also became concerned about the possibility of Nazi influence growing in the West Indian colonies. The main point of friction focussed on the French island of Martinique where two cruisers and the aircraft carrier *Béarn*, with 160 American-built planes aboard, had taken refuge. They had brought with them a large part of the French gold reserves which the British were very keen to acquire. Churchill sent a cruiser squadron to blockade the island after the Vichy Governor refused to cooperate but the Americans, anxious to avoid a clash, placed a naval squadron between the British and Vichy French.

Martinique was only one in a long line of strategically placed islands which American military strategists recognised as vital for the defence of the Western hemisphere. In this line of Atlantic islands from Iceland through Bermuda to the Caribbean and down to Trinidad, the United States had only three bases – at Puerto Rico, St Croix and St Thomas. In 1939 the British government had been prepared to allow American forces to use St Lucia, Trinidad and Bermuda but the isolationists now urged the seizure or purchase of these European possessions to satisfy unpaid war debts.

Isolationist opposition, aided by the communists, had stirred up a new wave of opposition in the University Campuses. In July students had made a peace march to the White House and demonstrated in New York and Chicago carrying thousands of white crosses symbolising the GI's who died in the First War. Their banners prominently displayed the slogan 'The Yanks are NOT coming.'

The rapid fall of France had been a severe setback to Roosevelt's hope at the beginning of the year that Germany could be contained by the 'Trinity of French land power, British seapower and American industrial power' but he still believed that Britain must be kept as the forward bastion of the United States defences. Now he set about reorganising the US armaments industry to step up its output to provide both nations with the weapons needed for their defence. He also shrewdly strengthened his political base by reorganising his Administration on a virtual coalition basis, bringing in two prominent Republicans, Colonel Frank Knox, a leading advocate of a strong fleet, as Secretary of the Navy and veteran Henry Stimson as Secretary for War. At the same time Congress was asked for 4 billion dollars to fund new rearmament.

91

The French collapse and the desperate situation of Britain had finally decided Roosevelt to take the unprecedented step of running for a third Presidential term and to calm isolationist fears he was careful to promise: 'we will not send out men to take part in European wars'. He also avoided raising the unpopular issue of selective military service, conscious that the approaching November elections had weakened his Administration's ability to act decisively.

Across the Atlantic Churchill was growing impatient with the cautious political course that Roosevelt appeared to be steering. On 26 June he informed Lord Lothian: 'We have really not had any help worth speaking of from the United States so far. We know the President is our best friend but it is no use trying to dance attendance upon Republican and Democratic Conventions. What really matters is whether Hitler is master of Britain in three months or not.' The Prime Minister also stressed the need for stepping up the level of US arms supplies in the long personal and secret telephone conversations he held almost nightly with the President. But he could do little to influence the complex political checks imposed on the White House by the forthcoming Election campaign.

Churchill's pessimism about the American political scene was to prove ill-founded. In the last days of June the Republican Party, chose an outsider – Wendell Willkie – as their presidential candidate on the sixth ballot. The national platform had originally stated, 'The Republican Party is firmly opposed to involving this nation in foreign wars', but Willkie had astonished the press when he told the Convention, 'as far as the assistance to the democracies is concerned, I am in accord with the national administration'.

Much of the success in changing the public mood was attributable to the anti-isolationist campaigners from the 'Committee to Defend America by Aiding the Allies', which was growing rapidly. It had allied itself with the exclusive and very influential 'Century Group', of media and business 'Ivy Leaguers' which had been founded by wealthy Lewis Douglas. It could call on the service of Pulitzer Prize writers and influential publishers like Henry Luce, proprietor of *Time, Life* and *Fortune* magazines as well as the powerful New York law establishment represented by Dean Acheson and Allen Dulles. The group also received the backing of Hollywood but it faced a vocal isolationist opposition as well as an influential body of pro-German industrialists and sympathisers who gathered in the New York's Waldorf Astoria Hotel at the end of June to celebrate the German victory over France.

There was little doubt in London and Washington that Hitler's next move would be to launch an invasion of England. This was precisely what the German generals wanted, but, to their surprise, the Führer was uneasy about the operation. His doubts were reinforced by Raeder who believed any cross-Channel invasion to be unnecessary, proposing instead a total siege of Britain, so that 'all possible energy and armaments should be concentrated against the enemy overseas supply lines'.

'We are marching against England!' The signing of the French Armistice made Hitler (left) master of Europe. The might of the Wehrmacht was now directed towards the destruction of Britain and Hitler's troops began practising for the invasion *Operation Sea Lion* (below). Raeder and the Naval War Staff repeatedly drew attention to the risks of the operation that should only be undertaken as 'a last resort'.

INDECISION OVER 'SEA LION'

Hitler's curiously ambivalent attitude was largely founded on a belief that Britain would soon see the futility of continuing the struggle alone. Nor had he any wish to provoke the collapse of her world empire, which he admired, hoping that one day it could become a useful ally of the Reich.

At first Hitler was inclined to accept the Navy's case against making a risky invasion attempt but by 7 July the Generals had persuaded him to reverse his decision and he ordered planning to begin for an invasion. This decision sent Raeder hurrying to the Führer's mountain retreat in the Obersalzburg where he pointed out the difficulties, reasoning that Britain could be made 'to ask for peace simply by cutting off her trade by means of U-boat and air attacks on her main supply centres such as Liverpool'. Hitler appeared to change his mind again by opting for a naval strategy, promising to restart work on the super-battleships and carriers together with a grandiose fifteen year programme that would transform Trondheim in Norway into the biggest naval base in the world. He also approved Raeder's scheme for expanding Atlantic operations by moving into the French African Naval base port of Dakar and concluding a deal with Spain to set up a U-boat base in the Canaries.

But Hitler's enthusiasm for a purely naval strategy against Britain was soon again dispelled by the arguments of the Army and orders went out for 'Preparations for the Invasion of England'. The landings were to be carried out on a wide front along the Channel coast from Ramsgate to the Isle of Wight. Everything was to be ready by mid-August when it was planned the RAF would be 'so reduced physically and morally that it is unable to deliver any significant attack against the German crossing'.

Raeder was now alarmed that the Navy, with nearly all its heavy ships under repair, would be given an impossible task. His blunt memorandum, warning of the immensity of the undertaking, influenced Hitler's 'appeal once more to reason and common sense in Great Britain' in a Reichstag Speech of 19 July. 'I can see no reason why this war must go on'. The Führer declared, 'I am grieved by the sacrifices.' He was much less confident than his generals who believed that 'Sea Lion' was 'little more than a large scale river crossing on a front stretching from Ostend to Le Havre'.

Next day, the British Foreign Secretary, Lord Halifax, rejected the new peace offer. 'Hitler may plant his swastika where he will, but unless he can sap the strength of Britain, the foundations of his Empire are built on sand.' Hitler could hardly climb down now and he directed that 'an attempt must be made to prepare the operation for 15 September 1940'.

Anticipating the worst, the British Chiefs of Staff made plans to deal with any invasion attempt. The Home Fleet was to be moved to Rosyth so that its heavy ships would be ready for an immediate dash to the south, extra destroyer flotillas were sent to the Channel ports, and in the skies over Southern England Fighter Command stood ready to contest critical air superiority. Across the home counties concrete pill boxes and fortification lines were hastily thrown up across the natural defences of rivers and canals.

Steel tank traps, minefields and barbed wire barricades were festooned across deserted coastal seaside resorts and the Army concentrated its forces in the South East of England, ready to repel the invader.

Destroyers and corvettes were taken off convoy duties to stand guard against the greater peril threatening across the Channel. Several French destroyers fitted with British Asdic had been thoroughly examined by German experts. Technical reports revealed the weaknesses of Asdic, encouraging Dönitz's plans to concentrate his forces on the weakly protected convoys. In July U-boat sinkings rose to over 200,000 tons and the monthly Anti-Submarine Warfare Report warned: 'July marked the beginning of serious attacks on convoys whilst Asdic-fitted vessels were actually present, these attacks have generally been on large convoys which, owing to the shortage of escort vessels, have only been guarded by an average of two Asdic-fitted vessels'.

For many merchant skippers the late summer of 1940 was remembered as the time when 'escorts were something you read about in books'. One Master recalled an occasion when a single corvette and one trawler arrived to cover an incoming thirty ship convoy. His cockney first officer called out from the bridge: 'Blimey! Look what they've sent us – a raft and a lifeboat!'

There was a bitter side to the joke. The waters of the Western Approaches were adrift with the rafts and lifeboats of torpedoed merchantmen, as the U-boats exploited the shortage of warships to raid the shipping lanes. Often with only a corvette and a slow trawler to protect a convoy covering twenty square miles there was little that could be done to interfere with the U-boat attacks. Even after a sudden explosion had revealed the presence of the enemy, a proper hunt could not be mounted since no escort commander dared leave his flock of ships totally unprotected in order to beat off the marauder.

During the three months from July to October 1940, when the Admiralty was obliged to concentrate the greater part of its destroyer flotillas on anti-invasion duties, the U-boats destroyed 217 merchant ships. Only two U-boats were sunk between July and October as the Germans jubilantly enjoyed their most successful period of the war, which they aptly called the 'Happy Time'. There was little that the Royal Navy could do to stop the slaughter in the Atlantic approaches. On 15 August Hitler proclaimed a 'total blockade, of the waters around Britain', calling on the neutrals to keep their shipping out of this 'War Zone'. Immediately sinkings rocketed, to peak in the final week of August 1940 at 110,000 tons – (their most successful single week's destruction in the war).

Thoroughly alarmed, the Admiralty was forced to consider giving protection of the convoys priority over anti-invasion measures. Such losses could not be allowed to continue without seriously jeopardising Britain's ability to continue the war but an even greater peril was posed by the thousands of invasion barges jamming the French Channel ports.

THE BROKEN EAGLE

All the Wehrmacht's efforts were being directed to the invasion of Britain. Everything turned on the air offensive, which had begun on 15 August, Eagle Day, when Goering threw 1790 aircraft against Britain's air defences. The orderly formations of Luftwaffe bombers swept across the Channel to attack RAF airfields and radar installations. On the first day of 'The Battle of Britain' the spirited defence of Fighter Command's Spitfires and Hurricanes presaged a bitter struggle for air supremacy. Radar early warning of the German Bomber fleets together with efficient fighter control allowed RAF Fighter Comand to concentrate their aircraft where they could cause the most destruction. The first significant penetration of the Luftwaffe Enigma codes by the Bletchley Park decrypting teams also provided additional advance information about the German objectives. This allowed Air Marshal Dowding to commit his dwindling reserves of fighters at crucial moments in the great battle of attrition that raged over Southern England. By the end of August, German losses were mounting badly but there was still no sign of Goering's promised victory in the air and the Navy's hastily assembled invasion fleet was also being harried by British bombers in the embarkation ports.

As the Luftwaffe massed its strength for an all-out attack, it was clear that the risk of sending more destroyer reinforcements back to protect the convoys could not be taken. All that could be done was to close the Channel and the South Western Approaches to shipping with coastal traffic diverted north around Scotland.

These measures had little effect. The U-boats were now able to operate from the French Atlantic bases and this saved them the long trek across the North Sea, doubling the time that they could patrol in the Western Approaches. Dönitz had wasted no time after the fall of France in securing what he termed 'a strategic position of the utmost importance'. Even before the French Armistice had been signed, lorryloads of technicians were already on their way to set up the first of Germany's Atlantic bases at Lorient in Brittany. Only the small number of U-boats available during the critical autumn months of 1940 saved British shipping from annihilation. There were fewer than forty operational boats, of which on average only fourteen were at sea. Only six of these could be on war patrol at any one time and it is not surprising that, looking back on the spectacular successes achieved by this handful of U-boats, Dönitz believed that if he had twice as many boats available during the 'Happy Time', they could have knocked Britain out of the war.

'What we sink today is what matters more than anything that we sink in two or three years time,' Dönitz told his men as they left on their patrols in July 1940, urging them to use their skill to make up for what they lacked in numbers. They did not let him down. From July to November 1940, the aggressive skill of the highly trained generation of U-boat commanders brought them tremendous individual success. It was the hey-day of the 'Aces'

The Few: In the 1940 Battle of the Western Approaches the handful of escorts could not stem the tide of the U-boat offensive In the skies over Southern England, it was a different picture. Although RAF Fighter Command had less than 700 aircraft to resist the 2,800 Luftwaffe fighters and bombers in the first ten days of the Battle of Britain, the Hurricanes and Spitfires inflicted several times their own losses on the enemy. At the end of the month, German losses were sufficiently great to make it clear that the Luftwaffe had failed in its bid to win the domination of the air that Hitler had set as a condition for launching *Sea Lion*.

like Prien, Kretschmer, Schepke, Schultze, Endrass, Bleichrodt and Rollman. Their names, faces and tonnage-scores became front page news in the Reich. Press and radio reporters flocked down to the U-boat bases to interview and photograph the new heroes. Programmes on German radio were frequently interrupted to bring listeners the latest – and often exaggerated – totals of tonnage sunk in the deadly contest being fought out in the Atlantic.

Lorient was soon to become famous throughout Germany as the 'Port of the Aces'. The first U-boat to arrive was none other than Kapitänleutnant Lemp's U-30 in the first week of July by which time Flotilla Headquarters had already been set up in the Prefecture. Dönitz flew in from Germany to supervise the arrangements personally, paying attention to the rest and recreational facilities being prepared for his crews. The cosy Hotel Beau Séjour, overlooking the Place Lorraine, was taken over for officers' quarters and the nearby School of Military Music was converted into barrack accommodation for the crewmen. Particular attention was given to improving French sanitary arrangements and naval medical teams toured the town's red light district. Special rest camps were established at the nearby coastal resorts of Quiberon and Carnac.

Whilst the officers toasted their successes in some of the 100,000 bottles of requisitioned vintage champagne in the Beau Séjour, their men made the most of the good French wine and pretty girls to be found in the back street cafes. In the heady weeks that followed, the more adventurous officers were soon discovering the pleasures of Paris, but during the months of the 'Happy Time' Dönitz worked his crews hard and shore leave was restricted to a few days, just long enough to refuel and rearm their boats. Patrols became shorter as increasingly skilful captains rapidly exhausted their twelve torpedoes.

One of the most celebrated of the Aces to operate from Lorient was Kapitänleutnant Otto Kretschmer who brought U-99 up the winding Scorff Estuary for the first time in mid-July after a patrol in which his boat had survived nineteen hours of almost continuous depth-charging. After a few days rest, during which his crew celebrated with a drunken spree long remembered in the town, the crew assembled for their next patrol wearing British army uniforms. These had been taken from the huge stock discovered

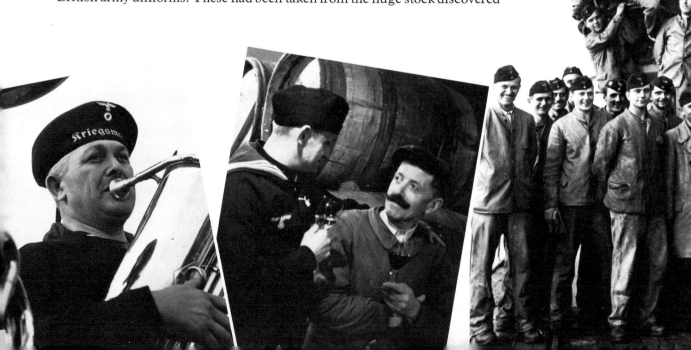

in the dockyard because the foul air endured inside the boat had made their own uniforms unwearable.

On 24 July, sporting two golden horseshoes on her conning tower, U-99 headed out into the Atlantic again on what was to prove an epic voyage of destruction. Two weeks later Kretschmer returned in triumph with seven horseshoe victory pennants fluttering from her periscope. A band and cheering German soldiers welcomed U-99 back from a record-breaking patrol on which Kretschmer had sunk 65,137 tons. He was awarded the Knight's Cross for his 'continuous determination and skill' and achieving the highest tonnage sunk to date on a single patrol. His crew were inspected by Admiral Raeder, who was astonished to find them smartly turned out in British army battledress.

Kretschmer's record patrol was to be followed up by the others as the rocketing successes of the 'Happy Time' saw Dönitz's U-boats coming close to proving the logic of a siege strategy against Britain.

The U-boats had switched their tactics and were now being directed against the convoys, attacking on the surface under cover of darkness. On 25 August the first of these new style attacks cost the inward-bound convoy HX 65 six heavily-laden vessels. The danger of the new night operations was dramatically underlined three days later when Kapitänleutnant Schepke torpedoed five ships in three hours from the outward bound OA 204. The convoy, consisting of 21 ships, was sailing in six columns protected only by a trawler, HMS *Gleaner*, and a corvette, HMS *Clematis*. They could do little to stop Schepke in U-100 picking off vessels at will, as the convoy report of that night records:

> At 23.25 about 175 miles from Bloody Foreland, the British SS *Hartismere* was struck on the starboard side underneath the bridge. One minute later the Commodore's ship, the SS *Dalblair*, was torpedoed amidship on her starboard side and sank in 10 minutes. HMS *Clematis* immediately commenced an Asdic sweep on the starboard side of the convoy, but she did not gain contact and at 0030 reached some of the *Dalblair*'s survivors. HMS *Gleaner* sighted the explosion and tried to cross ahead of the convoy, narrowly avoiding collision with several ships, which without any Commodore and without any orders, were scattering in all directions at full speed.

To gain a clear picture of Britain's chances of survival against such, Roosevelt decided to bypass Ambassador Kennedy and his pessimistic reports by sending his personal emissary, Colonel 'Wild Bill' Donovan, to London. Donovan was followed by a top level team of American staff officers who arrived in Britain during August under the cover title of 'The Standardisation of Arms Committee'. On 26 August they met with the British Chiefs of Staff, who had been warned by the Cabinet to be frank, but not so frank as to discourage the Americans from any thought of providing further aid. The Chiefs of Staff summed up the dangerous military situation as realistically as they could, telling the Americans that 'the economic and industrial co-operation of the United States was fundamental to our whole strategy'.

The night U-boat attacks on the poorly guarded convoys gave a new sense of urgency to the need for more destroyers which Churchill had already pleaded again for in his cable of 31 July:

> It has now become most urgent for you to let us have the destroyers, motor boats and flying boats for which we have asked. The Germans have the whole French coastline from which to launch U-boats and dive-bomber attacks upon our trade and food and in addition we must be constantly prepared to repel by sea action threatened invasion . . . Mr President, with great respect I must tell you that, in the long history of the world, this is a thing to do now. Large construction is coming to me in 1941 but the crisis will be reached long before 1941.

Roosevelt still felt he could not risk releasing the destroyers in the face of strong Isolationist opposition. The Committee to Defend America strongly campaigned with newspaper advertisements 'Between US and Hitler stands the British Fleet'. But it was the fertile minds of the Century Group's lawyers which eventually found a way through the legal barrier, by proposing the destroyers be traded for bases in the British Empire's Atlantic islands. On 13 August Roosevelt cabled Churchill:

> It is my belief that it may be possible to furnish to the British Government as immediate assistance at least fifty destroyers . . . for the use of Newfoundland, Bermuda, the Bahamas, Jamaica, St Lucia, Trinidad and British Guiana as naval and air bases by the United States in the event of an attack on the American hemisphere . . .

Churchill replied that he 'had not contemplated anything in the nature of a contract bargain or sale between us', but that he would be prepared to present the United States with the bases 'as a gift'. A compromise was reached; some of the bases were given away and some leased.

The news of the destroyer deal was finally given at an informal press conference aboard the Presidential train as it passed through West Virginia on 30 August. Reaction to the news was enthusiastic on both sides of the Atlantic. The *Christian Science Monitor* wrote, 'History may record 2 September 1940 as the beginning of the ebb of the totalitarian tide', while the *New York Times* declared: 'There is no question whatever about the indissoluble link that binds the United States to the fate of the British Isles and the

The Deal that Saved the West: Confident of the backing of US public opinion following Hitler's takeover in Europe and the nationwide advertising campaign of the American CDAA (above); on 30 August, 1940, the President announced

the deal for trading British bases for US arms and destroyers. A week later the first of the fifty reconditioned World War 1 destroyers urgently needed to stem the tide of the U-boat offensive was being handed over in Halifax.

Royal Navy.' Isolationist papers, however, attacked the scheme. The *St Louis Post Dispatch* placed an advertisement in the New York Times:

> Mr Roosevelt today committed an act of war . . . Of all sucker real estate deals in history this is the worst and the President of the United States is the sucker.

There was a month's more delay in getting the destroyers to Halifax, where the first eight arrived on 6 September to be taken over by the Royal Navy. The flush-decked, four-funnelled warships were old fashioned but still sturdy and after being reconditioned for the Neutrality Patrol, they were handed over in excellent condition. Their new crews found them spotlessly clean and the US Navy had generously added many extras, from pencil sharpeners to coffee machines and had stocked the ships with a wide variety of choice American food including clams, tomato juice and pumpkins.

The first destroyer to be handed over was appropriately re-named HMS *Churchill* but the ceremony was a curious affair. The US Navy crews lined up on the quay as the American ensigns were slowly lowered, they then turned about and marched to trains waiting nearby to take them to their home bases. The British crews then went aboard and the white ensign was run up on the eight ships, while the small parties of American officers and men who were to instruct the British in the use of their new ships stayed carefully out of sight below.

There was considerable teething trouble and a number of accidents and collisions as the British commanders tried to work up their unfamiliar ships for the Atlantic crossing. Only five of the first batch sailed by the end of September but although it would be well into 1941 before the ex-US destroyers were actually escorting the Atlantic convoys in any numbers, the Admiralty could plan on the Royal Navy's destroyer strength going up by over 30% – more than compensating for the heavy Dunkirk losses.

7. Siege by Sea and Air

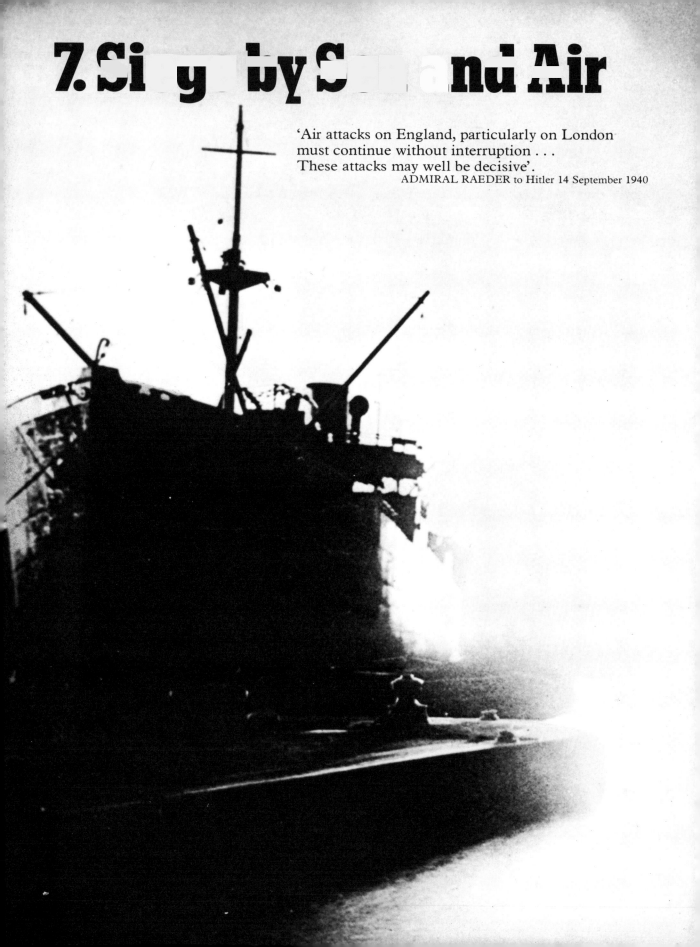

'Air attacks on England, particularly on London
must continue without interruption . . .
These attacks may well be decisive'.

ADMIRAL RAEDER to Hitler 14 September 1940

The Blitz began with a devastating 200 bomber raid on London docks on the night of 7 September 1940. The German Naval War Staff hoped that the 'considerable successes' of their U-boat campaign coupled with the Luftwaffe offensive would bring 'an attitude in the enemy which will make the *Sea Lion* operation unnecessary'. Meanwhile millions of British citizens began to feel the pressure of Hitler's siege as they queued for 'luxuries'.

The German siege of Britain tightened, as prospects for launching the invasion faded rapidly after the Luftwaffe failed to win air superiority which the Führer had set as a precondition for the invasion. Stung by a token RAF raid on Berlin, Goering ordered his vaunted air fleets against the British capital and on the evening of 7 September 1940, 200 heavy bombers roared over the Thames to begin the Blitz. Their mission that night, and every succeeding night for a month, was 'the complete destruction of London's harbours, docks, industries and supplies by means of continuous heavy air attacks.' Two weeks later, on 22 September, to the Kriegsmarine's immense relief, Hitler postponed the invasion in an embarrassing recognition of the Luftwaffe's failure to win the Battle of Britain.

Goering's bomber fleets were, however, having more success in achieving their new objective. After three nights of heavy bombing, in which thousands of tons of supplies were destroyed in the docks, the Port of London had to be closed to ocean-going shipping. Orders went out to divert all vessels from the Thames and the East Coast to the ports of Glasgow, Liverpool and Bristol. The War Cabinet had decided to switch the country's entire supply and distribution system, even at the risk of major problems for road and rail transport. The administrative and traffic chaos that resulted soon became known as the 'Battle of the Ports' as more ships arrived than could be dealt with by the already overcrowded West Coast dock facilities. Labour problems mounted, warehouses became jammed and the disruption of Britain's internal supply lines was soon causing a greater problem than the direct effects of the Blitz itself.

Meanwhile, the U-boat's 'Happy Time' continued unchecked. Many of the Royal Navy's destroyers were still tied down by the invasion threat and only fifty escorts were available to give minimal protection to the convoys, now facing increasing night attacks from the U-boats. Fortunately for Britain, the German strength had remained at 57 boats; the 28 new U-boats that had entered service during the first year of the war had only just kept pace with the losses. The arrival of the 27 boats of Mussolini's Italian Atlantic Flotilla during August had, on paper, reinforced the operational strength of his command, but Dönitz had serious doubts about the efficiency of the Italian submariners. His fears were soon justified by the poor results of the Atlantic Flotilla which operated from Bordeaux. The Italian U-boats were large and imposing, with big conning towers complete with fully-equipped galleys and lavatories. Such unnecessary luxury deeply offended Dönitz's Spartan notions and confirmed his worst fears about the temperamental unsuitability of the Italians to operate alongside his disciplined men. He immediately ordered the cutting down of their prodigious conning towers, an operation which took many weeks. Those boats that did go out performed poorly compared to the Germans, and Dönitz was soon insisting that they supply their own diesel fuel for these unproductive operations.

The highly individualistic approach of the Italian crews did not endear them to their stern German allies. The commander of the *Capellini*, Salvatore Todaro, aroused Dönitz's particular wrath for refusing to torpedo ships. He insisted on surfacing to fight a gentlemanly gunnery duel with mer-

102

that neither the unwieldy boats with their high conning-towers or the temperament of their commanders were suited to the tough Atlantic campaign.

chantmen which led to the C-inC's acid comment in the margin of his report: 'It's a pity that this officer is not commanding a gunboat'. But although the ebullient Todaro attracted scorn from the Germans he was a popular figure in Bordeaux. His fame reached new heights after he had towed a lifeboat full of survivors from a Portuguese ship 600 miles to safety in Morocco. A savage reprimand from U-boat Command was soon followed by a flood of fan mail from Portuguese ladies writing to tell him that he was 'an angel of goodness' and *'un chevalier sans peur et sans reproche'*.

The British Government might well have echoed these sentiments. In August, the Italians had sunk only four ships. An insignificant 17,000 tons alongside the German score of over a quarter of a million tons. After this failure Dönitz ordered the Italians to leave the Western Approaches convoys to patrol around the Azores, where it was hoped the absence of air and sea patrols would give them an opportunity to do better. In September they succeeded in sinking only three ships, and U-boat Command decided that their Italian allies could not be counted on to make a significant contribution in the war against shipping.

Dönitz had now moved his operational headquarters to France. First to a temporary command in an imposing Paris mansion at 18, Boulevard Suchet, and then later that autumn, to Kernevel near the main Lorient base. A former sardine merchant's villa, overlooking the Scorff Estuary had been taken over by U-boat Command transforming it into an efficiently-run nerve centre complete with an underground bunker in the garden. In a small operations room surrounded by Atlantic charts a small staff directed the U-boat war.

PERSONALLY HIRED BY DÖNITZ

Dönitz worked closely with his staff of half a dozen carefully chosen young officers, each with a particular responsibility for communications, operations or intelligence. They were all experienced U-boat commanders who had acquired a thorough grounding in operational tactics and they worked as a tightly knit team under the eagle eye and quick mind of the second in command, Staff Captain Godt.

At nine every morning Dönitz assembled his staff in the operations room in front of the large Atlantic charts with their markers indicating the up-to-date positions of the U-boats and the courses of convoys and shipping reported by B-Dienst intelligence and any Luftwaffe reconnaissance. A round-table discussion then took place to decide on the tactical operations for the next twenty four hours and orders were then transmitted out to the U-boats at sea.

To keep in touch with his crews Dönitz made frequent visits to the other flotilla bases which were soon established in the French Atlantic ports of Brest, St Nazaire, Bordeaux and La Pallice. After every boat returned from patrol he made a careful study of the commander's report before conducting a searching personal interview. This gave him the chance not only to encourage and criticise but also to get a 'first hand feel' of the way his men were carrying out their operations. It was also invaluable for building the strong sense of personal loyalty and trust that was a hallmark of his leadership;

'Great Successes'. Dönitz's *Rudeltaktik*, in which a number of U-boats were ordered to operate against a single convoy, soon proved extremely productive. He briefed his commanders on the three key rules for success:
'1. FIRST FIND YOUR CONVOY
2. REPORT YOUR SIGHTING
3. ATTACK TOGETHER.'

'every one felt that he, personally, had been hired by Dönitz'. At the same time the Commander in Chief gained a shrewd insight into the particular qualities of each officer to know how each would perform in the stress of battle.

This deep feeling for his men and the way they went about their operations was an important element in the way in which Dönitz and his staff now controlled the U-boat. They had to fight the convoy battles at a distance and it was appreciated that whilst HQ could direct the boats at sea onto the convoys it was going to be up to the individual commanders to make the *Rudeltaktik* work. The idea of concentrating as many attacking boats as possible to break up a convoy's defences was not new; Drake's fast Elizabethan men of war had employed it with devastating success against the 'flottas' of Spanish treasure galleons. Dönitz had seen that the U-boats could use it too. By taking advantage of their fast surface speed and low profile they could operate like torpedo boats, virtually unseen at night.

The two keys to the success of the *Rudeltaktik* as Dönitz had learnt from the experiences of the previous October were first to locate the convoy and then to concentrate as many U-boats as possible against it so that 'the distractions caused by a number of simultaneous attacks will break down the convoy's defences and open the way to the possibility of achieving great successes'.

FIRST WOLF PACK SUCCESSES

The first real success of what the British came to call the Wolf Packs was achieved on the same night as the Luftwaffe opened its Blitz on London when a four boat pack was concentrated round the 53 ships of the slow homeward-bound convoy SC2. Dönitz co-ordinated the first stage of the operation by radio, after the *B-Dienst* had intercepted signals from SC2 four days before it was due to meet its Western Approaches escort. The Ace Commanders Prien and Kretschmer were ordered to intercept the convoy, but it had been Kuhnke in U-28 who had first sighted the ships in heavy weather. His shadowing and homing signals brought the pack together, although it was then disrupted by the arrival of a Sunderland flying boat of Coastal Command which forced the U-boats down. This setback was overcome on the nights of 7 and 8 September when Prien and Kuhnke succeeded in making co-ordinated attacks which resulted in the sinking of five ships.

Wolf Pack operations directed from U-boat Command were soon increasing although the lone Aces were still able to attack the poorly-escorted convoys independently. The severity of the new night assaults on the convoys worried the British anti-submarine warfare staff, but it was the sinking of an 11,000 ton passenger liner which brought home the ruthlessness of the 'Happy Time' to newspaper readers all over the world.

The *City of Benares* was sailing independently with hundreds of children aboard in a scheme to evacuate them to the safety of North America. On 17 September she was 600 miles out in the Atlantic when Kapitänleutnant Bleichrodt in U-48 sighted her. At ten o'clock that night when many of the children were fast asleep, the torpedo struck.

Mr Cooper, the *City of Benares* Fourth officer, was woken by the alarm gongs and helped to get the children and passengers into the lifeboats before going to his own. Here he found six children and one of their escorts, Miss Cornish, waiting in the boat with other passengers together with members of the Lascar crew:

The Assistant Steward then reported that all the children had been cleared from the muster station in the children's playroom to their allotted boats. I sent him to make a further search to ascertain if there were any further children asleep in their cabins. He returned and stated that the cabins had been wrecked and the water being up to his waist, he shouted along the alleyway. Receiving no reply, he assumed that there were no children there.

There were now eighteen natives in the boat and nine Europeans and as the vessel did not appear to be sinking very rapidly I held on for approximately a quarter of an hour in case any stragglers happened to appear . . . At about 11 pm the vessel commenced to go down stern first; raising her bow out of the water, she appeared to list heavily to port and disappeared.

Noticing a person on one of the rafts we went alongside and took him aboard. The boat now contained six children, two escorts, one passenger, one cadet, one seaman gunner, the asst. steward, one naval signalman, 32 natives and myself.

There was a rough sea and heavy swell running. Noting a light which I took to be the rescue ship, I steered for it, but on approaching discovered it to be another lifeboat, the occupants of which hailed us and asked what ship. I replied *City of Benares* and they answered *Marina*. Seeing no sign of the remainder of the lifeboats we kept company with the *Marina*'s lifeboat and steered on an easterly direction before a strong wind, keeping sea and swell astern. We continued in company until dawn when the *Marina*'s boat set sail, parting from us.

As daylight came I had the canvas hood rigged forward for the children who were quite snugly wrapped in blankets of which there was an ample supply in the boat. The weather was so heavy that I decided not to set sail but carried on by means of the Fleming Gear, setting members of the crew on watch. At noon I put all the occupants of the boat on food and water rations, detailing the assistant steward to serve out the allotted quantities.

For the next week Cooper sailed the lifeboat on an easterly course in the hope of reaching land. When the weather blew up he rigged a sea anchor and tried to protect the children under the hood in the fore-end of the boat. On 23 September, as supplies of water and emergency rations were running low, the boat was sighted by a Coastal Command Sunderland on patrol 400 miles from land, which directed a destroyer to rescue them.

About 2 pm the flying boat again appeared and dropped a parcel containing food, also a note telling us that assistance was on the way. At about 4.30 pm we sighted a destroyer coming guided by the plane . . . All the children were in good form having, I think, looked upon the whole thing as a picnic, and only one child was suffering from trench feet. We had already travelled 200 miles and were still 400 miles from land when picked up.

Three days after the torpedoing of the *City of Benares* a big Wolf Pack was successfully assembled around the 41 merchant ships of the fast inward-bound convoy HX 72. It had first been sighted by Prien's U-47 who had been sent far out into the Atlantic on a weather patrol. Hardly able to believe his

The Children's Ship: – the evacuation of children to North America was halted after the torpedoing of the liner *City of Benares* on 27 September 1940 by U-48. Seventy seven children perished and half of the 13 children rescued were in a lifeboat that drifted for a week cared for by Miss Cornish (above).

good luck, but with only one torpedo left after his attacks on SC2, he signalled the position and course of the convoy to U-boat Command. He shadowed HX 72 for a day until Kretschmer, Bleichrodt and Schepke joined him on 21 September. Late that evening four of Germany's Ace commanders moved in for the kill. The convoy was quite strongly covered by a sloop and four corvettes, but the five inexperienced escorts were soon overwhelmed by the ferocity of the Wolf Pack's attack as the report of the senior escort officer, Commander Knapp, in the sloop *Lowestoft* recorded:

The night was light with a bright moon but with periodical heavy rain showers and low visibility. The sea was calm. About 22.20/21 a bright light was sighted which appeared to come from the starboard side of the convoy. This was followed shortly by a ship hoisting a red light (HAVE BEEN TORPEDOED). This light appeared to come from the starboard side of the convoy but NO explosions were either seen or heard . . . I immediately turned to the starboard thinking that attack had probably come from that side. I tried to signal *La Mouline* but could not see her and after signalling around the horizon I gave up and called the Commodore instead. I asked the Commodore for information regarding the direction of the attack. He acknowledged the signal but made no reply.

By this time I could see the torpedoed ship was near the centre of the convoy so at 22.27 I ordered the escorts by WT to search their own sides . . . I immediately proceeded over to port to a distance of about four miles from the convoy and fired starshells. As I could see nothing I turned back towards the rear of the convoy and I picked up the *Heartsease* who had, it subsequently transpired, only then discovered that the convoy had been attacked.

Whilst returning to the convoy W/T reports were received on two other ships torpedoed, one near the front of the convoy close to the centre, and the other, the rear ship of the port column . . . On getting astern of the convoy and sweeping across and down the wake it became apparent that the convoy had split up into two sections and very shortly after that the port half appeared to scatter. I then turned to sweep astern of the convoy at maximum speed."

The attack flared up again and the *Lowestoft* tried to round up her charges, but the panic-stricken scattering of the merchant ships gave the U-boat pack their chance:

At about midnight there was a very heavy explosion and a tanker burst into flames. She was about five miles on my port bow. I immediately steamed towards her with *Heartsease* and swept up her side away from the moon and fired a starshell. With the convoy scattered and ships proceeding on various courses at their maximum speed which, in many cases, was probably very little more than my own, my task became almost impossible unless given luck, and, having dropped astern to search the wake, I could not catch up sufficiently quickly to counter attack or to deal with a well-handled submarine on the surface whose maximum speed was probably in excess of mine.

Terrific explosions continued to punctuate the night as ship after ship was hit by torpedoes. Lacking the speed to catch the surfaced U-boats, the escorts were fighting a losing battle. The only way they could destroy a U-boat was to force it to submerge where it could be detected by Asdic and depth-charged. Yet only one depth-charge attack was carried out during the seven hours action which cost 11 merchantmen and sent over a hundred thousand tons of American supplies to the bottom of the Atlantic.

Slaughter of Convoy HX 72: The night of 21 September was lit up by the funeral pyres of ships when the four Aces – Prien, Kretschmer, Schepke and Bleichrodt joined in a devastating pack attack on the 41-ship convoy. Aboard the *City of Oxford*, A. McKellar, a DEMS gunner recalled: 'As darkness came it was attack after attack. The sea was lit with giant fires dotted over the ocean. The escorts seemed to be racing about in panic trying to protect the tankers which were the number one target of the U-boats. When they hit one it seemed to spur on their ego and our vessel – which somehow kept her position in the column – seemed at one time to be escorted by the U-boats themselves.'

Over the next days, the straggling remnants of the convoy had to battle their way to port through gales and heavy bombing by the Luftwaffe. That the escorts were not equipped to deal with the U-boat packs was made clear by Commander Knapp in the conclusions to his report of the convoy's misfortune:

> Submarines are now operating amongst convoys at night as surface vessels with the advantage of a minute silhouette and therefore extremely difficult to see in the dark, and the advantage of being able to dive quickly to avoid collision or make their getaway when sighted by merchant ships. Against this type of attack our Asdic is of little use, whether transmissions are used or not and the only effective countermeasures would appear to be to turn night into day and to use starshell, searchlights and flares from aircraft to carry out a high speed search in and around the convoy . . . Sloops, corvettes and trawlers are severely handicapped and are of little use in any night action.

There were differing views inside the Admiralty as to how best to counter the menace of the Wolf Packs. In October, Western Approaches Command formed eight escort groups to strengthen convoy defences but the Admiralty's Department of Trade Defence, which was responsible for co-ordinating merchant shipping, argued for more offensive action, maintaining that: 'complete immunity from attack cannot nor ever had been guaranteed with the number of escorts which are, or are ever likely to be, available and to this extent it is agreed that the escort is not intended to be a protective screen'. But the Royal Navy still had nothing like the numbers needed either to provide adequate escorts or to establish the powerful hunting groups of destroyers that the Trade Defence experts argued should operate on the flanks of a convoy to drive off the U-boats. Moreover, as long as escorts had no means of detecting the approach of surfaced U-boats at night, the advantage lay with the Wolf Packs.

In an abortive attempt to stop the spread of the U-boat war into the mid-Atlantic and the shipping lanes of the coast of Africa, Churchill had sent an expedition to occupy the Vichy French naval base of Dakar. But 'Operation Menace' was repulsed on 23 September and the next day, its failure gave Admiral Raeder an opportunity to press for a broader naval strategy to defeat Britain. In a long private session with the Führer, he set out the Naval Staff proposals for tightening the blockade of the British Isles by building up the U-boat arm. A powerful flank attack should also be mounted against the British position in the Mediterranean which, according to Raeder, had always been 'the key point of their world position'. A Mediterranean offensive should be undertaken 'quickly before the United States entered actively into the conflict'. He urged the Führer to seize Gibraltar and to land paratroops on the Canary Islands. At the same time the Italians were to be supported in a drive to the Suez Canal which would open the way for a thrust towards Russia or India.

Raeder at first believed that he had won Hitler's acceptance for his grand scheme. He was wrong, the Führer's own strategic dreams centred not on the Atlantic but Russia, and he wanted to postpone any decisions until the forthcoming Tripartite Pact between Germany, Italy and Japan had been

The Menace that Failed:
Churchill's scheme to take-over the West African port of Dakar failed. When General De Gaulle (below) arrived off Dakar with a British task force he was greeted with shells from the Vichy battleship *Richelieu*. On 25 September *Operation Menace* was finally called off and Roosevelt was told by Churchill 'I much regret that we had to abandon the Dakar enterprise. Vichy got in before us . . . several of our ships were hit and to persist with the landing in force would have forced us to an overwhelming commitment – when you think what we have got on our hands already'.

'Help our Shipping!'
As the U-boat offensive
mounted in intensity, it became
apparent that Britain's safety
depended on the steadfastness
of her 120,000 merchant
seamen (above, the helmsman
of an Atlantic freighter.)
Already they were suffering
heavy casualties and the
Ministry of Information
skilfully involved public
opinion in the growing
shipping problem (poster).

concluded. This would recognise 'the leadership of Germany and Italy in the establishment of a new order in Europe', in return for their accepting Japan's 'establishment of a new order in Greater Asia'. The 'Tripartite Pact', was signed three days later on 27 September 1940. The agreement's major objective was to ensure that the three nations would 'mutually co-operate in order not to allow the United States to interfere in regions other than the Western Hemisphere'. Raeder's hopes of achieving a combined Atlantic-Mediterranean Axis strategy had suffered a series of setbacks by the end of October. Marshal Petain refused to commit Vichy France to the Axis and Mussolini, after turning down Hitler's offer of German support against the British in North Africa, blundered into the invasion of Greece.

Although the full-scale naval strategy was never to be implemented, Dönitz's new Wolf Pack tactics were already threatening the British convoy system with disruption. In September they had sunk almost 300,000 tons of shipping and the Admiralty was urgently experimenting with measures to reduce the losses. Convoys were reduced in size and more escorts provided as destroyers were released from anti-invasion patrols. New defence tactics were introduced, with escorts stationed farther out on the wings of the convoys to keep the U-boats further away from the merchant ships. In the event of an attack, the escorts were to 'proceed outwards from the convoy at full speed firing starshell to illuminate the area where the U-boat was thought to be, in an attempt to force her to submerge and increase the chances of asdic detection'.

SLAUGHTER IN THE WESTERN APPROACHES

These new measures were soon proved less than adequate. Throughout October sinkings escalated as the autumn assault on the convoys reached a crescendo with the battle around SC7. Bleichrodt had sighted the slow homeward-bound convoy, but had broken one of the cardinal rules of the *Rudeltaktik* by deciding to attack without waiting for the pack to assemble. After he had sunk two ships, he lost contact with the convoy. Dönitz was determined not to let the prize escape and, predicting its likely course, he set up a patrol line of five U-boats across it. The line, which included several of the Aces including Kretschmer, succeeded in intercepting the convoy and might have achieved a devastating victory if the lone sloop escorting SC7 had not fortunately been reinforced with another four escorts for the passage through the Western Approaches. Even so, the pack made short work of the defences at Kretschmer's war diary recounted after he had torpedoed his first victim:

> Ship still burning fiercely with green flames
> 00.15 Three destroyers, line abreast, approach the ship, searching the vicinity. I went off at full speed on a southwesterly course and very soon regained contact with the convoy. Torpedoes from other boats exploding all the time. The destroyers are at their wits ends, shooting off star shells the whole time to comfort themselves and each other. Not that it makes much odds in the bright moonlight. I am now beginning to pick them off from the stern of the convoy.'

CONVOY HX. 79.
Attacks by U.Boats on night of
19~20th Oct 1940.

Scale

At 23.18 *Sitla* leader of the 7th column was hit by a torpedo on her starboard side.
Lady Elsa, Angle and *Heliotrope* all proceeded in the direction of the torpedoed ships. The first two picked up survivors, *Heliotrope* continued to escort the convoy.
At 23.22 four minutes after the *Sitla* was torpedoed, *Wandby* was torpedoed on her port side, followed one minute later by *Ruperra*. She was also hit on her port side. At 23.40 *La Estancia* was torpedoed on her port side. All these ships were making approximately correct station in the convoy. *Indira* stopped to pick up survivors. *Whitehall* having carried out a further search towards *Shirak* swept to the southward and at about midnight set course for the two tankers which were the victims of the 2nd attack on the convoy and which were by this time burning fiercely.

Convoy report HX 79

Kretschmer alone accounted for six of the eighteen merchantmen that were sunk in a running battle. The slaughter was made worse because the convoy had once again scattered under the fierce attack, leaving the stragglers to be picked off one by one. Over 80,000 tons of shipping and nearly hundred thousand tons of supplies were destroyed in one of the biggest convoy disasters that the war was to see. The magnitude of the U-boat's success was summed up in the final line of the senior escort officers report:

Friday 20 October: 1216 made my ETA Liverpool and informed CinC Western Approaches that *no* ships were in company.

This was the beginning of the most successful two days of destruction the U-boats were ever to achieve. On the morning after the rout of SC7, Prien's lookouts could hardly believe their luck when they spotted another large inward-bound convoy. This was the fast HX 79 comprising 49 ships loaded with American military supplies. Because of its importance HX 79 was well escorted with a destroyer, two sloops, two corvettes and four armed trawlers.

As an experiment the Dutch submarine O-14 had also been attached to the escort, but its presence was to prove totally ineffective against a Wolf Pack, and which included the four Aces Prien, Bleichrodt, Endrass and Schepke. In five hours during which the U-boats ran alongside the columns of merchant ships firing torpedoes to port and starboard, a fifth of the convoy was wiped out.

One of the many merchant seamen who were torpedoed that night was James Lee of the SS *Uganda*:

> The Maltese donkeyman Manuel Bonella and I were having some cocoa when we heard the first explosion. As we rushed on deck there was a second – and then we were the third to go. We were thrown about all over the place and when we pulled ourselves together we discovered to our horror that all the boats were missing, except one, and it was more by luck than judgement that we managed to get away and clear the ship.
>
> About an hour later a destroyer came along and told us over the loud hailer that he could not risk stopping, but about dawn a sloop arrived and stopped. It was a job getting aboard with the rise and fall of the boats and the sailors pulled us inboard by the hair or anything else they could get hold of. When we got aboard we discovered that this was not the first time of the night, she was loaded with so many survivors that she was down by the head.

Thirteen ships in all were destroyed, adding another 60,000 tons to the U-boats' score. By the end of the month, with total losses of over a third of a million tons, the Admiralty began to get really alarmed that the Germans were on the brink of defeating the convoys.

The Department of Anti-submarine Warfare launched an urgent inquiry which resulted in a demand for 'adequate numbers of escorting vessels on the flanks of the convoys' and for means of 'detecting the approach of the enemy and of locating him, forcing him to dive and then proceeding to his destruction by our well-tested methods'. But so long as the escorts had to wait for the U-boats to announce their presence with an attack, the only practical counter-measure was to illuminate the convoy with starshells before carrying out intensive sweeps. This 'hit and miss' technique could only be overcome by fitting the escorts with ASV (Anti-Surface Vessel) radar. Some ASV sets for escorts were already under development but their delicate electronics were causing many teething troubles. The importance of this equipment was reflected in the report: 'No effort is to be spared to clear up these difficulties and it is to be hoped that ASV will soon become effective and its use by escort ships universal'. Apart from spurring on the development of radar a new system of VHF intership communication for the escorts was given top priority.

The full magnitude of the U-boat threat now facing Britain as she struggled to survive the German siege was graphically brought home to Churchill who compared the United Kingdom to:

> The diver deep below the surface of the sea, depending from minute to minute on his air pipe. What would he feel if he could see a growing shoal of sharks biting at it? All the more when there was no possibility of being pulled to the surface. For us there was no surface.

The Luck of the Aces: Prien, Bleichrodt, Schepke and Endrass could scarcely believe their good fortune when, on 19 October, they were able to intercept and surround convoy HX 79. The Ace commanders were soon amongst the convoy columns and the rout that followed is clear from the official report of the second wave of the attack and track chart (left). Thirteen ships, amounting to 60,000 tons, were sunk in a night that was a triumph for Pack tactics. After Prien in U-47 led his flotilla (below) back to Lorient in triumph.

Under Pressure: Following the spectacular U-boat Pack operations against the convoys Churchill sent the First Lord of the Admiralty, A. V. Alexander (left) to Plymouth to visit Western Approaches Command and press for action from Admiral Sir Dunbar Nasmith (right)

After the shock of the two convoy disasters the Prime Minister took a personal hand in speeding up the necessary measures to drive the sharks away from the vital Atlantic lifeline. He directed that more destroyers were at once to be transferred from invasion duty in the Channel to the convoys, radar for the escorts was given top priority and, most important of all, the Admiralty was pressed to set up a completely separate command to direct the war against the U-boats. The Command organisation, in which the Western Approaches had been an adjunct of Admiral Sir Dunbar Nasmith's Plymouth Command, had proved totally inadequate to deal with the expanding scale of the Battle of the Atlantic. Henceforth, half measures were abandoned and a new high powered Commander-in-Chief Western Approaches was appointed as work got under way in preparing a large operational command post and headquarters organisation at Liverpool. At the same time, it was clear that if the convoy escorts were going to defeat men of the calibre of Kretschmer and Prien, there would have to be a radical shake-up of anti-submarine training. A special base attached to Western Approaches Command was to be set up at Tobermory in the Hebrides where the escorts and their crews were to be put through a rigorous course in convoy defence and anti-submarine tactics.

These measures would take several months to come into effect and throughout the winter crisis Churchill looked anxiously to the United States for the essential supplies to withstand the German offensive in 1941. Plans were discussed by the British Purchasing Mission in Washington for the production of 4,000 planes a month for the RAF and 2,000 tanks for the new British armoured divisions, but it was soon clear that there was not enough money to finance this. The British gold and dollar reserves were being run down in spite of the steady liquidation of holdings of North American securities. In August, the Chancellor of the Exchequer had forecast that Britain would run out of gold by the end of the year with the new American purchases which would cost one and a half billion dollars. By September 1940, Britain had only £897 million in reserve, of which £600 million was earmarked for payments to Canada.

'NO FOREIGN WARS'

The American Administration could do little to ease the financial crisis without getting Congress to modify the Neutrality Legislation which blocked loans for any supplies. The vital North American supply line with which Britain hoped to balance Germany's industrial superiority was at risk. Hoping to barter technology for supplies, the War Cabinet set about exchanging top level scientific information. In September, Sir Henry Tizard, Britain's leading defence scientist, headed a team to the United States. Among the secrets the scientists carried in their bags to Washington were the designs and prototype for the magnetron power valve – the key to advanced centimetric radar. Under the guidance of Admiral Bailey, a special Admiralty Committee was in contact with all the branches of the Royal Navy, channelling a mass of information to the Americans on Asdic, convoy organisation, signalling, anti-submarine warfare, the penetrating power of heavy calibre guns and anti-aircraft defence.

112

The piecemeal and directionless way in which the Americans appeared to be organising their armament production worried the British but Roosevelt was still unwilling to embrace the full implications of a war economy in the final stages of the Presidential elections.

The Presidential campaign of 1940 was a strangely muted affair and the clandestine injection of thousands of dollars of Nazi funds to try and spike Roosevelt's campaign had proved a total failure. The Republican candidate, Wendell Willkie, gave 560 speeches in fifty days, but Roosevelt stayed aloof in the White House until the last two weeks of the campaign. Then, with the opinion polls showing that his 10% lead was narrowing dangerously, the President emerged to make five key speeches appealing to the deep American instinct for 'No foreign wars'. Speaking in Boston, before a largely Boston-Irish audience on 30 October he said: 'And while I am talking to you, mothers and fathers, I give you one more assurance. I have said this before but I shall say it again and again; your boys are not going to be sent into any foreign wars.'

On the night of 5 November, as the results were declared it was soon plain that Roosevelt's tactics had paid off. For the first time in history an American President had been elected to a third term of office with 27,243,466 votes against Willkie's 22,304,755. Churchill immediately cabled Roosevelt:

> I did not think it right for me as a foreigner to express any opinion upon American politics while the election was on but now I feel that you will not mind me saying that I prayed for your success and that I am truly thankful for it . . .

Presidential Promises: In the final stages of the 1940 Presidential race, although both candidates (right, Wendell Wilkie campaigning in Chicago) were committed to aiding Britain, both promised to 'stay out of foreign wars'. Roosevelt (below) stayed aloof for most of the campaign but a last-minute intervention was enough to secure him a five million majority on 5 November 1940 for an unprecedented third term in the White House.

The success of the German assault on Britain's lifelines
was registered by the destruction of 4 million tons of
merchant shipping in 1940. With less than one million tons
of new construction this meant an alarming fall of 3 million
tons of cargo capacity in twelve months. Moreover, the
casualty rate amongst merchant seamen was also rising; In
1940, 5622 merchant seamen perished out of the 23,922
who were forced to abandon ship. There was usually little
time to get the lifeboats away. Often it was a case of
clinging to a life-raft and unless rescue came rapidly, cold
water and exposure soon extinguished life. The U-boats
were expressly forbidden to save survivors, and there was
little that the crew of U-124 could do for one of their victims
adrift in the mid-Atlantic early in 1941

8. A Time of Trouble

'If Britain should go down, all of us in all America would be living at the point of a gun'
PRESIDENT ROOSEVELT, broadcast 29 December 1940

The Happy Time for the U-boat men reached its peak in the last days of October 1940 when the quayside at Lorient echoed to the brass bands, and popping of champagne corks that greeted the arrival of the Aces back from their Atlantic hunting grounds. The crews arrived back to garlands of flowers and film star welcomes. German press and radio boasted to the world that their intrepid submariners were winning the war against Britain by sinking a thousand tons of shipping a day.

In the blacked-out austerity of British ports there were no bouquets and champagne waiting for Britain's merchant seamen when they returned to bombed wharves after running the gauntlet of the U-boats in the Western Approaches. Many hundreds returned physically and mentally exhausted after surviving the terrible ordeal of days or weeks adrift in open boats. Others did not come back at all. Nearly six thousand British seamen perished in 1940 and that winter their casualty rate climbed to frightening proportions, outstripping that of their uniformed comrades in the Royal Navy.

The British press carried the all too frequent stories of the personal heroism of seamen who had survived torpedo attacks and Churchill was to suggest that a special medal be struck in recognition of acts of unassuming bravery being displayed daily by the civilian seamen. The Admiralty insisted that the Merchant Navy would be better protected – in international law at least – if nothing was done to prejudice their legal position as non-combatants. But torpedoed or not, almost all the seamen returned with a quiet pride to sign on again.

'You just came to terms very quickly with the situation', was a typical reaction of one of these seamen, Urban Peters from Liverpool.

> You never saw many sleeping in their clothes for instance, it was always pyjamas. You just didn't mention being torpedoed. It always happened to the other fellow, not to you. Life went on as life does at sea. The usual beer at night, card playing, bawdy stories – the usual sailor talk of wine, women and song, although not so much concern for the song as the other two!

Like many seamen Peters hated being 'a sitting duck on a ship that was attacked and not being able to hit back,' so he volunteered for a special RNVR gunnery course. After he had got his certificate he joined the banana boat SS *Mopan* as a seaman gunner 'and imagined myself in all sorts of brave situations', but shortly after he had rejoined Peters missed the only chance he had to hit back at the Germans during a heavy night raid,

> We couldn't fire our gun because the standby Naval gunner had left the key to the ammunition locker at his digs. When we sailed the next day things started to go wrong. As we were going through the dock gates the second cook and baker jumped ashore grasping his suitcases and disappeared up the dock road. He must have had some sort of premonition.
>
> We carried twelve passengers on this trip as well. I can recall on the first night out one passenger asking for a banana. On being told there were no bananas he blew his top shouting, 'What! A banana boat and no bloody bananas!'

There were 70,000 stems of bananas aboard during the return trip but it was the *Mopan*'s fate to encounter the pocket battleship *Scheer*. Captain Krancke

Raider at Work: After sinking the *Mopan* (below) the pocket battleship *Scheer* (above) encountered the fierce resistance of the *Jervis Bay* (right) as her convoy scattered. All but 5 of the 37 ships escaped, including *San Demetrio* (bottom) which limped into port with the aid of a school Atlas.

had broken out unobserved into the Denmark Strait on 1 November 1940 and headed out into the Atlantic in search of the unescorted and vulnerable mid-ocean convoys. *Scheer* encountered the *Mopan* by chance as Krancke searched for the homeward-bound convoy HX 84 which *B Dienst* intelligence had warned was in the vicinity. The *Mopan* had the ill luck to have sailed on ahead of the long lines of merchantmen on her passage back across the Atlantic from Jamaica.

Shortly after 2 pm on the afternoon of 5 November Urban Peters was shaken awake. The *Mopan* had been stopped by a warship and as he rushed to his gun position Peters recalled hearing the naval gunner declare:

> 'It's alright, it's one of the Royal Oak class.' This served to calm us down for a moment and another voice said, 'She is flashing a morse signal to us!' This pearl of information turned out to be gun flashes because there was a loud explosion. The lifeboat just above us shattered and the debris and shrapnel covered the hatch behind us – miraculously, nobody received a scratch. Everyone was stunned into a deathly silence, except the Refrigerating Engineer who for some unknown reason whispered 'It's a bloody Jerry'.
>
> Whisper or not, this galvanised us into action. We of the guns' crew followed our naval leader to the gun deck just in time to see a shell land there; as a man we all turned tail and fled the scene. By this time the warship started to circle our ship, and we in turn to do the same, only inside. In the panic the chaps did inexplicable things. The assistant cook opened up the ovens and took some chickens out, not to put them in the lifeboat, but to stop them burning! Another went to his locker and put on his raincoat and trilby hat and I for some reason put on my uniform jacket, a raincoat and put 50 cigarettes and my razor, of all things, in my pocket.
>
> As there hadn't been any 'abandon ship' order we all eventually made for the boats. It must have been the most chaotic 'abandon ship' on record. The skipper's boat was the first to leave. Somebody in our boat shouted the phrase 'Women and Skippers First!' The three boats eventually pulled away.

As they were herded aboard the *Scheer*, Peters suddenly realised that the 37 ships of convoy HX 84 were following the same course home and would soon fall victims to the *Scheer*'s 11″ guns.

> Someone said that if we'd got a message out they would have scattered by now. The Radio Officer squashed these hopes when the skipper refused him three requests to be allowed to send a warning.

It was now too late to do anything to save HX 84 and it was only a matter of hours before *Scheer*'s lookouts sighted the smoke of the convoy. At first, Captain Fegen in the armed merchant ship *Jervis Bay* that was acting as ocean escort, could not make out the identity of the warship. He made a request by signal light that she should identify herself. Krancke ignored the signal and closed, when the range was down to four miles he threw off all pretence and opened fire on the *Jervis Bay*. The unarmoured 14,000 ton liner was no match for a pocket battleship, but Fegen did not hesitate. Signalling the convoy to scatter, to give it time to escape he started to close the enemy. The liner's 5.9″ guns began exchanging fire with the *Scheer*'s 11″ guns. In twenty minutes it was all over. The heroic *Jervis Bay*, reduced to a blazing hulk, capsized and sank.

The *Scheer*'s dramatic appearance in the mid-Atlantic for a time dislocated the entire convoy system as sailings were cancelled and convoys drastically re-routed, until the battleships from the Home Fleet arrived to act as mid-ocean escorts. The renewed campaign by the German surface warships came at a critical time for the Royal Navy, which was overburdened in its attempt to check the U-boat assault on the convoys. This continued throughout the month, the biggest success coming after the inward-bound SC 11 and the outward-bound OB44 were simultaneously trapped by two packs of U-boats on 21 November. Fifteen ships were sunk bringing the month's total to over 200,000 tons. This was a significant fall from the high figures of October and attributable to the slackening pace of the attacks because Dönitz only had a dozen operational boats. As the submarines that had achieved the great victories of the previous months returned to refuel and re-arm, Raeder went to Hitler to explain the fall off in successes and to complain that the cutback in naval construction meant that by the end of 1940 '37 fewer U-boats will have been completed than were originally planned'.

British counter-measures also contributed to the decline in successful operations against the convoys. Evasive routeing and a steady increase in the number of new corvettes were making it less easy for U-boat packs but the year's accumulated losses of over a million tons were beginning to make themselves felt. Tanker losses had been especially serious, oil imports were cut in half and needs were only met by drawing heavily on reserve stocks. It was not only the bloody battle at sea that was taking its toll of Britain's supplies. Congestion in the ports and the resulting slowdown in the turn-around of shipping produced a drop of 10% in imports. Lack of cranes, dock space and the poorly organised loading of ships on the other side of the Atlantic all contributed to the delays. Steel piled up at the quayside because there was a shortage of the large railway waggons needed to shift the long American billets and the dockers added to the difficulties by resisting the introduction of more efficient shift patterns. Furthermore, the closure of the Mediterranean to merchant traffic, after Italy's entry into the War had extended voyages to the Far East by up to a third, thus reducing shipping capacity.

ACTION THIS DAY

The situation was becoming so serious that Churchill decided to step in. Firing off a stream of 'Action This Day' memoranda, the Prime Minister emphasised the need to keep supplies moving through the ports. The efficiency of the docks was as crucial to Britain's survival as the strengthening of the convoy escorts and the difficulties were exacerbated by the state of near warfare which existed between the dock employers and the unions. Churchill's coalition government was fortunate to include Ernest Bevin as Minister of Labour who used his immense experience and authority as a former General Secretary of the dockers union (The Transport and General Workers). Sitting on the specially set up emergency Port Clearance Committee this solid, John Bull-like figure urged sweeping changes to solve the long-standing problems of Britain's docks.

The Battle of the Docks: The Emergency Port Clearance Committee, set up to clear the congestion of Britain's over-crowded west coast ports like Liverpool (bottom left) and London (centre) was dominated by the tough Minister of Labour, Ernest Bevin (bottom right). He pushed through management reorganisation and higher pay for the dockers. A new 'over the side' port at Greenock (top right) was soon put into operation to speed up the flow of imports.

119

The British Cabinet was preoccupied with the crisis arising from the U-boat assault on the convoys and to Churchill's dismay, in the aftermath of the Presidential Election Roosevelt appeared to become more indifferent to Britain's growing plight leaving for a Caribbean holiday aboard the USS *Tuscaloosa* in early December accompanied by his close aide, Harry Hopkins. Nevertheless he still received his mail by Navy flying boat and on 9 December 1940 it brought a message from Churchill, described by the Prime Minister as 'one of the most important I ever wrote'. Bluntly it set out the prospects for 1941 and forced the issue of America's attitude to Britain's survival. Churchill told Roosevelt that it was essential 'in the common interest as also for our own survival to hold the front and grapple with Nazi power until the preparations of the United States are complete'. The objective throughout 1941 should be to build up 'such a supply of weapons, particularly aircraft, both by increased output at home in spite of bombardment and through oceanborne supplies, as will lay the foundation of victory'. To ensure final victory not less than three million tons of additional merchant shipbuilding capacity would be required. Only the United States could supply this need.

> The more rapid and abundant the flow of munitions and ships which you are able to send us, the sooner will our dollar credits be exhausted . . . The moment approaches when we shall no longer be able to pay cash for shipping and other supplies. While we will do our utmost and shrink from no proper sacrifice to make payments across the exchange, I believe that you will agree that it would be wrong in principle and mutually disadvantage us if, at the height of this struggle, Great Britain were to be divested of all saleable assets so that after victory was won with our blood, civilisation saved and time gained for the United States to be fully armed against all eventualities we should stand stripped to the bone.

The effect of this dramatic appeal on Roosevelt was not at first apparent. Harry Hopkins, the President's confidant, recalled: 'We didn't know for quite a while what he was thinking about – if anything. Then one evening he suddenly came out with it – the whole programme.' On his return to the White House on 16 December, Roosevelt took reporters aside for an impromptu press conference to announce the basis of Lend-Lease. 'In all history, no major war has ever been lost through lack of money,' he told them. 'Now what I want to do is to eliminate the dollar sign. That is something brand new in the thoughts of everybody in this room I think – get rid of the silly, foolish old dollar sign.' American industry, instead of fulfilling British contracts on a haphazard basis, would now have its output centrally contracted and controlled by the Administration, which would determine whether armaments were to be used by US forces or allocated to others fighting in the common defence.

In his fireside chats of 29 December the President explained the new commitment to the nation:

> If Britain should go down, all of us in all America would be living at the point of a gun, a gun loaded with explosive bullets, economic as well as military. We must produce arms and ships with every energy and resource we can command. We must be the great Arsenal of Democracy.

Eliminating the Dollar Sign: Roosevelt's plan to turn America into the 'Arsenal of Democracy' with the Lend/Lease Bill ran into stiff opposition from the isolationists. Colonel Charles Lindbergh (top) one of their leading spokesmen testified against Bill 1776 before the House Foreign Affairs Committee. He was countered by leading members of the Administration (above right). Isolationist newspapers accused the President of dragging America closer to war (cartoon) and there were demonstrations outside the White House (below right).

As the heated debate raged in Congress during January 1941, Wendell Willkie, was sent to London (right) with a note from the President quoting Longfellow:
Sail on, Oh Ship of State!
Sail on, Oh Union strong and Great
Humanity with all its fears,
With all the hope of future years
Is hanging breathless on thy fate.
To which Churchill replied:
GIVE US THE TOOLS AND
WE WILL FINISH THE JOB!

On 10 January the historic Lend-Lease Bill, appropriately coded HR 1776, was introduced into both Houses of Congress. It was based on a little known statute of 1892 which accorded the Secretary of War the right to lease military property 'when in his discretion it will be for the public good'.

At once the Bill came under fire from the isolationists who saw it as a sinister war plan, 'to plough under every fourth American boy'. Congressional Committees were soon locked in bitter wrangles and, as Britain neared the end of her dollar resources, some members of the War Cabinet began to wonder impatiently whether the lengthy American democratic process might not see its British counterpart suffocated first.

In January, as an emergency measure, the British Treasury raised the rate at which it was cashing in its remaining US securities from $2m. to $10m. a week and the Cabinet agreed to publish Britain's current holdings of gold and dollars to convince doubting Congressmen that she was approaching bankruptcy. So desperate had the situation become, that Britain had to tap her last emergency gold reserves in South Africa so that supplies could be kept flowing whilst Congress argued. On 5 January the cruiser USS *Louisville* called at Capetown to collect $150m of gold bullion.

THE FRONT MOVES WEST

The growing alignment between Britain and the United States and the news of the Lend-Lease proposals brought a warning from Germany that, 'the American policy of pin-pricks, challenges, insults and moral aggression has reached a point at which it is insupportable'. On 27 December Raeder revealed to Hitler his apprehensions that the Americans were dramatically increasing their war supplies to Britain and were likely to aid the Royal Navy by stepping up their naval patrols in the Atlantic. 'Very strong support will be forthcoming only at the end of 1941 or in the beginning of 1942', he advised; Germany now had less than twelve months in which to deliver a decisive blow against Britain.

To enable the U-boats to strike this blow, Raeder pressed Hitler to sanction an immediate and massive increase in the planned U-boat construction rate of 12 a month, but the Führer was already set on other plans. On 4 January 1941 he issued Directive No 21, ordering the Wehrmacht to prepare to overthrow the Soviet Union with a rapid campaign. This decision appalled Raeder, who was not satisfied with the promise that after victory in Russia 'everything can be concentrated on the needs of the Air Force and Navy'. The Naval War Staff's strategy for defeating Britain by a vigorous campaign at sea supported by the Mediterranean flank attack was crumbling fast. Mussolini's forces had suffered a series of defeats at the hands of the British when, on 11 November, the Duce's naval supremacy in the Mediterranean had been wiped out for the loss of only two aircraft in a brilliant strike against the Italian Fleet base of Taranto. A few weeks later the Italian threat to Egypt had been removed when General Wavell's 30,000 strong army defeated Graziani's 200,000 Italians at Sidi Barrani. To prop up the collapsing Italian Mediterranean front, Hitler had been forced to send German troops to Greece and North Africa at the risk of his plans for Barbarossa being delayed.

Hitler's prophesies of an early victory seemed unrealistic to U-boat Command. At the end of 1940 Dönitz could muster only two submarines actually on patrol to maintain some vestige of an offensive against Britain and his handful of U-boats was handicapped in delivering any decisive attacks by the appallingly bad weather. Evasive routeing, now being skilfully organised by the British, made it extremely difficult for the U-boat commanders to find the convoys but in spite of these adverse conditions, the Germans still managed to sink 37 ships during December 1940. The monthly tonnage sunk by U-boats had diminished from its October peak to 200,000 tons in December and nearly half the month's total had come from a six U-boat pack attack on HX 90. On 20 December the Admiralty decided to route convoys far to the north, away from the concentrations of U-boats. More escorts and aircraft were assigned to cover the convoys and the attacks declined throughout the month. The Admiralty Monthly U-boat Report noted with some satisfaction: 'These measures appear to have achieved the desired effect of increasing the difficulties of the enemy in locating convoys and the U-boats are being forced farther out into the Atlantic . . .'

The increasing pressure on Dönitz to move his U-boats further West

The Reconnaissance Problem: With the evasive routeing of convoys to avoid his concentrations in the Western Approaches, Dönitz appreciated that aerial reconnaissance of the Atlantic was essential. In February 1941, despite bitter opposition from Goering, Hitler directed that *Kampfgeschwader 40* in Bordeaux be placed at Dönitz's disposal. Yet the missions flown by the squadrons four engined Focke-Wolf Condors (above) were not very productive. The pilots were inexperienced and the aircraft proved difficult but they nevertheless became 'the scourge of the convoys'.

brought what he described as the 'almost insoluble tasks as far as finding of merchant shipping was concerned ... The problem of location urgently required better reconnaissance. The U-boat itself, with its extremely limited range of vision, was the worst possible medium. The most vital and necessary complement to the U-boat, which was our main instrument of battle, was the aircraft. Here the flaw in the conduct of the war at sea was revealed with painful clarity.'

At the root of U-boat Command's problem was Goering's persistent refusal to allow the Kriegsmarine to establish its own air arm or to control the Luftwaffe reconnaissance missions over the Atlantic. Since the outbreak of war Dönitz and Raeder had both tried to secure Luftwaffe co-operation. Dönitz's personal contacts with the Luftwaffe commander at Mérignac near Bordeaux had secured the daily services of one solitary FW 200 patrol over the Western Approaches, but this was frequently postponed through bad weather or mechanical defects. Frustrated by the situation on 2 January 1941 Dönitz flew to Berlin to enlist the co-operation of Raeder and Colonel-General Jodl. The need for a daily reconnaissance by twelve aircraft was sympathetically received by Hitler who, during one of Goering's frequent absences on a hunting trip, allocated *Kampfgeschwader 40* to U-boat Command operational control but they located few convoys and the decline in U-boat sinkings fell in January 1941 to 127,000 tons.

To keep up the pace of the war at sea Raeder proposed sending out the surface Fleet against the British convoys. The first moves began in early December when the heavy cruiser *Hipper* had been sent out to supplement the efforts of the *Scheer* which was still at large in the Atlantic. With a high fuel consumption and sophisticated machinery the sortie met with little success. On Christmas Day 1940 when *Hipper* finally intercepted a troop convoy, the sight of its battleship escort sent the heavy cruiser running to the French port of Brest.

The *Scheer* was more successful operating deep in the South Atlantic, making occasional rendezvous with supply tankers and the auxiliary raiders, *Thor* and *Pinguin*. In early February Captain Krancke reached the Indian Ocean, aiming to strike at the Australia-Cape Town run, but as he swept down the coast of East Africa one of the three ships he sank had managed to alert the Admiralty. The carrier *Hermes* and six cruisers were immediately despatched to the Indian ocean to trap the *Scheer* and the pocket battleship was sighted by the cruiser *Glasgow*'s aircraft but threw off the Royal Navy to arrive back in Bergen on 30 March 1941. This completed the most successful pocket battleship sortie of the war, which sank nearly a hundred thousands tons.

To distract the Royal Navy during the *Scheer*'s break-back to Germany, Raeder had sent the *Hipper* out for a brief foray into the Atlantic. This time she headed south to attack the Gibraltar convoy routes and soon intercepted the unescorted ships of a Sierra Leone convoy SLS 65. The *Hipper*'s 8″ guns destroyed seven freighters before heading back to Brest where the RAF continued its bombing of the ports to such good effect that the heavy cruiser was soon withdrawn to Kiel via the Denmark Strait.

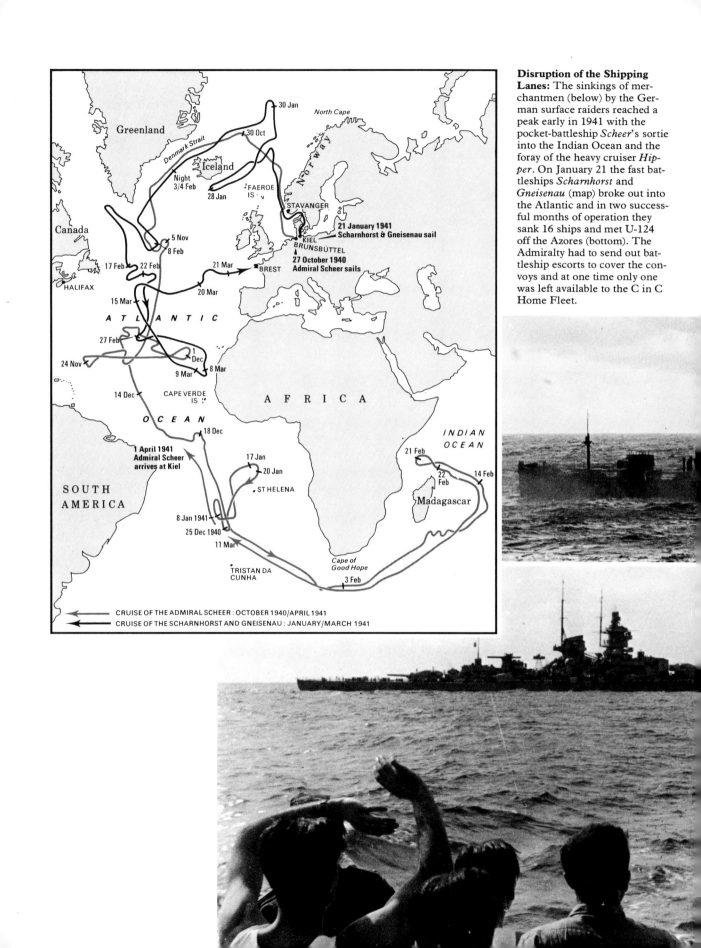

Disruption of the Shipping Lanes: The sinkings of merchantmen (below) by the German surface raiders reached a peak early in 1941 with the pocket-battleship *Scheer*'s sortie into the Indian Ocean and the foray of the heavy cruiser *Hipper*. On January 21 the fast battleships *Scharnhorst* and *Gneisenau* (map) broke out into the Atlantic and in two successful months of operation they sank 16 ships and met U-124 off the Azores (bottom). The Admiralty had to send out battleship escorts to cover the convoys and at one time only one was left available to the C in C Home Fleet.

Map labels:

Greenland

North Cape

30 Jan

30 Oct

Denmark Strait

Iceland

Night 3/4 Feb

28 Jan

FAEROE IS

STAVANGER

Canada

5 Nov

8 Feb

17 Feb   22 Feb

21 Mar

BREST

HALIFAX

20 Mar

15 Mar

A T L A N T I C

27 Feb

1 Dec

24 Nov

9 Mar   8 Mar

14 Dec

CAPE VERDE IS

O C E A N

A F R I C A

18 Dec

1 April 1941 Admiral Scheer arrives at Kiel

17 Jan

20 Jan

ST HELENA

INDIAN OCEAN

21 Feb

22 Feb

14 Feb

Madagascar

SOUTH AMERICA

8 Jan 1941

25 Dec 1940

11 Mar

TRISTAN DA CUNHA

Cape of Good Hope

3 Feb

21 January 1941 Scharnhorst & Gneisenau sail

KIEL BRUNSBÜTTEL

27 October 1940 Admiral Scheer sails

⟶ CRUISE OF THE ADMIRAL SCHEER : OCTOBER 1940/APRIL 1941
⟶ CRUISE OF THE SCHARNHORST AND GNEISENAU : JANUARY/MARCH 1941

Raeder was well satisfied with the success of his surface units and the ease with which they threw the Admiralty into confusion by tying down considerable numbers of British capital ships. Late in February 1941 he decided to escalate the campaign by sending out the two fast battleships *Scharnhorst* and *Gneisenau* under command of Admiral Lutjens. Avoiding the British cruiser patrols Lütjens broke through in the Denmark Strait and headed south until on 8 February he sighted eastbound convoy HX 106, but the battleship *Ramillies* was spotted escorting the merchantmen and in compliance with orders not to risk his ships Lütjens steamed off.

On the afternoon of 16 March the *Gneisenau* had better luck when she intercepted the MV *Chilean Reefer*, sailing independently. The Master was determined to alert the Admiralty and as the *Gneisenau* opened fire, the radio officer began to tap out the 'RRR' signal.

On 22 March the two battleships fell upon a recently dispersed convoy and sank five ships 500 miles east of Newfoundland. Realising that the hunt would now be on in earnest, Lütjen's headed south east, refuelling from a supply tanker in mid-Atlantic and then shifted his attack to the Sierra Leone convoys. The two elusive battleships, dubbed the 'Salmon and Gluckstein' by the British, were next spotted by carrier aircraft 350 miles north of the Cape Verde Islands but Lütjens doubled back to the North Atlantic routes. The convoys had been thrown into confusion as sailings had to be delayed until a battleship escort could be provided for each one. Using his supply ships as scouts, Lütjens soon located a convoy dispersing off Newfoundland and on 15 March sank sixteen ships.

The Home Fleet had been deployed to block *Scharnhorst*'s and *Gneisenau*'s return to Germany by the northern route, but aided by *B-Dienst* intelligence of the British trap, Lütjens steamed across the Atlantic. 'Salmon and Gluckstein' finally entered Brest on 22 March, 1941, leaving the Admiralty deeply embarrassed by the comparative freedom with which they had operated. The pair had sunk 115,000 tons of shipping but the disruption they caused to the convoys was even more devastating.

The Americans had watched apprehensively as the *Scharnhorst* and *Gneisenau* came closer to their shores. Churchill reported the latest activities of the German squadron to the President on 23 March, taking the opportunity of asking for Roosevelt's agreement to repair the torpedo-damaged battleship *Malaya* in an American yard. The President was able to accede, since the Lend-Lease Bill had finally passed the Senate in March on a vote of 60 to 31. Two days later it was passed by the House.

The new Act, which was signed by Roosevelt on 11 March 1941, was a milestone. American industry could now be mobilised by the Administration for all-out production to aid the democracies and rearm the United States. Churchill's jubilant recognition of this fundamental change in the course of the war was reflected on the day the President signed the Act. 'Blessings from the whole British Empire go out to you and the American nation for this very present help in time of trouble'.

9. Dig Harder to Beat the U-boats

'Backs to the land, we must all lend a hand
To the farms and fields we must go.
There's a job to be done,
Though we can't fire a gun,
We can still do our bit with the hoe'

Womens' Land Army Song

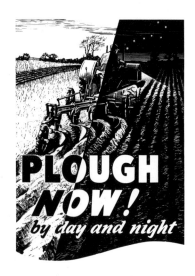

PLOUGH NOW! *by day and night*

The German siege of Britain began to bite deeply in February 1941 following Hitler's Directive No 23 'to concentrate every means of waging war by sea and air on enemy supplies'. The remorseless Luftwaffe blitz disrupted communications and industrial life ashore; at sea the Kriegsmarine's surface warships and U-boats stepped up the tempo of their attacks on the Atlantic life-line. Shipping losses soared again to over 400,000 tons by the end of the month in which 39 vessels were sunk by U-boats, 28 by surface raiders, 27 by Goering's bombers and 10 by mines. As the U-boat fleet steadily increased Dönitz had more operational boats with which to counter the evasive routing of the convoys and the terrible toll extracted on merchant shipping caused grave concern to Churchill and the War Cabinet, who recognised that the cumulative effect of the monthly losses was a 'mortal danger to our life-lines'. They were losing ships at the rate of over 7 million tons a year, more than three times as fast as the shipyards could build them. But as the Prime Minister observed, the yards were overwhelmed with repairs:

> At the beginning of March 1941 over 2.6 m. tons of shipping had accumulated of which about 930,000 were ships undergoing repair while loading cargoes, and nearly 1.7 m. tons were immobilised by the need of repairs.

The steady attrition of cargo-carrying capacity was affecting the import programme. It had been originally hoped to bring 43 m. tons of food and raw materials into Britain during 1941, but by mid-March this had to be cut nearly a fifth and then a further reduction of 5 m. tons had to be ordered. The biggest cuts were made in raw material supplies. Food imports were fixed at a safe minimum of 15 m. tons but even this had to be reduced later by nearly two million tons which meant slaughtering more livestock to reduce meat imports. If the current rate of loss continued, the Government was warned that the war economy could not be sustained through 1942. Churchill was to write: 'How willingly would I have exchanged a full-scale attempt at invasion for this shapeless, measureless peril, expressed in charts, curves and statistics'. The Prime Minister told Roosevelt his fears that: 'It is in shipping and in the power to transport across the oceans that in 1941 the crunch of the whole war will be felt'.

The crisis came to a head in March when Admiral Pound presented to the War Cabinet full figures for the February shipping losses. Churchill immediately saw the extreme danger of Hitler's siege tactics, which were now extending further than the battles being waged on the Atlantic. The German bombing threatened the efficiency of the country's port, transport and distribution systems. It was placing an unprecedented strain on its ship-building and repair capacity and most serious of all, by cutting into Britain's essential supplies of food and raw materials the Germans were challenging the nation's morale.

By 1941 the British people were being subjected to a state of total siege, with controls and rationing affecting every part of national life. The small buff ration-book had become the key to survival for every man, woman and child in Britain. In the twelve months since January 1940 bacon, ham, butter and sugar had not only been rationed, but the ration had been steadily

'**Dig for Victory**': Britain's food imports were halved as parks, gardens and allotments were brought into cultivation. Prince Albert looks down on rows of vegetables cultivated in Kensington Gardens (below).

reduced and most other foodstuffs, except bread, had been brought under tight control. Meat was rationed by price (each ration-book holder being allowed 2/2d worth) and cheese allocations fluctuated wildly. Eggs had almost vanished with an allowance of one per fortnight. The biggest blow came early in 1941 with the rationing of tea (a meagre two ounces per person per week) which prompted one BBC commentator to tell the listeners: ' . . . it's a grand gesture to throw in the face of Hitler. What, the English are prepared to go short on tea. Tea. He must be on his toes!'

The Ministry of Food's nutrition experts were unperturbed by these shortages since they had calculated for the average Briton's survival an emergency 'basal diet' of bread (12 ounces) potatoes (one pound) oatmeal (2 ounces) fats (one ounce) vegetables (six ounces) and milk (six tenths of a pint a day). Their plans never became official policy but there was a heavy reliance on bread as the staple of the British diet. Even though the hard Canadian wheat for it had to be transported across the Atlantic, white bread was never rationed during the war. The Ministry's dietary experts had attempted to cut down wheat imports by persuading the public to eat wholemeal bread made from British flour but extensive publicity had failed to persuade the consumers to accept the grey and spongy 'National Wholemeal Loaf' and jokes were made about it being 'Hitler's Secret Weapon'.

If Hitler hoped that the privations caused by the siege would bring about social unrest and defeatism in Britain he was totally mistaken. Shipping losses certainly affected the standard of living, but the efficient administration of food rationing allied to a skilful publicity campaign, won the support of the people. The success of rationing owed much to the leadership of Lord Woolton, the avuncular chairman of one of the country's biggest retail stores, who became Minister of Food in 1940. His understanding of the mass consumer market enabled his Ministry to strike the right note in getting people to make the best of food rationing.

All the techniques of advertising and public relations were applied by Lord Woolton when he launched 'The Kitchen Front' to involve housewives in the struggle against Hitler. An 'Eat More Potatoes' campaign featuring the cartoon figure of 'Potato Pete' led to a 60% increase in this valuable home produced vegetable and 'Dr Carrot' was projected as the great healthgiver, ensuring a clear complexion and good vision in the blackout. At 8.15 every morning the BBC gave housewives a daily menu, together with all kinds of hints and suggestions on new foods and recipes. 'Have you tried cabbage tops, swede tops and radish tops cooked as greens or the fronds of young bracken which tastes like asparagus?' asked broadcaster S. P. B. Mais. 'You don't want to be too cranky, but you do want to use what's handy, if it's palatable even if you've never tried it before.' Recipes were soon flooding in from all parts of the country which were ingenious – if hardly appetising – concoctions like mock bacon made out of lettuce and dripping and hundreds of recipes for eggless, sugarless cakes. There were also many suggestions for potato flour, pastry and even potato 'barley' for brewing into beer.

There was surprisingly little trading on the black market. Special investigators at the Ministry of Food kept a close lookout for swindlers and food

Fair Shares All Round: Lord Woolton's Ministry of Food mobilised the 'Kitchen Front' in a series of brilliant campaigns to eke out Britain's limited food supplies with rationing, – and imaginative use of vegetables. The Head Chef at the Savoy was asked to devise a meat substitute pie out of potatoes, cauliflower, swedes, carrots and onions that became nationally famous as 'Woolton Pie'.

'What would Lord Woolton expect me to have if he was taking me out to dinner?'

'How would you like your egg this month, dear?'

Eggs from the New World:
Lord Woolton (left) and Averell Harriman (right), Roosevelt's Lend/Lease Administrator, at Liverpool docks to receive the first cargoes of American food early in May 1941 including 6m. eggs which were a particular luxury in Britain. Soon housewives and chefs were to become accustomed to dehydrated egg powder, imported from specially built American plants in thousands of tons.

hoarders and there were severe penalties for any offender. High class restaurants did not escape the 'men from the Ministry' and only one main course per person could be served each meal. The public remained suspicious that London's luxury hotels found some way round the restrictions but an American magazine reported that the Ritz had 'cut its weekly butter consumption from 392 pounds to 77 pounds' and that Claridges 'now served 378 eggs a week compared to 9,100 before the war'.

Parallel with the Ministry's efforts to equalize distribution, there was a major campaign by the Ministry of Agriculture to increase production of home-grown food. Land under cultivation had risen from 12 m. acres in 1939 to 17 m. by 1941. County Agriculture Committees were set up to direct which crops were to be sown and farm machinery was shared on collectivist principles. A large army of volunteer Land Girls, dressed in stout corduroy breeches and jerseys, was mobilised to work on the farms. Many of them exchanged jobs in shops and offices for the rigours of country life and were unperturbed by coarse jokes about 'backs to the land'.

The efforts of the farm workers were supplemented by amateur gardeners. The slogan 'Dig for Victory', which had been coined in 1939, now appeared on hoardings everywhere. As well as private gardens and allotments, public parks and golf courses were dug up to grow more vegetables. Back gardens came to resemble miniature farms with rabbit hutches and chicken runs and the cluck of hens was heard in some of London's most fashionable residential squares. Rows of potatoes and cabbages were planted in Hyde Park and the Albert Memorial overshadowed a thriving market garden. As a result of all these labours Britain soon became self-sufficient in vegetables and her food imports were cut from two thirds of her total requirements to one third by the end of 1941.

The siege also hit the supply of raw materials needed for war production and there were national collections of waste paper and scrap metal. Railings were removed from the public parks and private homes; the cartoon 'Squander Bug' appeared to explain the need for national parsimony. Many appeals to save food and raw materials were directly linked to the need to import and an arresting poster campaign proclaimed 'Save our Ships'.

THE ATLANTIC COMMITTEE

For all the national efforts to become self-sufficient the Prime Minister knew that the outcome of the siege would ultimately be decided not in the allotments and kitchens of England but on the stormy waters of the Atlantic. In March 1941 he told Admiral Pound: 'We have got to lift this business to the highest plane over everything else. I am going to proclaim the Battle of the Atlantic.' On the 6th he issued a key directive:

> In view of various German statements we must assume that the Battle of the Atlantic has begun. The next four months should enable us to defeat the attempt to strangle our food supplies and our connections with the United States. For this purpose we must take the offensive against the U-boat and Focke Wolfe.

The Voice of the Blitz:
Broadcasting from London, as the bombs rained down in 1941, C.B.S. reporter Edward R. Murrow (below) brought the Blitz home to millions of Americans. He helped cement the unity of purpose proclaimed by the President. Rubble from the bombed London streets was used as ballast in ships sent to collect Lend/Lease supplies and found its way into the foundations of New York city streets.

The memorandum went on to order the fitting of merchant ships with catapult aircraft, and questioned the wisdom of docking the American destroyers for the 'second stages of their improvement'. It suggested that ships capable of speeds above 12 knots might be 'liberated from convoys'.

One of the most important sections of the Battle of the Atlantic directive was designed to deal with the congestion in the ports and dockyards. Every effort had been made, 'to reduce the terrible slowness of the turn round of ships in British ports. A saving of fifteen days in this process would be in itself the equivalent to 5 m. tons of imports or a tonnage equal to 1¼ m. tons of the importing fleet saved.'

Forty thousand men were to be released from the armed forces to be sent back into the shipyards and docks to clear the huge backlog of 800,000 tons of shipping awaiting repair. A propaganda campaign was to be launched to impress on them the importance of their contribution to the war effort. A trouble-shooting Committee made up of representatives of the Admiralty Trade Division, Ministry of Shipping and Ministry of Transport was to meet daily and report 'all hitches and difficulties encountered' to the Import Executive. Above these new operational committees the top-level 'Battle of the Atlantic Committee' was established to mastermind the whole campaign.

At the first meeting of the new Committee on 19 March, the ministries involved delivered their plans for dealing with the crisis. The First Lord of the Admiralty welcomed the 'high priority among bombing targets given by your directive to the U-boats and the Focke Wolfe works and bases'. RAF Bomber Command reluctantly agreed to increase the bombing raids on Brest and Bordeaux but the Admiralty wanted still more air support. Now, under the impetus of the Battle of the Atlantic directive, nine more squadrons were to be added to the Command's 31 and priority was to be given to the installation of 'ASV' radar. A joint Navy-RAF committee eventually agreed that Coastal Command should have priority in delivery of the new American long range Liberator bombers. Suitable merchant ships were to be converted to escort aircraft carriers and as an emergency measure, others were to be equipped with catapult Hurricane fighters, four of these CAM (catapult armed merchant) ships were to be ready by the end of April 1941.

The Prime Minister urged that heavier anti-aircraft defences be installed around the key ports because, the Luftwaffe had begun to switch the blitz in a determined effort to bomb the docks and shipyards to a standstill. Heavy and systematic air raids at the beginning of the month opened Goering's 'tour of the ports'. Portsmouth, Salford and Manchester were blitzed, before the bombers turned on Liverpool and the Clyde where the shipyards were severely dislocated and several hundred people killed. Worse was to follow. The Luftwaffe devastated large areas of Plymouth and Bristol and at the beginning of May Liverpool was blitzed for seven successive nights – 2000 people were killed, 7,600 made homeless and serious damage was done to the docks with 69 out of 144 berths disabled. Thousands of tons of valuable supplies were lost as ships and warehouses went up in flames.

The War Cabinet trusted that the United States could not stand idly by for much longer watching Britain being battered into defeat. There was good reason to hope for increased American support, since secret staff talks had begun in Washington during January. The US Naval Attaché in London had warned that the Royal Navy were 'very jealous of their long experience of successful naval leadership. They will expect to tell us what to do and where.' The British were satisfied with the outcome of the talks, known as ABC-1 (America-Britain-Canada) which, on 27 March, 1940, decided the fundamental strategic doctrine to defeat Hitler:

> Since Germany is the predominant member of the Axis powers the Atlantic and European War is considered to be the decisive theater. The principal US military effort will be exerted in that theater and operations of US forces in other theaters will be conducted in such a manner as to facilitate that effort.

At the end of March as the Washington talks reached their final stages, the siege of Britain began to ease as Hitler diverted his bombers east in preparation for the campaign against Russia. At the same time, the growing number of new convoy escorts joining Western Approaches Command together with the refitted American destroyers and intensification of Coastal Command patrols made March 1941 a significant turning point in the struggle at sea.

Shake-up at Western Approaches: **Shake-up at Western Approaches:** The new independent Western Approaches Command was set up early in 1941 at Liverpool under Admiral Sir Percy Noble (above right). After a number of trips to sea the new C-in-C ordered the formation of Escort Groups which were rigorously trained at Tobermory under the eagle-eye of Commodore 'Pug' Stephenson (right). His training stressed teamwork and co-operation which were encapsulated in cartoons (bottom) by Captain J. Broome, in the revised Instruction Manual, that became the blueprint for the counter-attack on the U-boats.

STRENGTHENING THE ESCORTS

The change in British fortunes was in no small part due to the establishment early in 1941 of Western Approaches Command Centre in Liverpool under the direction of a new Commander-in-Chief, Admiral Sir Percy Noble. Escort commanders, convoy commodores and ships' masters were now all based in the same port, which enabled them to get to know each other, making an important increase in morale and efficiency. The move to new headquarters in a heavily protected basement beneath the grimy waterfront office block of Derby House coincided with Admiral Noble's appointment to take over Western Approaches Command. The fifty-year old Sir Percy Noble had the reputation of being the 'best dressed Admiral in the Royal Navy' and he also possessed a powerful intellect. Although throughout his time at Western Approaches he would be desperately short of escorts and on the defensive

A lot depends on the teamwork of an escort group.

The first U-boat that sights you

against the U-boats, Noble inspired a radical rethinking of the Royal Navy's Anti-Submarine tactics.

The large operations room in Derby House soon became the nerve centre of the Atlantic campaign, where an overall picture of the situation out on the ocean was kept updated round the clock. The giant wallmaps were constantly revised with information from air reconnaissance, convoy reports and secret intelligence fed into Derby House by land-line from the Submarine Tracking Room and the Admiralty Operations Intelligence Centre in London.

Admiral Noble was extremely popular with his staff and he kept up his fastidious reputation by having a special bathroom fitted out for himself, with, it was rumoured, gold-plated bath taps. It was an extravagance that was repeated in the duplicate Western Approaches Command post that had been built ten miles outside the city of Liverpool under Lord Derby's country estate.

The headquarters of No. 15 Group Coastal Command were also moved to Liverpool from Plymouth and the close co-operation in the Western Approaches Operations Room was reinforced when the Chiefs of Staff agreed that Coastal Command should operate under the Royal Navy's control.

Under Noble's leadership the morale of the anti-submarine forces began to rise. One of his first steps was to end 'all the nonsense' of the shore headquarters trying to exercise too great a tactical control over the escorts. He had seen for himself the problems this caused during one of his trips to sea. Ashore, the operational plots could give the necessary overall picture for evasive routing of the convoys but once an action had started decisions had to be left to the man on the spot. He also saw the need for the escorts to work as a unified team and set about forming the ships under his command into 'Escort Groups'.

Intensive training of the escort forces now became one of the most important features of the new Western Approaches regime. It was of particular importance in this Command, because most of the officers and men who manned the destroyers, sloops and corvettes had been drawn from the Royal Naval Reserve of merchant service officers and former regulars, together with the 'week-end sailors' of the Royal Naval Volunteer Reserve. The ships always had a backbone of regular service officers and men, but by and large, the routine of convoy work had not attracted the top talent in the Royal Navy.

'When I say move, I mean MOVE!!'

convoy is bound to tell his friends.

Never hesitate to attack immediately.

133

In the U-boat everything was quiet. Those off duty lay peacefully in their bunks just waiting . . . Then they came at us again! The grinding noise of propellers became louder. The bearing remained static; that meant that the destroyer was coming straight at us. Then with our own ears we could clearly hear the rhythmic beat over our heads . . . Twenty seconds of oppressive, absolute silence and then with a roar and crash down came a pattern of depth charges helter-skelter all round us . . . The ship shuddered from stem to stern; shook herself; lockers sprang open; from here and there came the tinkle of splintered glass, but we suffered no serious damage, thank God.

We had begun to sink rapidly. Inexorably the needle of the depth indicator moved to the right 100 – 120 – 150 – it went on gathering speed. At the same moment came a report from the engine room aft 'LEAK!' 'Both motors, full ahead! Hydroplanes hard up! Everybody aft.' Would we be able to stop her dive – or were we plunging on and on into the depths? There were 3,000 metres of water below us, too deep even for us. Frenziedly the men off duty leapt through the bulkheads to transfer the weight aft and lift the bows . . .

With unusual clarity I suddenly realised our lives hung by a thread . . .

Kapitänleutnant Matz U-70

The U-boat's March offensive was to present a challenge to the new-found skill and morale of the escorts. The battle was being carried deeper into the Atlantic as Dönitz concentrated his forces south of Iceland where intelligence indicated that the convoys were now being evasively routed with the improving weather. Some of the most skilful and experienced U-boat Aces were sent out on patrol to form the spearhead of the attacks.

The campaign opened on 6 March, 1941, when Prien spotted the distant smoke of a convoy. This was the westbound OB 203 and Kretschmer in U-99 and Matz in U-70 began chasing, homed in by Prien's signals.

It was a measure of the increasing efficiency of the escort groups tactics that the destroyers *Verity* and *Wolverine* with the corvettes *Arbutus* and *Camelia* then managed to force under the whole pack of four U-boats and attacked them with sustained depth-charging. Kretschmer soon managed to take U-99 clear but Matz was less fortunate. After consulting his Chief Engineer he realised that, if all went well, he could stay down until late afternoon, but the batteries would not hold out after that. The initiative lay in the hands of the escorts as Matz kept his boat silent and barely moving at 300 feet.

A small leak had been sprung which meant precious reserves of air had continually to be blown into the tanks to keep U-70 in trim. Hour after hour the attack continued. The shock of the depth charges smashed all the light fixtures and broken glass littered the deck. The contents of lockers had been spilled out everywhere. Then the U-boat reeled under another well-placed attack which sent her plummeting down out of control to over 600 feet before Matz succeeded in bringing her to the surface where the escorts were waiting to finish her off.

The other U-boats had by this time renewed their attacks. Prien had caught up with the convoy and began running in on the surface to attack from the starboard flank. At twenty three minutes after midnight, Commander J. M. Rowlands in the *Wolverine* caught the whiff of diesel fumes at the same time as his hydrophone operator reported propeller noises close by. Seconds later the phosphorescent wake of Prien's U-47 was spotted and the destroyer swung over at full ahead in hot pursuit. As *Wolverine* prepared to ram, *Verity* fired starshell and Prien managed to crash-dive seconds before *Wolverine* ran over him to drop a full pattern of depth charges. For five hours the two destroyers depth-charged U-47, working as a team with one holding asdic contact as the other attacked. Remorselessly they followed Prien's every twist and turn. Their efforts were finally rewarded shortly after 04.00 when an oil slick came to the surface. An hour later the hydrophone operator reported loud clattering sounds. At 05.19 U-47 surfaced again, only to crash-dive when he spotted *Wolverine* preparing to ram. This time the full depth charge pattern resulted in a menacing dull red glow beneath the surface. This lasted for ten seconds before asdic contact was lost. It was the end of the Bull of Scapa.

The night's operations had cost the loss of two U-boats and brought about the destruction of Germany's leading U-boat hero and all his crew. But on top of this shattering blow for U-boat Command, a week later came the losses of

Destruction from the Surface: Before U-70 was forced to the surface and sunk (above) her crew had endured hours of depth charging (left). An accurate attack by HMS *Wolverine* destroyed U-47 and its Ace Commander Gunther Prien (below) in a dull red underwater explosion.

two more Ace commanders in the battle of convoy HX 122 which reached its climax on St Patrick's night 1941. The fast inward-bound convoy, heavily laden with North American supplies, was first sighted and attacked by Lemp in U-110 early on the morning of 16 March 1941. The beginning of the attack was vividly described by Captain Donald Macintyre whose destroyer HMS *Walker* was leading the seven warships of the 5th Escort Group:

> *Erdona*, a 10,000 ton tanker carrying petrol burst into a blinding flame casting a ghastly glare over the heaving waters. Then came the full detonation of the torpedo striking home. I had never seen this most appalling of all night disasters and on the bridge of the *Walker* we were shocked into silence by the horror of it . . .

Macintyre was relieved to find that no further attacks developed that night. The next day Lemp continued shadowing and by early evening he had homed a Wolf Pack onto the convoy which included the top Aces Kretschmer and Schepke. The first round in the night's battle went to the Germans with Kretschmer sinking six ships from the convoy in one brilliantly executed attack from his 'favourite position between the columns.'

Unable to locate him, Macintyre recalled, 'I racked my brains to find some way to stop the holocaust . . . Our one hope was to sight a U-boat's tell-tale white wake, give chase to force her to dive and so give the Asdics a chance to bring our depth charges into action.' After several false hunts, shortly before 1 o'clock the destroyer *Vanoc* succeeded in picking up a firm Asdic echo and with *Walker* acting as the directing ship the contact was plastered with depth charges. It was nearly half an hour before they realized they had been successful in forcing U-100 to the surface. An overconfident Schepke had dived too late and the heavy underwater explosions had badly damaged his boat. He tried to crawl away on the surface but there was to be no escape. *Vanoc* spotted the U-boat and turned at full speed to ram. According to the survivors who were later picked up, Schepke thought until the last minute that the destroyer would pass astern – it was his second fatal mistake of the night:

> Five seconds before the collision *Vanoc* stopped all engines and the destroyer struck U-100 nearly at right angles just below the conning tower. The side of the U-boats hull and conning tower were smashed in and the Captain caught and crushed between the stoved-in side of the bridge and the periscope. One officer and five ratings were rescued by *Vanoc*. The Captain was dragged under by the sinking U-boat.

While *Walker* circled the destroyer which had now stopped to inspect her badly damaged bows, Macintyre's Asdic operator picked up another contact:

Victory over the Aces: On the night of 16 March 1941 Captain Donald Macintyre's 5th Escort Group led by his destroyer HMS *Walker* (below) defeated an attempted Wolf Pack attack on convoy HX 122 and destroyed two U-boats. This finished the spectacular careers of two of Dönitz's leading Aces (right), Kapitänleutnant Schepke who was crushed to death when U-100 was rammed and Kapitänleutnant Kretschmer who was captured after U-99's golden horseshoes finally ran out of luck. For the first time the initiative in the Battle of the Atlantic had passed to the escorts.

This was thought to be a non-sub at first, but the Asdic operator insisted contact was firm and the echo rapidly improved. I decided to attack again. At 0343 a pattern of six charges was fired.

Contact was regained astern and the ship was turning towards the contact when *Vanoc* signalled that a submarine had come to the surface astern of her.

The badly battered U-boat turned out to be Kretschmer's U-99, which had defied all her crew's desperate attempts to stop the water pouring in and was sinking fast. Macintyre's destroyer was soon fishing out her survivors:

> The last to come over the side was obviously the captain, as he swam to *Walker* still wearing his brass-bound cap. We were soon to find out that we had made a notable capture, for the captain was Otto Kretschmer, leading Ace of the U-boat arm, holder of the Knight's Cross with Oak leaves and top scorer in terms of tonnage sunk.

Now it was the British commanders turn to sail back into port to be greeted by a rousing welcome at the Liverpool escort base. To everyone's surprise, when he was interrogated, Kretschmer did not live up to the popular image of a ruthless Nazi U-boat ace. He was 'quiet and deliberate, more like a student than a U-boat captain.'

At the Hotel Beau Séjour and the other haunts of the U-boat crews, which had been the scene of so many lively celebrations in recent months, there was a sombre atmosphere as rumours of the death of the top Aces spread. Their loss was kept secret for nearly two months until 24 May when Dönitz was finally allowed to release the press notice announcing the loss of Prien:

> The hero of Scapa Flow has made his last patrol. We of the U-boat Service proudly mourn and salute him and his men . . . they have become for us a symbol of our hard and unshakeable will to victory against England. In this spirit we shall continue the fight.

The scale of the setback to the U-boat offensive was revealed by the entry in Dönitz's war log for 19 March: 'With certainty we can now count on only three boats in the North Atlantic.'

The sinking of four U-boats in the space of ten days and the loss of three of the most brilliant commanders who had together accounted for 600,000 tons of shipping was the first major victory for Western Approaches Command. For Churchill it was even more significant:

> The elimination of these three able men had a marked effect on the progress of the struggle. Few U-boat commanders who followed them were their equals in ruthless ability and daring . . . the first round of the Battle of the Atlantic may be said to have ended in a draw.

Kapitänleutnant Schepke

Kapitänleutnant Kretschmer

Admiral Raeder hoped that a spectacular break by a battleship squadron into the Atlantic would have a 'decisive
effect' on the war at sea. Hitler expressed grave doubts but
Operation Rheinübung went ahead and even though the
Scharnhorst and *Gneisenau* could not take part, the 41,000
ton *Bismarck* sailed for the Atlantic together with the heavy
cruiser *Prinz Eugen*. They were spotted in the Bergen
Fjords by an RAF photo reconnaissance aircraft (inset) on
21 May, confirming intelligence reports that a major threat
was developing to the Allied life-lines.

10. Clash of Titans

'We shall fight to the last shell.'
Bismarck to Berlin, 26 May 1941

The simultaneous elimination of the three top Ace commanders, Kretschmer, Prien and Schepke in March 1941 marked the end of the 'Happy Time' for the U-boat men. Germany's most productive phase of the Battle of the Atlantic, when monthly sinkings had reached a peak of eight ships for every boat at sea, was over. Gloomily reviewing the new statistics that they were now destroying only two ships per boat per month, U-boat Command wondered whether the enemy might have developed some devastating new anti-submarine weapon. Yet the reversal of fortunes in the Western Approaches had come about largely through improvements in escort tactics and not a brilliant technological breakthrough. Increasing numbers of escorts had also stiffened the convoy defences to the point where Dönitz reluctantly decided 'to withdraw my forces from the area at the end of March and concentrate them further to the south west'.

The decision to call off the Wolf Packs from the bottleneck area of the Western Approaches made it easier for Western Approaches Command to use evasive routing to avoid the U-boats, this had to be balanced against the need to provide escorts farther and farther out into the Atlantic. As the monthly Anti-Submarine report warned, 'at the moment escort West can only be achieved at the expense of weaker escorts'.

The urgent need to protect the shipping lanes much further west was soon apparent from the fate of the slow home-bound convoy SC26, which battled through a seven-boat Wolf Pack for two days and nights before its Western Approaches escort joined on 5 April. Ten ships were sunk, but the reinforcements' arrival evened the score when they sank one of the attacking Wolf Pack. After this, the difficulty faced by U-boat Command in locating the convoys in the wide tracts of ocean meant that there were no further big attacks until the end of the month when they were able to concentrate a pack onto HX 121 and sink four ships. Unfortunately for the U-boats, this fast UK-bound convoy's powerful escort joined before the battle developed. Dönitz ordered them to carry out daylight submerged attacks but this made them vulnerable to Asdic and one U-boat was destroyed.

At the end of April 1941 another quarter of a million tons of British shipping had been sunk, but less than half the month's losses was the result of Wolf Pack operations and two U-boats had been sunk. As Dönitz continued sending his forces westwards, where the convoys were less well defended by sea and air patrols, Iceland became increasingly important. A naval base was set up in Hjalfjord on the bleak east coast for the escorts to refuel and extend their range out into the Atlantic, and Coastal Command was beginning to send squadrons of Lockheed Hudsons to replace the aged Fairey Battles which were operating under difficult weather conditions from the rough lava of the Icelandic airstrips. When the new aircraft arrived in June 1941, their 500 mile patrol radius allowed the convoys to be routed north to bring them under the protection of air cover for nearly half their journey across the Atlantic. At the same time, Western Approaches air patrols were increased using Whitley and Wellington bombers which had been reluctantly transferred by Bomber Command. Their patrol time was restricted and the only long-range aircraft available were the flying boats based in Northern

More Tools from America: The westward movement of the U-boats into the mid-Atlantic in the late spring of 1941 strained Britain's air and sea escorts to the limit. In April Churchill urgently requested more Lockheed Hudsons (above, being produced for the RAF in a Californian assembly line) to strengthen Coastal Command patrols (right). Secret discussions were also taking place for the US Navy to establish its presence in the Eastern Atlantic and at Gibraltar.

Ireland. The newly arrived Lend/Lease PBY Catalina's soon proved able to extend air cover beyond 700 miles, but, like the big Sunderland Flying boats which carried out most of the distant patrols, they carried only a small depth charge load. Aircraft were not yet effective U-boat killers and Dönitz's crews jokingly referred to the lumbering flying boats as 'tired bumble bees', but even if their sting was not sharp, most commanders rapidly crash-dived their boats when they saw one rumbling in over the horizon. This success in forcing the enemy to submerge made Coastal Command's new policy of patrolling the paths and flanks of the convoys more and more effective. The greater number of air patrols were an important factor in driving the U-boat packs out of the Western Approaches.

When the Battle of the Atlantic Committee came to review the overall situation at the end of April there was not much that they could be optimistic about. The Wolf Packs might have been driven out of the Western Approaches, but sinkings were still running much higher than new construction and the cumulative effects of lost cargo-carrying capacity was now threatening to disrupt Britain's import programme. The Ministry of Food warned of 'a sorry deterioration in the diet' and a crash programme was organised to save every available cubic foot of cargo space. Boneless-beef, condensed milk and dried egg began to make their appearance, accompanied by a stream of new recipes from the Kitchen Front.

The War Cabinet was only too well aware that the country could not withstand the German siege indefinitely and they sought an immediate increase in Lend/Lease aid. The British Purchasing Mission submitted a long 'shopping list' for more aircraft, food, merchant ships and munitions. Arrangements had already been made to repair British merchant ships and warships in US dockyards and on 2 April Roosevelt cabled, 'I have allotted funds for the building of 58 additional shipping ways and 200 additional ships', but what Churchill wanted was immediate US Navy support in the Atlantic. 'Beating the U-boat is simply a question of destroyers and escorts, but we are so strained that to fill one gap is to open another' he had cabled in reply, asking at the same time for ten US Coastguard cutters.

Whilst Churchill was confident that, given the rising scale of US aid, the siege could be broken, the American Chiefs of Staff were not all convinced that Britain could last out during 1941. Not only was her survival threatened by the sea and air siege but in North Africa the Germans had gone to the assistance of their Italian allies as General Rommel's Panzer divisions had swept the British army back to Tobruk. In Greece, the British troops had been rolled back by the German Twelfth Army and were facing another Dunkirk style evacuation and the convoy routes around the Azores were coming under increasing U-boat attacks. Averell Harriman, Roosevelt's aide in London warned the President, 'England's strength is bleeding. In our own interest I trust that our Navy can be directly employed before our partner is too weak'.

On 11 April 1941, the US Navy had already fired its first shots in anger when the destroyer USS *Niblack* depth-charged an asdic contact whilst rescuing survivors from a torpedoed merchant ship, but unhappily for Churchill, the incident did not result in an immediate American involvement. The President's reluctance to act disappointed Admiral Stark, the US Chief of Naval Staff, who had secretly planned that on 1 April 1941 'the navy would be prepared to convoy shipping in the Atlantic to England'. A high level mission under Admiral Ghormley had been sent to London to consolidate links with the Admiralty and to prepare for the construction of a US naval base in Northern Ireland and Stark had been building the Atlantic Squadron's strength by transferring three battleships and a carrier from the Pacific together with more destroyers. The President, however, was worried that Congress might not grant him the power to escort convoys.

The President's caution was reciprocated by Hitler who equally had no intention of being drawn into war with the United States on the eve of his attack on Russia. The Naval War Staff at the end of March had won their argument to extend the War Zone to Greenland in order to forestall any American attempts to supply Iceland, but on 25 April Hitler had reacted cautiously to the United States extension of her neutrality patrol area to 26 degrees west. All German naval forces had been ordered to avoid any incidents with US warships.

On the other side of the ocean, the British were disappointed by Roosevelt's caution. The monthly return of shipping losses was no longer published, since they revealed the harsh truth that for every new British ship built, three were sunk. Prospects had become so serious that in the last week of April the Prime Minister reflected:

> When you think how easy it is to sink ships at sea, and how hard it is to build them and when you realise that we have never less than 2000 ships afloat and 300 to 400 in the danger zone –and of the great armies we are nurturing and reinforcing in the east and of the world-wide traffic we have to carry on – when you think of all this can you wonder that it is the Battle of the Atlantic which holds the first place in the thoughts of those upon whom the responsibility for final victory rests.

Churchill would have been even more concerned had he known that the German Naval War Staff had come up with a bold plan to shake the Royal Navy's control of the Atlantic with a spectacular surface operation led by the Reich's new super battleship *Bismarck*.

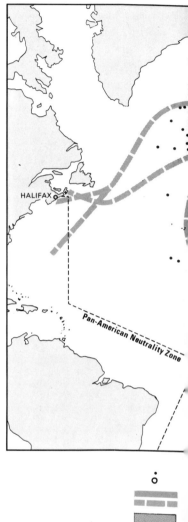

ALLIED SHIPPING LOSSES 1ST JUNE 1940-31ST MARCH 1941

OPERATION RHEINÜBUNG

Two weeks after the Fleet Commander, Admiral Gunter Lütjens had docked at Brest following his successful foray with the *Scharnhorst* and *Gneisenau*, he was ordered to transfer his flag to the *Bismarck* which had just completed six months working-up trials in the Baltic. The Admiral was informed that the pride of Hitler's navy would be accompanied into the Atlantic by the new heavy cruiser *Prinz Eugen*, and the *Gneisenau* from Brest. It had been planned that the *Bismarck*'s sister-ship *Tirpitz* would have finished her trials in time to take part in Operation *Rheinübung* which was intended to fulfil Admiral Raeder's long cherished ambition to send a German Fleet into the Atlantic powerful enough to defeat any British force.

The *Bismarck*, even by herself, presented a formidable naval threat. One of the most powerful warships afloat, she had four twin 15″ turrets firing very high velocity shells and a secondary armament of six 5.9″ turrets. Special Krupp 'Wotan' armour shielded the *Bismarck*'s decks and hull. She was also so intricately compartmentalised that her crew believed the ship to be 'unsinkable'; enemy shells and torpedoes would be 'mere bee stings'.

Hitler was uneasy about the operation but he finally accepted that a break-out had to be made before the nights became too short. He still hesitated, however, to give Raeder final permission to risk the Reich's biggest and newest military symbol. Admiral Lütjens also had his doubts when he was informed that the *Gneisenau* had been put out of action by the RAF, but the elaborate preparations for Rheinübung were already far advanced, with five tankers and two supply ships on their way to remote rendezvous points. They would join the weather ships strung out across the North Atlantic to give advance forecasts for the operation. On 5 May Hitler visited Lütjens and his staff aboard the *Bismarck* at anchor off the Baltic port of Gotenhafen. He showed little enthusiasm for the forthcoming operation and, once the battleship had sailed, Raeder deliberately omitted to report that *Rheinübung* was under way for two days in case the Führer changed his mind.

By this time British Naval Intelligence was already forewarned that a big operation was afoot. Heavy wireless traffic had been picked up from the north of Norway and German reconnaissance flights increased between Jan Mayen Island and Greenland. The intercepted naval Enigma was still unintelligible but it was clear from the complicated cyphers that a break-out by heavy forces was imminent. Since the *Scharnhorst* and *Gneisenau* were still penned in Brest, the Admiralty Operational Intelligence Centre predicted a foray by the *Bismarck* possibly accompanied by the *Tirpitz*. On 18 May the Home Fleet Commander, Admiral Tovey, signalled the cruiser *Suffolk* patrolling the Denmark Strait at the edge of the Greenland ice pack to expect enemy warships and within 48 hours, on 20 May, the Admiralty received a MOST IMMEDIATE telegram from Captain Denham, the British Naval Attaché in Stockholm. He passed on the dramatic news:

> Kattegat today, 20th May at 1500, two large warships, escorted by three destroyers, five escort vessels, ten or twelve aircraft passed Marstrand course North West.

143

Next morning Lütjens force arrived safely in Kors Fjord near Bergen, by which time he knew that his squadron had been spotted because *B-Dienst* radio intelligence officers aboard the battleship reported that British aircraft were being ordered to hunt for 'two battleships on a northerly course'.

At 1.15 that afternoon the *Bismarck* and *Prinz Eugen* were sighted from 25,000 feet by a reconnaissance Spitfire. The Admiralty acted immediately. By midnight the battlecruiser *Hood* and the brand-new battleship *Prince of Wales*, still with civilian technicians from Vickers Armstrong's yard on board, set course for the Denmark Strait with six destroyers. The cruiser *Norfolk*, relieving her sister-ship *Suffolk*, was ordered to patrol the Denmark Strait. The Iceland-Faroes gap was to be covered by the cruisers *Manchester* and *Birmingham* whilst the battlecruiser *Repulse* and new carrier *Victorious*, which were making ready to sail as cover for a convoy ferrying 20,000 troops to the Middle East, were ordered to remain with the Home Fleet.

Whilst the Home Fleet waited anxiously at their Scapa anchorages for definite news of the enemy, unbroken cloud halted all flights over the North Sea for 24 hours and it was not until the evening of 22 May that a courageous reconnaissance mission flown by Commander G. A. Rotherham from the Shetlands reported that the Bergen Fjords were empty. The *Bismarck* and *Prinz Eugen* were already far out into the Atlantic. At once Admiral Tovey decided to put to sea with the Home Fleet to take up a position between the sea passages north and south of Iceland.

Aboard the *Bismarck* and the *Prinz Eugen*, optimism was running high since the latest Luftwaffe reconnaissance reports had found the British Fleet still in Scapa Flow. Lütjens decided to save time by not refuelling and making a quick break out to take advantage of the fog banks reported North of Iceland. Through the day and night of the 23 May the *Bismarck* raced on at 24 knots skirting westwards along the edge of the Arctic ice. The thick overcast weather covered her dash as the *B-Dienst* listening teams aboard reported no suspicious increase in British radio activity, but on the evening of 23 May 1941, the Admiralty's suspense was ended. Admiral Wake Walker, commanding the 18th Cruiser Squadron in *Norfolk*, had just turned his two ships back from the edge of the ice pack towards the minefield west of Iceland when *Suffolk*'s radar picked up a contact. Minutes later the *Bismarck* loomed out of the mist seven miles away heading on the same southwesterly course. A 'MOST IMMEDIATE' signal was rushed off: 'One battleship one cruiser in sight bearing 020 degrees distant 7 miles course 240 degrees.' The hunt was up.

The German battleship opened fire on the *Norfolk*, forcing her to turn away under a smokescreen. A tortuous game of hide and seek now began as

The Chase is On: At 20.15 on 23 May 1941, the cruiser *Suffolk* (top) with the *Norfolk* contacted the German squadron in the Denmark Strait. Carefully keeping out of range, they shadowed her by radar as the *Hood* (below) and the brand new battleship HMS *Prince of Wales* steamed at full speed to intercept the enemy. Admiral Holland (right) who had only taken command of the squadron ten days before was eager for action, but he appreciated that his famous battlecruiser was vulnerable to the plunging shellfire of the *Bismarck*.

Bismarck tried to shake off her shadowers by dodging in and out of the fog banks. She did not elude the *Suffolk*'s radar and the two cruisers clung on tenaciously just outside the range of the battleship's guns. Aboard the *Bismarck* the *B-Dienst* officers were busily decoding the *Norfolk*'s reports and from other British signals, they were able to give Lütjens an accurate picture of the Admiralty's widespread operations to box him in.

Far to the south east, Admiral Somerville's Force H at Gibraltar had been ordered to raise steam and head into the Atlantic to protect the troop convoy to the south-west. The battleships *Ramillies* and *Revenge* were also instructed to leave their Halifax convoys and to sail east. Meanwhile the Home Fleet was steaming at top speed towards Greenland for what promised to be the biggest naval confrontation of the war. To block the southern entrance of the Denmark Straits, Admiral Tovey sent forward his fastest squadron, commanded by Vice-Admiral Lancelot Holland in the battle-cruiser *Hood*, the pride of the Royal Navy, accompanied by the *Prince of Wales*. *Hood*'s eight 15″ guns were equal in calibre to her more modern opponent, but the battlecruiser's armour protection had been sacrificed for speed. The Battle of Jutland in 1916 had revealed the fatal weakness in this class of warships, of which the *Hood* was one of the last and, for all her fine lines, the 23-year-old *Hood* was, in fact, obsolete. Constant pre-war cruising as the Royal Navy's showpiece had prevented any major reconstruction to increase her protection.

Holland took the *Hood*'s relative weakness against the *Bismarck* into his calculations as he closed Lütjen's squadron, guided by *Suffolk*'s reports. Wanting to avoid a night action, which he believed would put his ship at a disadvantage as the *Prince of Wales* was having mechanical problems with its triple 14″ turrets, he had altered course to the northwest to intercept the enemy at dawn next day.

When *Hood* finally sighted the *Bismarck* just before 6 am. on 24 May, Holland found that his approach had placed him at a tactical disadvantage. The German Squadron lay almost dead ahead and his two warships could only bring their forward turrets to bear against the enemy's full broadsides, 'fighting with only one hand when you have got two'. The British squadron was further handicapped because only five of the *Prince of Wales*'s six forward 14″ guns could be got in working order. Holland's intention had probably been to use his superior speed to close the range, minimising the risk of an engagement at long distance which would expose his weak deck armour to plunging shells but he went on to make two unfortunate errors which were to have serious consequences. Instead of dividing the fire of the two German ships by opening the distance between *Hood* and *Prince of Wales*, he now gave orders to manoeuvre in close order, so presenting the enemy with what was virtually a single target. Then he wrongly assumed that the leading ship was the *Bismarck* and ordered fire to be concentrated on her.

LOSS OF THE HOOD

At 5.53 on the morning of 24 May, 1941, HMS *Hood* fired the opening salvo of the engagement from her forward turrets. It was the *Prinz Eugen* and not the *Bismarck* which found herself at the receiving end. The flagship's mistake was spotted by the Gunnery Officer of the *Prince of Wales*, who had redirected his battleship's guns on to the second ship. No countermanding order was ever issued by Admiral Holland who almost certainly never engaged the *Bismarck*.

Observing the majestic gunnery duel on the Compass Platform of *Hood*, alongside Admiral Holland and his staff, was Ordinary Signalman Albert Edward Briggs.

When the *Hood* opened fire, the *Prinz Eugen* definitely turned away, and the *Bismarck* was thought to turn away. This I gathered from a conversation between the Admiral and the Captain. We altered course 30 degrees together and closed in to 12 miles range. We hit the *Bismarck* with our second salvo right amidships and the *Bismarck* did not open fire until we had fired about 4 or 5 salvoes. And then she hit us, according to the Squadron Gunnery Officer 'on the starboard side of the boat deck aft' causing a fire in the 4 inch ready-use lockers.

When *Bismarck*'s salvo struck the *Hood* Able Seaman Robert Tilburn was sheltering under the forward bridge:

A fire started and it was a very fierce blaze, a pinkish colour with not much smoke. There were fairly small explosions, rather like a big Chinese cracker. I heard the explosions but could not see any results of them. The order to put the fire out was given and then countermanded because of exploding ammunition.

After the fire had been going for a good while and about 6 salvoes had been fired altogether, when we started turning to round to port, we were hit somewhere and the ship shook all over and a lot of debris and bodies started falling all over the decks.

Bismarck's second or third salvo straddled the *Hood* and at least one of the shells plunged through the inadequately armoured deck amidships to the 4" magazine, causing a flash conflagration that spread in seconds down to the

The End of the Hood: The British battlecruiser's opening salvoes were concentrated on the leading German warship, the *Prinz Eugen*, where Captain Brinckmann (below) watched from the bridge. Minutes later a salvo from the *Bismarck* (bottom) straddled the *Hood* and the great ship was torn apart in seconds by a 'terrific explosion' (inset) leaving Seaman Robert Tilburn (right) one of the three survivors of the disaster.

after 15″ magazine. Its detonation tore the ship apart. On the Compass platform Briggs witnessed the battlecruiser's final moments:

> There was a terrific explosion, but the officer of the watch said to the Admiral that the compass platform had gone and the Admiral said move to after control. During that she had listed six to seven degrees to starboard and shortly after the Admiral spoke she listed right over to port. She had gone about twenty five degrees to port and the crew were trying to get away – by the crew I mean the men on the bridge – but the Admiral did not make any attempt to get away. I got out of the starboard door and there was the navigator just in front of me and the Squadron Gunnery Officer just in front of him. I had just got out of the door and the water by that time had got level with the compass platform. I do not remember anything more then until I found myself on the surface. The bows of the *Hood* were vertical in the water about 50 yards away and I was looking at the bottom of the ship.

Two hours later a destroyer picked up just three survivors, each on a separately Carley float, Briggs, Tilburn and Midshipman Dundas. Of the rest of the ship's company of 95 officers and 1,324 men there was no sign.

After the *Hood* had disappeared into the funeral pyre of smoke the *Prince of Wales* was suddenly faced with having to alter course sharply to avoid the wreckage. Now she came up against the concentrated fire of both German ships. Within minutes, one of *Bismarck*'s salvoes struck her and one 15″ shell killed or badly wounded everyone on the bridge except the Captain. *Prinz Eugen*'s 8″ guns had scored three hits when the British battleship's rear turret jammed and Captain Leach, now in the after conning position, decided he must save his ship by breaking off the action. At 6.13 am the *Prince of Wales* hauled away under cover of smoke.

The lucky few:
Robert Tilburn, (above) was one of only three survivors from the mighty *Hood*. The holocaust was witnessed by Able Seaman Usher aboard the *Prince of Wales*. 'All amidships seemed to lift up into the air. After that the ship was surrounded by yellow smoke . . . All along the upper deck it seemed to be bubbling up as if boiling. This was the foc'sle only, the deck of which seemed to be bubbling like a frying egg . . . The next thing I saw was the quarterdeck coming up into the air and I saw the screws. After that the quarterdeck disappeared and all I could see was smoke.'

CLOSING THE TRAP

Aboard the *Bismarck* there was jubilation. Many of the crew had crowded on the port superstructure oblivious to the danger. According to Ordinary Seaman Herbert Manthey cheering broke out: 'when it was announced from the bridge that the enemy were the largest British battleships. At the same time it was announced that the *Hood* had been sunk and that the *King George V* had turned away as well as the *Prince of Wales*. At the end of the action we learned that the *Bismarck* had received three hits . . . One was in the ship's side (at the bows). The second went through the starboard picket boat and detonated in the water. The third had gone into the port oil bunker. This damage did not impair the *Bismarck*'s fighting ability but the loss of oil and the urgent need to repair the bow forced Lütjens to reduce speed to 24 knots. He realised after receiving the full damage reports that he now had no choice but to abandon the break-out. At 8 am he broke radio silence to signal his intention to make for St Nazaire.

At this moment, the main British Fleet was still 300 miles away and with nineteen major warships converging across the Atlantic from different directions, it was crucial for Admiral Tovey that the *Prince of Wales* and Wake-Walker's shadowing cruisers should not lose contact. The *Suffolk*'s radar was performing well and she had reported that the *Bismarck*'s speed had dropped slightly and that the enemy squadron was now on a more southerly course. Realising that the Germans might still elude him, Tovey ordered the carrier *Victorious* accompanied by the 2nd Cruiser squadron ahead at top speed to launch an air attack.

Shortly after 6 p.m. Lütjens tried to un-nerve Wake-Walker's force by turning to face them. He also opened fire so as to create a diversion as part of a pre-arranged plan to cover the *Prinz Eugen's* break away to the south. Later that evening, with a worsening fuel situation, Lütjens abandoned his attempt to make for St Nazaire, and signalled that he was now on course for Brest. He asked for a line of U-boats to be set across his path to trap his pursuers.

The chase across the mid-Atlantic continued throughout the afternoon and evening until *Victorious* was close enough to launch an air strike. In thick weather nine Swordfish torpedo bombers of the Fleet Air Arm's 825 Squadron led by Lieutenant Commander Esmonde took off, followed by a flight of escorting Fulmar fighters, and headed southwest into the murky overcast. The Squadron report recorded:

> Radar contact made indicated vessel ahead and below, consequently Squadron broke through cloud to deliver attack. Vessel immediately recognised as United States coastguard cutter. *Bismarck* observed aircraft as they broke cloud, distance 6 miles, and opened fire with anti-aircraft guns.

The US coastguard cutter *Modoc*, which had been searching for convoy survivors suddenly found herself caught up in the *Bismarck* drama. Swordfish biplanes, with their torpedoes slung beneath them, bore down on the amazed American crew before Esmonde realised the mistake and climbed

Desperate Measures: Swordfish torpedo bombers were flown off the carrier *Victorious* in a bid to slow down the *Bismarck* and allow the Home Fleet to catch up. The 'stringbags' of 825 Squadron (top, on deck prior to their sortie) attacked at midnight on 24 May, watched by the crew of the US Coastguard cutter *Modoc* (below). For all the pilots' gallantry, the *Bismarck* was unscathed and three hours later she succeeded in throwing off the shadowing cruisers.

away. The *Bismarck*'s gunners were now fully alerted as Esmonde's planes reformed to make their attack:

> Aircraft went past a gap in the clouds and saw *Bismarck* who fired a salvo at that moment. A red glow was seen ahead, estimated 100 yards away. After leaving the clouds heavy bursts came up at once . . . Some bursts occurred behind, but they were always close. Two burst together 40 yards to starboard and below, shaking up the aircraft and setting it 90 degrees off course.

One torpedo struck *Bismarck* amidships, but the 'Wotan' armour lived up to its makers' claim and no damage resulted. The Swordfish pilots, whose squadrons were still officially under training, somehow managed to find their way back to their carrier through the half darkness but five of the escorting Fulmars were lost.

Commander Esmonde's attack, for all the gallantry displayed by his trainee naval pilots, had failed to slow down the *Bismarck*. Then, shortly after 3 am early on 25 May, 1941, Tovey suffered a major setback. Captain Lindemann had finally succeeded in shaking off his pursuers by a sudden change of course which caught the *Suffolk*'s radar operators off-guard. It was a bitter moment for Tovey as the *Bismarck* was then little more than a hundred miles to the west of him.

Frantic air and sea searches were mounted throughout the next day and night to find the battleship. At 10.30 am on 26 May the uncertainty was resolved when a Catalina Flying Boat of Coastal Command's No. 209 Squadron sighted a ship far below. The *Bismarck* soon removed any doubt that Ensign Leonard Smith USN, who was at the controls, may have had about her identity with a barrage of bursting shells which sent splinters through the aircraft's fuselage. The American officer was aboard as a 'Special Observer' and the Catalina's pilot, Flying Officer D. A. Briggs was soon tapping out the signal: 'One battleship in sight bearing 240 degrees distant 5 miles, my position 49.33N 21.77W'.

The Catalina's report put the *Bismarck* some 690 miles due west of Brest, which indicated that she would escape by the evening of the following day

Bismarck at Bay: After evading the ocean-wide hunt for more than a day and a half, the German battleship was spotted at 10.30 on 26 May by a Catalina flying boat (inset below) flown by a US Navy pilot. That evening, attacks by Swordfish from the carrier *Ark Royal* scored a lucky hit, jamming the *Bismarck* rudder. Unmanoeuverable and trailing fuel oil (below) Admiral Lütjens (above) realised the hunt was up.

when the Luftwaffe could provide massive air cover from the French bases. It was a desperate race for Tovey whose forces were more than 130 miles away and running low on fuel. The nearest British warship was Admiral Somerville's Force H still 70 miles away, whose battlecruiser *Renown* would not be able to take on the *Bismarck* alone, but Tovey saw the chance that a successful torpedo attack from *Ark Royal*'s aircraft might slow her up.

Orders went out to the carrier to launch an immediate reconnaissance. Two of the *Ark Royal*'s Swordfish finally located the *Bismarck* and shortly before 3 pm a strike was launched as the carrier's deck bucketed up and down in heavy seas. An hour later, the 14 Swordfish torpedo bombers dived through the cloud cover on a radar contact to launch their torpedoes. But the green blip which they had assumed to be the enemy ship turned out to be the cruiser *Sheffield*, sent ahead to shadow the *Bismarck* and now herself manouevring violently to avoid being hit.

A second flight of 15 Swordfish of Nos. 810, 818 and 820 Squadrons Fleet Air Arm led by Lieutenant Commander T. P. Coode were hastily brought to the carrier's flight deck and took off with orders to first make contact with *Sheffield* before making their attack. Just before 8 pm the Swordfish paired up and started a series of attacks on the *Bismarck* from all sides. Of the thirteen torpedoes launched, two hit. One exploded harmlessly on the heavy armour belt amidships, but the second struck the battleship's unprotected stern, jamming her rudders and wrecking the steering gear. All the aircraft managed to find the carrier but, with the *Ark Royal*'s flight deck rearing some thirty feet in the rough sea, four planes were wrecked in heavy landings.

First reports received in the tense and crowded Admiralty Operations Centre in London suggested that the attack had failed, but then revised signals from the *Sheffield* indicated that *Bismarck* was manoeuvring erratically and was clearly damaged. Lütjens was in trouble. Repairs to the rudder proved impossible in the heavy seas and his fuel situation was becoming desperate. He signalled, 'Ship no longer manoeuverable'.

DEATH OF THE BISMARCK

Just before 2 am on the morning of 27 May 1941 which happened to be Lütjens birthday, Hitler wirelessed a final message:

To Fleet Commander: I thank you in the name of the German people.

To the crew of the battleship *Bismarck:* The whole of Germany is with you. What can still be done will be done. The performance of your duty will strengthen our people in the struggle for their existence.

Shortly before 9 am on the morning of 27 May 1941 Admiral Tovey arrived in the *King George V* accompanied by the battleship *Rodney.* They closed and opened fire. Steering an erratic course *Bismarck* replied at a range of 16,000 yards. Her gunnery control was still lethally accurate and her first salvoes almost hit the *Rodney.* But, subjected to the concentrated British salvoes her firing rapidly deteriorated. By 10.15 *Bismarck*'s guns were silent.

As the pride of Hitler's navy was pounded into a blazing wreck, morale on board broke. Gunnery crews abandoned their turrets, saying 'Why should we stay here for target practice,' and others like Seaman Manthey prepared to abandon ship:

We had the impression that we were fired on from all sides. As the hits increased the anti-aircraft crews went under cover. First I was with a group of 20 men in the after gunnery position. After a few hits close-by we fled behind turrets C and D on the upper deck'.

It was left to the cruiser *Dorsetshire* to administer the coup de grâce. At 10.36 she deftly fired a torpedo into each side of the sinking hulk and, with her flag still flying, *Bismarck* disappeared beneath the rough Atlantic waves. Only 110 survivors could be hurriedly picked up before the threat of U-boats and aircraft forced the British to leave the scene. Of the ship's company, over 2,000 were lost.

The Kill: At dawn on 27 May 1941 Admiral Tovey (above) on his bridge in the flagship *King George V* watched the German battleship being pounded to pieces (below) by the combined weight of his ten 14″ and *Rodney*'s nine 16″ guns. After being torpedoed, the *Bismarck* finally capsized with her colours flying.

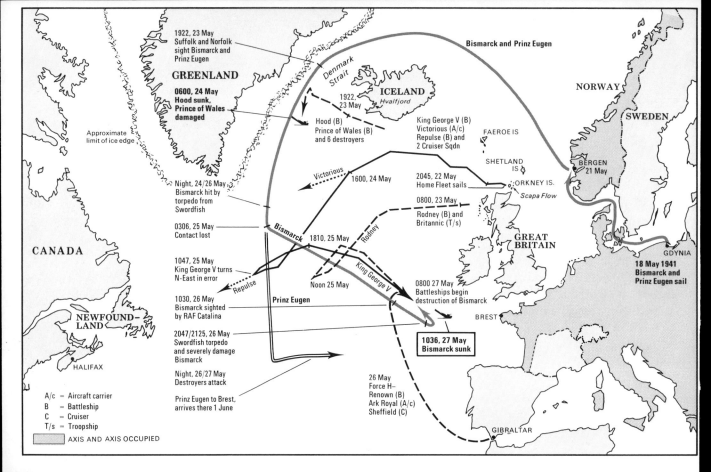

News of the destruction of the *Bismarck* was received with jubilation in Britain. The House of Commons burst into cheering after Churchill had interrupted the afternoon's business to announce that the *Hood* had been avenged. Churchill hoped that the *Bismarck*'s sortie, which had shaken up American opinion, would lead to even more dramatic 'additional measures. In a top secret note to the First Sea Lord, the Prime Minister stated:

> It would be far better, for instance, that she be located by a US ship, thus providing the incident for which the US government would be so thankful.

The Prime Minister's suggestion that the Navy should drive the German cruiser into a conflict with a US warship failed to bear fruit, but the sinking of the *Bismarck* had removed a major threat from the Atlantic life-lines. Hitler knew that Raeder's surface strategy had failed and he treated him to a gruelling interrogation. In acerbic mood, the Führer wanted to know why the *Prince of Wales* had been allowed to escape and made it plain that Raeder had talked him into the entire *Rheinübung* plan against his own better judgement. This resulted in a significant weakening of Hitler's confidence in Raeder and from now on both knew that the Battle of the Atlantic would depend on the U-boats. Unknown to them, however, they had already suffered a loss that was ultimately to prove as decisive in determining the ultimate course of the battle at sea than the destruction of the *Bismarck*. British intelligence had already seized the means to penetrate the German Naval Enigma cyphers.

'ULTRA' BREAKTHROUGH

The first of a series of steps that led to this breakthrough took place on 7 May 1941. Using information about the German Atlantic weathership operations gained from the capture of the patrol boat *Krebs* during a raid on the Lofotens, the weather ship *München* was captured by a strong cruiser and destroyer force in a carefully planned operation in the North Atlantic. A boarding party from the destroyer *Somali* had seized an intact naval *Enigma* coding machine and the all-important book of cyphers for setting the code wheels.

Within days, the equipment was in the hands of the experts of the 'Government Code and Cypher School' at Bletchley Park. The weathership *Enigma* codes were low-grade and did not provide the means to crack the complex *Enigma* cypher used by the German battleships or U-boats. But it provided an important series of clues for the brilliant team of mathematicians under Alfred Knox, a former fellow of King's College, Cambridge, and his colleague Allan Turing, who had studied under Einstein. Together they were working on a 'Universal Machine', one of the first computers, which would duplicate the rotor combinations of the Enigma code.

They badly needed an *Enigma* machine and a set of daily rotor settings for a U-boat. Since the beginning of the year, all escort commanders were instructed to try to capture a U-boat intact, but Dönitz's crews were well drilled in the need to scuttle their craft. To try to prevent this the Admiralty issued the escorts with instructions to shout at surrendering U-boats '*Boot hoch halten, sonst wird keiner gerettet!*' – 'Keep your boat afloat or you will not be picked up!' Also included were layouts of U-boat controls, assembled after careful interrogation of prisoners, and a chart showing which levers and wheels closed the sea cocks. Would-be U-boat captors were warned, 'the boat will be in darkness, so that an electric torch, a watertight one, will be essential'.

The long-awaited capture was finally made just two days after the *München* operation. It turned out to be the boat commanded by Kapitänleutnant Lemp – the man who had sunk the *Athenia*. On the morning of 8 May Lemp sighted convoy OB 318 soon after it had formed up off the Hebrides. The following morning he had joined up with Kapitänleutnant Schnee in U-201 and agreed on tactics before preceeding to attack independently.

Lemp manoeuvered on the surface for position ahead of the convoy. Shortly before midday, he fired three torpedoes in quick succession into the convoy. The fourth torpedo was aimed at a 15,000 ton whaling factory ship, but it failed to leave the tube. Lemp was preparing to attack the whaler again when he saw that he had been sighted by a corvette which was racing straight for him. He crash-dived in thirty seconds, but HMS *Aubretia*'s first well-placed depth-charges caused considerable damage.

Joined by the destroyer *Bulldog* and the sloop *Broadway*, two more accurate depth-charge patterns severely damaged U-110, putting the hydroplanes and rudder out of action, disabling the electric motor and the batteries which

End of the Bismarck: Some of the 110 survivors being picked up by the cruiser *Dorsetshire* (left) after the oceanwide hunt (map). They were all that were left of a crew numbering 2,100 whose commander had signalled: 'To the Führer of the German Reich Adolf Hitler. We fight to the last in our belief in you my Führer and the firm faith in Germany's victory.'

The map/chart shows positions labeled: AUBRETIA 1130, ST APOLLO 1130, BORGFRIED [94], AELYBRYN [93], EMPIRE CLOUD [92], ESMOND [91], GREGALIA [71], BENGORE HEAD [71], H.M.S. RANPURA, BROADWAY 1130, NIGELLA 1130, COLONIAL [4] 1130/9, BULLDOG 1130, DANEMAN 1130, HOLLYHOCK 1130, AMAZON 1130, U.110, U.110 surfaced 1235, ESMOND [91] 1200, BENGORE HEAD [71] 1200, U-BOAT "B", BROADWAY and AUBRETIA hunted U-Boat in this area until 1845/9

The Secret Capture: Two weeks before the *Bismarck*'s break-out, Royal Navy escorts achieved an even more significant victory in the Battle of the Atlantic, which was to remain a closely guarded secret for 30 years. On May 8 1941, a skilful attack (chart above) ended the career of U110 and the life of Kapitänleutnant Lemp – the commander who had sunk the *Athenia*. The rush to abandon U110 allowed a boarding party from *HMS Bulldog* to capture the U-boat as well as her code books and Enigma machine before she sank. This gave British cryptanalysts their first chance to penetrate the complicated U-boat codes.

started to emit gas. As the boat filled with choking fumes the crew panicked. U-110 started to plummet to the depths and there was a rush to reach the bows to restore the balance. Lemp ordered the main tanks to be blown, but the vital wheel controlling the valve had been broken off and was found lying on the floorplates. For several minutes the boat continued to sink and her crew despaired, then inexplicably she began to rise. Minutes later, U-110 broke surface to find herself surrounded and under a hail of fire which was so devastating that one of the observers who saw it reported: 'The battle of Trafalgar must have been like a snowball fight compared to this'.

The sloop HMS *Broadway* closed in to drop shallow depth-charges and increase the panic as the Germans started abandoning ship. Commander Baker-Cresswell in HMS *Bulldog* saw his chance to capture or at least board the U-boat before it sank. He raced in at full speed. This action caused Lemp and the last of his crew to jump from the conning tower convinced that their boat was about to be rammed and sunk. But HMS *Bulldog* sheered off, boats were lowered and the survivors were quickly picked up and hurried below, before a boarding party made for the U-boat. Lemp himself was still struggling in the water when, to his horror, he realised that U-110 was not sinking but was about to be boarded. In a desperate bid, he started swimming back to try to get aboard and complete the scuttling. Before he could clamber up the

154

slippery, wet casing he was spotted and shot dead by the boarding party who were determined that nothing would stop them.

When British sailors gingerly climbed down the narrow conning tower hatch they were amazed to find that no attempt had been made to scuttle the U-boat or destroy her confidential code books, papers and the vital Enigma machine. This was intact with its sets of spare rotor wheels, current daily rotor setting, diary and patrol signals.

Appreciating at once the importance of his capture, Baker-Cresswell gave strict orders to prevent the bedraggled survivors, now safely below decks, from knowing anything about his group's success or that U-110 was being taken in tow. His hopes for a triumphant return were dampened when the U-boat sank the next morning, but the Admiralty radioed orders for him to observe the strictest secrecy in avoiding any mention of the operation and to make for Scapa Flow at full speed.

The first complete Naval Enigma machine to be captured with a full set of the U-boat cyphers and current rotor settings was to prove one of the most important single intelligence breakthroughs of the whole war. The heavily-guarded packages, when they reached the teams of cryptologists at Bletchley Park, provided an insight into the secrets of the Atlantic U-boat codes. This added a new dimension to the growing stream of Enigma decodes emanating from Bletchley Park, providing information that was so top-secret that it had been given its own code name 'ULTRA'.

The breakthrough was to play a decisive role in the Battle of the Atlantic. By the end of May 1941 the importance of 'Special Intelligence' was apparent after the first erratic decoding of the U-boat signals clattered into the Admiralty's Operational Intelligence Centre on the secret teleprinter lines from Bletchley Park. These intercepts were only snatches of the overall traffic but they gave Commander Roger Winn and his team of U-boat watchers running the Submarine Tracking Room a picture of techniques that Dönitz used to run his campaign. For more than two years penetration of the U-boat Enigma traffic was neither continuous nor very complete. There were often gaps of days, weeks – and in 1942 a ten month blackout – when the Bletchley Park teams failed to break the Enigma codes but the 'Z Signals' added an important new dimension to the war against the U-boats. Sometimes the Tracking Room did receive enough advance warning of the operations that Dönitz was directing to successfully route convoys around a patrol line of U-boats and, if the 'Special Intelligence' arrived too late to save a particular convoy from a U-boat Pack, the analysis of the signals sent during the operation gave a valuable insight of their opponents' tactics. More important still was the Tracking Room's ability to build up gradually a clear picture of how Dönitz HQ operated, so that even if it was not possible to decode an actual set of signals they could identify the different patterns of the Enigma signals – whether it was for example 'E bar' or B bar' – and decide immediately if the reporting U-boat was sending a position signal or shadowing a convoy. This bank of intelligence experience made the 'intuitive guess work' of the Tracking Room very accurate, so that from May 1941 Dönitz's use of radio to control the U-boats proved to be U-Boat Command's Achilles' heel.

Special Intelligence: Commander Roger Winn, in charge of the Admiralty's Submarine Tracking Room, received an invaluable source of intelligence on Dönitz' dispositions and tactics as a result of the Enigma breakthrough,. A barrister in civilian life, Winn brought his keen intellect to the task of providing a steady stream of accurate intelligence for the senior Allied Commanders which enabled them to evade the U-boat concentrations.

The Battle for the Atlantic was going at full blast in Britain's hard pressed shipyards as the American industry prepared to help with the burden. Repairing damaged merchant ships and building new ones drew many women into the yards in the fight to beat the U boats on the slipways.

11. Charter for Survival

'The Battle for the Atlantic now extends from the icy waters of the North Pole to the frozen wastes of the Antarctic. . . . The blunt truth is the present rate of Nazi sinkings of merchant ships is more than three times as high as the capacity of British shipyards to replace them; it is more than twice the combined British and American output of merchant ships today'.

PRESIDENT ROOSEVELT broadcast June 1941

In June 1941, more than three million German troops together with a massive concentration of tanks and artillery supported by 2000 aircraft were poised for a titanic assault on the Soviet Union. 'When Barbarossa begins the world will hold its breath', Hitler had prophesied to his generals in February. 'You have only to kick down the door and the whole rotten edifice will come crashing down'. The Führer explained that a rapid campaign against Russia would realise his dream of limitless *Lebensraum* and destroy Communism. He was also convinced that a Nazi triumph would unnerve the United States, leaving an isolated Britain with no choice other than to sue for peace.

The German intentions were known in London and Washington – as well as Moscow. For months British intelligence had been following the build up from decyphered Enigma traffic and in February 1941, a disaffected Army officer had leaked the 'Barbarossa' plans to the US Commercial Attaché in Berlin. Warnings had been passed to the Kremlin, together with discreet suggestions of possible Anglo-American aid should Stalin pre-empt the German attack, but he chose to ignore all the warnings. In March the Kremlin had even discounted reports from Tokyo by their own master-spy Richard Sorge of *Barbarossa's* timing and objectives.

If the Russians continued to believe that their treacherous ally might still be bought off and were determined to do nothing to provoke the German attack, Hitler was even more anxious not to give the United States any excuse to increase its involvement in the conflict. But his hopes had already been imperilled by American reaction to the killing of her citizens in the South Atlantic on 19 May when the neutral Egyptian freighter *Zamzam* was sunk by U-boats followed, two days later, by the destruction of the clearly identified US merchantman *Robin Moor*. Together with the panic caused by the *Bismarck*'s sortie into the Atlantic these incidents led Roosevelt to issue a declaration of 'an unlimited national emergency' on 27 May. He followed this by an order on 14 June that froze German and Italian assets in the United States and another which closed the Axis consulates. Although the President's policy was to wait for Hitler to fire the first shot before openly committing the US Navy against the U-boats, on 17 June he optimistically cabled Churchill: 'I have a distinct feeling in my bones that things are looking up with you and with us. After freezing the German and Italian assets on Saturday, I closed the German consulates and agencies yesterday and the reaction here is, I should say 90 per cent favourable.'

Three days later the actions of an over zealous U-boat commander almost brought about the very incident that Hitler most feared – giving the United States the excuse to begin a shooting war in the Atlantic.

Kapitänleutnant Mützelburg in U-203 was patrolling between Greenland and Iceland on 20 June when he sighted the American battleship *Texas* accompanied by a destroyer screen steaming ten miles inside the War Zone where the Germans had declared that all shipping was in danger of being sunk on sight. Without waiting for U-boat Command to reply to his sighting report, he tried to get into a position to attack, but after chasing the American squadron for 140 miles, heavy seas and its zig-zag course foiled his plan. The next day he appreciated his good fortune, when he received the signal:

The Undeclared War: Two days before the German armies rolled into Russia (above) the United States was nearly precipitated into the war when Kapitänleutnant Mützelburg in U-203 (right) tried to torpedo the battleship USS *Texas* off Iceland. Incidents such as the sinking of the US freighter *Robin Moor*, led to President Roosevelt declaring an 'unlimited national emergency' on 27 May and closing the Axis consulates on 14 June. However on 29 July the Senate was assured 'there is not an undeclared war, a hidden naval war as far as we are concerned'.

BY ORDER OF THE FUHRER: All incidents with the United States must be avoided in the coming weeks. Until further notice, attacks may not be made on battleships, cruisers and aircraft carriers unless positively identified as hostile.

The urgent signal had been sent out to all U-boats following Hitler's meeting with Raeder that afternoon, during the course of which, the Führer had been furious to learn that U-203 had nearly wrecked his whole strategy – just two days before *Operation Barbarossa* was due to begin. The Admiral had received a stern lecture and the strictest instructions:

> to avoid any incidents with the USA. After a few weeks the situation will become clearer. America will have less inclination to enter the war, owing to the threat from Japan which will then increase. If possible, therefore, all attacks on naval vessels in the war zone should cease . . .

At 3.00 am on the morning of 22 June 1941, eight hours after this stormy conference, an artillery barrage of 6,000 guns announced the opening of *Operation Barbarossa* and 120 German divisions rolled across the Soviet frontier. Britain's prospects for survival were transformed. Within hours Churchill was broadcasting a public offer of an alliance with Stalin.

> Any man or state who fights against Nazidom will have our aid. Any man or state who marches with Hitler is our foe . . .
> The Russian danger is therefore, our danger, and the danger of the United States, just as the cause of any Russian fighting for his hearth and home is the cause of free men and free peoples in every quarter of the globe.

There was no immediate response from the Kremlin to offers of help until 3 July when Stalin, broadcasting to the Russian people, referred to 'the historic statement of the British Prime Minister, Mr Churchill regarding aid to the Soviet Union, and the declaration of the United States Government signifying their readiness to render aid to our country. . . .' On 12 July the Soviet-British mutual assistance pact was signed in Moscow, diverting some of Britain's precious Lend-Lease supplies direct to Russia and proposing joint naval operations. But there was embarrassingly little that Britain or the United States could immediately give and military chiefs in both London and Washington privately agreed that Russia would not survive the German onslaught. However, to stave off the Red Army's defeat, on 25 July the British War Cabinet agreed to release 200 US built Tomahawk fighters, together with other essential war materials including 'three million pairs of boots'. Four weeks later, on 21 August, the first Russian convoy sailed from Reykjavik for Archangel escorted by the Royal Navy.

In his preoccupation with the eastern campaign, Hitler had failed to grasp how rapidly the United States was preparing for war in the west. At his June meeting with Mussolini in the Brenner Pass, he had dismissed as 'childish statements', reports that the United States was planning to produce 400 tanks a month and 18,000 aircraft by 1942. His convictions were confirmed by a Foreign Ministry assessment that 'without knowing what Japan will do, the President cannot dare enter the war; he cannot bring about entry into the war, which, under the Constitution can be declared only by Congress, in opposition to the predominant public opinion among his people.'

This under-estimated the American mood, for while the US Congress was still opposed to initiating an open conflict, it had shown an increasing hostility to Germany by approving a Presidential order freezing all Axis funds in the US and closing their consulates. Roosevelt was confident that he could now get Congressional backing if the Germans began a shooting war in the Atlantic, but he was equally determined to avoid the dangers of a simultaneous conflict with the Japanese in the Pacific and the Germans in the Atlantic. To the concern of the British he initiated discussions with Tokyo, and he explained his policy of playing for time with the Japanese – 'it is terribly important for the control of the Atlantic to help keep the peace in the Pacific. I simply have not got enough navy to go round. . . .'

The President's solution to this problem was 'Hemisphere Defence', which was popular with most Americans as a way of insulating their country from foreign wars. Even before Germany's invasion of Russia, Roosevelt had decided to extend the plan to Iceland and Admiral Stark was directed to provide 4,400 Marines for an Expeditionary Force. The operation had to be delayed until the 'Althing', the Icelandic parliament, could be persuaded to 'invite' American protection and *Task Force 19* finally sailed on the day Hitler invaded Russia. As it steamed towards Iceland the military chiefs in Washington had second thoughts and advised its recall. News of the operation had 'leaked' in the Senate where it was roundly denounced by the isolationists. However, Congress gave its approval and public reaction was more favourable than expected. This encouraged Roosevelt to issue orders to the Navy to deal firmly with any German forces that presented a 'threat' to communication between the United States and Iceland.

Now the Americans were firmly established in Iceland less than 500 miles from Britain it was clear to the world that the United States had moved much closer to belligerency. This new move sent Raeder hurrying to the Führer's field headquarters at Rastenburg in East Prussia to ask if 'from a political point of view the occupation of Iceland by the USA is to be considered an entry into the war'. Hitler dashed the Admiral's hopes by insisting on the observance of existing orders and demanding that the U-boats should avoid 'all incidents' since a 'victorious campaign on the Eastern front would have a tremendous effect on the whole situation and certainly on the USA'.

Many of the President's closest advisers were hourly anticipating the incident that would allow the United States to deal a blow against Hitler, while 'his back was turned in Russia'. Roosevelt, however, was determined to move more cautiously and, disturbed at Churchill's recent supposition in the House of Commons of imminent naval co-operation, he dispatched Harry Hopkins to London with strict instructions 'No talk of war!'

At one of his first meetings with the Prime Minister, Hopkins, who was accompanied by US military observers, raised the issue of the failure of British Mediterranean strategy. Crete had fallen to the German paratroops with heavy losses and General Wavell's long heralded desert offensive against Rommel had just collapsed. As Hopkins put it, 'Our Chiefs of Staff – the men who make the big decisions on all matters relating to defence – believe the British Empire is making too many sacrifices in trying to maintain

No Talk of War! After the occupation of Iceland by US forces at the end of June, Roosevelt sent his confidential aide Harry Hopkins (right) on a mission to London and Moscow to prepare for a summit meeting with Churchill. After his daunting flight to Moscow Hopkins immediately travelled back to America aboard the *Prince of Wales* as the Prime Minister (below with Field Marshal Sir John Dill) prepared for the historic meeting with Roosevelt.

an indefensible position in the Middle East'. The President's aide emphasised, 'the Battle of the Atlantic is the final, decisive battle of the war and everything has got to be concentrated on winning it'. Churchill launched into a robust statement of the vital role the Mediterranean played in the Empire's defence.

But Anglo-American plans suddenly became academic with the dramatic arrival of the Soviet Ambassador bringing a message from Stalin demanding the immediate opening of a Second Front to save Russia from military collapse. Given the weakness of the western powers, this was an impossible request but Roosevelt, anxious to give the Soviet leader some demonstration of support, sent Hopkins on a hazardous flight to Moscow to judge the position at first hand. 'Give us anti-aircraft guns and aluminium and we can fight for three or four years', Stalin told him in 'straight and hard' talks.

Encouraged by Russia's obvious determination to resist the Nazi onslaught, Hopkins flew back to accompany Churchill on his clandestine voyage across the Atlantic, to the first summit meeting with the President. On 4 August the battleship *Prince of Wales*, still bearing the scars of her action with the *Bismarck*, sailed in conditions of total secrecy from Scapa Flow.

MEETING 'GOD'

'You'd have thought Winston was being carried up to the heavens to meet God', wrote Hopkins of the British Prime Minister's exuberant mood during the voyage. As the great battleship and her strong destroyer escort zig-zagged their way across the North Atlantic at high speed Churchill revelled in the experience, exploring the great warship like a schoolboy, playing gin rummy and watching films like '*Lady Hamilton*'. Some members of the party were apprehensive about the outcome of this face-to-face contact between the two towering personalities. Churchill, however, was convinced that the conference would be a prelude to the long-awaited announcement of cobelligerency by the United States. On the day they left, he had cabled the President, 'It is twenty-seven years ago today that the Huns began their last war. We must make a good job of it this time. Twice ought to be enough. . .'. Roosevelt was determined not be hustled into the conflict before he judged that public opinion would support him. Elaborate steps had been taken to fool the American press into believing that he was still aboard the presidential yacht *Potomac*, while he transferred to the cruiser *Augusta* for the voyage to Placentia Bay and the historic rendezvous with Churchill's battleship.

On Saturday 9 August 1941, the *Prince of Wales*, steamed round the misty Newfoundland bay before dropping anchor alongside the American squadron. The bands of both flagships were playing and the decks of the US ships were lined with cheering sailors. Shortly before midday the *Augusta's* band struck up 'God save the King' and 'The Star Spangled Banner' as Churchill climbed the gangway to greet Roosevelt under the quarterdeck awning. The two men took an instant liking to each other. After a convivial lunch 'the long cigarette holder and the long cigar were at last being lit by the same match', and the President and Prime Minister settled down to begin three days of critical discussions.

That night, after dinner aboard the *Augusta*, Churchill presented a vivid resumé of the war, in which he stressed the British strategy for containing Germany in the Middle East, with the United States providing the means to sustain Soviet resistance and deterring Japan in the Far East. The discussions then broke up into a series of meetings in which the military chiefs conferred with their opposite numbers, while the two leaders discussed broad strategy. The British were soon disappointed to discover that the Americans stopped short of making any commitment that would involve them in actual shooting. The delicacy of the President's position was clearly impressed on the British during the last day of the meetings when news was received from Washington that the House of Representatives had passed the important bill to extend selective army service by a majority of one vote.

The British delegation did, however, succeed in convincing the Americans of the need to support the Mediterranean strategy, to take a firm stand against Japan and to agree to occupy the Azores if Germany invaded Spain. Roosevelt also put forward 'Naval Plan 4' proposing that American ships should take over the escort of convoys on the Halifax-Iceland leg of the Atlantic, 'thus giving us relief equal to over fifty destroyers and corvettes'. The talks gave expression to the Anglo-American determination to keep the Atlantic free of Nazi domination.

After nearly two years of war, the floodlighting of the camouflaged British battleship alongside the pristine US squadron brought an air of festivity to the occasion and, to the delight of the British sailors, 1,500 cartons were delivered by the *Augusta's* boats to the *Prince of Wales*, each containing fresh fruit cheese together with 200 cigarettes and a card: 'The President of the US of America sends his compliments and best wishes.'

The underlying unity of the two nations was given expression on the Sunday, when the talks were adjourned for a joint Church-parade held on the quarterdeck of *Prince of Wales* under the shadow of her great 14″ guns. The bleak grey hills of the Placentia Bay echoed to the voices of British and American sailors joining the Royal Marine band in the familiar hymns 'For Those in Peril in the Sea' and 'Onward Christian Soldiers'. It was a moment of deep emotion for everyone present and, as one of the President's party recorded, it 'gave meaning to the conflict between civilisation and arrogant, brute challenge; and gave promise more powerful and binding than any formal treaty could. . .'.

Churchill was much moved by the occasion and later described its profound significance in a broadcast,

> When I looked upon that densely packed congregation of fighting men of the same language, of the same faith, of the same ideals and to a large extent of the same interests and certainly in different degrees facing the same dangers, it swept across me that here was the only hope but also the sure hope of saving the world from merciless degradation.

The main, and unexpected achievement of the meeting was a declaration of Anglo-American War aims. 'The Atlantic Charter'. What soon came to be regarded as one of the most significant declarations of the war originated in a press release entitled a 'Joint Declaration'. Intended as a statement of broad idealistic principle, rather than specific war aims, it was originally drafted under Churchill's supervision to express British support for Roosevelt's 'Four freedoms'. It was revised by the Americans, who nearly soured the occasion by insisting that it carried some reference to relaxing Britain's imperial role. However, it was finally approved by the British Cabinet who were kept from their beds whilst the two sides haggled over an acceptable wording for a trade-liberalization clause. The Atlantic Charter, which was to become one of the principal foundation stones of the United Nations, also declared that 'all men in all the lands may live out their lives in freedom from fear and want.' Postwar disarmament and the 'abandonment of the use of force' were to provide for the 'establishment of a wider and more permanent system of collective security.'

Armed with this proclamation Churchill sailed for home in the *Prince of Wales,* accompanied as far as Iceland by US Navy destroyers, which, he cabled to London, 'are not considered escort, but will chip in if any trouble occurs'. To the Prime Minister's dismay, no U-boats were rash enough to attack, but he was uplifted when the battleship steamed majestically through the ranks of a 71 ship convoy before reaching Rekjavik. Here he inspected the new American garrison before sailing for home, reaching London on 19 August.

The Special Relationship:
The President's gift boxes to the British seamen (above) symbolised the underlying unity of purpose between Britain and America at the Argentia Conference. It was recorded in the autographed picture (left) showing General Marshall, The President, The Prime Minister, Admiral King and US Naval Chief of Staff Stark, relaxing informally after the Sunday service aboard the *Prince of Wales*.

During their historic meeting, neither the President nor the Prime Minister had forgotten Stalin. They both believed that Hitler could not be defeated unless Russia were kept in the fight and, to this end, Harriman and Beaverbrook were despatched on a joint mission to Moscow in September to 'offer all we could spare and dare'. Stalin demanded a 'Second Front' and a massive Lend-Lease programme, including complete armaments factories. As Soviet pressure increased, Churchill was astonished to learn that 'our new ally, surly, snarly, grasping,' was suggesting that 30 British army divisions be sent to fight alongside the Red Army. It was only after a series of stormy meetings that Harriman and Beaverbrook had to agree to provide Stalin with aid on a far greater scale than originally intended. The British feared that this would threaten their own Lend-Lease supply and that the burden of covering the convoys to Russia would fall on their already over-extended escort resources. The Americans also were displeased to find that Stalin had driven such a hard bargain, insisting on the same Lend-Lease terms as the British, which meant that the Administration had difficulty getting the legislation through a strongly anti-Communist Congress.

The Anglo-American deliberations had little effect on the Germans. Hitler's High Command discounted Anglo-American aid to Stalin and was confident that Moscow would fall before the winter. Only the Naval Staff disagreed, believing that any delay in the planned early victory would have serious consequences. The progress of the Russian campaign particularly concerned Dönitz, who saw it as a swing away from the all-important Atlantic strategy. He concluded that, 'For the naval command, whose strategic interests had been turned entirely to the war against England and her sea communications, this new development was particularly painful.'

Since the collapse of Raeder's surface strategy, Dönitz warned that the final outcome of the Battle of the Atlantic was now more dependent than ever on the number of U-boats at sea. The enormous resources required for *Barbarossa* had badly affected naval construction with output of new U-boats falling from the planned twenty to less than fourteen a month. Shortages of copper and steel plate were blamed, but the shipyards were also desperately short of 25,000 skilled workers who had been drafted for service on the Eastern front.

With fewer U-boats coming into service, the pace of the attack on Britain's seaborne life-line was certain to slow down and the Luftwaffe had also been diverted from its raids on British ports and internal communications. Yet four weeks after *Barbarossa*, Hitler assured Raeder that he had no intention of lifting the 'Siege of England'. He still stressed the need to keep America out of the conflict and handicapped the U-boat commanders by reiterating the orders which forbade attacks on warships 'not positively identified as British'.

Dönitz's warnings were proved during the summer months of 1941 as the U-boat successes fell from over 300,000 tons of shipping sunk in June, to little more than 90,000 tons in July and even less in August. The reason for this 75% drop was not, as the Germans believed at the time, just the result of greater numbers of British escorts or American patrols, but because the U-boats' Enigma traffic had been broken following the capture of U-110.

164

'Special Intelligence' now provided a steady stream of accurate information about U-boat movements on which Western Approaches Command acted so that most convoys could be routed well clear of the Wolf Pack concentrations. The Submarine Tracking Room's new accuracy also increased the efficiency of the convoy defences. Escorts could now be concentrated around those convoys which were threatened and Coastal Command aircraft sent to intercept known U-boat concentrations instead of patrolling hundreds of square miles of empty ocean.

The first proof of the value of 'Special Intelligence' came on 23 June 1941 when the Tracking Room received advance warning from Bletchley Park that ten U-boats were gathering to attack the homeward-bound convoy HX 133, which had been sighted by U-203 south of Greenland. Orders were immediately radioed from Western Approaches Command to change the convoy's course. At the same time HX 133's escort was reinforced by ships from two nearby westbound convoys which the Tracking Room confirmed were not in immediate danger. Air patrols were concentrated ahead and on the flanks of the convoy so that the gathering U-boats were continually forced to submerge. For five days the Wolf Pack was beaten off by the strong escort defences and two U-boats were destroyed for the loss of five merchant ships. Although the U-boats intercepted OB 336, one of the now weakly escorted westbound convoys and sank three empty freighters, it was an important reverse. For two months Dönitz did not attempt another pack attack on a protected Atlantic convoy. Instead he sent his forces to the Azores to attack the less well defended Freetown convoys.

3

The Convoys Hit Back:
The penetration of the U-boat Enigma radio traffic in June 1941 allowed Western Approaches Command to reinforce threatened convoys. These measures proved very successful in beating off the attack on convoy HX 133 at the end of the month, when two U-boats were destroyed. The destruction of U-556 on 27 June was recorded by the corvette *Gladiolus* whose accurate depth charging (1) forced the U-boat to the surface to be shelled by two other corvettes (2) so that by the time *Nasturtium* closed to ram (3) the German crew were already abandoning the sinking boat (4 & 5) leaving the bedraggled survivors to be picked up (6 & 7).

6

7

SPY MANIA

To their consternation, Dönitz's staff soon found that their change in tactics appeared to have been pre-empted by the British when the mid-Atlantic supply ships and tankers started vanishing. 'Special Intelligence' had revealed the positions of the Kriegsmarine's secret ocean supply system and, at the end of May, Royal Navy cruisers were detailed to sink the weather ships and three tankers which had been sent out to support the *Bismarck* and which were now being used by the U-boats. At the end of the first week in June, the *Esso Hamburg* and *Egerland*, waiting in the supposedly secret mid-Atlantic 'Andalusian' rendezvous area to refuel the boats operating off the Azores, were surprised and sunk.

These attacks were a severe blow to the Germans since the supply ships were supporting not only U-boats but also blockade runners and surface raiders. They had been an integral part of U-boat Command's operations in the South Atlantic, which, since early 1941 had been deploying their large 1,200 ton Type IX U-boats to prey on independently routed ships off the Azores and the African coast. Replenishment at sea saved the 4,600 mile round trip to the Biscay ports and effectively doubled the Type IX's patrol capabilities. The seven in the South Atlantic had already sunk 74 ships, but Dönitz's attempts to extend his offensive into distant waters were frustrated. As an answer he planned to build a fleet of 1,700 ton supply U-boats, the so-called Milch cows.

The disruption of the supply system had alerted Dönitz to the possibility of a breach in security. His suspicions appeared to be confirmed by the rapidly declining success rate which had fallen below one sinking per U-boat per month for the first time – in spite of the fact that 25 operational U-boats were at sea, more than ever before. In a thorough investigation into the reasons for this 'meagre success', Dönitz's staff paid particular attention to security at their bases. There had already been a disturbingly high number of sabotage attempts ranging from water and sand in lubricating oil to the deaths of three crewmen after serious tampering with the diesel exhausts of U-101 had been tampered with. Investigations had revealed that disaffected Germans were responsible, but, the French dockyard workers were obvious suspects. They had been forced to adopt subtle ways of interfering with teutonic efficiency, after direct methods had led to terrible reprisals. In December 1940 the disappearance of an armed Naval patrol in Lorient resulted in the Germans ordering the municipal authorities to supply the names of all Frenchmen in the city above the age of 19 years. Victims were selected from this list and ten Frenchmen were shot for every rating killed and 25 for every officer. After this incident the U-boat crews were not allowed out in Lorient in groups of less than four and were warned to carry arms.

The disappearance of U-138 on 18 June off Gibraltar, soon after she had set out on patrol, caused 'spy mania' to sweep the U-boat bases. A search was mounted for an informer and particular suspicion fell on the Italians at Bordeaux who were given long lectures about the dangers of talking to the 'women of the town who play a most important part in Italian seaman's life'.

The End of the Happy Time in Warm Waters: Since April 1941 increasing numbers of the new large Type IX U-boats had been sent to attack unconvoyed shipping off Freetown. It was a successful time for Kapitänleutnant Hessler and his crew in U-107 and the absence of patrols allowed them time for bathing (below right) and a leisurely rendezvous with other boats (above, U-69 and UA). The group was supplied by surface tankers, the *Nordmark* (below) camouflaged as the US *Prairie* refuelling U-107 on 5 May in the *Andalusian* mid-Atlantic zone. Operations were cut short when the British sank all the tankers in June, forcing Dönitz to recall the six U-boats. When U-107 returned, Dönitz decorated his son-in-law Hessler for achieving the highest sinkings in any single operational patrol of the war – 86,699 tons – during three months at sea.

The Germans had tried to counter the operations of latter-day Mata Haris in the whore-house by getting the Todt Organisation to construct special 'rest camps' like the 'U-boat Holiday Home' complete with Bierkeller décor, overlooking Quiberon's sandy beaches but the men still preferred to fraternise with the local girls. For the officers, Paris was particularly tempting and Kapitän Meckel on Dönitz's staff was aware at the time that the city was a security risk:

> There was one club, the Scherazade, which was a particularly favourite place to celebrate a successful patrol. It was a Russian Club with attractive girls who sang delightfully and who also spoke good German. There was one particularly attractive girl called Tania who vied for the favours of some of our senior commanders. I was certain she was really out for information, but in spite of all our efforts we could never trap her.

Dönitz's investigations in the bases failed to produce any proof of a leak and he eventually concluded that the source of information had been one of the weather ships. Naval High Command, believed that this could not have produced any serious breakthrough into the communications system because their Enigma machines were designed only for the low-grade codes. The vital U-boat cypher, they believed, was still secure, since all officers had been instructed to pass back the information with specially chosen code words in Red Cross letters if a U-boat had been captured. The taking of U-110 was never discovered because the one man who witnessed it – Captain Lemp – was dead and the other survivors were kept below decks.

CAPTURED BY A BOMBER

It was through this secret channel of communication that the Germans discovered that a U-boat, but not the Enigma cyphers, had been captured. In one of the most astonishing events of the war a Coastal Command Hudson of 269 Squadron secured the capture of U-570 on 27 August 1941. Squadron Leader J. Thompson's log described how he obtained the surrender which occurred 80 miles south of Iceland:

> Sighted U-boat on surface 1,200 yards away to port quarter on course of 09 deg. 6 knots. Aircraft at once dived from 500 to 100 feet releasing 4 depth charges, the explosion of which enveloped the U-boat which was beginning to submerge.
>
> One minute after water disturbance subsided, the U-boat fully surfaced in slightly bow-heavy position and 10 or 12 of crew came out of conning tower wearing yellow life-saving jackets and stood on deck. The aircraft made an attack on them with front turret and belly guns. Crew ran back inside conning tower and aircraft continued attacks with guns firing about 2,000 rounds. A white flag was then waved from the conning tower and on deck displaying a large white board. The aircraft signalled to base asking for air and surface assistance and circled until 13.45 when Catalina of 209 Squadron arrived and took over watch. Rescue and salvage taken over by the Navy.

Damaged and unable to dive, U-570 had barely enough power from the leaking batteries to keep her pumps working and the very rough seas deterred the crew from abandoning ship. Just before 11 o'clock that evening the circling aircraft were relieved by the armed trawler *Northern Chief* which arrived and flashed to the U-boat: 'If you make any attempt to scuttle I will not save anyone, and will fire on your rafts and floats'. To this the luckless Commander of U-570, Korvettenkapitän Hans Rahmlow signalled back in English: 'I cannot scuttle or abandon; save us tomorrow please.'

At first light next day, Rahmlow and his clearly nervous and inexperienced crew were taken off their U-boat, which was then brought in tow and beached in an Icelandic cove. The Royal Navy now had its first complete U-boat, a major prize, even though its secret codes and intelligence papers had been dumped overboard. After a complete refit U-570 was commissioned into the Royal Navy as HMS *Graph* and carried out experimental patrols.

Aircraft Captures U-boat: The remarkable feat of Squadron Leader Thompson in effecting the surrender of U-570 is recorded on the camera of his Hudson aircraft (below). The capture presented the Royal Navy with its first real chance to thoroughly evaluate the performance of the principal weapon in the Battle when the U-boat was commissioned as HMS *Graph*.

British experts were able to get a complete analysis of a U-boat's operating capabilities, and some astonishing discoveries were made, principally that the Germans had 'produced the strongest hull known in marine architecture'. It was made of 1″ high tensile steel with every joint carefully riveted and welded so that it was capable of withstanding the 14 tons per square foot of water pressure at 500 feet. This appreciation of the deep-diving capabilities of the enemy submarines resulted in the immediate modification of the detonators on all depth charges so that they could be triggered below 600 feet.

The capture of U-570 marked the high point of British fortunes in the Atlantic during 1941 and four months after it had first been convened, the Battle of the Atlantic Committee was able to take a cautiously optimistic view of the progress made since it was set up in the midst of the March crisis. The increased strength of the escort by June had made it possible for Western Approaches Command to introduce end-to-end convoying for the first time. The participation of the Royal Canadian Navy was steadily expanding, as their shipyards turned out more warships and they were to take a larger share in the burden of the Atlantic escort shuttle which had its western headquarters based in the Newfoundland port of St Johns.

At the eastern end of the Atlantic air escort was having a significant effect and the Chief of the Air Staff reported that 'our methods, in particular the use of aircraft, were driving the submarines farther to the west'. Twenty of the new US-built Liberator bombers arrived in June. After modification, they were found to be the ideal aircraft for Coastal Command's need for a long-range convoy escort capable of patrolling over 700 miles into the Atlantic packing the powerful punch of 24 depth charges in their large bomb bays. In September 1941 the first Liberator squadron became operational in the Western Atlantic patrolling between Iceland and Britain. But the need for long-range aircraft was desperate and by October Coastal Command's squadron was reduced by half as valuable Liberators were transferred to RAF Ferry Command and BOAC as transatlantic transports for senior officials flying between Britain and America. Coastal Command found itself pushed to the back of the queue when RAF Bomber Command and the US Army Air Force also discovered the Liberator's outstanding performance, although they had neglected the plane for years.

Aircraft v. U-boats: The newly-appointed C-in-C of Coastal Command, Air Vice Marshal Joubert de la Ferté (above) was determined that his planes would play an effective part in the campaign. He set in motion new training programmes as well as beginning an offensive in the Bay of Biscay, but Costal Command was short of the long range aircraft needed to patrol far out into the Atlantic. The potential of the new Consolidated Liberator bombers (below), which first arrived in September 1941, soon became apparent. But for two years Coastal Command was to be deprived of adequate numbers .

A new C-in-C at Coastal Command, Air Marshal Sir Philip Joubert de la Ferté, was instilling far greater drive into the RAF's campaign against the U-boat. With a total strength approaching 200 aircraft, he was understandably keen that air crews should start sinking U-boats instead of merely forcing them to submerge. None of the 41 U-boats so far sunk had been the direct victims of an aircraft attack although they had brought surface escorts into successful kills. Joubert therefore decided to use some of his medium-range aircraft to patrol intensively the transit areas from the Biscay bases and the North Sea, where the U-boats travelled on the surface, in the hope that a greater frequency of sightings would bring a successful sinking.

Bomber Command was also pressed by the Battle of the Atlantic Committee to concentrate its attacks against the U-boat construction yards in Germany and the French bases, where reconnaissance had shown that the Germans were building huge shelters. These structures were erected by the Todt Organisation, using millions of tons of concrete reinforced by vast quantities of steel. The largest shelter at St Nazaire was 25 feet thick, nearly a thousand feet long and 80 ft high. It could house 26 U-boats. To his surprise, Joubert's commonsense request was fiercely resisted by Bomber Command, who believed that attacks on the Reich's industrial plant and shipyards was a better use of air power. In this they were mistaken. Raids on U-boat yards continued for over three years before they could be made sufficiently intense to affect production but when heavy raids began on the Biscay bases early in 1942, the U-boats were immune inside their completed pens.

Coastal Command had been quick to take advantage of Special Intelligence to give maximum cover to threatened convoys rather than a thin protection to all. But Joubert's greatest problems were the great shortage of long-range aircraft and the difficulty of locating the U-boats at night when they usually delivered their attacks. By the autumn most aircraft had been fitted with Mk II ASV radar, although aircrews were inexperienced in its use. This system also had a number of short-comings and to remedy these a series of 'brains' trust' sessions called 'Sunday Soviets' brought operational aircrew, scientists and civil servants together at the Telecommunications Research Establishment at Swanage, to hammer out ways of improving the equipment. At the same time, a series of promising experiments were being conducted by Squadron Leader Humphrey de Vere Leigh to adapt a searchlight for aircraft use during the final minutes of a night attack when the radar echo disappeared in the clutter of close-range sea reflections.

These new airborne anti-submarine systems were bound to increase the capability of aircraft to destroy U-boats but in 1941 surface escorts were still the main killers. As their number increased, it became possible to provide most of the big Atlantic convoys with both an inner and outer screen. Asdic training became a high priority after a report revealed that over 80% of U-boats escaped because of the failure to deliver an accurate attack. London buses were hurriedly converted into mobile attack teachers complete with Asdic simulators; a 'bridge' on the upper deck contained the Asdic control whilst the 'lower deck' was fitted as a plotting room. Anti-Submarine weapons were also being steadily improved and work was progressing on the

170

Industrial Might: Whilst the Reich's Organisation Todt poured thousands of tons of steel and concrete into the gigantic U-boat pens in France (above), on the other side of the Atlantic the huge 'Ships for Britain' programme was in full swing (below) with the launching of the *Ocean Vanguard*.

development of an ahead-throwing weapon called the 'Hedgehog', to allow the escort to maintain Asdic contact during the final critical moments of an attack.

A far more unusual device was the Admiralty Net Defences, a First War idea in which hanging nets would stop the U-boats' torpedoes, but the first AND ship was hit by a torpedo which went straight through. An improved class of ocean escort, the River Class sloops, were ordered in July. They were nearly twice the size of the Flower Class corvettes, and faster at 20 knots. Radar sets, rugged and reliable enough for the surface escorts, were also coming into service, and by the autumn the more efficient Type 271 was available which, could detect a surfaced submarine at 5,000 yards or 8 feet of periscope at 1,300 yards. Shipborne HF/DF 'Huff-Duff', (High Frequency Direction Finding) was also installed so that an escort could take a fix on a U-boat's radio.

The Battle of the Atlantic Committee's efforts had not only been directed to improving the fighting services, its most immediate effect had been felt in the docks and shipyards of Britain. By mid-July, a reduction of 700,000 tons had been made in the tonnage under repair and port efficiency had been dramatically improved, with substantial time being saved in the turn-around of shipping. Air defences had been increased with additional anti-aircraft batteries and fire-fighting services. A novel scheme for camouflaging the Liverpool docks by spreading a thin film of coal dust over the harbour entrances at the rate of ten tons of coal per hour was 'nearing a solution'.

In view of this brighter picture, Churchill had to issue a warning to the Cabinet: 'There must be no complacency. Nothing should be said in public that the Battle of the Atlantic had been won, since there might well be surprises in store for us.' He was one of the few who knew that the advantages of Special Intelligence could be destroyed if an entirely new set of cyphers was introduced for the Enigma coding machines.

STOP HITLER NOW!

Meanwhile, in the United States' shipyards the US Maritime Commission, directed by the tough-talking Admiral Emory S. Land, was struggling to obtain enough steel plate to fulfil his ambitious 'Ships for Britain' programme. It had been launched with a great fanfare the previous year with a £10 m. order for 60 cargo ships placed with construction magnate Henry J. Kaiser. On 17 August, 1941, the 10,000 ton *Ocean Vanguard*, the first of the new fleet, launched herself prematurely before the Admiral's wife Betty could make her speech. Fortunately she had the presence of mind to smash the bottle of champagne as the hull slid down the ways.

American industry was gearing up for war, but public opinion still favoured staying out. The interventionists had redoubled their efforts during the summer of 1941 to persuade the Americans to 'Stop Hitler Now', only to be faced by equally noisy isolationists whose sympathies sometimes bordered on open support for the Nazis.

In the autumn of 1941 it looked as though Hitler might be proved right in his sceptical view of American productive capacity, but the President took a personal hand and General Marshall was requested to examine American war needs and to formulate a distribution system which would satisfy the requirements both of the US forces and their allies. It was an opportunity for the Chiefs of Staff to draw up a strategic assessment revealing the full implications of American involvement in the shooting war. In his report, prepared with the assistance of Admiral Stark, Marshall concluded that:

> Germany and her European satellites cannot be defeated by the European powers now fighting against her. Therefore, if our European enemies are to be defeated, it will be necessary for the US to enter the war and to employ a part of the armed forces offensively on the Eastern Atlantic and in Europe or Africa.

He advised that plans should immediately be made for a simultaneous war in both the Pacific and Atlantic, warning that an 'inconclusive peace' would be just as dangerous for American security, since it would give Germany the opportunity 'to reorganise Europe and to replenish her strength'.

If Roosevelt still clung to the belief that the Axis might be defeated by a sea strategy alone, Marshall dashed his hopes with the unpalatable fact the US could not hope to avoid involvement in a major land campaign because, 'by themselves naval and air forces seldom, if ever, win important wars. It should be recognised as an almost invariable rule that only land armies can finally win wars.

This judgment, and Marshall's gigantic estimates for equipping an army of 8 m. men, shook the President. For the first time the staggering costs of global war had been spelt out. Before Roosevelt received Marshall's final study, the Germans had already fired their first shots against the United States.

The isolationist 'America First' organisation was active but was now opposed by a strong new interventionist group, the 'Fight for Freedom' which abandoned the gentlemanly approach of the 'Century Group'. In July, a 'Stop Hitler Now' campaign was launched, with 'V for Victory' slogans, car stickers, buttons and badges. Using a comic strip style, advertisements were run by Fight for Freedom in the main newspapers. American readers were told that Hitler and his team of 'Berlin Bullies', 'Fats' Goering, 'Spider' Goebbels, 'Heel' Hitler, 'Rats' Ribbentrop, 'won't tolerate baseball games or football or basketball or anything else that smacks of sportsmanship or fair play . . .' 'There's something sacred about the right to call a player a bum or to dub a rookie 'Stinky'. We've got to protect these rights. Beat the hell out of Hitler!'

The isolationist campaign was to suffer a severe setback after a bitter speech by Charles Lindbergh, one of its leading lights, who, in September at Des Moines, threatened: 'Instead of agitating for the Jewish groups in this country should be opposing it in every possible way, for they will be the first to feel its consequences . . .'

Not all the isolationist campaigners had restricted their activities to speechmaking, some, like Texas oil dealer William Rhodes Davis, had worked for two years as a Nazi undercover agent. Using his Eurotank refinery in Hamburg and German funds channelled through Zurich banks, he had tried to set up a secret oil supply route from Mexico to the Reich. In 1939, as a

The Berlin Connection: Oil man W. R. Davis (above right). His secret dealings with the Kriegsmarine and his association with the isolationist opposition to Roosevelt, particularly Union boss John L. Lewis (above) was exposed shortly before his sudden death in June 1941. The activities of the pro-German pressure groups had little effect on the Administration which agreed to the repair of the battleship HMS *Malaya* (below) in Brooklyn Navy Yard to relieve the strain on British yards.

one-man peace mission, he had tried to enlist the President's support and failed. A year later Davis was the agent through which $1½ m. of Nazi money was spent trying to prevent Roosevelt being re-elected. He had associated with leading isolationists as well as enlisting the support of the influential left wing Union leader, John L. Lewis of the United Mineworkers in an attempt to raise five million workers' votes against the President. His sudden death raised rumours of foul play, but the FBI discreetly discouraged any official enquiry.

The campaign against the Nazi agents and undercover business interests in the United States had been conducted with discreet efficiency by the 'British Security Coordination Office' headquartered in New York's Rockefeller Plaza under William Stephenson, an influential and well-connected Canadian whom Churchill had code-named 'Intrepid'. With the tacit approval of the White House, who found it a useful way to keep track of Nazi American activities, BSC had been responsible for the press exposure of the German business connection of firms like ITT. The steps taken by the President to freeze all Axis funds had finally cut off what had been a lucrative financial connection for quite a few American corporations.

However neither German agents nor the hard-line isolationists had been able to prevent the American Administration from supplying a significant part of all British food imports by late 1941. Much of these Lend-Lease supplies were 'luxuries' for the British, such as canned fruit, beans, condensed milk, cheese and the celebrated Spam (chopped ham). These were made available on a special points rationing system, 'borrowed' from Germany.

A study of the American food programme in the US by Dr J. T. Palmer pointed out that the Americans had committed themselves to 'furnish one fourth of the food supply of Great Britain in 1942, enough to feed 10 m. people'. On Britain's shopping list were 500 m. dozen eggs, 18 m. pounds of chicken, 750 m. pounds of pork and lard as well as millions of cases of canned fruit and vegetables. Britain was able to get most of her supplies of wheat, sugar and other bulk products from Canada and other Empire sources, but the US planned to supply 'rich concentrated foods such as milk, eggs and cheese rich in protein and vitamins which conserve shipping space'. Since America had no beef surplus, and cattle took five years to rear, it was decided that '9 m. hogs' would provide an important supply of protein and the Ministry of Food set to work to popularise the new foods, 'Spam Fritters' and dried egg omelettes became the subjects of a major publicity campaign on the BBC and in cinema newsreels.

Whilst the British and American governments could be confident that the food situation was proceeding well, the position with regard to munitions was far from good. British studies by the North American Supply Council had shown that: 'By the end of 1942 the much vaunted American production will not be much greater than that of our own and Canada combined,' and Lord Beaverbrook had complained to Averell Harriman in September that now they were faced with a vastly expanding aid programme to Russia ' . . . many of our munitions requirements cannot be met'.

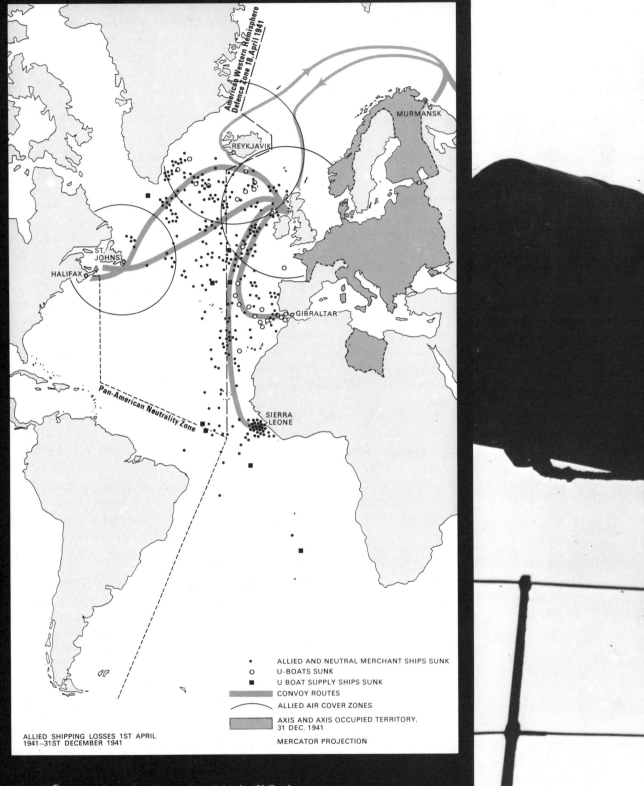

American Western Hemisphere
Defence Zone 18, April 1941

MURMANSK

REYKJAVIK

ST.
JOHNS

HALIFAX

GIBRALTAR

Pan-American Neutrality Zone

SIERRA
LEONE

- ALLIED AND NEUTRAL MERCHANT SHIPS SUNK
○ U-BOATS SUNK
■ U BOAT SUPPLY SHIPS SUNK
CONVOY ROUTES
ALLIED AIR COVER ZONES
AXIS AND AXIS OCCUPIED TERRITORY,
31 DEC. 1941

ALLIED SHIPPING LOSSES 1ST APRIL
1941–31ST DECEMBER 1941

MERCATOR PROJECTION

Aboard a US Navy destroyer a seaman stands by the 'Y Gun'
depth-charge thrower ready to give a hostile reception to any
U-boat entering the American Hemisphere Defence zone.

12. Damn the Torpedoes– Full Speed Ahead!

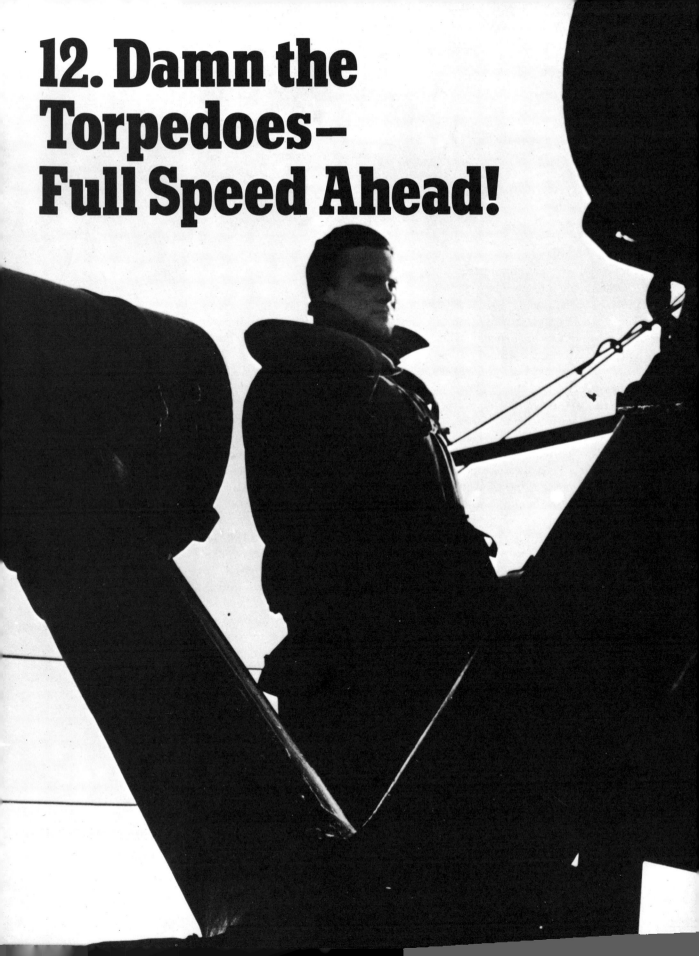

'We are starting considerable operations between North America and Iceland and the Good Lord knows, if the Germans want an excuse for war they can have plenty.' So wrote Admiral Stark, the US Chief of Naval Operations, at the end of August 1941, anticipating that the Atlantic Fleet deployment to Iceland would soon bring the 'incident', which, as Roosevelt had promised Churchill, would allow United States naval activity to be stepped up. The American patrols ranged over three-quarters of the North Atlantic ocean and had explicit orders to deal aggressively with the 'threat of attack' which was to be presumed from the presence of any Germans discovered in the vast expanse of ocean that Roosevelt had now deemed 'our side'. At the beginning of September, Hitler was given his first 'excuse' when an incident occurred between Greenland and Iceland, in a U-boat infested area called 'Torpedo Junction' by the merchantmen.

Early on the forenoon of 5 September 1941 the old flush-deck destroyer, USS *Greer*, was intercepted some 125 miles from Iceland by an RAF Hudson which urgently signalled by lamp that a U-boat had just crash-dived directly on her course. Unable to decide whether the destroyer would join in the hunt, the pilot headed off to circle the spot where the enemy had submerged. The senior officer aboard the *Greer*, the Commander of Destroyer Division 61, rapidly decided that the 'proper action' was to track the U-boat which was presenting a 'threat' to US shipping and began an Asdic hunt, only to find his ship the target for two torpedoes.

The *Greer* carried on the search for over four hours before regaining contact and delivering a final depth charge pattern. Oberleutnant Fraatz, commanding U-652, extricated his boat by going deep and later radioed to base that he had been attacked by what he had taken to be a British destroyer.

A report on the incident was immediately radioed to Washington reaching the Oval Office desk within a matter of hours. After studying it the President decided to move cautiously as it was clear that the *Greer* had provoked the attack and it was not until 11 September that an indignant Roosevelt broadcast to the nation on the 'piracy, legally and morally' of the attack, which he presented as part of a 'Nazi design to abolish the freedom of the seas and to acquire absolute control and domination of the seas'.

Accusing Hitler of attempting to destroy 'the bridge of ships, which we are building across the Atlantic and over which we shall continue to roll the implements of war to help destroy him', the President now promised that the US Navy would 'protect all merchant ships – not only American ships but ships of any flag – engaged in commerce on our defensive waters . . . ' The President presented his case with vivid imagery:

> When you see a rattlesnake poised, you don't wait until it has struck before you crush it. These Nazi submarines and raiders are the rattlesnakes of the Atlantic. They are a menace to the free pathways of the high seas. They are a challenge to our sovereignty . . . In waters we deem necessary to our own safety American warships and planes will no longer wait until Axis submarines lurking under the water, or Axis raiders on the surface of the sea, strike their deadly blow first.

The US Navy now found itself in a state of undeclared war, as Admiral Stark wrote 'So far as the Atlantic is concerned, we are all but, if not actually, in it.'

Proper Action: On 5 September 1941 the USS *Greer* (above in heavy seas) encountered U-652. Captain Laurence Frost USN logged the action he took to deal with the 'threat':

1032 British plane attacked submarine which was then dead ahead of *Greer*.

1240 Bearing of submarine changed rapidly to left and then to the right. Range decreased rapidly as if submarine were heading towards ship.

1247 (about) Lost sound contact at 150 yards, bearing broad on the starboard bow. The disturbance visible in the water as the submarine approached the ship was reported to Captain.

1248 Ship was going ahead 10 knots on port engine. Torpedo impulse bubble sighted 25 yards abeam of bridge to starboard. All engines ahead 25 knots, full left rudder. Torpedo track sighted on port quarter.

1250 (about) Commander Destroyer Division 61 ordered *Greer* to attack. Full right rudder changed course approximately 180 deg. in order to attack submarine.

1256 Attacked with eight depth charges without aid of sound.

1258 Sighted torpedo track broad on starboard bow and which passed well clear to port – about 300 yards. *Greer* began search of area, speed 15 knots.

In London, Churchill was delighted by the news. 'The dispositions made by the President must certainly lead to conflict with the U-boats,' he noted, anticipating that the 'shoot-on-sight' orders must force Hitler to declare war. To his intense disappointment there was as yet no reaction from Berlin. It was apparent that Hitler, preoccupied with the Russian front, was not looking for excuses to start a war with the United States. Admiral Raeder felt differently and, accompanied by Dönitz, flew to Hitler's Rastenburg headquarters on 17 September to try and persuade the Führer to remove the restrictions on attacking American shipping. Raeder argued forcibly that, 'German forces must expect offensive war measures by these US forces in every case of an encounter. There is no longer any difference between British and American ships.'

Hitler did not agree. He was not prepared to be provoked into attacking the United States and was still confident that 'September will bring the great decision in the Russian campaign'. The Admirals were told to 'avoid any incidents in the war on merchant shipping before the middle of October'. He also instructed that an immediate signal should be sent out to the U-boats informing them of the necessity for strictly obeying their existing orders. This came as a severe blow to U-boat Command who were planning to renew their offensive against the North Atlantic convoys.

On the day that Hitler vetoed any lifting of the restrictions on his U-boat commanders, the US Navy took over protection of the Newfoundland to Iceland leg of the convoy routes. To the cheers of the local Canadian escort, the destroyer USS *Ericsson* steamed to the head of 51 heavily laden ships of convoy HX 150 for the first stage of their eastward passage across the Atlantic. Four days later Captain Deyo USN was safely handing over his charge to the British escort at a Mid-Ocean Meeting Point (MOMP) with the signal, 'As in the last war I know our people afloat will see eye to eye'.

The first US convoy had been fortunate in getting through unspotted by the concentration of seventeen U-boats already patrolling between Greenland and Iceland. The seven most westerly boats, code-named *Markgraf*, were combing the convoy routes like a giant rake. With some twenty miles between each U-boat to aid reconnaissance, the group was able to sweep 200 miles of ocean and, the slow east-bound convoy SC 42 which had sailed before HX 150 ran straight into the teeth of the trap.

The Admiralty Tracking Room was aware of the U-boat concentration in 'Torpedo Junction' but could not fix the precise position of the *Markgraf* group in time to save the convoy. This serious lapse in 'Special Intelligence' resulted directly from the recent introduction of new cyphering instructions for the U-boats' Enigma machines. Now the decrypting teams at Bletchley Park were having to wrestle for many days before any part of the U-boat traffic could be decoded. Even so, the Canadian escorted convoy might have escaped had not U-85 sighted its smoke by chance as she headed for her station at the northern end of the *Markgraf* line, 60 miles from Greenland's barren Cape Farewell. Early on the afternoon of 9 September the signal went out from the Kernevel U-boat HQ ordering the Markgraf group to concentrate on 'U-85's convoy' for a pack attack that night.

ATTACK AND SINK

Unfortunately for Lieutenant Commander Jackson RCN, leading the three corvettes in the Canadian destroyer *Kenogami*, the night was clear with a full moon which assisted four U-boats to press home a fierce attack. His report reveals the difficulties confronting the slow escorts that allowed the U-boats to penetrate the defensive screen and get amongst the ships.

> A submarine was sighted, proceeding away from the convoy towards the coast. We endeavoured to overtake it but our speed was not sufficient to do so, and at 2310 it disappeared. We also lost Asdic contact at the time. During the rest of the night frequent attacks took place but we obtained no more contacts.

Eight ships were torpedoed that night and three more sunk next morning as the convoy changed course time and again in a vain effort to throw off its attackers. The U-boats clung on, as Dönitz radioed 'This convoy must not get through. U-BOATS PURSUE, ATTACK AND SINK.'

Some U-boats were already reporting that they had run out of torpedoes and the more distant *Markgraf* boats were racing to join the battle. Not all reached the convoy. U-501 had the ill fortune to run across two Canadian corvettes, HMCS *Chambly* and *Moosejaw*, on a training exercise. They managed to sink the U-boat in a carefully co-ordinated hunt before arriving in the middle of a night attack. These reinforcements were badly needed since four more U-boats reached the convoy at dusk just as the last escorting Catalina flying boat departed. Seven more ships were sent to the bottom before the following morning when the returning air patrols and five fresh British escorts arrived.

Although the battle of SC 42 cost two U-boats, the sinking of 16 of the convoy's 64 ships was regarded as a notable success for U-boat Command and it raised morale at a critical time. It had shown that, given sufficient numbers, a Wolf Pack could break through the escort and cause havoc. As Lieutenant Commander Jackson RCN reported, 'The submarines showed great daring in their attacks and had no hesitation in coming to the surface. They often surfaced among the convoy and raised their periscopes even in daylight.'

The battle of SC 42 convinced Dönitz that the key to success against the Atlantic convoy routes lay not in fixed dispositions of U-boats, whose location might be discovered or harassed by aircraft, but by deploying U-boat patrol lines in the waters off southern Greenland where the convoy routes bunched outside the range of air cover before swinging north for the passage across the Atlantic. His calculation that the new area was 'particularly favourable' for Wolf Pack operations was confirmed a week after the assault on convoy SC 42 when the *Brandenburg* Group sank four ships from the slow eastbound convoy SC 44. But on the other side of the Atlantic, 200 miles off the coast of Ireland, the *Seawolf* Group was far less effective. Their patrol line was frequently broken up by Coastal Command aircraft forcing the boats to submerge and *B-Dienst* reported that the enemy, 'is aware of the patrol line and can avoid it'. U-boat Command soon abandoned attempts to operate

War in Warm and Cold Waters: In the autumn of 1941 when the large-scale attacks were resumed against the Atlantic 'Mainline', the crews of U-boats and escorts (top), standing by the depth-charge traps of a Canadian destroyer, battled against appalling weather. It was very different for the large Type IX U-boats operating off the West African Coast (below) whose crews had plenty of time to enjoy the tropical weather.

submarine groups in the Eastern Atlantic within range of the air patrols from Britain.

Dönitz now switched his attentions to the waters off the Azores and the Cape Verde Islands as seven of the large type IX boats were sent south to intercept shipping on the way to the Cape route. At first they were successful when convoy SL 87 lost 9 ships after a three-day chase by four U-boats. After this, the U-boat commanders discovered that convoys were few and far between because the Admiralty had diverted independent shipping west into the American Neutrality zone where it was safe from attack.

The difficulties experienced in locating merchant shipping in the South Atlantic gave Dönitz strong grounds for believing once more that the British had penetrated his communications systems. His suspicions grew stronger when two U-boats, arriving for a refuelling rendezvous at remote Tarafel Bay in the Cape Verde Islands, narrowly escaped a salvo of torpedoes from the British submarine *Clyde*.

In spite of this interference with his supply system, Dönitz was determined to press ahead with plans to attack the heavy shipping on the Cape route and in October, three more long-range U-boats set out for the Cape together with the supply ship *Python*, to join boats which had successfully refuelled on the second attempt in the Cape Verde Bay. The Admiralty Tracking Room were well aware of what was afoot and of the German plans to refuel the U-boats from the returning raider *Atlantis* and the *Python* at secret mid-ocean rendezvous points. After weighing the possible risks of exposing ULTRA, the Admiralty decided that the only way to protect the Cape from the impending blitz was to smash the U-boats' supply system.

The first interception took place on 21 November 1941, when the cruiser *Devonshire* interrupted the rendezvous between the *Atlantis* and U-126. The Kriegsmarine's star raider, which had accounted for 22 ships in her long cruise, was soon in flames and U-126, which had managed to crash-dive, before the shelling began, surfaced to carry out rescue operations. With 305 survivors aboard, the raider's lifeboats were towed for two days to a new rendezvous with the supply ship *Python*. It was bad luck for the *Atlantis'* survivors when ten days later, as the *Python* was busy replenishing U A and U-68, the British cruiser *Dorsetshire* steamed over the horizon. The supply ship was scuttled and the U-boats, which had crash-dived in panic, surfaced to pick up survivors. Two other U-boats in the area were ordered to join the rescue and each packed with over 100 extra men, they started their 2,500 mile voyage home.

These disasters cut short Dönitz's offensive against the Cape and the loss of the supply ships increased his fears that the British might be reading his signals. Yet whenever he raised this possibility with Berlin he was bluntly told: 'This matter is being continually examined by the Naval War Staff and is *considered out of the question*.'

'A GREAT VICTORY'

If the U-boat offensive was failing in the south, Dönitz was able to balance this against the success of operations against the Gibraltar convoys where the mounting scale of attacks by both U-boats and Luftwaffe worried the Admiralty. Special Intelligence had revealed that the Focke Wulf Condors were employing successful new tactics; instead of attacking the convoys the aircraft now circled round them, transmitting homing signals for the U-boats. These tactics made it almost impossible to route convoys around patrol lines on the Gibraltar run and the Germans received good intelligence whenever a convoy sailed from their agents in Algeciras armed with powerful Zeiss binoculars.

The British were severely handicapped by Coastal Command's inability to maintain continuous air cover on the Gibraltar run. The CAM ships had only a very limited effect because their Hurricane fighters could only be launched once and it was not until the escort carrier *Audacity* arrived in September, that air cover improved and her US-built Martlet fighters began shooting down the Focke Wulfs. But she could not cover every convoy.

Casualties on the Gibraltar run mounted alarmingly during the autumn of 1941 and after sinking five ships and the destroyer *Cossack* from HG 75 in October, the Admiralty decided to suspend the convoys until a sufficiently strong escort could be assembled to fight the ships through.

The showdown battle began on 14 December 1941 when the 31 ships of HG 76 sailed from Gibraltar with a formidable escort of 16 warships; two destroyers, four sloops, nine corvettes, the escort carrier *Audacity* and the CAM ship *Darwin*. The convoy's defences were centred around the experienced 3rd Escort Group commanded by the redoubtable Lt. Commander F. J. Walker RN in the sloop *Stork*. Tall and gaunt, 'Johnny' Walker was the Royal Navy's leading anti-U-boat tactician.

The assembly and sailing of HG 76 and its powerful escort were duly reported by the German agents and Dönitz was ready. The seven U-boats of the *Seeräuber* Group patrolling west of Gibraltar were immediately signalled to intercept and the Focke Wulf Condors of 1 KG40 from Bordeaux began to search for the convoy. It was not until two days had passed that they first sighted HG 76, because Walker had set his course far to the south, after

In Good Hands: After months of heavy losses on the Gibraltar run, HG 76 sailed on 14 December 1941 for Britain with the Royal Navy's most dedicated U-boat killer, Captain 'Johnny' Walker (below) prepared to give no quarter in a showdown with the Wolf Packs and Focke Wulf's. The large escort under his command included a CAM ship (bottom) with its single Hurricane and RAF pilot ready to challenge enemy reconnaissance bombers.

Don't mind me, I'm only the pilot.

receiving intelligence warnings. By dusk, the most southerly U-boat of the *Seeräuber* Group had made contact and a second arrived during the night of the 16 September. First blood went to the escort the following morning, when U-131, shadowing the convoy, tried to shoot it out with Martlets from the *Audacity*, only to be sunk by the destroyers before she could dive.

Two more of the *Seeräuber* Group arrived during the second night but three U-boats were not enough to penetrate Walker's heavy escort disposed in an outer screen of five and an inner barrier of eight warships. After an undisturbed night the convoy Commodore signalled: 'Never mind the gathering storm. With the score one for nil, the convoy is confident it is in good hands.' This was shortly to be made two nil when U-434, the only U-boat still shadowing, was spotted early that morning and sunk.

The U-boats had now lost touch with the convoy and throughout the daylight hours *Audacity's* fighters tried to keep the Focke Wulfs away, but shortly before nightfall the German pilots managed to home the U-boats back on to target. That night Dönitz radioed new tactics and U-574 and U-108 moved into position to attack the escorts and punch a hole through the convoy's defences. This soon became evident to Walker. He had just finished signalling the destroyer *Stanley* 1½ miles on his port quarter when, 'she went up, literally in a sheet of flame, several hundred feet high. It was reported to me later that torpedoes had passed astern of *Stork* at about the same time'.

The destruction of one of his destroyers brought Walker racing to the attack like an avenging angel. Turning 16 points at full speed he quickly picked up an Asdic contact and made two fast depth-charge runs which brought U-434 to the surface. The hunt became fast and furious, vividly described in Walkers' report:

> The ensuing chase lasted 11 minutes and I was surprised to find later by the plot *Stork* had turned three complete circles. The U-boat appeared to be turning continuously to port just inside the *Stork's* turning circle at a speed of only 2 or 3 knots less than the latter's best. I kept her illuminated with Snowflakes – which were quite invaluable for their unusual action. Some 4″ was fired from the forward mountings until the guns could not be sufficiently depressed, after which the gun crews, reduced to fist-shakings, roared curses at an enemy who several times seemed to be a matter of feet away rather than yards. A burst of two machine gun rounds were fired when these could bear; but the prettiest shooting was made by my First Lieutenant (GTS Gray DSC RN). With a stripped Lewis gun over the top of the bridge screen, he quickly reduced the conning tower to a mortuary.

Eventually I managed to ram her just before the conning tower from an angle of about 20 deg on her starboard quarter, and roll her over. She hung for a few seconds on the bow and again on the Asdic dome and then scraped aft where she was greeted by a 10 charge pattern (9 only fired) at shallowest settings. I was informed that a Boche in the water, holding up his arms and crying "*Kamerade*", received the contents of the thrower in his face instead.

At first light the Focke Wulfs returned to home in more U-boats and the air battle flared up with HMS *Audacity's* Martlets airborne all day driving them off. In one battle the fighters dived and climbed as an enemy plane, 'attempted to escape first in the clouds and then to the water. They presently returned leaving a very dead Wulf'.

In spite of these strenuous efforts, five U-boats had been homed in by nightfall and Walker knew that, 'the net of U-boats around us seemed at this stage to be growing uncomfortably close'. He decided to try to outwit the Wolf Pack by a drastic alteration of course, relying on a mock battle with starshell and depth charges as a diversion. Unfortunately the plan 'was a flop'. A panicky merchant ship let off a 'Snowflake' by mistake, at once revealing the convoy's true position and:

> The balloon went up at 22.33, one ship was heard, and vaguely seen, to be torpedoed on our starboard bow. Off went all the 'snowflakes' again, but no rockets from the casualty.

Then a few minutes later the U-boats struck a devastating blow at Walker's defences by torpedoing *Audacity*. Most of the carrier's off-duty crew were playing tombola, but Seaman Gunner George Parr was on watch on the port forward pom-pom, when his 'blood froze, for coming straight for our port quarter was a thin streak of tell-tale bubbles – a tin fish'. He just had time to warn the gun's crew before the torpedo struck. The lights went out and the ship lurched to port.

> The captain ordered all boats and floats to be lowered to the water when there came a shout to open fire on the port beam. The U-boat had been spotted a few hundred yards off. I managed to get the gun to bear and depressed on the port side. I had fired one round when another row of bubbles came streaking towards us and all hell broke loose. Flames and smoke blotted out everything. The whaler that was being lowered forward of me just shot skywards, taking the injured man and the crew up with it in a shower of splinters. The ship groaned horribly, water rushing in everywhere. The order came to abandon ship. Two of my mates shouted 'Stick by us!' I never saw them again.
>
> There was a huge rush of water along the upper deck. I dived straight over. I came to the surface and struck out for a Carley float. I managed to clamber aboard and just lay gazing with awe at the last of my ship; as she slipped below the waves there came a final cheer as a salute from the men in the water. Then silence.

The loss of the carrier was a serious setback for Walker, and disaster almost overtook his own ship when the *Deptford* rammed her the following afternoon. However, he was relieved to find that, 'The damage was serious enough but not vital. *Deptford's* stem had walked straight into the temporary prison and two of the five Boches were pulped literally into a bloody mess'. Walker managed to get under way but with the number of U-boats increasing 'it was difficult not to take a somewhat gloomy view of the situation'.

However, only one merchant ship had so far been lost and, although it was not known at the time, U-567 had been destroyed by the *Deptford*. The convoy was now in range of the UK-based Liberators but preparing for that night's attack Walker decided, 'there was clearly one thing not to be done and that was to hold the convoy on a steady course and passively await attack. I could think of nothing better than last night's ruse.'

This time the strategy worked. As two escorts fought a diversionary mock battle with starshell and depth-charges, the convoy turned on to a new course. 'All went according to plan and a quietish night ensued'. His report noted 'there were some very angry [U-boat] captains on the morning of the 23rd.'

The Germans had suffered a severe defeat with the loss of four of Group *Seeräuber's* seven boats, it was made more bitter for Dönitz by the destruction of one of the few surviving ace commanders, Kapitänleutnant Endrass in U-567. The escort had also suffered but only one merchant ship had been lost and HG 76's Convoy Commodore was in no doubt who had won the battle, he signalled Walker, 'You have won a great victory. On behalf of the convoy deepest congratulations and many thanks.'

The defeat of the attack on HG 76 added to U-boat Command's increasing frustration as it became clear that the offensive on both sides of the Atlantic was not yielding the anticipated success. September's total sinking of 200,000 tons had dropped to 156,000 in October and a mere 62,000 tons in November, the lowest for 18 months, but it rose again in December to 156,000 tons.

The principal reason for the failure was the diversion in October of a substantial part of Dönitz's force to set up operations in the Mediterranean. The Middle East campaign had brought unexpected benefits to the Atlantic war as the U-boats were moved, on Hitler's direct orders, to counter the Royal Navy's drive against Rommel's sea supply line. In mid-November, Dönitz protested to Raeder that the Führer's new orders to send 25 of his 29 operational boats into the Mediterranean 'Mousetrap' would bring heavy losses just getting them through the heavily patrolled Straits of Gibraltar and that such a transfer of his strength threatened 'a cessation of U-boat activities in the main Atlantic theatre of operations'.

Dönitz received no support from his Commander in Chief. Raeder still considered the Mediterranean strategy to be of decisive importance, pointing to the spectacular successes already achieved by their U-boats in sinking the carrier *Ark Royal* and the battleship *Barham*. Nor was there any immediate prospect of improving the chronic shortage of U-boats due to the slow rate at which they were entering service and being repaired. Little could be done to remedy the situation in the face of Hitler's refusal to give naval construction top priority and as more and more men were drained off by the Eastern Front. Raeder certainly had no intention of accepting Dönitz's radical plan set out in his 26 November memorandum for stopping all repair work on the large

Casualties of Battle: HMS *Audacity* (below) the Royal Navy's first escort carrier, converted from the captured German merchantman *Hanover*, was torpedoed on the last night of the battle. But her US built Martlet fighters had performed a valiant service in shooting down the shadowing Focke-Wulfs (above). Another victim of the 21 December was U-567 commanded by Kapitänleutnant Endrass (left) the Ace whose boat was the fourth to be destroyed in *Seeräuber* Group's defeat.

warships so as to release workers for the U-boats and the year ended, as Dönitz wrote, 'in an atmosphere of worry and anxiety for U-boat Command'.

In less than 12 months the U-boat triumphs of the first quarter of 1941 had declined into the 'meagre successes' of the summer and the final collapse of the autumn offensive. Since the end of March only 325 ships had been sunk for the loss of 28 German and Italian U-boats in the Atlantic, an exchange rate not much better than one in eleven. The same period had also seen a marked improvement in the efficiency of the British Anti-Submarine effort. In the last half of 1941, one out of every three U-boats attacked by surface craft was being badly damaged and one out of every seven sunk. The number of U-boats in commission had increased from about 50 to nearly 200 but this was insufficient to offset the transfer of strength to the Mediterranean and the general decline in their sinking rate – which had been halved since March. Moreover, the weight of American intervention was being increasingly felt.

AMERICANS UNDER FIRE

The United States was still maintaining an official neutrality but her Navy was now very much in evidence on the North Atlantic convoys. American ships took over from the local Canadian escorts at a Western Ocean Meeting Point (WESTOMP) south of Newfoundland and covered the convoys to a Mid Ocean Meeting Point (MOMP) off Iceland, where the British assumed responsibility. The US warships would then refuel in Iceland ready to shepherd another convoy back to Newfoundland.

The American commanders were very inexperienced and, against British advice, had adopted a close escort policy in placing their destroyers less than a mile from a convoy. This, as the Royal Navy had discovered in the early days of the war, gave the U-boats the advantage of being able to press home their attacks at close quarters.

The weakness of the American tactics was revealed in the first battle in which their escorts faced a big U-boat attack. Five US destroyers were sent to reinforce convoy SC 48, a 50-ship slow convoy which had sailed into heavy weather. Eleven ships were lost as stragglers ran into a U-boat patrol line on 15 October 400 miles south of Iceland. The first ship to be hit by a torpedo, fired by Kapitänleutnant Thurmann in U-553, was the 6,000 ton British freighter *Silvercedar*. Aboard was Able Seaman Hughes who remembered:

> The starboard lifeboat had been blown away with the explosion. I could hear the cries of the two youngsters, Faulkes and Peters trapped in their cabin on the boat deck as their cabin door was jammed – I had kept mine ajar on a hook as a precaution. At that moment the ship broke in half. I was submerged being sucked down and down, but eventually I broke surface and it was wonderful to gulp air and realise that I was alive. Everywhere was lit up like daylight by the chandelier-like flares and there was a tremendous amount of gunfire and explosions. My mind at this point went back over the years. I was very frightened at the prospect of dying and not seeing my mother again and although I was not a religious person I prayed to God to save me. I banged against the sides of the ship, someone at that moment must have been drawn into its propellors as I could hear screams and the threshing as they came out of the water.

The other torpedo of Thurmann's salvo sank the 5,000 ton Norwegian freighter *Ila*. Just before sunset next day on 16 October SC 48's reinforcements arrived. They were the five US destroyers *Plunkett*, *Livermore*, *Kearny*, *Greer* and *Decatur* together with the British destroyer HMS *Broadwater* and the Free-French corvette *Lobelia*, detached from a westbound convoy. Taking advantage of the American destroyers' proximity to the convoy and their lack of radar, the Wolf Pack closed to torpedo range and loosed off salvoes unmolested. The Norwegian freighter *Evriken* and the tanker *Teagle* were hit, followed by the corvette *Gladiolus*. Then nerves broke and the escorts started indiscriminately firing starshell and Snowflake which blinded look-outs and made it easier for the U-boats to sight their targets. The merchantman *Rym* was the next to be sunk and Schultze in U-432 arrived to torpedo the large 12,000 ton Norwegian tanker *Barfonn*:

> A colossal flash leapt from the convoy. In a moment it resolved itself into a tremendous flame which shot upwards from the water, accompanied by a roar like the passing of an express train. The great column of fire, whose diameter might have been equal to the length of the ship from whose tanks it sprang, seemed almost to reach the cloud base. The whole convoy was lit up by its brilliance.

Swinging out to avoid a Canadian corvette, the new US destroyer *Kearny* presented a perfect target for Kapitänleutnant Preuss in U-568 as he fired a spread of three torpedoes. One struck the destroyer's starboard engine room, killing seven men, and four more died as the explosion ripped through the deck carrying away the starboard wing of the bridge. The destroyer's siren had been jammed open and its high-pitched scream added to the confusion as *Kearny*'s captain, Lieutenant Commander Anthony L. Davis, struggled to keep control of his stricken ship with engine room equipment, compass and steering gear smashed. The bulkheads of the flooded starboard engine room were shored up by the damage control parties and under power from the port engine and escorted by the USS *Greer*, Davis was able to get his ship, all but cut in two by the torpedo, back to Iceland.

Five minutes after the *Kearny* had been hit the British destroyer HMS *Broadwater* was torpedoed by U-101 and, not so stoutly constructed as the new American warship, she soon sank. The attack on SC 48 had been highly successful for U-boat Command with nine merchant ships, two destroyers and one corvette sunk. Casualties were high and the 11 crewmen killed in the *Kearny* had brought the first American naval fatalities of the war.

The torpedoing of the *Kearny* occurred at a singularly inopportune time for Hitler because Congress was debating the Presidential request that the last remaining restrictions of the Neutrality Act be lifted.

'We have tried to avoid shooting', Roosevelt broadcast on 27 October, 'but the shooting war has started. And history recorded who fired the first shot': Hitler reacted to Roosevelt's statement by announcing:

> I have ordered German ships not to shoot when they sight American vessels but to defend themselves when attacked. I will have any German officer court martialled who fails to defend himself.

Three days later the Führer's determination not to be dragged into a war, and the President's resolve that Germany should provide the excuse to declare one, were to be tested when the American-escorted convoy HX 156 was sighted by Kapitänleutnant Erich Topp in U-552. His first torpedo slammed into the side of the American destroyer USS *Reuben James* just ahead of the forward funnel. 'With a terrific roar', a column of flame leapt into the air. When it disappeared every ship in the convoy saw 'a great black pall of smoke licked by moving tongues of orange.'

All the ship forward of number 4 stack had disappeared. One of the handful of survivors was Fireman Robert Carr who had a miraculous escape:

> There was a blinding flash. I felt I was swimming. Then I realised I couldn't feel any water under me. I turned my head down and I realised I was 25 feet above the water. Then I landed smack on my back. Parts of the ship, steel and jagged sections were flying through the air and hitting the water all around me.

The sea was soon covered with a filthy choking film of fuel oil which made it almost impossible for those struggling in the water to climb aboard the few rafts or grasp the scrambling nets of the four destroyers which came to their rescue. Only 46 survivors were picked up alive looking like 'black shiny seals' as one of the rescuers in the USS *Hilary P. Jones* vividly remembered:

> They were blown up and choking with oil and water, they're like small animals caught up in molasses. We are now in a black circle of water, surrounded by a vast silver ring of oil slick. The men to port are drifting towards us and the heaving lines are slipping through their greasy hands. Soon many eager hands are grasping the cargo net but our ship's upward roll breaks their weak slippery hold.

A hundred and fifteen American sailors were dead and Berlin waited anxiously for Washington's reaction. Hitler believed that war would be declared by the United States, but Admiral Stark, who had long felt and stated that 'the sooner we get in the better', noted, 'Events are moving rapidly towards a real showdown. . . The Navy is already in the war of the Atlantic but the country doesn't seem to realise it. . . . . Apathy to the point of open opposition is evident in a considerable section of the Press. . . . Whether the country knows it or not *we are at war*'.

Yet the President still waited. Churchill explained to South African Prime Minister, Jan Smuts, 'He [Roosevelt] went so far as to say to me 'I shall never declare war. I shall make war. If I were to ask Congress to declare war they might argue about it for three months'. Britain would have to be patient.

The tide might be inexorably edging the United States into war, but the increasingly dangerous interaction between the two great oceanic theatres began to present both Prime Minister and President with even greater problems. On 17 October 1941 the militarist War Minister, General Eiki Tojo, had become Japan's Prime Minister in a move which made conflict in the Pacific more likely as America tightened her oil embargo. The British were relying heavily on the Americans to protect their own and Dutch possessions in the Far East as well as the Dominions of Australia and New Zealand, but General Marshall had already warned the President that there would not be sufficient US army reinforcements to repel an attack on the Philippines by

Shooting but not War: The sinking by U-126 of the clearly identified US freighter *Lehigh* (above) off the West African coast on 19 October followed two weeks later by U-552's destruction of the destroyer *Reuben James* in the North Atlantic, led the President to announce on November 1 'The shooting war has started' – but he still hesitated to declare open war on Germany.

December 1941. A still more pessimistic Admiral Stark could not muster a strong force to counter the Japanese fleet until February 1942 at the earliest. 'We are at our wit's end in the Atlantic with the butter spread extremely thin and the job continuously increasing in toughness', he had written to his Pacific Fleet Commander, Admiral Husband E. Kimmel.

The Royal Navy were overstretched too, but had reluctantly fallen in with Churchill's proposal to send a powerful squadron to reinforce Singapore consisting of the battleship *Prince of Wales,* battlecruiser *Repulse* and the carrier *Indomitable*. 'This ought to serve as a deterrent on Japan. There is nothing like having something that can catch and kill anything' he had cabled the President on the 7 November 1941. 'The firmer your attitude and ours, the less chance of their taking the plunge.'

On 7 November 1941 the US Secretary of State, Cordell Hull, seeking a compromise solution to the rising tension in the Pacific with Ambassador Nomura and Tojo's envoy Saboru Kurusu, warned 'We should be on the lookout for a military attack by Japan anywhere at any time.' His fears were soon substantiated by the US intelligence 'Magic' which intercepted and decoded Tokio's secret wireless communications with their negotiators in Washington. On 22 November, following a meeting between the Japanese emissaries and the President, 'Magic' indicated that Tojo had already decided that an accord had to be reached by the 25 November – (it was later extended by 4 days) – 'After that things are automatically going to happen'. On 27 November 1941, the US Army and Navy were put on war alert in the Pacific as Britain and America expected the Japanese attacks to be launched in the Malay Peninsula.

GLOBAL WAR

It came as a devastating shock when news reached Washington on Sunday, 7 December 1941 that waves of Japanese carrier planes were bombing the Pacific Fleet in Pearl Harbour. Hopkins remarked that, if it were true, the Japanese 'had made the decision' for the President. It was late evening in England where Churchill happened to be entertaining the American Ambassador, John Winant, and Averell Harriman to dinner at Chequers. When they received the startling news on the radio, the Prime Minister wanted to declare war on Japan immediately. Winant cautioned him, 'Good God, you can't declare war on a radio announcement,' and insisted on putting a call through to the President. After Roosevelt had confirmed the bare facts, Churchill took the phone and asked, 'Mr President, what's all this about Japan?'. The familiar voice replied 'It's quite true. They have attacked us at Pearl Harbour. We are all in the same boat now.' Roosevelt expected that Congress would confirm his declaration of war against Japan the next day.

In Berlin the news of the Japanese attack was received with equal surprise. Ribbentrop, the German Foreign Minister, was officially 'delighted' and assured the Japanese Ambassador that 'immediate participation in the war by Germany and Italy was a matter of course'. But the Germans were surprised to discover that the President of the United States did not automatically include them when he went before Congress next day to announce the declaration of war on Japan. For three days the world wondered and waited. Roosevelt, worried that a demand for a formal commitment to the European war so soon after the traumatic shock of Pearl Harbour would stir up a divisive debate, hoped that Hitler would declare war first. But although the President anticipated this in his war speech to the nation, there was no certainty that Hitler would jump into war with America right away. The Führer's strategy was very definitely to avoid war with the United States until the Soviet Union had been crushed.

Yet, after two days of careful deliberation Hitler decided to go to war because he appreciated that 'sooner or later, the United States would come into the conflict'. His views had begun to change before Pearl Harbour when the full details of General Marshall's 'Victory Program' became known to the German High Command. In one of the most amazing – and potentially most damaging – newspaper scoops of the century, the isolationist Colonel McCormick's *Chicago Tribune* had published on 4 December all the significant details of the 'blueprint for total war', under the banner headlines 'F. D. R.'s WAR PLANS'. The details had been leaked by Burton K. Wheeler, the leading isolationist in the Senate. He had been brought the Secret 'Victory Program' briefs by a young Army Captain in the War Plans Division

Hitler's Move: In the aftermath of the Pearl Harbor (above, launches rescuing survivors from the *West Virginia*). Roosevelt waited two days for Hitler to declare war on the United States before signing the American declaration of hostilities against Germany (right). Hitler's decision had been strongly influenced by the *Chicago Tribune*'s publication 3 days before Pearl Harbor of the United States war strategy (below).

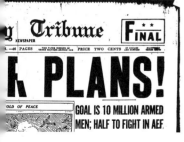

who had been fired by a determination to stop the President dragging America into what he passionately believed was the wrong war. Wheeler at once realised the potential damage that this could do the President and committed what was tantamount to treason, by passing all the details on to his contacts in the anti-Roosevelt press.

The revelations that the United States was determined to crush Nazi Germany was accepted in Berlin as 'incontrovertible intelligence' and Hitler's military advisers called for a revision of German strategy. Admiral Raeder pressed for a concentration on his Atlantic strategy and called for a series of co-ordinated operations with Germany's Axis partners striking the US Navy hard while it reeled from Japan's attack. He argued that

> All the calculations of the United States War Plan as published by the Chicago Tribune have now come to naught in view of the recent developments. A Pacific War, two or three years before the completion of a Two Ocean Navy, at a time when the army is not yet fully equipped and the giant armament machine has not yet gained momentum, must be most unwelcome to the United States Government.

It was this consideration which probably weighed above all others in confirming Hitler in his decision to declare war on the United States. On 11 December 1941 he addressed the Reichstag and after denouncing American War plans, he declared that Germany had been 'provoked' into declaring war on America because 'our patience has come to the breaking point'.

Germany had now taken on the world's largest industrial power. Outline proposals were put to Hitler for a new strategy to concentrate the maximum effort on eliminating Britain from the war before America could use her as a springboard for launching a massive invasion of Europe. This new thinking called for a major Mediterranean offensive in 1942 and an intensification of the Battle of the Atlantic, which was to be made the central campaign of the war.

But it was clear that Germany could only find the military resources to switch back to the West if she could effect a rapid stabilisation of the Eastern front. The Führer at first appeared to agree to this radical change in strategy. Five days later, however, he returned to his command headquarters in the Rastenburg Forest to find his generals were advising withdrawal of the mauled Panzer divisions from the Russian front. Instinctively he believed that a defensive posture against the Red Army would result in a demoralising debacle for the Wehrmacht. In stormy meeting with his Army Commanders the new strategy was dismissed as 'drivelling nonsense'.

Two days later Hitler sacked von Brauchitsch, his Army Commander, and took over the Army himself. At the same time he countermanded the new plans for a Western offensive. This, together with his declaration of war against the United States a week earlier, was Hitler's biggest mistake. He had rejected the one strategy that could have decisively disrupted the Anglo-American war effort.

13. The American Shooting Season

'Reports from the coastal waters off North America indicate that the U-boat campaign there will be successful for much longer than anticipated. U-123 signals that they have achieved results far above expectations'

DÖNITZ'S WAR DIARY, 17 January 1942

The first six months of Operation *Paukenschlag* were more successful than Dönitz dared to hope as more than 2 million tons of Allied shipping were sunk in the blitz that was unfolded from the St Lawrence to the Gulf of Mexico by successive waves of U-boats. Tankers were prime targets, their wrecked hulls could only be photographed by the few US air patrols which were unable to halt the tide of destruction. For the victorious U-boatmen the return to their bases was a time of champagne and flower celebrations. The crew of U-582 with their trophies from the US freighter *Stella Lykes* (right). Kapitänleutnant Vogelsang of U-132 celebrates with Moet & Chandon (far right).

'So we had won after all,' Churchill wrote of the climactic turning point in the war in December 1941. 'Many disasters, immeasurable cost and tribulation lay ahead, but there were no more doubts about the final outcome.' At the time, the Prime Minister was deeply worried that the US Chiefs of Staff and American public opinion might demand action to restore their prestige in the Pacific. Fearing that this might threaten the agreed 'Europe First' strategy the Prime Minister cabled the President suggesting a summit meeting 'to review the war plan in the light of reality and new facts'.

Churchill's suspicions that the Pearl Harbour attack might be influencing a redirection of American strategy increased when Roosevelt proposed postponing the meeting. On 9 December he cabled the President, 'it would be disastrous to wait another month before we settle common action in the face of the new adverse situation in the Pacific, I hope to start tomorrow night . . .' Two days later Roosevelt replied, accepting the need for another summit.

The alarming pace of the Japanese advances had changed Roosevelt's mind. Shanghai was captured within hours of Pearl Harbour; Hong Kong and US bases in the Philippines were bombed; Bangkok had fallen and a Japanese army was storming down the Malay Peninsula towards Singapore. Early on the morning of 10 December, Churchill was woken by a telephone call with the bitterest blow of all. 'In all the war I never received a more direct shock,' he wrote of the news that the *Prince of Wales* and the *Repulse* had been sunk by Japanese torpedo bombers in the Gulf of Siam.

As the British and Americans faced this disaster in the Far East, Dönitz and his staff were planning to deal an even greater blow to Allied seapower. Senior U-boat commanders were being briefed for an offensive off the Eastern Seaboard of the United States.

The Naval War Staff had already been asked to allocate at least twelve of the large Type IX U-boats with the long range necessary for the American offensive which had been code named *Paukenschlag* – 'Operation Drumroll', but Dönitz was dismayed that the Berlin staff was undermining his chances of achieving a 'spectacular success' when they only allowed him to deploy six boats. He was ordered not to withdraw those operating off Gibraltar or in the Mediterranean. As it turned out, only five Type IX boats were operational by mid-December and ready to set out for America, so that Dönitz now renewed his battle with the Naval Staff to step up operations in the Atlantic. He stressed the unacceptably high casualty rate in getting U-boats through to the Mediterranean and forcefully argued that it was unprofitable to send any more forces to the Arctic to attack the Russian convoys. He reminded his superiors in Berlin:

> If one considers the battle against Britain as decisive for the outcome of the war, then the U-boats must be given *no* task which diverts them from the main theatres of this battle. The war in the Atlantic has been suspended for weeks now – the first objective must be to resume it with new forces as soon as possible.

On 12 December, four days before the first of the *Paukenschlag* U-boats sailed for American waters, the new battleship *Duke of York* put out from the Clyde. Aboard were the British Prime Minister and his top advisers. With the war situation 'molten', Churchill was worried that the United States had

Europe First: In the days after Pearl Harbor some Washington critics argued for an all-out effort against Japan (above) but after Churchill had addressed Congress (below) on 26 December 1941, the Prime Minister was confident that American opinion was wholeheartedly behind the President's strategy of defeating Hitler first.

'**Victory Program**': The gigantic scale of the war effort was brought home to Americans when the President asked Congress for 17½ billion dollars in his 1942 budget. It had been increased dramatically after Victory Program Administrator Donald M. Nelson (below) had to double his targets for aircraft, shipping and tank production at the insistence of the British Minister of War Production, Lord Beaverbrook (above).

'embargoed everything for the present'. 'I hope to loosen them up' he told Foreign Secretary Anthony Eden, who was dispatched to Russia with strict instructions 'not to make any promises beyond our agreed quota of supplies.'

Dodging reported U-boats, the great battleship and her destroyer escort ploughed through heavy Atlantic storms within range of Luftwaffe bombers. Battened down for most of the voyage and observing strict wireless silence, Beaverbrook, the British Minister of War Production, complained they might 'just as well have travelled by submarine!'

The British team arrived in Washington on 22 December 1941, well-briefed to deal with 'the danger that the United States might pursue the war against Japan in the Pacific and leave us to face Germany'. When the formal sessions of the Arcadia Conference began between the Christmas festivities, the British pressed their strategy for a Mediterranean offensive followed by the liberation of Europe and both sides understood that their common plans could only become effective 'if British and American superiority in the Atlantic is maintained, if supply lines continue uninterrupted and if the British Isles are effectively safeguarded against invasion'.

The British were immensely relieved to find that General Marshall supported their fundamental argument, that 'Germany is still the prime enemy and her defeat is the key to victory.' This principle was reiterated and the strategic war plan, agreed at Arcadia, coincided almost exactly with the British objectives. The Axis powers were to be contained by strengthening the ring of steel around them, 'by sustaining the Russian Front, by arming and supporting Turkey, by increasing strength in the Middle East and by gaining possession of the whole North African coast for the prevention of German eruptions towards the Persian Gulf or the West Coast of Africa or elsewhere.' American troops were to be sent to relieve the British garrison in Northern Ireland and US bombers would join the RAF in an air offensive against the industrial heart of the Reich and the U-boat bases. To co-ordinate the allied war effort, a combined British-American Chiefs of Staff organisation was to be set up in Washington.

In a major political gesture of the new unity of purpose 22 nations, including the Soviet Union, agreed to sign the 'Declaration of the United Nations' on 1 January 1942 pledging an all-out effort against the Axis powers.

The realities of the allied strategy now depended on the American 'Victory Program' of war production and mobilisation together with the transportation of these supplies and troops across the Atlantic. If either of these elements failed, all Anglo-American plans would collapse. Yet even before the conclusion of the Arcadia talks, Lord Beaverbrook's supply experts from the Ministry of War Production expressed alarm at the lack of realism in American production estimates which were far too small to cope with a 'resourceful and determined enemy.' The British team then set about persuading Donald M. Nelson, the former Vice-president of the Sears-Roebuck mail-order corporation who was in charge of the Victory Program, to revise all his targets. American industry would have to support the Allies, expand its own armed forces and equip a 2 m. strong army for the Liberation of Europe in less than two years.

A HARD TIME

When the President announced the new production targets in his New Year message to Congress, the nation was at first stunned by the scale of effort required. Aircraft production was to be doubled in the current year and doubled again to 100,000 machines by 1943; tank production was to double to 45,000 and then rise to 75,000; ship construction was raised to 8 m. tons and then 10 m. and there were equally sky-high targets for military supplies.

The American public were already beginning to feel the squeeze on consumer production, and the announcement of tyre rationing that came with Japanese seizure of Malayan rubber, was only the first of many sacrifices that would have to be made in consumer goods. Churchill was confident that these sacrifices would be made, for when he had addressed Congress on 26 December he had sensed that the 'might and will power of the American nation' was now totally committed to victory. The optimistic mood of the 67-year-old premier was undiminished by the slight stroke that he had suffered while at the White House and, after a brief spell of recuperation, he gamely decided to fly across the Atlantic in one of the giant Boeing flying boats.

However, when Churchill reached No. 10 Downing Street on 16 January 1942, his high hopes faded. He faced a gloomy military situation; the Japanese advance in the Far East continued unchecked and reports from the Mediterranean were even worse. Rommel was forcing the British army back in Libya, and Malta was cut off.

Then the blow fell on the other side of the Atlantic. On January 12 Kapitänleutnant Hardegen in U-123 opened Operation *Paukenschlag* with a flourish by sinking the British steamer *Cyclops* 300 miles off Cape Cod. Next day, Kapitänleutnant Kals in U-130 torpedoed two freighters off Halifax, and on 14 January U-123 sank the 10,000 ton Panamanian tanker *Norness* within sight of the Nantucket lightship. The war had arrived at America's shores with a vengeance. The US press was alive with rumours of hundreds of U-boats prowling off the East Coast and German spies on the coast.

With few warships and aircraft available there was little that could be done to police the 2000 mile stretch of coastal waters from Maine to Florida. Facing public hysteria, the recently formed Eastern Sea Frontier's handful of

East Coast Slaughter: The havoc caused to shipping between Cape Cod and Cape Hatteras by the first wave of U-boats in January 1942 provoked a furious outcry in the press. Yet with the meagre Anti-Submarine forces at his disposal there was little that Eastern Sea Frontier Commander, Admiral Adolphus Andrews (above) could do. Hardegen in U-123 was able to carry out surface attacks on shipping by day and night (below, a tanker exploding in a pillar of flame off Cape Hatteras). Within weeks the huge losses of supplies were endangering the war effort.

Coastguard cutters was joined by four Navy 'Blimp' airships and twenty available aircraft; their wild goose chases followed hundreds of false sighting reports. Apart from barring the broadcasts of weather forecasts little could be done other than to share the hope of the *New York Times*: 'It is not believed ... that Germany could keep up widespread warfare of this sort'.

They were wrong. Dönitz had carefully calculated that his Type IX U-boats would have at least several weeks' fuel after crossing the Atlantic and he had briefed his commanders to conserve their 14 torpedoes, attacking only large ships and making tankers a special priority. Hardegen had already sunk two tankers and another freighter when he was joined on 18 January by Zapp in U-66 who sank the American tanker *Allen Jackson* off New York. Hardegen then closed in on the busy harbour, joking with his crew that he could make out dancers on the top of the Empire State building through his binoculars. The following night, after sinking an American freighter off Cape Hatteras he logged:

> It is a pity that there were not twenty U-boats here last night, instead of one. I am sure all would have found ample targets. Altogether, I saw about twenty steamships, some undarkened; also a few tramp steamers all hugging the coast.

The five U-boat commanders now on station were amazed to find the waterfront lights burning brightly. It was to be nearly three months before a coastal blackout was enforced in the face of protests from the Florida resorts that their tourist season would be ruined. After battling with the heavily defended Atlantic Convoys, the commanders were radioing reports of how easy it was to sink ships off the American coast. Their successes spoke for themselves. In two weeks 25 ships, totalling 200,000 tons, were sent to the bottom, over 70% being tankers. The spectacular achievements of the five Type IX's far exceeded Dönitz's expectations and the Naval War Staff gave permission for seven standard Atlantic Type VII U-boats to be sent into American waters, allowing four of the Type IX boats to be detached to open up the operations south of Cape Hatteras.

The growing 'U-boat Blitz' was a painful time for Admiral Adolphus Andrews, the 62-year-old Texan commanding the Eastern Sea Frontier. He knew that the U-boats were torpedoing tankers with impunity almost within sight of his Headquarters at 90 Church Street in downtown Manhattan. Early

The Cost of Sinking
If a submarine sinks two 6,000 ton ships and one 3,000 ton tanker, here is a typical account of what we have lost: 42 tankers, 8 six-inch howitzers, 88 twenty-five-pound guns, 40 two-pound guns, 24 armoured cars, 50 Bren carriers, 5,112 tons of ammunition, 600 rifles, 428 tons of tank supplies, 2,000 tons of stores and 1,000 tanks of gasoline.' Official Report

in the beginning of January Andrews had warned Admiral King, newly promoted on 20 December to be C-in-C US Fleet: 'Should the enemy submarines operate off this coast, this command has no force available to take action against them, either offensively or defensively'. In the face of mounting criticism the Navy did its best to restore confidence, maintaining on 24 January that 'an unspecified number of U-boats' had been sunk off the Atlantic coast but that 'details are to be kept secret to injure Nazi morale'. This contrasted oddly with the Army's willingness to parade airmen who claimed to have sunk enemy submarines.

When the U-boat blitz began, the British Admiralty had cabled Washington to ask what defensive measures were being put into operation to protect the shipping lanes. The Trade Division in London was horrified at the replies and the 'inadequate' state of the US Navy's defences. The Director of Trade Division, Captain B. B. Schofield, found it 'quite incomprehensible' that the Americans were so ill-equipped to deal with the U-boats. The US Navy had been kept fully briefed on anti-submarine warfare and a liaison officer had observed how the Trade Division ran the convoy system. Now, as the days passed with sinkings rocketing to unprecedented heights, and Admiral King appearing to order no effective action, Trade Division 'found it extremely difficult to be polite about it'. On 3 February 1942 King had turned down British suggestions to set up a unified command system for the Atlantic convoys. A week later Admiral Pound, the First Sea Lord, again cabled King, advising that a convoy system was the only way to deal with the U-boats and even proposed 'helping out' with 24 Royal Navy trawlers. Three days later, the American C-in-C replied frostily that 'continuous consideration was being given to coastal convoys, but that this would invite trouble unless adequate and suitable escorts were available', which was 'not the case at present'.

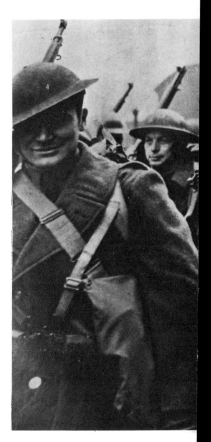

Admiral King's refusal of the British offer to provide sufficient escorts to make a start with an East Coast convoy system was received with amazement. His attitude was endangering the whole Atlantic supply system. Half the shipping casualties were occurring before joining or after leaving the convoys, with the net effect of reducing the total tonnage available for the Allies.

Soon it was the Royal Navy's turn to suffer a major blow to its prestige. In the late evening of 11 February 1942, the battleships *Scharnhorst,* and *Gneisenau* and the heavy cruiser *Prinz Eugen* broke out of Brest. The Führer had overidden his naval advisers and ordered the two battleships to sail up the Channel to join *Tirpitz* in Norway, where they could counter invasion threats and menace convoys carrying supplies to Russia. Hitler also believed: 'If the ships remain at Brest they will be put out of action by the enemy air force'.

The gamble paid off. Operation *Cerberus* took the British completely by surprise and the German squadron was not spotted until it reached Boulogne on 12 February. By then there was little that could be done to stop the warships racing through the Straits of Dover under a heavy fighter umbrella.

When they finally reached Wilhelmshaven, the Admiralty were relieved that the German ships could no longer threaten the Atlantic from Brest, but British public opinion did not easily accept the Navy's view that the episode was 'a tactical defeat but a strategic victory'. People were outraged at the German impudence and even the normally temperate London *Times* commented: 'Nothing more mortifying to the pride of seapower has happened in home waters since the 17th century.'

The British setbacks were only just beginning. News soon came that the Japanese had taken Singapore. Coming on top of the escape of the German battleships and news of Rommel's advances in North Africa, the mood of Britain became even blacker. To make matters worse, Churchill found himself in the middle of a political crisis. 'All in all it's a dark moment for him' Harriman cabled Washington as the embattled Prime Minister faced pressure from the Labour Party leaders to bring in Sir Stafford Cripps, who had made a considerable mark as Ambassador to Moscow, into the War Cabinet. Then the Minister of Production, the fierce Lord Beaverbrook, resigned after differences between the two about aid to the Soviet Union. A weary Churchill, in the midst of the crisis, cabled Roosevelt, 'Democracy has to prove that it can provide a granite foundation for war against tyranny'.

The only bright spot for the British during the dark weeks of early 1942 was the arrival of the first G.I.'s in Northern Ireland. 'YANKS HERE' were the only two huge words of welcome on the *Belfast Telegraph's* front page.

The mountain of rubbish that had been collected on the deck of one US transport was too much for the austerity-bound dockers. A Navy crewman recalled the race for the rubbish: 'Americans being rather wasteful, each longshoreman ended up with a grocery bag full of food to take home from that trash pile'.

This brought home the reality of a war economy to the Americans who had not yet experienced life under strict rationing. Appreciating the need to prevent shortages and stop inflationary price rises, the US Government had already printed and stockpiled millions of ration books. Voluntary economies were, however, being tried and advertisements told housewives not to throw away tin cans. The War Production Board introduced a 'Victory Style' fashion for men's suits, saving cloth by banning trouser cuffs, pleats, patch pockets and the double-breasted style made popular by film star Clark Gable. The big changeover to war production by the vast plants of the automobile industry had already led to a reduction in the number of new cars reaching the showrooms. All over the United States factories, producing everything from toasters to toys, swung over to war contracts. In a feature on Detroit in the second week of February, the *New York Times* reported, 'It is hard to find any visible reminder of the assembly lines that made more than 5 million automobiles last year.'

Whether many of these war supplies would ever reach Britain was open to doubt. In the middle of February a second wave of U-boats arrived off the Florida coast to continue the *Paukenschlag* offensive – often within sight of coastal homes.

On 16 February 1942 the U-boat blitz hit the Caribbean when Donitz

YANKS HERE!: On 26 January 1942 the first contingent of American soldiers landed in Belfast to a rousing welcome (above). But on the other side of the Atlantic, things were going badly for the US Navy whose C-in-C, 64-year-old Admiral Ernest King (left) was totally unprepared for the German onslaught. A tough and uncompromising character (Roosevelt claimed 'he shaved with a blow torch') King refused to introduce a convoy system in spite of British pressure.

launched operation *Neuland,* a carefully planned series of strikes at tankers off the Caribbean islands and at the local oil industry. Curaçao's Aruba harbour was defended only by a converted Dutch whaleboat when Kapitänleutnant Hartenstein nosed U-156 in under cover of night to attack its oil storage tanks and refinery. Two small tankers were sunk and US army officer Captain Robert Rudkin witnessed the opening shots of *Operation Neuland.* 'Flaming oil spread over a wide area under a steady wind. We dashed outside. I could hear cries out in the waters which I learned were infested with barracuda. There came a steady stream of tracer bullets from the dark of the ocean – aimed at the refinery.' The first night of *Operation Neuland* was a success as the three other U-boats sank seven tankers. By the end of February this had risen to 17 – most of them tankers.

Admiral Hoover's Caribbean Sea Frontier force with its HQ in San Juan, Puerto Rico, was powerless and could only deploy a couple of destroyers and two old patrol boats to defend the long stretch from Key West to Trinidad. This was more than the strength of the neighbouring Gulf Sea Frontier, which had three coastguard cutters and a motor yacht to patrol the whole Gulf of Mexico, the Yucatan Channel, Cuba and the west coast of Florida.

In the face of such weak defences, the Caribbean blitz increased in tempo. On the night of 19 February, Kapitänleutnant Achilles took U-161 into Trinidad's Port of Spain harbour, which he knew well as a merchant ship officer, to sink a tanker and a freighter. A month later, he repeated the operation at St Lucia, where he sank two freighters riding at anchor in the harbour. Soon, Kapitänleutnant Bauer in U-50 arrived on the scene and in two weeks in the Windward Passage and the old Bahamas Channel sank nine ships before running out of torpedoes.

Hitler was delighted by the success of *Paukenschlag* and congratulations were telephoned to Dönitz, who was now encouraged to send every available U-boat to join the campaign. The returning U-boat commanders, their morale boosted by the easy successes in the warm waters of the Gulf and Caribbean, jokingly referred to it as 'The Second Happy Time' or 'The American Turkey Shoot'. Yet Dönitz was unable to exploit this breakthrough which was crippling the Allied merchant marine, since Hitler still insisted on keeping 20 boats in Norway. This left Dönitz with only half a dozen boats to deploy in American waters.

By the third week of February 1942 the offensive concentrated off the harbours of the Carolinas, Georgia and Florida. At the same time, U-boat Command was careful to keep operations going against the Atlantic lifeline and on 24 February, four boats intercepted a westbound convoy, ON 67, approaching Newfoundland. The determined Wolf Pack, up against the inexperience of the US Navy escort, sank six ships but nearly 80% of the 430,000 tons sunk in February 1942 was destroyed in US coastal waters. The month ended in spectacular style with the torpedoing of the 10,000 ton tanker *R.P. Leasor,* 'a grim spectacle for early morning watchers of the Jersey coast. Flames leapt 200 feet into the air', reported the *New York Times.*

Funeral Pyres: Successive waves of U-boats arriving in American waters made tankers their prime targets and the columns of black smoke from blazing oil became familiar sights along the coast from New Jersey to Florida. It was a time of ordeal for the US seamen, and Captain Robert E. Christy (top left) was lucky to survive the torpedoing of his 8,000 ton tanker *Pan Massachussets* on 19 February off Cape Canaveral: 'The sea was afire for half a mile or a mile around us as the gasoline and oil spread. Instantly the doorway was framed with fire. There was no gasoline explosion for our tanks were full, and full tanks don't explode. I then got down some heavy towels, wet them and wound them round my head, face and hands. I threw open my door and made my way forwards. We talked the situation over and got a heavy mooring line which we made fast and put the end over the bow. We waited until the bow was clear of the flames, then slid down into the sea and swam away from the ship. I thought there wasn't a chance for life. All lifeboats were burned.'

THE AMERICAN CRISIS

It was only when the destroyer *Jacob Jones* was torpedoed within sight of the New Jersey coast with only 11 of her crew surviving, that US Navy Headquarters in Washington were stung into taking urgent action. At last, Admiral King ruled that more destroyers and patrol boats were to be made available to the coast defence commands. By coincidence, on 1 March the Navy finally succeeded in sinking its first U-boat, significantly by an air attack, when the Hudson of Ensign William Tepuni USNR successfully depth-charged U-556 off Newfoundland.

The might of American industry was now turned against the U-boat. With the slogan 'Sixty Ships in Sixty Days', a programme for the war production of anti-submarine coastal craft was launched in early April. Other important steps were taken, including the establishment in Miami of the Subchaser Training Center under Lieutenant Commander McDaniel a former Atlantic Fleet escort officer. Soon McDaniel's 'Academy' was putting the eager young sub-chaser crews of what came to be known as 'The Donald Duck Navy' through an intensive anti-submarine training programme in conjunction with the Asdic school at Key West and a team of lecturers from the University of Chicago. At the same time, the Anti-Submarine Warfare Unit was set up at Boston Navy Yard where it was to play an important backroom role in developing tactics and new weapons against the U-boats. It brought together the skills of experienced naval officers and civilian scientists under Dr Philip Morse of MIT who applied the principles of Operational Research to convoy actions and U-boat sinkings, in order to improve the efficiency of anti-submarine operations in the US Navy.

It would be months before the new sub-chasers started to come into service in sufficient numbers and in March the US Navy accepted the offer of the Cruising Club of America to loan thirty auxiliary sailing vessels manned by volunteer crews. This 'Hooligans' Navy carried out duties as a Coastal Picket off the East Coast harbours. It was good for morale but did little to stop the U-boats. The Civil Air Patrol was more successful with its volunteer pilots, flying their own light aircraft carrying red pyramid identification insignia and patrolling for thousands of hours from coastal airstrips.

Unfortunately, the burgeoning American Anti-Submarine air efforts were seriously hampered by inter-service rivalry between the Army and the Navy. The responsibility for providing anti-submarine air cover was divided between the 83 PBY Flying Boats and Hudsons of the US Navy and the 84 Army Air Force bombers based on 18 airstrips from Bangor, Maine, to Jacksonville, Florida. At first, co-operation between the two services was good, but four months later, when both services were equipping with squadrons of the new Liberator bombers, a conflict was smouldering. Each service had its own ideas of anti-U-boat tactics and it was only after a bitter clash that Admiral King finally won tactical control of the Army Anti-Submarine aircraft in June 1942 – but their crews stayed with the Army Air Force.

It would be some time before the US air forces could be effectively organised against the U-boat, but in March 1942 the Americans finally

Emergency Measures: In March 1942 the US Navy Department belatedly reacted to the U-boat crisis by ordering a crash programme of Anti-Submarine vessels. Work went on round the clock turning out subchasers for the 'Donald Duck' Navy of coastal patrol craft whose officers and men were to be trained by Lieutenant-Commander J. D. McDaniel (right) at the Anti-Submarine 'University' at Miami.

accepted British help when Royal Navy anti-submarine trawlers arrived on the Eastern Seaboard. They were badly needed. Sinkings had now risen to an average of over 10,000 tons a day.

Many of these heavy losses were caused by the total lack of an American convoy system. The situation was so bad that the Admiralty had offered to send a complete escort group of corvettes to help get convoys started. By 12 March Churchill stepped into the picture, cabling Hopkins, 'The situation is so serious that drastic action of some kind is necessary and we very much hope that you will be able to provide additional escort forces to organise immediate convoys in the West Indies and Bermuda area by withdrawing a few of your destroyer strength in the Pacific until the ten corvettes we are handing over to you come into service.'

Admiral King, summoned to report to the White House, made it clear that he was not going to take instructions from the British. He still did not find the case for a full convoy system on the American coast 'entirely convincing' and persuaded Roosevelt to ask the British instead to make 'heavy attacks on submarine bases and building and repair yards, thus checking submarine activities at their source and where submarines perforce congregate'.

With March sinkings now approaching the half-million ton mark, the British War Cabinet were alarmed about their oil supplies. Four large tankers a day were needed to keep the British war economy going and, with much of the oil coming from US Gulf ports and Venezuela, tankers became the particular target of the U-boat as they passed up the East Coast. By the end of April another 400,000 tons of losses brought the total destruction of Allied shipping in the first four months of 1942 to almost a million tons, and Churchill feared that the blitz in US waters must lead to a crippling shortage of ships, imposing 'severe limitations upon our efforts throughout 1942'. The need to keep the Russian convoys sailing was imposing an additional strain on shipping resources, severely overstretched in sending reinforcements to the Mediterranean and keeping India and Ceylon supplied. All this was on top of the 26 million tons of cargo capacity needed to keep Britain's industry and people from starvation. Already Allied strategy was suffering and the 1942 landings in North Africa had to be postponed until the late autumn.

In the spring of 1942, the German Naval War Staff could glimpse victory. If the U-boats continued to sink ships faster than the Allies could build them then the Battle of the Atlantic would be won. In his February report to the Führer, Raeder emphasised: 'Time and again Churchill speaks of shipping shortages as his greatest worry', and he produced an analysis to show that the Axis partners had to sustain a sinking rate of 600,000 tons a month to negate the estimated 7m. tons of annual ship construction planned by the Allies. A month later he was even more confident that his goal was within the U-boats' grasp, since intelligence assessments had concluded that American ship-building claims were largely propaganda and even better results could be expected as more U-boats became available. Of Dönitz's 288 strong fleet, 122 were now operational, with 81 in the Atlantic. Hitler was pleased but he still did not give the priority Raeder requested to step up the U-boat construction programme.

On 1 April 1942 the hard facts of the attrition of American coastal shipping finally forced Admiral King to accept what the British had been telling him for three months and he ordered the introduction of a 'partial convoy system' for the 120 ships a day passing through the Eastern Sea Frontier. With only 28 escorts available, Admiral Adolphus Andrews had to resort to 'The Bucket Brigade' which convoyed the merchantmen up the East coast in 120 mile stretches during daylight, anchoring every night in the protection of the harbours. As more warships became available, the 'Bucket Brigade' was to be gradually replaced by a full convoy system, so that by the end of June it was possible for ships to be protected from Halifax to Key West. A dramatic improvement followed. Losses in the Eastern Sea Frontier fell from 128 ships in the first quarter of 1942 to only 21 in the second, and no losses at all were suffered for the rest of the year.

The 'Second Happy Time' for the U-boat commanders did not end with the introduction of Eastern Sea Frontier convoys. By late April Dönitz marshalled 18 U-boats for an all-out assault on independently sailing ships in the waters off Florida and another nine Type IX's were ordered to the Caribbean to hunt in the sunny waters between the Bahamas and Trinidad. U-boat Command now had the means of sustaining the distant offensive by sending the first of the 1,700 ton Milch-cow U-boats across the Atlantic with 700 tons of spare fuel and torpedoes – sufficient to keep a dozen U-boats operating deep in the Caribbean. The first refuelling took place on 22 April 1942 when U-459 met U-108, 500 miles north-east of Bermuda. Within two weeks she had topped up the tanks of twelve Type VII boats, and two Type IX's. Two more Milch-cows were then despatched to enable the offensive to be carried right across the Gulf of Mexico as far as the Panama Canal. For Rear Admiral Hoover, Commander of the Caribbean Sea Frontier, May and June 1942 became a 'nerve shattering period' as sinking in his area rose to 148.

In addition to the long-range strikes into the Gulf of Mexico, Dönitz ordered his commanders to make for the Mississippi delta ports of New Orleans and Mobile, where he knew that there was a rich traffic in tankers and bauxite carriers supplying the United States' most extensive concentration of refineries and aluminium smelters. The new offensive was designed to disrupt these industries, which were crucial to the whole of the US war effort. On 6 May 1942 Kapitänleutnant Schacht in U-507 struck the first blow by sinking the 8,000 ton bauxite carrier *Alcoa Puritan* a hundred miles south of Mobile, Alabama. Chivalrously he surfaced to tell the survivors, 'Sorry but I had to do it. Hope you make it.' They did.

The same day, the Gulf was declared a danger zone where no ships were to sail unescorted, but the Gulf Sea Frontier headquarters in Key West were hopelessly ill-equipped to carry out this plan. Only two destroyers, a handful of smaller craft and a score of planes were available for escorting all the shipping in the area; soon U-507, joined by U-506, were sinking a ship a day. The number of U-boats operating in the Gulf of Mexico never rose above six, but 41 ships were sunk. The 220,000 tons lost was double the casualty rate of any month on the Eastern Sea Frontier and, to make matters worse, over half the tonnage was tankers. These losses were soon felt in the Eastern United States, where petrol rationing had to be introduced on 15 May 1942, limiting consumers to three gallons a week.

As the U-boat blitz raged in the southern waters of the United States, General Marshall, could contain himself no longer. On June 19 1942, he sent a strong letter of criticism to Admiral King. 'The losses by submarines off our Atlantic seaboard and in the Caribbean now threaten our entire war effort.'

Admiral King sent an icy reply, cataloguing the shortage of subchasers and

A Question of Fuel: The refuelling operations of Milch cow U-459 (below) allowed Dönitz to carry the U-boat blitz deep into the Caribbean and Gulf of Mexico. With only a few escorts the heavy losses of tankers forced the US Government to introduce fuel rationing on the East Coast in May and the soaring shipping losses caused General Marshall to warn Admiral King the following month:

I am fearful that another month or two of this will so cripple our means of transport that we will be unable to bring sufficient men and planes to bear against the enemy in critical theatres to exercise a determining influence on the war.'

Red Glorioles: Although the convoy system gradually spread throughout the US coastal waters there were still many unescorted ships for the U-boats to attack (top Kapitänleutnant Möhlmann in U-571 notches up another success). A confident Dönitz declared that the U-boats were operating so close to the American shore 'that bathers and sometimes entire cities are witness to that drama of war, whose visual climaxes are constituted by the red glorioles of blazing tankers.'

escorts which had forced the Navy to 'improvise rapidly and on a large scale'. Only recently, he complained, had the Eastern Frontier possessed sufficient escorts to begin convoys and; 'Since 15 May our East Coast waters have enjoyed a high degree of security . . . ' The Admiral then went on to offer the hope that losses outside the East Coast zone would be reduced as air cover became available and in a telling final paragraph revealed his complete volte-face about the need for convoys:

> I might say in this connection that escort is not just *one* way of handling the submarine menace; it is the *only* way that gives any promise of success. The so-called patrol and hunting operations have time and again proved futile.

It was left unexplained why it had taken the US Chief of Naval Staff six months to reach this conclusion, during which time the U-boats had been able to sink well over a million tons of shipping. The effects of the slaughter were not only threatening to undermine Allied strategy, but were being personally felt by US citizens as coffee, sugar and gasoline were growing scarce. The President's broadcast appeals for everyone to 'cut their driving in half' were echoed in Britain, where the loss of a quarter of a million tons of tanker tonnage had created a desperate fuel situation and the First Sea Lord flew to Washington in a final effort to persuade Admiral King to agree to a series of emergency tanker convoys from the Caribbean. In this extremely serious situation, Admiral Pound offered to provide the necessary escorts by reducing the number of Royal Navy Escort Groups on the North Atlantic to ten, a bare minimum for safety.

It was not until 10 June 1942 that Admiral King finally accepted the need for a full convoy system throughout the Caribbean which, he agreed, would be organised with the assistance of British Escort Groups withdrawn from the Atlantic and a Squadron of RAF Coastal Command Hudsons to operate from Trinidad.

Five days later, the urgent need for a total convoy system was dramatically emphasised when two large freighters were torpedoed off Florida's fashionable Virginia Beach resort, a spectacle witnessed by thousands of sunbathing holidaymakers. Whilst it was achieving such spectacular successes in US waters, U-boat Command was careful not to let up the pressure on the North Atlantic. Observing that the British were using the shorter, great circle route to save fuel and make more efficient use of the Escort Groups a series of successful pack attacks were directed against the convoys. In May 1942 ONS 92 lost seven ships; the following month another Wolf Pack cost ON 100 a corvette and four merchantmen, whilst five ships from HG 84 were sunk on the night of 15 June.

The U-boats also struck in other ways. Attempts were made to mine the American harbours and on 13 June a party of four saboteurs were landed at Amagansett Beach, Long Island, with orders to destroy aluminium plants and railway bridges. They managed to get as far as New York before being picked up by the FBI. A second team of four German agents, including two US citizens, was landed at Jacksonville, Florida, and reached Chicago before being captured.

In the late summer, the blitz began to peter out as escorted convoys grew

Iron Rations: The German victories were bought at the price of severe deprivation of the U-boat crews. Their diet was mainly tinned food (seen being loaded aboard U-123) and one supply officer recalled. Black bread was an essential item in the needs of the German sailor and it kept badly. Experiments were made with tinned bread, bread baked on all sides and bread wrapped in cellophane but after six weeks, U-boat personnel had to eat hard tack. The fresh potatoes were hung up in nets but the bad air in the U-boats soon spoiled them.

more numerous and Anti-Submarine patrols took a steadily rising toll of the U-boats. The strain of operating over four thousand miles from their home base was beginning to tell on the U-boat crews. Weeks of continuous patrolling in the tropical heat of the Caribbean made the tin-can atmosphere of a cramped U-boat particularly arduous for the crews to endure. Food and the necessities of life were the principal worries of Kapitänleutnant Reinhard Suhren, who commanded U-564 in the Caribbean.

> The diet for the first eight days was quite good, we always left our base with a lot of fresh fruit, vegetables and meat. The second lavatory was used as a larder, but there were disadvantages; 46 men to one lavatory is not really adequate! When all the fresh food was used up, we turned to our supplies of tinned food, but no matter whether it was fresh or tinned it always tasted of diesel oil. The biggest problem was the bread; in the damp and sweaty atmosphere it rapidly went stale. The loaves would soon look like rabbits, covered in fluffy mildew. We just removed as much of it as possible before eating it.

Food was always a big problem for U-boat crews on cruises lasting three months or more, and many commanders like Suhren would try to relieve the

850   60

1350   10   240

ALLIED AND NEUTRAL MERCHANT SHIPS SUNK
○ U-BOATS SUNK
CONVOY ROUTES
ALLIED AIR COVER ZONES
AXIS AND AXIS OCCUPIED TERRITORY, 31 JULY 1942
MERCATOR PROJECTION

ALLIED SHIPPING LOSSES 1ST JANUARY 1942-31ST JULY 1942

Paying the Price: By the end of July 1942 when the impetus of Operation *Paukenschlag* began to fall off with the introduction of the Interlocking Convoy system, nearly 2½ million tons of shipping had been lost (map), much of it valuable tankers. The particularly nasty ordeal of abandoning ship in the tropical waters of the Caribbean was described by Captain Donald Blyth whose tanker the SS *San Gaspar* was turned into a blazing inferno by a torpedo from U-575 off Curacao on the 18 July: the 18 July:

'I gave the order "Jump for it!" and we all jumped overboard and swam for dear life away from the ship. One young sailor unfortunately got caught by the flames, but the rest of us managed to swim clear . . . It was necessary to keep swimming strongly most of the night to keep just outside the flames.

'Whilst swimming, we were

attacked by barracuda which tried to bite us, and as I had no clothes and the others were wearing very little, we made an attractive bait for them. Shoals of small dogfish also attacked us, but we managed to keep swimming through the night. At daybreak we saw a Catalina aircraft which flew over us, but took no notice. There were huge flames from the ship and the smoke from the oil was rising thousands of feet into the air. Tiger sharks appeared and joined in the attack; I took off my lifebelt, which was chafing me and rested my chin on it. By kicking vigorously, I was able to keep the sharks away temporarily, but they became bolder as the day went on. Towards noon we were nearly exhausted, when two bombers dropped a rubber dinghy within twenty feet of us. When in the dinghy the sharks became bolder and we had to stab at them with the aluminium paddles to keep them away.'

strain by allowing the men to swim off the isolated Caribbean Islands. It was a relief from the crowded environment of the submarine, where temperatures rose to barely tolerable levels in the engine compartment.

For the many men of the Royal Navy's BS Escort Group assigned to operate with the US Navy in the Caribbean, their new duties seemed more like a holiday cruise after the bleak, stormy waters of the Atlantic. It was only when a U-boat attacked or survivors were picked up from shark infested waters that the crews were brought face to face with the unique horrors of war in these tropical seas. Signalman J. Lisle of the corvette HMS *Pimpernel* recalled the night of 18 August 1942 when convoy AW 13 was attacked off Trinidad.

> Three ships were lost. There were no survivors from the tanker which was struck by a torpedo and immediately burst into flames from stem to stern. The convoy left her to burn herself out, the whole ship was a mass of flames and her sides were white hot. The crew would not have stood a chance.

The increasing tempo of the U-boat offensive in the waters off Trinidad in July and August was endangering the heavy coastal traffic sailing along the Brazilian coast. This threat to vital mineral supplies – and almost as vital coffee – led the Americans, with Brazilian permission, to despatch US Marines to set up a series of airstrips on the largely undefended 4,000 mile coast where there was a real fear that the Germans might build secret supply bases in isolated coves to support the U-boat offensive on the mid-Atlantic.

Hitler had already offered the Brazilian Government millions of captured US dollars in return for their co-operation, but he had been furious to find that, on Washington's advice, all Axis sympathisers had been promptly rounded up. In June, the Führer eagerly agreed with Raeder's proposals to extend the U-boat operations down Brazil's coast.

It was to prove a serious blunder. After five of her merchant ships had been sunk in three in three days, Brazil declared war on Germany and Italy on 22 August 1942. Admiral J. H. Ingram's South Atlantic Force quickly moved into the valuable Brazilian bases to control the important mid-Atlantic Narrows and the US Navy's protection of the coastal shipping off South America was the final link in a comprehensive Allied convoy network.

'The Interlocking System', as the network came to be known, was operating with the efficiency of a railroad timetable by the autumn of 1942. All northbound convoys were scheduled on five-day cycles to connect up with the departure of the trans-Atlantic 'main line' from Halifax. This divided at New York, with one main line running to Key West and the other to Guantanamo, Cuba. From Key West, a ten-day cycle served Galveston and the Mississippi ports and from Guantanamo the convoys ran across the Caribbean to Panama, Venezuela and Curaçao then south down the Brazilian coast.

After August 1942 the curtain came down abruptly on the 'Second Happy Time'. In the succeeding three months 1,400 ships were convoyed through the 'Interlocking System' and only eleven were sunk. The US Navy had learned the hard way, that it was the well-escorted convoy that had once again defeated the U-boats.

14. Winning the War with Ships

'A miracle of God and the genius of free American workmen'

HENRY J. KAISER at launching of 10 day Liberty ship
Joseph N. Teal, October 1942.

In July 1942, the Allied shipping stock showed a net gain for the first time in the war, thanks to the huge output of the American 'Ships for Victory Program' which in September produced nearly a million tons – equal to the whole of its output in 1941. This colossal achievement was one of the principal factors in securing victory in the Battle of the Atlantic and was largely realised through the prefabricated Liberty Ship construction programme. Assembled in sections like cars (left) the standardised designs were, by the autumn of 1942, sliding down the slipways in record time. The visit of the President (bottom) to Henry J. Kaiser (sitting behind Roosevelt) and his West coast yards in October 1942, was marked by the launch of the *Joseph N. Teal*. The ship had been completed in 10 days and the US Maritime Commission announced that it had reached its goal of launching 3 ships daily.

The U-boat blitz on American waters was only one of the major setbacks that afflicted the Allies in the first half of 1942. Until May, Japanese expansion continued unchecked and in April, the German armies launched a new Russian offensive in the south which was soon sweeping towards the Caucasus oilfields. These first months of global disaster were gloomily reviewed by Churchill:

at this moment in the world struggle no-one could be sure that Germany would not break Russia or drive her beyond the Urals and then be able to come back and invade Britain – or as an alternative spread through the Caucasus to join hands with the Japanese vanguards in India.

The first Allied success came on 7 May 1942 at the Battle of the Coral Sea, when the US Navy checked the Japanese expansion south towards Australia. This paved the way for the US Pacific Fleet Commander, Admiral Chester W. Nimitz to prepare his united forces for the biggest confrontation in naval history which came a month later at the Battle of Midway. By the end of the year, the United States had taken the offensive in the long and bitter 'island hopping' campaign that was to drive Japan back across the Pacific.

It was to be many more months before the Allies reached the decisive turning-point in the European war. The spring and summer saw the German Panzers racing unchecked towards Stalingrad and the Wehrmacht launching a concerted drive to remove the British from the Mediterranean as Rommel's Afrika Corps advanced to threaten Cairo. Furious air and sea battles raged around Malta as the Axis forces made a determined effort to bomb and starve this vital bastion into surrender. Only after a heavy commitment of British and American naval strength to Operation *Pedestal* were the supply convoys fought through to save the island fortress from falling. The Mediterranean operations, coming on top of the campaigns in the Pacific and Atlantic, drained increasing Allied naval and shipping resources from the Atlantic mainline on which Allied Strategy turned. As Churchill was later to record:

The Battle of the Atlantic was the dominating factor all through the war. Never for one moment could we forget that everything happening elsewhere, on land, at sea or in the air depended ultimately on its outcome.

By 1942 the Atlantic convoys had become not only the means of ensuring Britain's survival, but that of the Soviet Union as well. Dominating all military calculations was the knowledge that Hitler could only be defeated by an invasion of Europe, the armies and equipment for which, would have to come across the bridge of ships. Faced with the shipping losses, the British planners saw no way in which a successful invasion could be launched against the European mainland in 1942. The Americans felt otherwise – and so did Stalin. The Chief of US Army Plans, General Eisenhower, put the matter bluntly:

We've got to go to Europe and fight – and we've got to quit wasting resources all over the world and, still worse, wasting time. If we're going to keep Russia in, save the Middle East, India and Burma, we've got to begin slugging with air at Western Europe, to be followed by a land strike as soon as possible.'

The Kola Run: The extreme weather conditions faced by the merchant vessels making the journey to the North Russian ports required special protection from ice for ships and men. Early in 1942 the increasing tempo of German sea and air attacks meant that the convoys had to be heavily escorted (map) through the enemy dominated seas off Norway. The final defence of the merchant ships depended on their own armament. The guns of American ships were manned by the Armed Guard, which often had more than 20 men aboard each ship, under their own commander (below, the crew of an AA gun). The British ships were served by reservists of the Defensively Equipped Merchant Ships (DEMS) organisation backed up by the ships' own crews. The demand for gunners became so heavy that a special Maritime Regiment of the Royal Artillery was formed, whose 14000 men performed sterling service on the most threatened routes.

In spite of American pressure, the British Chiefs of Staff refused to commit themselves to what they regarded as a suicidal attempt to relieve pressure on the Red Army. On 8 April 1942, General Marshall, accompanied by Harry Hopkins, arrived in London to push the British into a cross-Channel attack and to make plain the political reality that, 'If public opinion had its way the weight of American effort would be directed against Japan.' A compromise was reached and contingency plans were drawn up for Operation *Sledgehammer*. This was planned as a limited British cross-Channel attack for 1942 to be launched if the Russian situation deteriorated and was to be followed up by a major invasion, Operation *Roundup*, the following year. To the relief of the British Chiefs of Staff it only proved practical to mount the token Dieppe Raid in August before Allied offensive preparations concentrated on the autumn invasion of North Africa.

In the absence of a Second Front, with the Soviet Forces reeling before the new German offensive, both Allies realised the importance of the Arctic supply route in keeping Russia in the war. Ever since the Beaverbrook-Harriman mission to Moscow in October 1941, regular convoys had been running to the ice-free port of Murmansk on the bleak Kola peninsula. By the end of the year 110 ships had made the journey through wintry seas to bring 799 fighters, 572 tanks, 1,404 vehicles and 100,000 tons of military supplies.

Until the spring of 1942 the Germans had not seriously attempted to interfere with the Russian convoys but, even without enemy attacks, ships and men faced a terrible ordeal in the Arctic winter. Ships needed special oils, toughened bows and steel propellers to cope with the ice. Thick insulation was installed, together with gyro-compasses in key ships, since the convoys would be passing close to the magnetic pole. To provide protection for the crews, the Ministry of Shipping issued thick gloves, padded duffel coats lined with lambswool and thick hoods with eye-slits.

The Russian convoys were soon facing more than bitter Arctic weather as Hitler reinforced the German sea and air forces in Norway, convinced that the Allies were secretly planning an invasion of Scandinavia. There was a build up of heavy fleet units, including the mighty *Tirpitz*, and an increase in the strength of the Luftwaffe. These powerful forces were in an ideal position to menace the convoy route to Russia.

The first challenge came on 6 March 1942 when the *Tirpitz* sailed from Trondheim, accompanied by three destroyers, to intercept convoy PQ 12 and the homeward-bound PQ 8, 80 miles south of Jan Mayen Island. The convoys moved north into fog and the *Tirpitz* failed to make an interception and only managed to sink a single straggler. On her way home she was attacked by aircraft from the carrier *Victorious*, but the battleship avoided the torpedoes and shot down two of the attacking Albacores.

The next convoy, PQ 13, was also heavily attacked, this time by the Luftwaffe bombers and destroyers 85 miles off the North Cape of Norway, losing six ships.

In the face of increasing German pressure and the growing hours of daylight, Admiral Pound argued that the Russian convoys were becoming too risky but Allied leaders insisted that they should go on and Roosevelt sent 'Task Force 39', which included the battleship USS *Washington* and the carrier *Wasp*, as reinforcements for the Home Fleet in April.

The attrition of the Russian convoys continued, with the brunt of the attacks falling on the escorts. Fourteen ships of PQ 14 turned back because of heavy ice and the returning QP 10 lost four. In May the double movement of QP 15 and QP 11 saw the modest loss of four merchant ships after furious battles between the heavy escort and U-boats, destroyers and Luftwaffe. The cost to the Royal Navy was high and included the sinking of the cruisers *Edinburgh* and *Trinidad*. 'These Russian convoys are becoming a regular millstone round our necks', Pound told Admiral King.

The Arctic convoys were seriously affecting Atlantic operations, as shipping delays caused congestion in Iceland. The convoys were therefore increased in size and their outward and return movements synchronised so that the heavy naval escorts could cover both through the critical waters of Norway. It was a move that delighted the Luftwaffe. On 25 May 1942, the outward-bound PQ 16, passing the homeward QP 12, ran into heavy air attacks. In one day, 108 successive waves of German aircraft kept up a relentless bombing attack. When the convoy struggled into Murmansk, eight ships out of 25 had been lost, but a quarter of a million tons of vital military equipment were soon unloaded and being sent down the single line railway track to the Red Army fighting fifteen hundred miles to the south.

Attrition in Arctic Waters: German bombs and torpedoes extracted a 20% toll of the merchant ships bound for Russia in appallingly cold weather (above, signal bridge of a cruiser). Losses rose to a disastrous 70% for the ill-fated PQ17 (below photographed by the Luftwaffe shortly before the convoy was ordered to scatter on 4 July 1942).

The 20% shipping casualty rate on the Russian route was by now surpassing even the heavy toll extracted on the bitterly contested Malta convoys. The Admiralty pressed for a halt during the continuous daylight of the Arctic summer but Churchill made it plain: 'Not only Premier Stalin but President Roosevelt will object very much to our desisting from running the convoys now.'

PQ 17 set sail from Iceland on 27 June 1942 bound for Archangel with 34 ships (22 American). Its escort included six destroyers, two A.A. ships, two submarines and eleven corvettes, minesweepers and armed trawlers all commanded by Captain John Broome in the destroyer HMS *Keppel*. He was also able to call on a close support force of four British and American cruisers and a distant heavy support force of a British and American battleship and three cruisers with their destroyer screens – more warships covered the convoy than the number of merchant ships sailing in it. Broome's instructions from the Admiralty stated: 'Our primary object is to get as much of the convoy through as possible, and the best way to do it is to keep it moving to the eastward, even though it is suffering damage.'

The Germans had been waiting since early June to spring Operation *Rösselsprung* (Knight's move) involving a surface strike led by the *Tirpitz*, and when the Luftwaffe sighted PQ 17 on 1 July as it passed east of Jan Mayen Island, Raeder ordered the *Tirpitz* north to Alten Fjord to await the convoy's arrival off the North Cape and Hitler's final permission to launch the attack. PQ 17 soon came under heavy air attack which continued over the next three days. Two ships were sunk and a Russian tanker damaged, but the Luftwaffe was beaten off and Captain Broome described how the spirits of his convoy rose: 'I went out astern of the convoy to have a close look at the Russian. Her crew were singing and smiling. A couple of lusty dames waved cheerfully from her bridge ... My impression on seeing the resolution displayed by the convoy and its escort was that, provided the ammunition lasted,

PQ 17 could get anywhere.' But Admiralty intelligence knew that the *Tirpitz* was ready to strike at the convoy. Although Special Intelligence had no firm indications to show that the battleship was at sea, Pound acted on his own judgement and signalled to Broome at 9.23 on July 4th: 'Immediate. Owing to the threat of surface ships convoy is to disperse and proceed to Russian ports.' Thirteen minutes later, the First Sea Lord's urgency was apparent from his signal: 'Most Immediate. My 9.23 of the 4th: Convoy is to scatter.'

It was a fatal error. The *Tirpitz* was still in Alten Fjord awaiting Hitler's approval to sail. Pound's signal caused consternation in the convoy. One of the destroyers signalled to Broome, 'Captain to Captain: What part of the bloody War Plan is this?' Broome regretfully signalled the Commodore: 'Sorry to leave you like this. Goodbye and good luck. It looks like a bloody business.' His words proved a tragic understatement. Within hours, the Luftwaffe and U-boats were remorselessly hunting down the scattered merchantmen, many of which were racing north for the pack ice. Only 11 of the convoy and two rescue ships were to survive the ordeal. The *Tirpitz*, the most powerful element in Operation *Rösselsprung* played no part in the destruction. PQ 17's decimation cost 100,000 tons of supplies, 3,350 vehicles, 430 tanks and 210 aircraft, and after the disaster, the Admiralty suspended all further sailings to Murmansk for the summer.

THE SHIPPING CRISIS

After the PQ 17 disaster the Russians and the Americans increased their pressure on the British to make a cross-Channel attack that summer. The American Chiefs of Staff now faced a powerful lobby urging concentration on the Pacific and on 17 June 1942 Churchill flew to Washington for a vital meeting with Roosevelt, to protect the Europe-first strategy. The weak British position was further undermined in the middle of the delicate talks when Roosevelt passed the Prime Minister a cable: 'Tobruk has surrendered with 25,000 men taken prisoner.' It was a black moment, Churchill realised that little stood between Rommel and Alexandria. The President generously offered 300 tanks to replace the heavy losses, but neither he nor the US Chiefs of Staff were yet prepared to commit themselves to a full agreement for the North African invasion in the autumn.

Any invasion was now crucially dependent on the shipping reserves which, with the German campaign of attrition, had now become very depleted. The sending of reinforcements to the Middle East was badly affected, and Britain had taken a cut of 250,000 tons in her import capacity to help Operation *Bolero* – the build-up of the US army and supplies in the UK. Troopship capacity was increased by about a third, simply by cramming more soldiers on board, and skilful routing cut down port delays to a minimum, yet cargo-carrying capacity had become so scarce that exports were given a low priority.

A cut-back in Britain's food supplies seemed inevitable. The British diet was already miserable by 1942, with the disappearance of fresh fruit and huge reductions in meat and butter, but careful planning by the Ministry of Food

Keeping the Ships Moving: By 1942 the whole of the Allied war effort turned on the efficient utilisation of every square foot of cargo space (above) and maximum co-ordination of vessels by the Ministry of Shipping (top). The importance of this effort was marked by Allied cartoonists (right).

and the Scientific Food Committee ensured that the average English family was eating the same number of calories, 3,000 per head, in 1942 as they were in 1939. In the case of protein, many of them were better fed.

Nevertheless, the Ministry of Food had to report: 'The four main foods on which our survival depends are flour, meat, fats and sugar. All these foods are dependent to a large extent on imports,' and the Ministry's experts predicted that, if imports were cut off:

> we could continue to survive for not less than four months without imports and might continue for six months. More stringent rationing of all foods at the commencement might stretch some of the less important commodities in such a way that a siege could be continued for a longer period.

To co-ordinate the dwindling reserves of Allied cargo-carrying capacity, a Combined Shipping Adjustment Board had been set up early in 1942 under Admiral Emory S. Land, Director of the US War Shipping Administration, and Sir Arthur Salter of the Ministry of Shipping. It faced a formidable task. Since the beginning of the war, the Allies had lost 3,000 ships and new construction was not keeping pace with sinkings.

The Shipping Adjustment Board began to co-ordinate resources skilfully, switching vessels from ocean to ocean. Slower and more ancient cargo ships were used in the Indian Ocean and faster ones in the North Atlantic where U-boat attack was more likely. Trooping operations were organised separately, using the 'Monsters', large ocean liners like the 80,000 ton *Queen Elizabeth* and *Queen Mary*, which could each transport over 10,000 troops across the Atlantic at nearly 30 knots.

Whilst Allied Shipping Control avoided the worst effects of the crisis, the only certain way to win the war was to build ships faster than the enemy could sink them. Britain alone was losing this crucial struggle. In the first six months of 1942, her net shipping loss was over ½ m. tons and there was the huge task of repairing the 2½ m. ton backlog of damaged merchant ships which was absorbing half the total shipyard workforce.

The output of Britain's shipyards had been dramatically increased from the pre-war slump conditions, but it was recognised that they would never be able to produce more than 1¼ m. tons a year. New intensive shift patterns and manning agreements had been hammered out with the unions and large numbers of women had been recruited for the yards where they worked in the open, exposed to the hard northern winter and air raids. Skilled shipwrights were exempted from military service to keep the ships sliding down the ways and the Ministry of Information organised a publicity campaign to bring home to the shipyard workers that they were in the front line of the battle against the U-boats. The popular BBC lunchtime variety programme 'Workers' Playtime' was frequently broadcast from shipyard canteens, and men who had been torpedoed and survived gruelling ordeals were taken to address lunchtime gatherings under the shadows of half-completed hulls.

The Americans also raised the tempo of their ship construction programme. On 19 February 1942, the President called a top level conference on shipping which took place in his White House bedroom. Here he set in motion 'the greatest shipbuilding programme in world history'. Admiral

Land, appointed to head the War Shipping Administration, was charged with producing 24 m. tons of new ships before the end of the year. This was 21 times the tonnage delivered in 1941 and Land noted: 'To meet the stiff quota of 750 ships before the end of the year, and about 1,500 vessels in 1943, American yards would have to increase their delivery of ships from one to three per day.'

A huge government-sponsored programme was already under way to build more shipyards – by the end of the war 99 completely new yards with a total work force of over 1½ m. would be in operation – but yards alone were not enough, and it was clear to the Maritime Commission that an entirely new way of building ships had to be found. Traditional methods could not cope and industrialists from the construction industry like Henry J. Kaiser, who had built the Boulder Dam and the San Francisco-Oakland Bay Bridge, were attracted into the ship-building race by multimillion dollar contracts.

The key to the success of Kaiser and other American yards lay in the application of the mass-production techniques of the car assembly line, working to a standard design and using all-welded construction and prefabricated assembly. The principal standardised vessel was the 10,000 ton EC2 (Emergency Cargo 2/large capacity) which had been adapted by Land's staff from an old British tramp steamer blueprint originating in 1879. Roosevelt had personally leafed through the proposed designs. 'He came to the profile sheet', Land recalled, 'backed away from it and said: 'Admiral, I think this ship will do us very well. She'll carry a good load. She isn't much to look at, though is she? A real ugly duckling?' The Admiral's comment at the time was: 'Liberty ships are slow, but hell they'll float, and by God they'll get there!'

The first Liberty ship, appropriately named *Patrick Henry*, was launched at the Bethlehem – Fairfield Yard at Baltimore on 27 September 1941. Before the end of the war 2,700 would be built in the United States and to cope with this production, the labour force in the US yards had to be increased from 100,000 to over 700,000. Training schools for platers, shipfitters and welders were opened and, as in Britain, thousands of women were recruited. 'Women,' as Admiral Land went on record as saying, 'make excellent welders.' To the women it was like a sewing machine job and 'Rosie the Riveter' soon became a national heroine.

A carefully designed cash incentive scheme boosted output, with yards receiving a fast delivery bonus of between $60,000 and $140,000 for each $1½ million Liberty ship. Construction time soon shrank from six months for the first Liberty ship to two months per ship in the spring of 1942, and finally to just over a month. The publicity conscious Kaiser Corporation achieved a spectacular record production time in November 1942 when No: 440 was completed in just 4 days 15 hours. On the 8 November, the hull was assembled from 250-ton prefabricated sections with the engine in place. At the end of the second day the upper deck was completed; on the third day the superstructure fittings, masts and derricks and, after final welding, wiring and painting, she was launched on the fourth day to a fanfare of national publicity. Three days later the *Robert E. Peary* was picking up her first cargo.

216

Teamwork: At the height of the 'Ships For Victory' programme nearly 30% of the workforce in Kaiser's West Coast yards were women. 'Rosie the Riveter' (above left) was immortalised by Norman Rockwell. Her statuesque defiance borrowed from Michelangelo caught the spirit, if not the feminine charm, of the real-life 'Rosies' (far left). The efforts of women workers boosted output in the yards and the *Robert E. Peary* was launched (above) at Richmond, California on 11 November 1942, having been assembled in four days 15 hours. Film stars like Madeleine Carroll (left) joined Admiral Emory S. Land at publicity launches.

217

The German High Command had grasped the importance of shipping to Allied Strategy – but had completely underestimated the huge industrial capacity of the United States to build unprecedented numbers of ships. In May 1942 Dönitz had set out the targets he had established for his U-boat arm to win the war:

> The total tonnage the enemy can build will be about 8·2 m. tons in 1942, and about 10·4 m. tons in 1943. This would mean that we would have to sink approximately 700,000 tons per month in order to offset new construction; only what is in excess of this amount would constitute a decrease in enemy tonnage. However, we are already sinking these 700,000 tons per month now

Dönitz revealed the flaw in his calculations with the statement that: 'The construction figures quoted are the maximum amounts ever mentioned by enemy propaganda as the goal of the shipbuilding programme. Our experts doubt that this goal can be reached and consider that the enemy can only build about 5 m. tons in 1942.'

He was wrong. The United States alone was building ships faster than the Germans were sinking them by the late summer of 1942. In the autumn of that year there was a net gain for the first time of over 700,000 tons in Anglo-American tonnage and this was repeated in the next quarter. In the first quarter of 1943 it was doubled to nearly 1½ m. tons and the balance of new construction over losses never fell below 2 m. tons throughout 1944.

Misled by the spectacular success of the 'Second Happy Time' Dönitz had failed to discern that by August 1942 the U-boats had all but lost the tonnage war. He realised that increasing protection given to shipping in American waters would force the U-boats to challenge the Atlantic convoys in a decisive showdown, but he hoped that improved magnetic torpedoes would 'considerably speed up the sinking of a torpedoed ship and thus save torpedoes'. The ships would not only sink faster but there would be a greater loss of crews and, as he reflected 'This increase in personnel losses will no doubt make it more difficult to man the many ships America is building'.

That summer the Germans had only 101 U-boats ready for operations, of which a daily average of 59 were at sea; the long transit across the Atlantic meant that only about 20 were actually operating against shipping. U-boat Command's plans were also disrupted by Hitler's insistence that boats should be deployed to protect the Atlantic islands like Madeira and the Azores. In spite of these limitations on his U-boat fleet, Dönitz planned a series of diversionary attacks to draw Allied escorts away from the North Atlantic. On 1 August the *Eisbär* (Polar bear) Group of four large Type IX boats U-68, 156, 172 and U-504 set off for the Cape, together with a Milchcow. On the night of 12 September, 500 miles north of Ascension Island, Kapitänleutnant Hartenstein in U-156 torpedoed the British troopship *Laconia*. She was carrying 1,700 Italian prisoners of war captured in North Africa and a worried Hartenstein radioed U-boat Command: 'So far 90 fished out . . . Request instructions'. Realising the serious impact this might have on their Axis partner, Dönitz radioed the *Eisbär* boats to go to the rescue and Hartenstein signalled in clear English on the international shipping distress band, 'If any ship will assist the shipwrecked *Laconia* crew I will not attack her, provided I am not attacked by ship or air force. I picked up 193 men 04.52 S 11.26 W. German submarine'.

For two days, Hartenstein struggled to keep boats and survivors together under impossible conditions. U-156 was unable to dive with 200 people crowded below and on deck, including British survivors. At noon on 15 September a Liberator with American markings spotted the strange assembly and signalled to the US Navy Air Base on Ascension Island that he had sighted a U-boat with 50 people on deck surrounded by four lifeboats. The pilot was commanded to sink the U-boat and returned to carry out his orders, ignoring the fact that U-156 was flying a Red Cross flag. The bombs only straddled her but they fell among the lifeboats. Faced with the possibility of imminent destruction, Hartenstein ordered all survivors off the boat. According to A. V. Lange, a South African who described the Commander as a 'Hatchet-faced little man with scars on his cheeks':

> Our own folk began to file out on deck . . . The U-boat ran slowly forward and submerged. As it went down it fouled the lifeboats full of Italians and wrecked it. Those who had been on the U-boat, including women and children, were left in the sea some hundreds of yards away from us.
> The two remaining boats filled themselves to capacity picking them up.'

As a result of this tragic incident Dönitz radioed on 17 September:

> 1. All attempts to rescue members of ships which have been sunk, including attempts to pick up swimmers, or to place food and water, will cease. The rescue of survivors contradicts the elementary necessity of war for the destruction of enemy boats and their crews.
> 2. The order for the capture of captains and chief engineers remains in force.
> 3. Survivors may only be rescued when interrogation may be of value to the U-boat.
> 4. Be severe. Remember that in his bombing attacks on German cities the enemy has no regard for women and children.

Ordeal in a Lifeboat: The conditions recorded by E. R. Pearce, Chief Officer of the SS *Avila Star* which was torpedoed by U-207 five hundred miles off the Portuguese Coast on 6 July 1942 were typical of many.
'We have chocolate, milk tablets, pemmican and 48 gallons of water in my boat, sufficient for 24 days. I rationed the water to a 5 oz dipper on the morning of the first day and the same amount in the evening, nothing during the heat of the day. Everyone ate the pemmican and we all liked the Horlicks Milk tablets. The nights were a little chilly . . . some of the people had on very few clothes whilst others were covered with fuel oil, so we shared out the clothes.'
One of the survivors was 18 years old Miss Johnny Ferguson who was praised for her outstanding fortitude in nursing the injured and scalded survivors. She was one of those rescued when *Avila Star's* No. 2 life-boat was finally sighted by a Portuguese frigate, and its survivors including the courageous Miss Ferguson was rescued (below) after 20 days adrift.

THE BOMBER ROW

Realising that a new autumn U-boat offensive was imminent, the Admiralty feared that their overtaxed convoy escorts might be overwhelmed without a rapid build up of long-range air cover. Pointing to the loss rate which was running at over half a million tons a month and the ominous growth of the U-boat fleet to over 200 boats, Admiral Pound informed the Chiefs of Staff on 24 June that 'the gravity of our position at sea increases day by day'. His request for 'more land-based squadrons of heavy aircraft as a matter of supreme urgency' was opposed by Air Marshal Sir Charles Portal, Chief of Air Staff who pointed out that Bomber Command needed every available bomber for its all-out air offensive against Germany and that too many had already been diverted to the Atlantic. Portal was supported by the tough C-in-C. of Bomber Command, Air Marshal Harris, who maintained that 'The naval employment of aircraft consists of picking at the fringes of enemy power . . . of looking for needles in a haystack.' In his view, it was much better to 'cut the artery' with strategic blows against U-boat bases and construction yards than to 'sever each capillary vein one by one'.

The row continued to dominate the meeting of the Battle of the Atlantic Committee with Pound finding it difficult to hold his own against the political skills of Portal. Even when the Committee adjudged that 'the submarine campaign against our shipping has reached a point beyond our capacity to contain', Portal refused to agree to the release of more long-range aircraft and had the support of the Prime Minister for his stand. Churchill was anxious to maintain the momentum of the bomber campaign, which was the main British offensive against the Reich and a valuable counter to Stalin's arguments that the Anglo-Saxon powers were shunning a direct confrontation with Germany.

Ironically the row reached its peak at a time when Coastal Command's aircraft, equipped with the combination of ASV radar sets and the 'Leigh Light', were beginning to achieve major successes against the U-boats. In the dark hours of 4 June, the Italian submarine *Luigi Torelli* was charging her batteries on the surface, when she was suddenly surprised by a blinding white light projected from a diving aircraft. After three passes, Squadron Leader J. Crosswell's *Wellington* succeeded in damaging the U-boat in the first successful attack using ASV radar in conjunction with Squadron Leader Leigh's airborne searchlight to illuminate the target. Only five 'Leigh-Light' equipped Wellingtons were in service but they soon proved their value when on 5 July, Pilot Officer W. Howell, an American pilot in coastal Command, made the first kill, sinking U-502, in the Bay of Biscay.

U-boat Command reacted swiftly to the new danger, issuing on 16 June an emergency order: 'Because the danger of attacks without warning from radar-equipped aircraft is growing by night and day, in future U-boats are to surface by day . . .' It was a bad miscalculation; Coastal Command sightings doubled and the RAF made four kills before the end of September. None had been sunk in the previous five months in the Bay of Biscay, but now it seemed as if the radar and search-light equipped aircraft might wreck Dönitz's

Battle of Rival Technology: The advantage gained by the radar/Leigh Light equipped Coastal Command Wellington Bombers (top) in June 1942 was soon countered by the German *Metox* detector receiver (above). But Dönitz was already planning a revolutionary new U-boat based on the Walter experimental V.80 submarine (below) which during test runs at Kiel in 1940 had achieved underwater speeds of 14 knots.
Hitler was informed by Dönitz at

his Naval Conference of 28 September 1942 that two of the smaller revolutionary Walter U-boats had been ordered as prototypes for a fleet of 24. A larger boat was also to be developed for mass production. High hopes were placed on the new boats whose 'great underwater speed . . . enabled it to come within shooting range of the convoy in spite of the enemy escort vessels. It will also enable the submarine to elude its pursuers quickly . . .'

forthcoming Atlantic offensive. Then, in September, the number of sightings abruptly dropped, following U-boat Command's successful development of a receiver capable of detecting radar transmissions, which had been rushed into production by the Paris firms of *Metox* and *Grandin*. The receivers were rapidly installed in the U-boats with a makeshift wooden aerial called a *Biscaykreuz* by the crews, who had to dismantle it rapidly before their boat crash-dived in the few minutes available after the high-pitched buzz from the set warned the commander of approaching aircraft.

Dönitz may have found a temporary answer to the radar threat but he had become persuaded that the air menace could only be mastered by a technological leap forward with a new submarine design capable of operating submerged for lengthy periods. The new U-boat had to be a true submarine and not a submersible like the Type VII and IX, which surfaced frequently in order to recharge their batteries and whose underwater speed was also limited to a few knots. To make reasonable headway the U-boats used their diesel engines on the surface, but this made them vulnerable to air attack. Already, on 24 June 1942, Dönitz had pressed Raeder for a new high speed U-boat based on the design of Professor Walter, a brilliant and independent engineer whose Kiel works had already demonstrated the capabilities of his new hydrogen peroxide propulsion system with two small experimental boats. Dönitz argued that 'the immediate development and testing and most rapid construction of the Walter U-boat is in my opinion an essential measure and one which may well decide the whole issue of the war.' But Naval High Command had so far failed to provide resources for developing new submarine technology, after Hitler's directive early in 1940 cancelling work on experimental weapon systems that could not be in service by 1941. This had been a disastrously short-sighted decision whose impact was to seriously affect the U-boat arm which had to face a constant stream of new antisubmarine technology from the Allies. In August 1942, Dönitz took matters into his own hands and summoned a meeting attended by his senior engineer officer 'Papa' Thedsen, Germany's leading U-boat designers Schürer and Bröking, as well as the forceful Professor Walter. The conference was held in the U-boat Command headquarters which had been moved to an imposing mansion in the Avenue Maréchal Manoury in April 1942 after the daring British raid on St Nazaire had persuaded Hitler that the next target might be Dönitz's command post at Lorient.

The decision was taken that work should be started on an experimental Walter boat which promised high submerged speed and Dönitz took the opportunity of raising the matter of a new U-boat programme directly with Hitler at the Naval Conference held in Berlin on 28 September 1942. Taking care to emphasise the successes that the U-boats were currently enjoying, he outlined plans for the new underwater fleet based on the Walter design.

Hitler approved starting mass production of the new U-boats as soon as the designs were ready and at last accepted that 'the submarine plays a decisive role in the outcome of the war'.

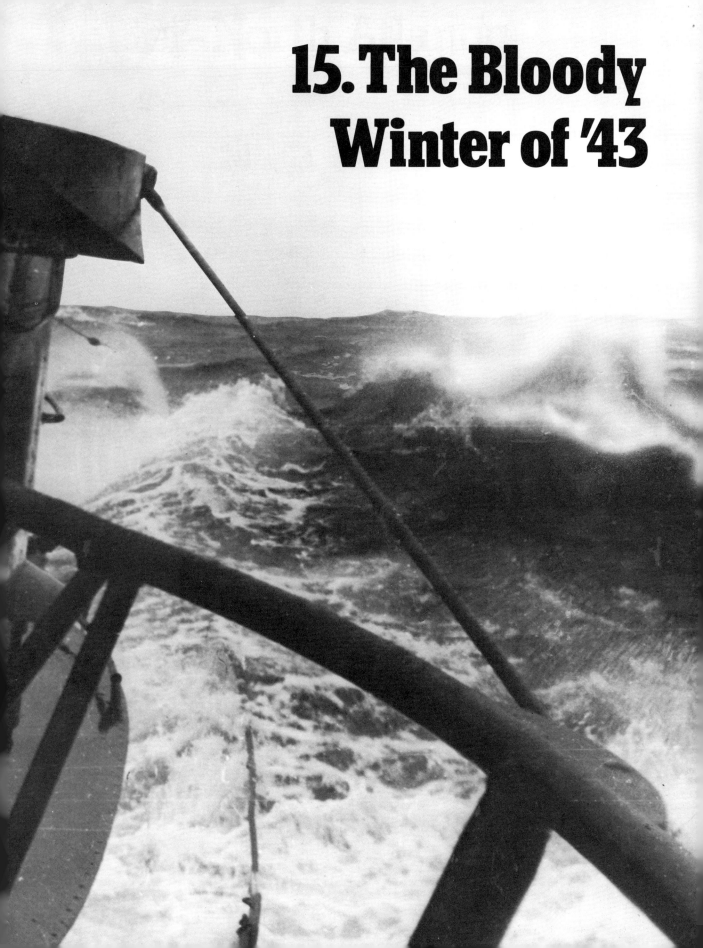

15. The Bloody Winter of '43

Improving air and sea defences in the Western Atlantic had brought the 'American Turkey Shoot' to an end and Dönitz decided that 'the war on shipping had now to be switched back to operations against the convoys to and from Britain in mid-Atlantic where they are beyond the range of land-based aircraft.' In mid-July two patrol groups, each of nine U-boats, put out from their Biscay bases to begin the new offensive. The decisive phase of the Battle of the Atlantic was about to begin.

Dönitz's U-boat arm was at last approaching the 300-boat strength that he had predicted in 1939 would be needed to strike a decisive blow. Thirty U-boats a month were now joining the Command, but Dönitz was also acutely aware that time was running out. It had taken three years for the German Supreme Command to give priority to the U-boat as a war-winning weapon, but already the vast Allied technical and industrial effort committed to its defeat was beginning to make an impact. Escorts were growing more numerous, aircraft were an increasing threat and radar had removed the U-boat's cloak of invisibility. Dönitz noted in his War Diary a concern that

> The ever increasing difficulties can only lead to high and indeed intolerable losses, to a decrease in the volume of our successes and to a reduction of our chances of ultimate victory in the U-boat war.

It was this fear of heavy casualties, coming on top of the unparalleled triumphs off the American coast that prompted the Admiral to request permission to broadcast in order 'to counter the exaggerated hopes that had been raised among the German people by the speeches and radio accounts of the tremendous successes of the previous months'.

When on 27 July 1942, the crisp voice of the Admiral himself was picked up in Britain, broadcasting a warning of 'harsh realities' and 'difficult times ahead', alarm bells rang in the Admiralty. This 'tip from the horse's mouth' was seen as confirming Admiral Pound's prediction that 'another turning point in the U-boat war is approaching' and a week later, the new offensive began when a Wolf Pack was successfully directed on to the slow eastbound convoy SC 94 as it passed through the Air Gap on 5 August. Although the Canadian escort sank U-210, the operation against SC 94 convinced Dönitz that, by forming a patrol line to intercept the convoys as soon as they had left the protection of the Newfoundland and Iceland air patrols, he had found the 'deciding factor which justifies the continuation of our war on the convoys'.

U-boat Command's strategy for the offensive of the autumn and winter of 1942 was to set up patrol lines on either side of the 300 mile wide mid-

Atlantic Air Gap to intersect the movements of the east and westbound convoys. In the 'Devil's Gorge', as the U-boat commanders came to call it, the Wolf Packs could carry out their attacks unhampered by Allied aircraft. At first the advantage lay with the Germans because the Atlantic escort forces had been reduced to protect the American coastal convoys and the African route which was threatened by Dönitz's long-distance diversionary thrusts towards the Cape. For nearly six months U-boat Command also held another tactical advantage, when they discovered that the Allied convoys were being regularly routed on the same great circle track across the Atlantic to save fuel. Furthermore, as a result of brilliant intelligence work by the *B-Dienst*, Dönitz staff would know the sailing date and routes of the important eastbound convoys at the same time as Western Approaches Command. As soon as the Convoy and Routing Section of the Commander-in-Chief, US Fleet (COM-INCH), transmitted any encyphered radio message, it was now picked up and decyphered by the *B-Dienst*. 'Never forget', Dönitz was to inform Captain Bonatz whose team was responsible for providing this invaluable intelligence, 'that you are the only reconnaissance on which I can rely'. Bonatz served his Commander well; *B-Dienst* continued to break the Allied Convoy traffic, in spite of a complete change of Allied codes in August.

Whilst the U-boat Command knew more or less where the convoys were, the British, by contrast, were suffering a serious intelligence blackout. The 'Special Intelligence' intercepts fed to the Submarine Tracking Room had dried up after the German Naval High Command had completely revised its Enigma cyphers early in February 1942. After months of effort, the decrypting teams at Bletchley Park had failed to achieve their previous level of penetration of the naval traffic. Moreover, the cypher that proved the most complex was the so-called *Triton* Enigma which controlled the movements of the Atlantic U-boats. Without advanced Special Intelligence giving Dönitz's precise instructions and the positions of his patrol lines, attempts to steer convoys around the Wolf Packs depended on 'inspired guesswork'. This blackout lasted ten months, until Bletchley Park finally broke back into the U-boat codes in the second week of December 1942. There were, nevertheless, ways of building up an intelligence picture according to Patrick Beesly, a member of Commander Winn's team in the Submarine Tracking Room:

Decisive Factors: In the autumn of 1942, as the Battle moved towards its climax with 100 U-boats at sea, the Allies could deploy 140 escorts to protect the convoys (below, escorts at the Londonderry base). Much depended on the skill of the Admiralty plotting rooms (above) in being able to route the convoys around the U-boat concentrations, but because the *Triton* Atlantic U-boat code was not cracked for 10 months, operations relied on the 'inspired guesswork' of Commander Roger Winn's team in the Tracking Room and his deputy, Lieutenant Commander Patrick Beesly (left).

> Fortunately we could still read the cypher used by the vessels that escorted the U-boats into and out of their bases, so we could establish whenever a U-boat left or returned from patrol – if it arrived back safely. Radio Direction finding also played

an important part in our calculations, since it continued all the time and was instantaneous. Moreover, by this time we could recognise the various different types of signals – not all of which were in the Enigma code – and could establish whether the U-boat was making a 'short sighting signal' or a 'sinking report'. Using all this information, and by estimating the time of passage, we could marry up the significant events, such as sinkings, with the boats known to be at sea with a fair degree of accuracy.

The German successes of August 1942 continued into September when the westbound convoy ON 127 lost nine ships and the Canadian destroyer *Ottawa* in an action lasting nearly a week. Dönitz then tried to marshall the twenty operational boats in the area for an assault on the next eastbound convoy, SC 100; but his move was frustrated by heavy air patrols and bad weather after only three ships had been sunk.

In the two months after the resumption of the campaign on the North Atlantic the U-boats sank over one million tons of shipping, almost 50% of which was in convoy. There was clearly a need to reinforce the eleven Escort Groups (one American, four Canadian and six British) protecting the North Atlantic mainline since, without heavier escorts, effective counter-attacks could not be made against the large U-boat packs.

A solution to provide freelance Escort Groups to carry out the hunter-killer role was tried with Escort Group B 20, but these developments had to take second place to the need to cover the North African invasion convoys in late October and early November.

THE MURMANSK RUN

The drain on Allied naval resources worsened following the resumption of the Russian convoys in September. Since the disaster of PQ 17, only the heavily escorted US cruiser *Tuscaloosa* had made the trip, but now a renewed effort was believed to be essential to stave off the collapse of the Soviet Army. The original Liberty ship, *Patrick Henry*, was one of the 40 merchantmen loaded with tanks, fuel and aircraft which set sail on 6 September 1942 from Loch Ewe on the West Coast of Scotland. PQ 18's close escort was the heaviest ever assigned to a convoy, and was made up of the cruiser HMS *Scylla*, 29 destroyers, the escort carrier HMS *Avenger*, five armed trawlers and three rescue ships.

Yet even this massive defence was insufficient to prevent heavy losses in the fiercest convoy battle of the entire war which began on 13 September off the barren island of Spitzbergen in the Barents Sea. In the forenoon, the U-boats sank two merchantmen and the real destruction of PQ 18 began in the afternoon when the Luftwaffe attacked like 'a huge flight of nightmare locusts'. The *Avenger's* few Hurricanes valiantly tried to disrupt the attacks which also met an intense hail of anti-aircraft fire, but it was not enough as Lieutenant Wesley N. Miller USNR, of the Armed Guard aboard the American freighter *St Olaf* recorded:

> The ring of destroyers, the flak cruisers and the merchant ships gave them everything they had from a thousand guns. The noise was deafening. The aircraft carrier was trying desperately to get into position for the Hurricanes to take off into the

Nightmare Convoy: A third of PQ 18 was destroyed by the Luftwaffe (below, an ammunition ship is hit) in the war's fiercest convoy battle during the third week of September (bottom, Medical Officer standing by during the action). This halted the convoys until winter darkness set in.

wind. On and on came the torpedo planes in an endless line. They darted up and down, to confuse the aim of our gunners. Some of the planes were painted solid black with the tips of their wings orange or green. They were weird and awful.

Lieutenant Maynard commanding the tiny anti-aircraft battery aboard the US merchantman *Schoharie* reported 'The Heinkels were carrying only torpedoes which they let go at point-blank range, and then strafed the gun's crews as they zoomed up and away'. His crew managed to shoot down one of the German planes whose bombs were so devastating. 'In this attack one ship completely disintegrated upon being hit and nine others were sinking or too badly damaged to proceed.'

The convoy steamed on leaving a trail of debris floating in the Arctic Ocean as the air attacks continued for nearly a week. Although none were so serious as that first wave of bombers, by 17 September the ships' crews were approaching the exhaustion experienced by Lieutenant Miller:

I have not slept longer than two hours at night for the past three nights. My food is brought to the bridge. I do not leave even to visit the head. And so it went with the majority of the ship's crew, including the merchant crew. It was 21 hours duty out of every 24 if one wanted to live.

It was to be six more days before the surviving ships, which included the *Patrick Henry*, finally made the Russian port of Archangel on 21 September still harrassed by German bombers. Out of 40 ships, 13 had been sunk – 10 by air attack – and 80% of the casualties were American. At the same time the returning 15-ship convoy QP 14, had managed to dodge the air attacks by steering far to the north, but it ran into a U-boat pack. Four merchant ships, the British destroyer *Somali* and an escorting trawler were sunk.

The Admiralty cancelled all further Russian convoys until the darkness of the Arctic winter could give some cover against the Luftwaffe; to keep a trickle of supplies moving to the Soviet Union they tried instead sending fast merchantmen sailing independently, many of which got through. The German success against the Allied shipping in the Arctic was followed up by the U-boat in their operations in the North Atlantic during the second week in October when SC 104 lost eleven merchantmen to the Wolf Packs which concentrated around it in the 'Devil's Gorge' followed two weeks later by HX 212's loss of nine ships. The biggest convoy battle of the month took place in the mid-Atlantic when the Freetown-bound SL 125 lost twelve freighters to a ten U-boat pack that chanced across the convoy's course. At the end of the month, Dönitz was gratified that total destruction of Allied shipping in October was only just short of the 700,000 ton target.

The sacrifice of the ships from SL 125 turned out to be more than counterbalanced by the fact that they had drawn a group of southward bound U-boats away from the large troop convoys which were converging on North Africa for Operation *Torch*. The Allied landings involved some 350 merchant ships supported by 200 warships which crossed the mid-Atlantic in the last weeks of October almost completely unmolested by the U-boats, mainly because German intelligence services had failed to give any advance warning of this massive concentration of Allied shipping which was to land 70,000 men on the North African coast.

In the crucial first week of November, U-boat Command were fully occupied on the North Atlantic running their biggest convoy battle of the war so far. *B-Dienst* had given advance warning of the sailing of SC 107 a slow convoy of 43 ships laden with supplies for Britain, which was escorted by five Canadian escorts and the US Coastguard cutter *Gemini*. Dönitz had sent out the boats of Group *Violet* in a long patrol line to intercept the convoy as it passed out of range of the Newfoundland air patrols. The U-boats intercepted SC 107 in the small hours of 2 November and the Wolf Pack soon found that the inexperienced Canadian escort left plenty of gaps for them to get in amongst the convoy columns. US Coastguard Lieutenant John M. Waters witnessed the results from the *Gemini*:

> First came the dull shock as a torpedo hit *Empire Sunrise* three miles away, then the shrill clanging of the *Gemini*'s general alarm bell. In the compartment, illuminated only by a dim red light, men piled out of their bunks, attempting simultaneously to don clothing and life jackets. On the main deck they were greeted by an unforgettable sight. Every ship in the convoy was firing snowflakes, lighting the scene like daylight, and as they burned the noise of depth charges was heard again.

The battle raged on all night and saw the destruction of twelve merchant ships. Waters remembered men aboard his cutter greasing their feet in case they had to swim in the cold waters but his most vivid impression was 'a scene of stark unreality' and he wrote:

> as the months passed, this feeling would become engraved in the minds of many as one of the prime ingredients of a night combat action at sea. The usual reaction to the crash of a torpedo is fright, a sudden natural animal fright, accompanied by the pounding pulse, cold sweat and, as time goes on, by paradoxical yawns. Men forced to wait under extreme stress often tend to yawn, and on the deck of *Gemini*, bathed in a flickering light from the snowflakes and the burning *Dalcroy*, the yawning spread contagiously

The pack continued ravaging the convoy on and off for three more days until it reached the other side of the 'Black Pit', having lost fifteen ships. But the Germans had little enough time to celebrate their victory for on the early morning of 8 November 1942 news came that thousands of Allied troops were pouring ashore at Casablanca on the North African Atlantic coast as well as at Oran and near Algiers. The *Torch* landings followed hard on the British desert victory at El-Alamein on 4 November and within a week, the

The Führer's Will: After spectacular October successes in the North Atlantic, Dönitz failed to move the Wolf Packs south in time to operate against the huge *Torch* convoys (below). It was only after the landings were well under way that a force was sent against them with the orders: 'We must relentlessly carry out the Führer's will with our tested and brutal methods of attack.' Forced to operate submerged (above) because of heavy air and sea patrols, the U-boats were unable to achieve much success in the shallow waters.

German advance through Southern Russia was halted in the fierce hand-to-hand fighting at Stalingrad.

The North African invasion marked the turning point of the war in Europe. The Germans found their Mediterranean strategy threatened with collapse and Hitler's hasty decision to occupy Vichy France to prevent it joining the Allies, resulted in the scuttling of the surviving heavy ships of the French Fleet in Toulon. Only the U-boats could threaten the Allied landings, and Dönitz was instructed to dispatch 15 for an all-out attack, but they achieved little success. Operating in the shallow water against heavy anti-submarine defences and air patrols, two of the U-boats were sunk and six more were seriously damaged. After receiving instructions to send reinforcements Dönitz dispatched a strong protest to Berlin:

> To employ U-boats as suggested would have disastrous results on the war against shipping in the Atlantic which U-boat Command has always regarded, and still regards, as the primary task of the U-boat arm.

This time the Naval High Command gave in and drastically reduced the number originally insisted on by the Führer.

Dönitz's tactics appeared to be justified by November's record sinking of over 700,000 tons of shipping. This peak total, when taken together with the 160,000 tons destroyed by aircraft and other action, was the worst single month's losses for the Allies during the whole war. For the second month in succession, U-boat Command believed that they had outstripped their 700,000 ton target. If this could be sustained then even the phenomenal ship construction programme might not be sufficient to get the Allies through the coming winter.

THE ANTI-U-BOAT COMMITTEE

Even before the Admiralty statisticians had begun compiling the grim figures for November, the rocketing losses had shocked Churchill into action. In characteristic vein the Prime Minister set up the 'Anti-U-boat Warfare Committee', composed of his Service Chiefs, the Ministers of Production and Transport as well as the Prime Minister's scientific *alter ego* Lord Cherwell. This powerful group first met on 4 November 1942, under orders to hold weekly sessions. Churchill called for 'stronger escorts for our convoys' to face the growing number of U-boats expected in 1943 which he predicted 'would be operating in all the oceans, moving from one to the other' and appointing Sir Stafford Cripps as Deputy Chairman, he ordered a thorough review of all aspects of the anti-submarine campaign.

It was clear from the first meeting that air cover was the key to countering the new U-boat offensive. The First Sea Lord, Admiral Sir Dudley Pound, stressed the most urgent requirement for very long-range aircraft to cover 'the blind spot in the centre of the North Atlantic where no air cover is provided and where most of our heaviest losses occured.' Yet neither Prime Minister nor Air Staff were at first prepared to strengthen Coastal Command's forces at the expense of the air offensive against Germany. Air Marshal Harris, Commander-in-Chief of Bomber Command, went to great lengths to show that the bombing offensive was slowing U-boat production by 'up to six months', pointing to the raids on the MAN Diesel plant at Augsburg, the Deutz diesel works at Cologne and the frequent heavy raids on Hamburg shipyards.

In fact, the huge British and American bombing effort had so far done very little to interfere with either U-boat production or operations. By May 1943, when some 18,000 sorties had been made and 33,000 tons of bombs dropped the sacrifice of 882 bombers and their crews had not stopped a single U-boat going into service. It would be the proud boast of the Kriegsmarine's principal yard, Blohm & Voss at Hamburg, that it had consistently turned over a new U-boat to its crew every Tuesday without a single week's interruption. Nor were the heavy raids against the U-boat bases any more successful. USAAF daylight attacks did no damage to the concrete U-boat pens and RAF attempts to disrupt the Biscay bases by bombing the surrounding areas did little except destroy French houses and cause the Germans to order the night-time evacuation of all dockyard workers.

Bomber Command refused to accept that their squadrons were not achieving results and that Coastal Command's aircraft were having a greater effect by attacking U-boats at sea. Yet Coastal Command argued that, 'only about 10% of the aircraft attacks on U-boats are now lethal,' they pointed out, 'if this figure can be increased to 20–30% then the U-boat problem has been solved'.

Coastal Command's statistical analysis was the product of months of careful work by a high-powered team of scientific advisers set up in late 1941 under Nobel Prizewinner, Professor P. M. S. Blackett. This team of top flight young scientists was pioneering the use of operational research in the war against the U-boat. Theirs was not the traditional boffin's role of inventing new weapons, but the revolutionary one of applying scientific analysis to strategy and tactics in order to improve current methods.

Among the achievements of the Operational Research team was an improvement in the kill-rate against U-boats merely by fixing far more shallow settings for airborne depth-charges. Careful scientific analysis of attacks on surfaced U-boats by aircraft had shown that the 'kill rate' could be dramatically increased from 4% to 20% by the simple measure of reducing the firing-pistol settings on the depth-charges from the usually accepted 100 ft to the shallower 25 ft optimum. Within eighteen months the scientists had

Wasted Effort: The Allied bombing offensive against the French Biscay ports came too late. The 30 ft thick concrete U-boat pens withstood thousands of tons of high explosive (below, the USAAF raid Lorient on 21 October 1942). The RAF carried out a heavy campaign against the construction yards and diesel engine works in Germany but Air Marshal Harris's (right) predictions that his aircraft had caused a six month delay in output proved wrong.

improved this, with the introduction of a new bombsight and increased spacing of the depth-charge pattern, to the point where nearly half the attacks made by aircraft on surfaced U-boats were lethal. At the same time, operational research methods were being applied to develop a 'Planned Maintenance' programme for Coastal Command which would increase its flying effort by over 60%, by making more efficient use of air and ground crews and aircraft servicing.

It was to be many months before this increase in operational efficiency increased the number of hours flown by every aircraft and during this time, the Anti-U-boat Warfare Committee was locked in a fierce debate over the competing claims for new aircraft between Coastal and Bomber Commands. The Admiralty argued strongly for increasing the number of aircraft at sea before the Battle of the Atlantic reached a critical point. It had been found that the new Mark III Liberator's patrol range could be increased to over 800 miles by fitting extra fuel tanks in one of the three bomb bays and reducing the depth charge load to 16. Just two dozen or so of the Very Long Range (VLR) Liberators would enable the Air Gap to be closed, but Bomber Command, with the support of the Prime Minister, was determined that nothing was going to stop them getting the new American bombers for the offensive against German industry. They also refused to relinquish any of the first 80 sets of the new 10 centimetre radar due in January. Tests on this new equipment, which had been developed by the Americans from the British cavity magnetron, had indicated a dramatic technical improvement on the British or German sets then in use. When an ASV version finally found its way into a Coastal Command plane in March 1943, pilots were astonished to find that they could easily distinguish the profile of a trimmed-down U-boat running on the surface at night; aircraft 'kills' rose accordingly. If just a handful of the sets had been available in early 1943, they might have been significant in the course of the battle, but Bomber Command maintained their exclusive right to the new weapon, code-named *H2S*.

The Anti-U-boat Committee did, however, agree that the Air Gap must be closed. Since the Admiralty reported that neither its 13 Merchant Aircraft Carriers nor the 5 US-built escort carriers could be operational before the late spring of 1943, Churchill had once again to make a personal appeal to Roosevelt for aircraft. On 20 November, he cabled Washington for '30 Liberators with centimetre ASV equipment' promising that 'these aircraft would be put to work immediately where they would make a direct contribution to the American war effort'. The President replied that the only long-range Liberators available were those already allocated to General Eisenhower in North Africa, which could only be used with his permission. It was accepted that they would only operate from Morocco and for another three months the Air Gap was to remain dangerously wide.

If the Allies faced the prospect of having to fight the U-boat battles without adequate air cover, the surface escort situation was not much better. Admiral King had demanded the immediate return of destroyers transferred from the Pacific to cover the initial stages of the North African landings, placing an increased burden for protecting the vital supply convoys on the Royal Navy. Allowing for a fifth of the total strength to be refitting at any one time only 108 would be available in the North Atlantic after the *Torch* convoys and the Freetown route had been covered. The escort building programme in the United States, Canada and Britain was going ahead as fast as possible without interfering with the vital repair and construction work on merchant ships. Production of the large new twin-screw *River* Class escorts had been slowed down when it was found that they were too big for the slips in many of the small yards and a new *Castle* Class design had been rushed through.

However, every step was being taken to step up the efficiency of those escorts that *were* in service and this reached a new pitch after the appointment of Admiral Sir Max Horton, as C-in-C Western Approaches on 19 November 1942.

A THIEF TO CATCH A THIEF

The new man running Britain's war against the U-boats was a suitably tough and ruthless professional ex-submariner who drove his staff hard – in complete contrast to the urbane Admiral Noble who had achieved his results with skill and persuasion. Max Horton had acquired his fiery reputation as a dashing young submarine commander who had flown the 'Jolly Roger' after sinking a German cruiser off Heligoland in the First World War. Since 1940, he had been commanding the British Submarine Flotillas and had even turned down the chance to command the Home Fleet. But such was his reputation for inspired leadership that the Board of Admiralty decided to put him in charge of the Battle of the Atlantic at the critical time. Putting the leading British submariner against Dönitz was 'setting a thief to catch a thief' and it paid off handsomely in the coming months.

Horton's prickly reputation had preceded him to Derby House and it was a little time before the staff adapted to his 'quite ruthless and quite selfish' manner. 'He knew everyone's job, but provided you knew your job a little better than Max then you were all right'. A devout Roman Catholic, Horton's aloof manner came with an equally fierce determination to succeed inherited from his Jewish forbears. His dealings with the thousand strong Staff at Derby House were soon running smoothly, thanks to the tact and charm of 30-year-old Kay Hallaran who had been born in Cleveland, Ohio, and who had been selected as his Flag Lieutenant. Kay Hallaran was a perfect foil for tempering Horton's aggressive manner and according to the Superintendent of Wrens at Derby House 'She had immense poise and savoir faire and never got rattled. . . . I doubt if Sir Max ever realised how much she did for him. He never showed much consideration for his staff and she carried out an exacting job with immense patience and cheerfulness.'

Horton lost little time in making his strong personality felt when he informed the Admiralty, soon after taking command on 5 December, of the urgent need for 'Support Groups'', which he believed should be composed of fast sloops and destroyers rather than slow corvettes. 'The immediate objective must therefore be: to raise the standard of the less efficient group',

Ruthless Determination: The arrival at Derby House of the ex-submariner Admiral Sir Maxwell Kennedy Horton (with his able Flag Lieutenant, Kay Hallaran) marked the beginning of a ruthless drive against the U-boats. He put great store on escort training and all the escort captains in his command had to take part in regular sessions at the Tactical School (below) playing 'The Game'.

Horton decided, and called for a special officer responsible for training to be attached to his Command. As a submariner, he realised the importance of seagoing tactical training. The former luxury yacht of millionaire Tom Sopwith, HMS *Philante*, was soon doing duty as a 'convoy' while the escorts practised anti-U-boat tactics against mock attacks made by two old submarines. Coastal Command pilots joined in these exercises which were obligatory for every Escort Group before putting to sea for its next spell of duty.

The Admiral paid particular attention to the exercises conducted in the Western Approaches Tactical School established in January 1942 on the top floor of the Exchange Building close to Derby House. Here, all officers in Western Approaches Command were obliged to take a six-day course in the theory of U-boat and escort tactics. Young officers were tested in their skills by playing 'The Game', which consisted of simulating the bridges of escorts with curtained booths from whose narrow slits they could see model convoys and escorts being moved over the floor by Wren plotters. Ironically, the first time that Horton played 'The Game' he took the role of a U-boat Commander, and, much to his chagrin, found himself 'sunk' on every enemy attack by a particularly skilful escort. His staff did not reveal that the 'escort' commander who sank the former submarine ace was a Wren Third Officer!

The importance of training when it came to defending the convoys out on the North Atlantic was emphasised by the markedly lower casualty rate achieved by the British Escort Groups. In the six months since June 1942, the six Western Approaches Command Groups had escorted 63 convoys for the loss of only 23 ships, compared to the 53 ships which had become casualties in convoys escorted by the four Royal Canadian Navy Groups and the 10 lost by the one US Navy Group.

The relatively poor showing of the Royal Canadian Navy was, in part, the result of the tremendous expansion that had occurred in little more than three years from 2,000 men and a handful of warships to a peak of 90,000 men and 400 warships. Although the Canadian shipyards had performed a magnificent feat in constructing hundreds of corvettes, it needed more than vessels to create a naval tradition. Many of the enthusiastic young Canadians had come straight from the farms of Alberta and Ontario, and naturally found it difficult to cope with life aboard a bucking corvette in mid-Atlantic. Most had undergone only a rudimentary training course before finding themselves in the midst of one of the fiercest sea struggles in history.

The rigorous discipline of the Royal Navy was certainly not very apparent in the democratically run Canadian warships and one British escort commander was appalled when an RCN corvette hauled alongside with the words 'WE WANT LEAVE' painted in large letters on her rust-streaked sides. Many British officers believed that their partners would have done much better to have trained and run mixed escort groups with the Royal Navy, instead of insisting on keeping their national units together whenever possible. In many ways this reflected the fiercely independent spirit of the Canadians who were trying to run their own show in the shadow of the mighty US Navy. However they were steadily improving with experience and

SAILOR 1942

He's college-trained for America's merchant marine: Ready to sail, save lives or fight!

Front-Line Casualty Rates: In 1942 nearly 8,000 seamen lost their lives in British ships alone. With such high casualty rates and the increasing tempo of the German attack the authorities on both sides of the Atlantic were apprehensive about morale. In America the US Maritime Commission was able to pay the new young sailors it advertised for (above) very high rates for the risks they ran. The British concentrated on cutting down the 30% death rate experienced in crews of torpedoed ships by developing rubber immersion suits (top right) and introducing more specially equipped Rescue Ships (right) into service.

by the end of 1942 the RCN warships had built up the creditable score of six U-boats destroyed.

The US Navy also did not prove receptive to British proposals for rationalising the north Atlantic convoys under a single Command. Even though the US Navy had only a single operational Atlantic Escort Group, Admiral King was determined not to relinquish control of it or the convoys, which came under operational command of the C-in-C US Atlantic Fleet when they passed the 26 degree 'CHOP line. This added to the difficulties of shepherding the convoys through the growing number of Wolf Packs in the Air Gap. After much pressure Western Approaches Command was granted an extension of their control when the CHOP line was moved 500 miles further west to the 35 meridian on 12 November 1942.

'ADMIRABLE AND WONDERFUL'

The British Ministry of War Transport was always fearful that the high casualty rates in the Merchant Service might break morale. Reports of men 'jumping ship' were scrutinised for any increase and special questionnaires were drawn up by psychologists and circulated to try to discover how the seamen were reacting to the strain. Nothing significant was revealed – except a general grouse about the poor food at sea. By the middle of 1942 the Ministry of Shipping could confidently report, 'Morale has not so far been affected and the only thing one can say with conviction on the subject is that it is admirable and wonderful.'

The spirit and courage displayed by the Merchant Service was truly remarkable and was admired by the men of the Royal Navy who sailed alongside them. It certainly was not pay or conditions that kept them coming forward to man the ships, in 1942 the wage for an able seaman was set at £22.12s.6d a month including danger money. What kept men at sea even during the blackest months of the Atlantic struggle in 1942 was a quiet and deep bond of common purpose that was shared by the youngest cabin boy to the most weatherbeaten old skipper. They knew that Britain's survival depended on a determination to fight their vessels through the worst that the U-boats and the ocean could hurl against them.

It was this same sense of purpose, coupled with a sense of adventure, that attracted many thousands of seamen volunteers in the United States. Many were 16-year-olds, fresh from high school. At first the powerful seamen's Labour Unions resented the way in which the Maritime Commission tried to turn out thousands of seamen in the semi-military 'boot camps' established in Brooklyn, the Great Lakes and San Francisco. To counter their restrictive labour practices, Admiral Land had to do some tough talking. In May 1942 he had warned that the Maritime Commission was not 'engaged in settling some industrial argument but in staving off a terrible defeat at sea'.

The seamen's Unions succeeded in driving a tough bargain in pay, and ensured that all their 60,000 pre-war members were taken on first, before allowing the Maritime Commission to go ahead with recruiting the ¼ m. new men. One result was that the US seamen earned twice the British wage, he

234

was paid a basic $90 a month, plus overtime, plus a 100% bonus for sailing in the North Atlantic and free Federal life insurance of $10,000 was thrown in. This huge discrepancy in pay frequently led to trouble when British and US seamen found themselves drinking in the same bars.

The relatively good pay and conditions on US ships were not only the envy of the British seamen, as Admiral Land discovered when a delegation of women, anxious to join up, invaded his Washington office:

A blonde with a very short skirt and bare legs led a female contingent of fifteen to twenty to the Commerce building. The ladies who surrounded my desk were of mixed nationalities and included a couple of coloured women. In a lengthy conference that followed, I listened to their arguments, one of which was that Russian women were at sea and that at least one Russian skipper was a woman.

After exhausting all my negative efforts, I finally told them that the question of their morals must be considered. To this the blonde leader angrily retorted 'Damn you, Admiral. You take care of your morals and we'll take care of ours.'

Women did not serve – at least officially – with the US Merchant Marine, but there was a notable exception in the British service when Victoria Drummond from Lambeth qualified as a Second Engineer. She was awarded the OBE and became a popular war hero after she took command in the engine-room of her ship which had been bombed in the Channel. When her ship safely crossed the Atlantic to Norfolk, Virginia, the US Press gave her a great reception.

The Atlantic in the winter of 1942/43 was no place for a woman, and this was made plain by a chilling piece of propaganda in the Christmas issue of *Volkischer Beobachter* which carried a large map of the Atlantic liberally sprinkled with red dots:

> The red dots on the chart of the Atlantic Ocean look like drops of blood. Each one of them marks the position of the sinking of an enemy merchant ship or transport by German and Italian U-boats in the period 1st January to 17th December 1942 . . . Every ship sunk is like a heavy loss of blood to reduce the fighting power of England and the USA . . .

The German claims to have sent sixteen million tons of Allied shipping to the bottom of the ocean since the beginning of the year proved to be a propaganda 'doubling' of the actual figure. Moreover, the total losses in December had fallen to less than half a million tons for the first time in a year.

U-boat Command had only been able to mount two large pack operations in the month because of the atrocious weather conditions and the Allied return to evasive routing. A pack of 22 U-boats, directed against the fast eastbound convoy HX 217, had arrived on 8 December as the convoy passed under the cover of the Iceland air patrols: only two ships were lost for the cost of one U-boat sunk by the aircraft. The need for air cover to defeat the Wolf Packs was soon proved by the fate of the slow eastbound convoy, ONS 154, which was directed onto a southerly course to escape the worst of the weather. Unfortunately, this took it well beyond the range of the Iceland-based air patrols for too long and its 45 ships became the easy target for an eleven boat pack that was able to carry on a running battle for three days. The Canadian escort managed to sink U-356 but their convoy had lost 14 ships by 30 December.

MADDENING HABITS

The extension of Western Approaches Command's operational control was a considerable advantage to Admiral Horton as he set about bringing his own very personal direct style to the way he ran the British end of the Battle of the Atlantic. The daily routine of their new C-in-C took some members of his staff by surprise:

> He had some maddening habits, he would play golf all afternoon then return, dine and play a rubber of bridge and then come down to his office overlooking the Operations Room at about 11.30 pm.

The Admiral's insistence on his daily round of golf even though the U-boat packs might be converging on a convoy out on the Atlantic ocean, caught the imagination of the American public after a *Life* Magazine photographer had caught Horton's stocky figure in cap and tweed trousers teeing off on the Hoylake course overlooking the approaches to Liverpool. It epitomised the tradition of Sir Francis Drake, who had calmly finished his game of bowls before sailing to defeat the Spanish Armada three and a half centuries before.

Whilst Horton prepared to direct the night convoy battles with an afternoon on the golf course, in Paris, Vice-Admiral Karl Dönitz was to be found most afternoons walking alone in the Bois de Boulogne or listening to an organ recital in Notre Dame. After a morning's work, dominated by the 9 am conference at U-boat Command Headquarters in the Avenue Maréchal Manoury Dönitz and his staff organised Wolf Packs. As one of his staff officers, Captain Meckel, recalled:

> Dönitz would always make a point of going out accompanied by his adjutant or be driven around Paris for two hours. He liked to retire early and would go upstairs to his room after dinner, usually about 10 o'clock. Only on special occasions would he stay up late and go to the Opera or celebrate his birthday or an award to one of the senior commanders. Then we would all accompany him to a Paris Club where he would be very generous at entertaining all of us, although he took care not to drink too much himself.

> If an alarm occurred or a convoy came under attack and we happened to be out during the evening, couriers would arrive to bring him and the staff back to the operations room. This occurred on one memorable occasion in the middle of a Paris Opera performance of the *Magic Flute*. The alarm came just after Sarastro's aria *In diesen heiligen Hallen, kennt man die Rache nicht*' – (Within these holy walls, vengeance is banished).

As Dönitz and his staff officers hurried back to their operations room to wait for the radio signals from the U-boats reporting their sinkings, a bloody battle would be raging on the wintry Atlantic Ocean. From his service in Royal Navy escorts, Nicholas Monsarrat wrote of the stark reality of the destruction wreaked by the German torpedoes:

> The first thing you notice when a ship goes down is a hateful smell of oil on the water. (We grew to loathe that smell; as well as a ship sunk, it meant survivors drenched with fuel oil, coughing it up, poisoned by it). But there is always an amazing amount of stuff left on the surface – crates, planks, baulks of wood, coal-dust, doors, rope ends, odd bits of clothing – a restless smear of debris, looking like a wrecked jumble sale, on which the searchlight plays. Here and there lights may be flickering: too often they are not the ship's you are hoping for, but empty rafts with automatic calcium flares attached to them, burning uselessly, mute witnesses to disaster. . . .

Few U-boat men who witnessed the destruction their actions caused remained immune to the experience. 'To torpedo a ship and see all those people flying through the air and getting burned was always a horrible sight that made many of us feel physically sick' admitted one U-boat petty officer, 'But we had to get used to the fact that war is very hard.' Everyone aboard a U-boat knew that their end would be just as horrifying if an escort accurately dropped depth-charges that split their hull apart underwater. Yet those who suffered most were the crews of the merchantmen, who faced little better than a 50-50 chance of survival if their ship sank under them. Whenever possible Rescue Ships sailed with the convoys, and these specially equipped vessels fitted with medical facilities and nets to scoop up survivors, saved over 4,000 seamen during the war. Unlike the U-boat men or the escort crews, the Allied seamen were strictly civilians. They were the real heroes of the Battle and nearly 8,000 Allied seamen lost their lives in the slaughter of 1942.

Off Duty: For the two men running the Battle of the Atlantic, the afternoon brought the opportunity for a few hours' relaxation. Horton (left above) played golf whilst in Paris (left below) Dönitz took an afternoon stroll. On the Atlantic the seaman's daily routine left them little time to come to terms with the risks as D. Willet recalled:
Leaving home for my next trip walking to the bus stop in the village of Danbury, Essex, my kit bag used to feel like lead. But once on the train on my way to Liverpool or Greenock where I had to join a new ship I used to feel better. Once at sea we were always wrapped up with the routine of watches. Off duty time was spent mostly sleeping, playing cribbage or the ever-popular tombola. Whenever the convoy was under attack by U-boat I always felt uneasy myself and tried to think of home – never of actually getting torpedoed – 'THE HAMMER' – as we used to call it.

January
The Wolf Packs Unleashed

The New Year started well for U-boat Command when Dönitz directed the *Delphin Group* to intercept a tanker convoy after a chance sighting by a U-boat shortly after it sailed from Trinidad. The nine tankers of TM 1 were bound for Gibraltar defended by the British B 5 Escort Group which had been operating alongside the Americans in the Caribbean. Failure to take the evasive course signalled after the Tracking Room had warned of the U-boat concentration off the Azores, brought the convoy right into the jaws of the Wolf Pack. With many of the escorts' radar, and HF/DF out of action, they were ill-prepared to stand up to the ferocious two-day battle in which the *Delphin* pack sank six of the nine valuable tankers. Only the timely arrival of air patrols from Gibraltar on 10 January 1943 prevented the U-boats wiping out the convoy completely.

The loss of so many tankers and so much valuable oil came at a galling moment for the British Government, which was facing a fuel crisis. Domestic consumption was cut back and the already stringent petrol ration was reduced by another 10% which put many bus services in England off the roads. 'This does not look good at all', Churchill had commented in the margin of a report that suggested that the Fleet might be immobilised to allow its reserves of bunkering fuel to be used to keep the convoys running.

Once again, the Prime Minister had to turn to the President to save the situation by begging the loan of some fast US tankers to run an emergency series of 'greyhound' fuel convoys from the Caribbean direct to Britain. But the heavy protection for these valuable tankers could only be found at the expense of reducing the escorts and the frequency of the Atlantic convoys, whose cycle was opened out from eight to ten days.

The first days of 1943 saw the Battle of the Atlantic taking an ominous turn for Britain, faced by fuel crisis and a shortage of ships and escorts. The Soviet Ambassador could not have chosen a worse time to press a demand for more and bigger Arctic convoys. 'I am getting to the end of my tether with these repeated Russian naggings,' Churchill wrote in a curt minute to the Foreign Secretary, 'our escorts all over the world are so attenuated that losses out of all proportion are falling on the British Mercantile Marine.'

It was not only the delicate balance of the British supply situation that was being threatened by the increasing tempo of the U-boat war in the Atlantic. On 2 January 1943 the Combined Chiefs of Staff in Washington warned that they were 'deeply concerned' about the disruption of Allied strategic planning if sinkings continued at the rate of ½ m. tons a month.

The Anti-U-boat Warfare Committee on 5 January 1943 faced the grim fact that, but for the million tons of new shipping produced by United States yards in December, British cargo-carrying capacity would have been reduced by another 600,000 tons.

An Admiralty memorandum warned that there were neither shipping nor escorts available to keep both Britain supplied with 33⅓ million tons of imports and to carry out the build-up of the US army in Britain. It was clear to Churchill that only the United States could provide the aircraft and ships necessary to prevent a collapse of Allied strategy and a list of requirements was drawn up for the Anglo-American summit in Casablanca.

Tanker Disaster: After the victory of the *Delphin* U-boat Pack against convoy TM 1 the Admiralty recorded: 'This convoy lost 7 ships out of 9, the highest percentage loss that any convoy has suffered by U-boats alone in this war'. For the survivors of tanker torpedoings (left) the suffering was immediate and the loss of their oil shipments was a severe blow to Britain now plunged into the worst fuel crisis of the war. Churchill was brought face to face with the possibility that the Fleet's fuel reserves might have to be used in an emergency to keep the convoys running.

On 12 January 1943 Churchill flew into the newly liberated Moroccan city with his staff for two weeks hard bargaining with Roosevelt and his Service Chiefs. Both sides were aware that future strategy was dictated by their dependence on the Atlantic supply line. The President and Prime Minister also knew that Stalin had been promised the Second Front by the end of the year, although they could take some comfort from the fact that the first of a new series of Russian convoys had arrived to keep the supply line open to the Red Army.

The *Symbol* conference took place in the ugly Hotel Anfa overlooking the white walls and palm trees of the old city. Churchill and Roosevelt carefully stayed apart from the main staff discussions which sometimes became heated. The Americans soon realised that the shortage of ships would force them to abandon their original strategy of a European invasion in 1943. The British argued that this was an opportunity to expand the Mediterranean offensive with landings in Sicily and Italy but General Marshall was reluctant to change his plans. His fellow Service Chief, Admiral King was undismayed by the strategic dilemma over Europe, and believed that far more emphasis should be given to the Pacific.

After a series of hard debates, the British won acceptance for a limited extension of the Mediterranean offensive with *Operation Husky* – the invasion of Sicily. There was to be no switch to the Pacific, instead the US Navy

Priorities at Casablanca: At the SYMBOL Conference, the Allied Chiefs of Staff were deeply concerned about the impact of the U-boat campaign on their overall strategic plans. Although measures to defeat the U-boat were given priority, the American Service Chiefs did little to speed up the delivery of the urgently needed VLR Liberators to close the mid-Atlantic Air Gap.

Left to right: Admiral King, C-in-C US Navy; General Marshall, Chief-of-Staff US Army; two staff officers; Major-General Sir Hastings Ismay; Admiral Lord Louis Mountbatten, Chief of Combined Operations; Admiral Sir Dudley Pound, First Sea Lord; General Sir Alan Brooke, Chief of Imperial General Staff; Air Marshall Sir Charles Portal, Chief of Air Staff; Field Marshall Sir John Dill.

was to increase its commitment to the Atlantic, by providing the escorts to cover the *Bolero* troop convoys. An important factor in winning over the Americans was a key British Naval Staff report, *Security of sea communications in the Atlantic and its repercusions on our strategy*. This warned that still heavier U-boat attacks were expected and that 'the enemy has spotted our weak spot, namely, air cover from Newfoundland'. The Americans were told, 'surface escorts are at present quite inadequate to meet the threat against our convoys', and 'We are short of V.L.R. aircraft generally and, in particular, the shore-based air forces in the western half are insufficient in types, numbers and training to provide the desired protection in the Newfoundland area.'

In two succinct pages the report made it clear that unless the USA met the 'requests' for 65 additional escorts, 12 escort carriers and 'as many as possible of the Liberators to be delivered under the existing agreement in January and February' – the Atlantic supply line could not be kept running at the level demanded by Allied strategy. In return for the US commitment on the Atlantic, the British agreed to keep open the possibility of launching a limited cross-Channel attack (*Sledgehammer*) in 1943, should the Russian situation become desperate. At the final plenary session, attended by Roosevelt and Churchill on 23 January 1943, the primary Anglo-American objective was unanimously agreed. 'The defeat of the U-boat must remain a first charge on the resources of the United Nations'.

THE FALL OF RAEDER

Hitler had also come to clear decisions about the future of the war at sea by realising that the time had come for Admiral Raeder to be replaced. The Führer had become increasingly dissatisfied with the intransigence of his elderly Commander in Chief, and the poor performance of the Kriegsmarine's heavy ships in Norway against the supply line to Russia.

Matters had been brought to a head with the sailing, on 15 December 1942, of the first of a new series of Arctic convoys to take advantage of the winter darkness. They were now being split into two halves and the Admiralty's decision to re-classify them JW appeared to have reversed the ill fortune of the previous PQ series since the 16 ships of JW 51A were to get through unmolested by the German warships. Sailing a week later the second section, JW 51 B, became the target for *Operation Regenbogen*, but the heavy ships *Hipper* and *Lützow* encountered fierce resistance from the convoy's escorting destroyers led by Captain Sherbrooke in HMS *Onslow*. Admiral Kummetz's task force was forced to abandon its objective after a confused mêlée in poor visibility, in which his flagship *Hipper* was damaged. The convoy escaped, unharmed, because the timely arrival of the British cruiser covering force sent Kummetz running for home on the assumption that they were the vanguard of the Home Fleet.

Operation Regenbogen was a humiliating defeat and Hitler's rage knew no bounds. When Raeder arrived to report at the Führer's Rastenburg headquarters on 6 January he was 'well aware that quite a clash was about to take place'. After 'a spiteful and quite unobjective attack on the Navy' Hitler told the Grossadmiral that the surface fleet had no further part to play and was to be paid off at once. The Führer, encouraged by Goering, believed that the warships' steel could be used to build tanks for the Eastern front.

Raeder went away to prepare a simple 'Guide to Seapower' in which he argued, that to abandon the surface ships would be a 'victory gained by our enemies without any effort on their part. It will be viewed as a sign of weakness and a lack of understanding of the supreme importance of naval warfare in the final stage of the war.'

But Hitler's decision was 'irrevocable' and Raeder had no alternative but to tender his resignation. Advising the Führer on a suitable choice of successor, he put forward the names of Admirals Carls and Dönitz, informing the Führer that 'if he wished to emphasize that the U-boat arm was now of primary importance, the choice of Admiral Dönitz would be fully justified'. This was indeed the Führer's view and on 30 January 1943 the Commander of the U-boat arm took over the helm.

At first Dönitz welcomed the chance to pay off the big ships, which he had consistently recommended as a way of releasing men and materials for the Atlantic war. At the same time he was determined to give the priority to the U-boat arm and in order to remove opposition in the Naval High Command, he retired all the senior Admirals and set about bringing 'personal influence to bear on Hitler himself'. In a series of long visits to headquarters Dönitz soon cut through the military entourage and established direct access to the

Defeat and Resignation: The *Hipper*'s ill-fated sortie through the Arctic seas (above) against convoy JW 51A on 31 December 1942 was followed by Hitler's demand that all the remaining big ships should be paid off. It was the final humiliation for Grossadmiral Raeder (left) who had such high hopes for the surface fleet that he tendered his resignation, as C-in-C of the Kriegsmarine.

Führer with whom he discussed his plans, carefully presenting his objectives 'in bold lines on a broad canvas in such a way as would excite Hitler's vivid powers of imagination'. Hitler, relieved not to be lectured, reciprocated the confidence and, approving of the ruthless dedication of the Kriegsmarine Commander-in-Chief, he promised to give top priority to the rapid expansion of the U-boat fleet. News of Dönitz's appointment had sent morale plummeting in the surface ships and a bitter joke had gone the rounds that a picture of an empty expanse of sea was to be titled: 'The German Naval Review of 1950 – Nothing but U-boats all submerged'.

After his first conference with the Führer on 8 February 1943, Dönitz had indeed advanced a plan to pay off all the large ships, including the *Tirpitz*, by the autumn of 1943. However, three weeks later he had begun to appreciate the strategic role they played in Norway and had modified his proposals. Dismantling them would also be a major task, absorbing 7,000 men working in five dockyards for 18 months, therefore Hitler finally agreed to spare the surviving battleships and cruisers. Dönitz now placed maximum emphasis on the U-boat campaign and got all personnel engaged in U-boat production and maintenance exempted from military service. He also quickly reached agreement with Reichs-Armaments Minister, Albert Speer, for the increased steel supplies to raise U-boat production and for priority to be given to development of the new Walter designs.

As Commander-in-Chief, Dönitz was now in a position to deal with a matter that had been causing him serious concern after the U-boat sinkings had fallen again in January; the possibility that the British might be reading the German signal traffic. At his first meeting with Hitler he had, with the aid of maps, pointed out that the enemy had 'found out the locations of our U-boats, and in some cases, even the exact number of boats'. This indicated either that the Atlantic U-boat *Triton* Enigma had been penetrated by British Intelligence; that 'undetected reconnaissance planes' were locating the U-boat patrol lines, or that a traitor was at work. The Naval Staff still refused to believe that it was possible to break their codes, and Dönitz informed Hitler that 'all necessary steps had been taken' to detect the traitor.

Captain Meckel, Dönitz's staff communications officer, was one of those who was intensively watched:

It went so far that the Chief of Staff, Admiral Godt, had all his staff officers observed by military intelligence. After we had been cleared, he apologised. No traitor was discovered and Dönitz jokingly said to Godt, "Now it can only be you or me".

In fact, after the ten month black-out, British intelligence had succeeded in again penetrating the Atlantic U-boat Code. The decrypting teams at Bletchley Park finally began breaking the signal traffic in the second week of December 1942, and by the end of January they were decoding substantial parts of the U-boat communications, often in hours rather than days.

This major breakthrough into the complicated *Triton* Enigma was achieved with the aid of large numbers of the new model electromechanical computers called 'Bombs' to solve the daily rotor setting on the German coding machines. One of the Wrens who operated one bank of 'Bombs' was Helen Rance:

> When we had plugged up each 'Bomb' with a possible setting, it was switched on and it started off 'clickety-click-clickety click' as the wheels on the front of the machine turned round all the time. Whenever the machine had a stop, we used to note the settings down on a piece of paper and hand it to the other girls with the checking machines. If it was a good stop we used to phone it through immediately to Bletchley Park and they would tell us whether or not 'The Job had come up'.

The right setting of the Enigma rotor wheels would then allow the deciphering of a whole day's signal traffic on the British-built duplicate machines. Sometimes the right combination was found within hours – at other times they were unlucky and the 'Bombs' could take a week of endless clicking to come up with the plug-settings. Even with the aid of the 'Bomb' computers, the successful decrypting of the Enigma messages still relied on a great deal of careful detective work. The decrypting teams almost certainly gained valuable clues in late 1942 from another successful boarding of a U-boat. On 30 October in the Eastern Mediterranean, five escorts forced U-559 to the surface after nine hours of depth-charging. Within minutes HMS *Petard* had raced alongside so that a boarding party was able to jump aboard and were soon inside searching for papers.

It is more than possible that some of her secret cypher codes and parts of the new model Enigma machine survived and were soon being rushed to Bletchley Park. The Mediterranean boats communicated with the so-called *Medusa* Enigma but the decrypting teams would have received valuable clues to assist them in unravelling the secrets of *Triton*.

Aided by the growing number of computers, the task of decrypting the Atlantic U-boat traffic was nevertheless arduous and time-consuming, and a complete or instantaneous breakdown of all signals was never possible. There were often delays and large gaps in 'Special Intelligence'. Fortunately members of Commander Winn's team, like Lieutenant Commander Patrick Beesly, could often fill in the gaps from their other intelligence sources:

> From January 1943 to May 1943 Special Intelligence was some days current, frequently two or four days in arrears, and in some instances up to a week behind. But it was always possible to tell what kind of signal was being made, and this allowed us to come to general conclusions. For example we could tell rapidly – as soon as we received the intercept – if the signal had been a position report or a convoy sighting report or if U-boat Command was ordering the boats to take up new positions. This was generally clear from the grouping of the letters, the length of the signal and the type of Enigma code employed.

As a further complication in the work of keeping the Admiralty's large table plot up to date with the positions of all U-boats, the secret Atlantic grid code letters for the position reports were often changed on a daily basis so that Winn and his staff had to deduce the new co-ordinates from previously known positions. It was in this work that radio intelligence played an increasingly important part in the spring of 1943, both in intercepting Enigma traffic and in obtaining the direction fixes of U-boat transmissions. A network of listening posts searched the Atlantic, operated by thousands of trained and highly-skilled radio-telegraphists. On listening watch for six hours or more they had to sit with headphones on, notepads ready for the demanding task of searching and picking out the U-boat Morse from the static and jumble of radio signals crowding the ether.

The listeners would take down the Morse code groups and the bearings of the signals would also be passed on by others with special receivers to a central control which gathered all the British reports, collated them and passed on the relevant information to Bletchley Park and the Admiralty Operational Intelligence Centre. Similar networks were being set up in North America, where the US Navy had followed the Admiralty's example and established a U-boat Tracking Room in Washington. These centres kept in touch constantly, updating each other with a flow of intelligence information on the U-boats' movements.

READING THE GAME

Every morning, Winn's small team gathered at 7.30 in the Tracking Room to sift through the latest 'Special Intelligence' radio intercepts and direction fixes in order to establish the daily U-boat movements. Any gaps would be filled in by the collective intuition of the staff which, after two years working to keep one step ahead of U-boat Command, was very reliable. Winn had constantly urged his Staff to take the German tactical view by 'putting themselves in Dönitz's shoes'. They all studied background intelligence material, gleaned from German radio and press reports, and, above all, the interrogation reports of captured U-boat Commanders. Often they gained a valuable insight into the personalities of the leading U-boat personalities and could predict with confidence how they would react in operations at sea.

This ability to get into their opponents' minds proved invaluable when the Tracking Room had to 'back a hunch' about the movements of a patrol line in order to save a convoy. Winn's up-to-date information about enemy dispositions played a most important part in the daily conference conducted by scrambler telephone with Western Approaches Command. This took place at 9 o'clock every morning, when Admiral Horton in his glass-fronted office overlooking two huge Atlantic wall plots was joined on the line by Coastal Command Headquarters and the Admiralty Trade Division Convoy Plot. After a full appraisal of the situation, his staff would dispose their air and sea forces to counter the U-boats' predicted movements. Convoys would be diverted to avoid U-boat patrol lines, air patrols directed to stop the build up of Wolf Packs and reinforcements sent to threatened convoys.

In the Western Approaches operations room and U-boat Command headquarters, the Battle of the Atlantic took on the character of a monstrous chess game, with each side trying to anticipate and check their opponents' moves. Dönitz's command post had been moved from Paris to the Hotel-am-Steinplatz in Berlin's Charlottenburg district five minutes by car from his office in the Kriegsmarine on Tirpitz Ufer. It was much smaller and manned

Atlantic Chessboard: The 30ft long Western Approaches Plot at Derby House, Liverpool, was kept permanently updated by Wren Plotters (top right) and was overlooked by the glass-fronted offices of the C-in-C and Coastal Command (right). This contrasted with the makeshift headquarters of U-boat Command where Dönitz (above flanked by Kapitänleutnant Schnee and Admiral Godt) planned out his moves.

by only a handful of staff. Yet as Captain Meckel, his Communication Staff Officer, observed:

> It was the same game, we knew it. In the main operations room there was a big chart of the Atlantic on the wall. The convoys were plotted in red and U-boat positions marked with blue pins. It was brought up to date every morning after the daily conference at nine o'clock.
>
> The staff was small and was attended whenever possible by the Commander in Chief, but his Chief of Staff, Admiral Godt, was in charge of day to day operations at sea. There were only about six of us and the advantage of a small staff was that we had been working closely together day and night for years and we knew exactly how our Admiral thought. Each one of us could write a memorandum exactly in his style.

This close-knit team met every morning to review the reports from the U-boats and go over the *B-Dienst* intelligence messages giving the intercepted British convoy movements and signals. Dönitz described his method of operations:

> At our command post we drew up each day a 'U-boat Disposition Chart' which showed the U-boat dispositions as we presumed the enemy might deduce it from the sighting reports and radio interceptions which he had received. We then asked ourselves: in the enemy's place how would we react to these dispositions? Would he try to avoid them by altering the courses of his convoys or allow them to sail straight on, on the assumption that we had already redisposed our forces in anticipation of the evasive action we expected of him.
>
> These appreciations 'in the first and second degree' as we used to call them, were necessary to enable us to counteract in good time the measures which we anticipated that the enemy would take. In 1942 our efforts in this direction had met with repeated success. But at the beginning of 1943, it seemed to us that this game of chess had become vastly more complicated.

Dönitz was getting *B-Dienst* reports of convoy sailings as well as the British 'U-boat Situation Report'. This daily bulletin, transmitted by Western Approaches to the escorts, proved to be of the 'greatest value' in revealing where the enemy intelligence placed the U-boats. These dispositions could then be changed so as to trap convoys that the British thought safely diverted.

Thousands of miles away on the stormy waters of the Atlantic, the opposing strategic calculations were put to the test. Then it was the skill of the U-boat crews which confronted the defensive tactics of the escort groups, the endurance of Allied aircrew and the dogged determination of the merchant seamen to fight their ships through. In these bitter battles it was often luck, courage and sheer seamanship in appalling weather that decided the result of the convoy battles.

As Good As We Get
January–February

Briefing for Battle: A Convoy Commodore addressing the pre-sailing conference of ships' masters which was also attended by representatives of the sea and air escorts.

The climactic months of the Battle in early 1943 took place in the worst weather conditions experienced on the North Atlantic for half a century. Frequent hurricane-force winds whipped up towering seas and the storms which prevailed for 116 days out of 140 during the winter affected both U-boats and convoys.

The Germans were at a disadvantage in getting sufficient advance warnings of the storm fronts, which frequently broke up patrol lines as mountainous seas blotted out visibility and forced the boats under. Apart from weather signals from the U-boats themselves, the Germans' only detailed meteorological reports came from the *Holzauge* station which had been secretly established on the east coast of Greenland in September 1942. This transmitted 1,500 weather reports during the winter but could not give a complete picture of the capricious North Atlantic weather and a big storm often allowed a convoy to sail unspotted through a waiting patrol line of U-boats.

Even though the Allies had more accurate weather forecasts, they could not take advantage of them to route the convoys south into calmer zones. This took the merchantmen beyond the range of the Iceland air patrols, increasing the opportunity for the Wolf Packs to assemble and attack unhindered. So the convoys had to continue to struggle through the gales and heavy seas which brought a rise in the number of weather-damaged ships, sometimes causing merchant ships to break up and sink without trace. More often the weather disrupted the orderly convoy columns and increased the number of stragglers. The drop-outs then had to be collected and routed on courses at least thirty miles away from the main body, to avoid revealing the convoy's course to watching U-boats.

The escorts also suffered severely from storm damage. Their Asdic domes could be easily damaged by heavy seas, their sensitive radar and HF/DF sets and aerials dislocated by the constant buffeting of storms. Throughout the winter months there was a depressing rise in the number of Escort Groups under strength because ships were being repaired. Particularly vulnerable were the older destroyers as one officer of an ancient S class wryly commented in his log: 'She celebrated her 24 birthday fighting as gamely as ever the only battle known to her – trying to beat to the Westward in the teeth of an Atlantic gale.' By January 1943 they had suffered so much serious damage that the Admiralty had to replace them with the new River Class frigates.

The Allied Anti-Submarine forces were now facing a German U-boat arm with a total strength of 400 boats, but nearly half of these were training or working up at any one time and with the continuing commitment to the Mediterranean, less than 200 U-boats were available for Atlantic operations. In the first quarter of 1943 never more than 120 boats were serviceable for the Atlantic operations at any one time. Many of the larger U-boats were carrying out distant operations off the coast of Brazil in the west and down the Cape routes off Africa. In addition to the Arctic boats, which operated against the Russian convoys from Norway, Dönitz also maintained the pressure on the mid-Atlantic convoys with another powerful concentration of U-boats between Gibraltar and the Azores. He was, therefore, able to concentrate some fifty boats in his chosen battleground of the North Atlantic

– the 'bottleneck area' between Greenland and Iceland through which he knew all the North Atlantic convoys had to pass. Here the U-boats would be strung out in long patrol lines, which would snare the convoys and then close in for a mass attack.

In the middle of January 1943, the Tracking Room began to detect signs of a steady build up of U-boats in the 'bottleneck' off Greenland. So far, that month had seen relatively few convoy attacks and sinkings fell to less than 200,000 tons – the lowest level for nearly two years. This calm before the storm did not deceive the Admiralty whose Anti-Submarine Report forecast:

> Now that Grand Admiral Dönitz is Supreme Commander of the German Navy we may expect all units to operate in support of the U-boat warfare. It is certainly going to be a grim fight in 1943 and, though we are not as ready for it as we should like to be, there have been plenty of examples in 1942 to demonstrate that, even with our present inadequate scale of air and surface escort, with good training and team work, it is possible to fight a convoy through a pack of U-boats and give as good as we get.

Even before Dönitz had taken over the leadership of the Kriegsmarine, he was preparing to get as many boats to sea as possible for an all-out offensive to smash the convoy system. Throughout January and early February, droves of U-boats left the French bases to battle their way across the Atlantic through heavy weather to concentrate off Greenland but the Allies were using their 'Special Intelligence' to good effect and at first the U-boats found it difficult to intercept the convoys which were being evasively routed over a wide area to avoid the patrol lines. However, by the third week in January they were confident that, with over thirty boats concentrated in three main groups, they would soon be intercepting the convoys again. Their break came on 23 January, when intelligence reports gave the course of eastbound convoy HX 223. Dönitz immediately ordered all fifteen U-boats southeast of Greenland to form a patrol line to trap it. It seemed that nothing could prevent the convoy heading into the 450 mile long barrier across its path, but when HX 223 was only 150 miles from the middle of the patrol line a hurricane-force storm swept down on both convoy and U-boats.

In conditions like those experienced by Executive Officer Herbert Werner in U-230 operations rapidly became impossible:

> Water poured in through the open hatch and sloshed around our feet, and the high humidity within the hull caused food to rot, the skin to turn flabby and our charts to dissolve. The smell was brutal. The extra fuel we carried in our bilges sent out a penetrating stench; our clothes reeked of it and our food took on the taste of oil and grease. The perpetual rocking and swaying of the boat was too much for those

unaccustomed to the Atlantic or unequipped with cast-iron stomachs; most of the men lost their appetites and often more than that . . . When we were on watch, the wind punished us with driving snow, sleet hail and frozen spray. It beat against our rubber divers suits, cut our faces like a razor, and threatened to tear away our eye masks; only the steel belts around our waists secured us to boat and life. Below, inside the bobbing steel cockleshell, the boat's violent up and down motion drove us to the floor plates and hurled us straight up and threw us around like puppets.

The hurricane-force winds blotted out all visibility and the American escorted convoy passed through the U-boat line unseen on the night of 24 January 1943. US Coastguard Lieutenant John M. Waters Jr. was buried by green water crashing aboard as he made his way to the wheelhouse of the Coastguard cutter *Ingram*:

The sight was one never to be forgotten. Though the night was pitch black, and the thick low clouds hurled by overhead, the ocean surface, beaten to a nearly solid white by the fury of the storm, was clearly visible. The ship was heading directly into the storm and ahead of it loomed great rolling mountains of water, each threatening to come down and break the ship. Though the bridge was 35 feet above the waterline, the seas towered up at a 45-degree angle above that. As a new wave loomed up, *Ingham* rose to meet it, climbing steeply up the front; as the sea slid past, her bow was left momentarily hanging in the air before dropping sickeningly into the next trough, where it buried with a resounding impact, sending shock waves throughout the ship to add to the vibrations of the screws racing madly as they came out of the water.

The fierce storm had taken its toll of the convoy which had been split into two sections; eleven ships were missing and one freighter had broken apart and sunk in the raging seas. The U-boats were able to pick off three of the stragglers but it was hardly the great success Dönitz had hoped for.

The North Atlantic defences in mid-January depended on just twelve Escort Groups (seven British, four Canadian and one American) which covered the convoys during their dangerous mid-ocean passage. The paper strength of an Escort Group needed to guard a convoy of up to 60 merchant ships was three destroyers, a frigate and six corvettes. That winter, the Groups were sailing 30% under strength because of the increasing number docked for repairs and this wastage became worse as the winter wore on. To increase the endurance of those escorts that were operational the Admiralty had introduced the policy of sailing special oil tankers with the convoys wherever possible, but the frequent spells of heavy weather seriously interfered with attempts to refuel at sea. Western Approaches could also deploy two Support Groups of fast sloops and destroyers to hunt down U-boat concentrations, when they could be released from escort duty. They were joined at the beginning of March by a US Navy Group whose escort carrier, USS *Bogue*, showed how effective its aircraft could be in covering convoys. A further seven US Navy Task Groups were deployed farther to the south to protect the mid-ocean convoys to North Africa. Responsibility for protecting the emergency UK 'greyhound' tanker convoys was at first undertaken by the Royal Navy whose Groups were already overstretched covering the Gibraltar and Sierra Leone traffic. After UC 1 was badly mauled by a Wolf Pack at the end of February the US Navy decided that it could give its valuable fast tankers better cover and took the convoys over.

THE BLACK PIT

If the weather hampered the surface escorts, its effect on the Atlantic air patrols was even more severe. During the winter the casualty rate climbed as aircraft crashed when trying to land in high winds or disappeared without trace. Hurricane-force winds and blizzards often grounded all flying from the bases in Iceland for days. At this time Coastal Command's total strength of aircraft for the Atlantic patrols was never more than 200 aircraft, of which never more than two thirds were serviceable at any one time. Much of Coastal Command's effort was deployed on patrols up to 600 miles out into the Atlantic from bases in the United Kingdom and Iceland with squadrons of Hudson and Wellington bombers. The Sunderland and Catalina flying boats could get farther, but their depth-charge load was small. By the end of February 1943, the British possessed only 23 of the important VLR Liberators that could fly patrols into the 'Black Pit' of the Air Gap southeast of Greenland where most of the sinkings were occurring. On the western side of the Air Gap the situation was worse. Neither the Canadians nor the Americans had *any* aircraft in Newfoundland that could get beyond 600 miles and, to close the gap in the convoy defences, Coastal Command had resorted to a desperate effort to operate a squadron of Hudsons from the American Bluie West 11 airstrip in Greenland. But the attempt was called off in the face of high casualties caused by the dangerous mountain approach which had to be flown in the frequent bad weather. So, with fewer than a dozen aircraft capable of providing any air protection in the eastern part of the Air Gap, the 'Black Pit' for the convoys was looming dangerously large.

Less than a week after this failure the next fast convoy HX 224 also slipped through a gap in U-boat Command's patrol lines, losing two ships to a shadowing U-boat. It was a survivor picked up after U-632 had torpedoed the tanker *Cordelia*, who incautiously volunteered the information to Kapitänleutnant Karp that another slow convoy was following HX 224. This was a stroke of luck for U-boat Command who found that the intelligence tallied with *B-Dienst* information on the sailing instructions given to the slow convoy SC 118. At once Dönitz signalled to all sixteen U-boats off south east Greenland to form a patrol line, Group *Pfeil*, across the convoy's route.

The 53 slow merchantmen had been plodding forward at six knots protected by the Royal Navy's B2 Escort Group of three destroyers and three corvettes accompanied by the US Coastguard Cutter *Bibb* and the Free French corvette *Lobelia*.

Atlantic Chessboard: Dönitz's headquarters plot clearly shows the Group *Pfeil* patrol line set up in the bottleneck south of Greenland to trap convoy SC 118 in February 1943. The pack's subsequent movements as it closed in for the kill is also clearly marked. Such massive pack attacks could only be defeated by closing the Air Gap which was not achieved until April 1943.

By a stroke of luck the convoy passed right through the *Pfeil* Group's patrol line in the pitch black night of 4 February, but as it was slowly pulling out of the danger zone, a Snowflake rocket was accidentally set off by a seaman in the SS *Anik* which was seen by U-187 twenty miles away. The news was immediately signalled to U-boat Command and, although the U-boat was promptly sunk by a destroyer, it was too late to save the convoy as the sixteen *Pfeil* Group boats astern and five boats of the *Hardegen* Group to the south were ordered to concentrate into a big Wolf Pack. Throughout the rest of that night and the following day, all the skilled teamwork of the escorts was required to keep the Pack at bay. Whenever HF/DF bearings revealed that U-boats, hungry for a kill, were closing in, an escort was sent out along the bearing to give chase. That morning, too, the Tracking Room signalled an urgent warning about the large Pack building up around the convoy and reinforcements were ordered to sea from Iceland.

On the night of 5 February 1943, the Wolf Pack missed a good opportunity to strike when the convoy was inadvertently broken in two parts by a communications failure, but by daybreak the escorts had successfully kept the wolves at bay and shepherded the convoy together. The reinforcements from Iceland also began to arrive and that afternoon, the merchantmen were protected by the heavy air cover provided by Iceland-based VLR Liberators.

Night Action: Convoy actions were still bitterly fought at night when the U-boats moved in on the surface to attack targets outlined by blazing tankers. Escorts, in their turn, fired star shells (inset) to illuminate their attackers and force them to dive, where they were depth-charged for many hours.

The Wolf Pack had now been fought off for three days during the most critical part of the passage without air cover through the 'Black Pit' for the loss of one straggler but that night the convoy's luck ran out. Eleven of the *Pfëil* Group were still in contact by early evening when they torpedoed another straggler, and the urgent exhortations of U-boat Command fired the determination of the Commanders to smash the convoy's defences once and for all. They made repeated thrusts to draw off the escorts and, shortly before midnight, U-262 penetrated the port flank to torpedo a freighter. Hours later, in pitch darkness early on 7 February 1943, the real destruction began when the Ace commander – Kapitänleutnant Siegfried von Forstner in U-402 – saw a chance to break in through a gap on the starboard flank, created by two of the escorts as they raced out to attack a radar contact. He torpedoed two ships in quick succession, one of them the convoy rescue vessel *Toward*, and in the resulting confusion U-614 also sank another freighter before Forstner had torpedoed his third victim.

The ferocity of this attack finally broke the co-ordination of the escorts and two hours later, von Forstner was able to take advantage of another gap to torpedo three more ships, including the trooper *Henry Mallory* with heavy loss of life among the 384 US soldiers and marines on their way to Iceland. One was a young army officer who had been writing to his bride of a few weeks: 'There have been a lot of explosions and firing tonight, and we don't know what is going on. We are all pretty frightened.' The sodden letter, unsigned and unfinished, was taken from his corpse several hours later.

Lieutenant John M. Waters Jnr. was sent out in one of the *Ingham*'s boats to help the USS *Bibb* in the grim search for survivors:

> I saw a body ahead and ordered, 'Give way together!' As we neared the body, I swung the sweep oar to turn the boat and felt it hit something. Turning I saw a sergeant bumping against my oar, his mouth open and his eyes staring. He bobbed stiffly. Rigor mortis had already set in. We were in the midst of perhaps half a dozen bodies. Taking in our oars, we began dragging the people alongside. In a short time the bodies began to interfere with the crew's rowing. Ahead we saw more, but there was little room left in the boat. . . .
>
> I looked carefully at each man's eyes. My hands were too frozen to feel for a pulse, so when their eyes and face looked dead, we tore off their ID tags and cast their bodies adrift. Soon there was room in the boat and we resumed searching for survivors.

Less than 40% of the troopship's complement were saved. It was the second such disaster for the United States in a week, five days earlier the trooper *Dorchester* had been torpedoed 300 miles to the northwest with the loss of 605 lives.

The battle had not gone entirely in the U-boats' favour. The Free French corvette *Lobelia* had destroyed U-609 and, next day, the combined work of escorts and the Liberators unnerved the surviving members of the *Pfëil* Wolf Pack. At nightfall, it was only the indomitable von Forstner who again got close enough to sink his seventh victim. Throughout the next day he clung on, trying to find a target for his last torpedo, encouraged by Dönitz:

> Forstner well done. Stay there and maintain contact. More boats are on their way. The depth charges also run out. Stay tough. This convoy is extemely important.

255

All day, Coastal Command aircraft kept forcing the remaining *Pfeil* boats under; von Forstner himself had to submerge seven times. U-624 did not crash-dive fast enough when a Liberator from 220 Squadron Coastal Command spotted her in time to launch an accurate attack:

> Three depth-charges were seen to enter the water on the U-boat's port bow. . . . The aircraft tracked right over the conning tower and one member of the U-boat's crew was seen looking up through the open hatch. Explosions blotted out the U-boat from view, but as the spray settled her bows were seen rising out of the water. The U-boat then rocked forward and the stern broke surface. After this it sank bodily on a more or less even keel. The depth charge scum and explosion eddies faded away slowly, giving place to a large patch of bubbles and under water disturbances which persisted gradually increasing in intensity.

The patch was still boiling when the Liberator left for its Iceland base forty minutes later. There was nothing to mark the tomb of U-624's fifty-strong crew except several light brown cylinders, a few planks of wood and a black box that bobbed incongruously up in the centre of the disturbance. Already it had attracted 'numerous white seabirds' which were observed diving for stunned fish and other flotsam that floated up from the depths.

The Tracking Room reported that the attack was petering out:

> A total of 20 U-boats operated or attempted to operate against SC.118. Ten or more of these have abandoned the operation because of defects or shortage of fuel. U-187 was sunk and prisoners taken and an aircraft may have finished off or severely damaged another. Urgent exhortations have been addressed to this group to fight on for the sake, *inter alia*, of the Eastern Front and they have orders to continue vigorously until dawn 9 February and then to move off.

'It was perhaps the hardest convoy battle of the whole war' Dönitz was to note of the U-boats' success in sinking 13 of SC 118's ships. Von Forstner was awarded the Knight's Cross for raising his total score to over 100,000 tons, but the U-boats' victory had not been without its heavy cost. In the battle for SC 118 the Germans had lost three boats and two others had been severely damaged. There were also compensations for the Allies, since a large proportion of the U-boats operating to the west of the air gap had been drawn out of position. This, together with a run of accurate 'Special Intelligence' to the Tracking Room, allowed the next two eastbound convoys from Halifax to be routed through without any loss. But for the first time Dönitz now had sufficient strength to bring up new boats rapidly to replace those lost or heading back to base after a large-scale operation. In this way the momentum of the offensive was maintained and two Milch-cows were stationed in mid-ocean so that more boats could be kept in the critical bottleneck area.

U-boat Command was now hoping to deploy the group stationed at the Iceland end of the Air Gap to engage the next two westbound convoys. They already knew from *B-Dienst* intelligence that one convoy had picked up its ocean escort at EASTOMP on 12 February 1943.

Battling through heavy storms, it was not until 21 February that the U-boats finally located the 63 ships of ON 166 heading west under the protection of the American Escort Group A3 led by Captain P. R. Heineman

USN. The incessant radio chatter of a growing number of U-boats told Heineman that he was surrounded by a large Wolf Pack in spite of the combined efforts of the Liberators and his aggressive tactics of sending escorts to run down the closer HF/DF fixes. That evening, the first round went to 'Heineman's Harriers', when the Coastguard Cutter *Spencer* successfully depth-charged U-225, one of three U-boats sighted by the last aircraft that the convoy would see for three days.

That night as it entered the 'Black Pit', seven U-boats closed in. During the mêlée, one freighter was torpedoed and, shortly before dawn, two more ships were sunk including the rescue vessel *Stockport*.

More U-boats were diverted to the struggling convoy by Dönitz, but as the convoy steamed on 'Heineman's Harriers' successfully beat off the U-boats for the loss of only two more merchant ships before it reached the safety of the Newfoundland air patrols on 25 February. Rough weather had made refuelling difficult and one corvette, HMS *Dianthus*, only just made St Johns with bone-dry tanks after her crew had 'emptied 120 gallons of Admiralty Compound into Number 6 Tank, also all the gunnery oil, paint mixing oil and two drums of special mineral oil.' The protracted thousand-mile running battle had cost five ships lost in convoy attacks and another six stragglers. But the U-boats had paid dearly and two had been sunk.

As February 1943 ended, shipping losses were again rising to over 300,000 tons and the U-boats had shown that they were capable of mounting sustained Pack operations against heavily protected convoys. Dönitz had sufficient strength both to maintain strong patrol lines in the main North Atlantic battleground and to strike powerful blows in other areas like the Azores and the Cape. The Admiralty's monthly Anti-Submarine bulletin commented:

'Never before has the enemy displayed such singleness of purpose in utilizing his strength against one objective – the interruption of supplies from America to Great Britain. As a result, engagements were embittered and successes against U-boats reached a record peak; it was probably the best month ever in respect of U-boats sunk.

Fifteen of Dönitz's U-boat fleet had been destroyed in the Atlantic alone during the month but this made little impression on the large force of over 100 boats that he could throw into the battle. The chances of a German victory seemed bright and the Admiralty feared that convoys could well be overcome if twenty or more U-boats were concentrated against them in each Pack attack. They concluded that:

in such conditions a purely surface escort is bound eventually to be overwhelmed by sheer weight of numbers. Bad weather and the practice of evasive routeing have contributed to the favourable outcome of the month's experiences, but both of these factors are played out and will supply little help in the next months. What is needed – and is being supplied – is the assistance of an increased force of VLR aircraft.

Disrupting the Packs: The sudden appearance of an aircraft followed by a stick of depth-charges (left) before the conning tower hatch could be closed (above) was a major hazard for the Wolf Packs. But in the Air Gap the escort could be equally deadly as Oberleutnant Schuenemann of U-606 recalled:

Immediately we crash-dived, but even before the conning tower hatch had been properly closed, we collected our first load of depth charges. These did quite a bit of damage and leaks started. We tried to escape by going deeper and deeper down. The water was pouring in all the time.
Everybody in the control room was looking at the depth gauge. When it reached 220 metres I thought 'this is the end!'

The Hammer March

ALLIED SHIPPING LOSSES 1ST AUGUST
1942–31ST MAY 1943

•	ALLIED AND NEUTRAL MERCHANT SHIPS SUNK
○	U-BOATS SUNK
▬	CONVOY ROUTES
⌒	ALLIED AIR COVER ZONES
▨	AXIS AND AXIS OCCUPIED TERRITORY, 31 MAY 1943

MERCATOR PROJECTION

MURMANSK
REYKJAVIK
ST. JOHNS
HALIFAX
NEW YORK
GIBRALTAR
SIERRA LEONE
PORT OF SPAIN
NATAL
ASCENSION I.

Target for Torpedoes: By March 1943, the Battle was reaching its peak of intensity (map) straining merchant navy morale. The seamen were only too well aware when a convoy attack began that the sickening crunch of a torpedo would find them clinging desperately onto life in icy seas. (below)

On 3 March 1943 the British War Cabinet received a grim reminder of the current state of play in the Battle of the Atlantic from Lord Cherwell, Churchill's Scientific Adviser: 'we are consuming ¾ m. tons more than we are importing. In *two months*, we would not meet our requirements if this continued.' The threat was not so much to food but to the oil and military supplies that were essential if Britain was to fulfil her commitments required by Allied strategy. It was clear that the war of attrition on the Atlantic was fast approaching its crisis.

If there was mounting apprehension in Downing Street, there was also growing concern at U-boat Headquarters, in Berlin, where it was anxiously noted that the U-boats' February score was still less than half the 700,000 tons set as the monthly target to win the shipping war. Every day over a hundred U-boats were at sea on the Atlantic, but in the preceeding four weeks no fewer than nine convoys had successfully evaded their patrol lines and only two main line and one tanker convoy had been intercepted.

Weather conditions had certainly aided the enemy, but this lack of success was even more puzzling when account was taken of the accurate advance information received from *B-Dienst* about convoy sailing plans. Somehow the enemy seemed to be getting an accurate picture of German dispositions. As Dönitz put it, 'my opposite number, Admiral Horton, was able to take a look at my cards without my being able to take a look at his'.

Continued assurances that the Enigma Code was unbreakable led Dönitz to wrongly assume that there was 'all but certain proof that, with the assistance of his airborne radar, the enemy is able to discover U-boat dispositions with sufficient accuracy to enable his convoys to take evasive action.' Accordingly on 3 March 1943, a new operational order was transmitted to all U-boats to submerge for at least thirty minutes after their *Metox* receivers gave warning of the approach of radar-equipped aircraft. This temporary expedient still further reduced the U-boats' movement and reconnaissance ability and made the Allied air patrols doubly effective.

The long-term solution to Dönitz's intelligence problem depended on getting effective aerial reconnaissance of the Western Atlantic and on 26 February 1943 he had flown to the Führer's advance headquarters at Vinnitsa in the Ukraine to ask that Reichmarshall Goering be directed to fulfill his many promises to provide the necessary squadrons. Hitler was sympathetic even though there was little hope of any very long range aircraft becoming available. The so-called 'Amerika' bombers, the Heinkel 177 and Messerschmitt 264, had been designed to allow the Luftwaffe to bomb New York. Had they been ready, their fuel reserves would have enabled them to patrol the Western Atlantic, but mounting technical problems had undermined confidence in the new aircraft.

The Allied navies were well aware of the serious threat developing in the Western Atlantic, and an important conference was held in Washington at the beginning of March to try and eradicate some of the shortcomings and inadequacies in the anti-submarine campaign. The meeting was convened by Admiral King, in pursuit of the instructions of the Casablanca Conference which had stipulated that 'the defeat of the U-boat must remain the first charge on the resources of the United Nations.' In his opening address he had told representatives of the British, Canadian and American navies of the 'grave responsibility of exploring our capabilities for waging war against the U-boats'. When he followed this with an equally strong warning about U-boats in the Pacific, the British officers present began wondering just how committed Admiral King really was to the Atlantic, particularly when he went on to condemn the proposals for a unified convoy command:

> It is a great pleasure to me to work with our Allies, and we can always learn something from each other, but, nevertheless I have had what to me is exclusive proof that these advantages are more than nullified by the handicap of effort that is inherent when forces of different customs and systems are brigaded together.

The British had not forgotten how it had taken a million tons of shipping losses before King had finally set up the coastal convoy system. It was left to Admiral Sir Percy Noble tactfully to press the urgent reform of the command system for the Atlantic convoys arguing 'Too much shipping is in danger of being destroyed. And at this moment the situation is causing grave anxiety to all concerned'. Then, speaking with all his experience as a former Commander-in-Chief of Western Approaches, he placed before Admiral King the overriding importance of air patrols:

> The submarine menace, to my mind, is becoming every day more and more an air problem. We haven't had enough aircraft during the first two years . . . My experience is that the provision of air cover is the only way to enable a slow-moving convoy to escape a pack of U-boats which has been following it. The aircraft causes the U-boats to submerge, thereby allowing the convoy to use evasive tactics.

Admiral King already had the solution in his power. Coastal Command had only 23 of the specially modified VLR Liberators operational, but the US Navy controlled 112 of the big bombers, 70 of which had been sent to the Pacific to carry out reconnaissance missions in non-combat areas and the other squadrons were operating from California and the Caribbean. No US Liberators were operating from Newfoundland bases although in no other area was the U-boat danger as great as in the North Atlantic. As later experiences revealed, just two squadrons of VLR Liberators based in Newfoundland would have been enough to break up the U-boat packs.

The British had come to the Conference well prepared to argue the need for increased air cover. They based their case on a detailed study of convoy escort and control undertaken by Professor Blackett, now Head of the Admiralty's Operational Research Department. His analysis had shown that losses could be cut by 65% if air cover were increased by an average of four sorties a day in the threatened areas. This led the sub committee on air escort at the Conference to call for a minimum of 120 VLR aircraft to be sent to provide convoy air escort 'at as early a date as possible, bearing in mind that early assignments will bear greater returns proportionally than the same assignments later.'

When he received all the recommendations on 14 March 1943, no immediate action was taken by Admiral King. His decision, that was to cost many lives and ships, was partly explained in a brief drawn up by King's staff prior to the Conference. 'There is the urgent need for immediate assignment of more long-range aircraft to anti-submarine duty in the Atlantic', the report concluded, but it recommended, 'In the view of the situation in the several theatres of warfare, it seems that the only possibility is to divert these planes from the bombing of Germany.' It was a clear indication that the US Navy would not divert any of its own aircraft from the Pacific to the Atlantic – even temporarily. The responsibility was to be offloaded on to the US Army Air Force. So adding a new source of friction to the running feud between the US Navy and Army that continued in spite of the previous June's agreement to give operational control of Anti-Submarine aircraft to the Navy.

The President himself finally had to intervene before the Air Gap was narrowed from the American end, after heavy convoy battles in March and an urgent appeal from Churchill. King agreed to send a single squadron of Liberators to Newfoundland although it was not the US Navy planes that belatedly flew to the Gander airfield but the 6th Anti-Submarine Squadron of the US Army Air Force in early April.

The Air Gap was closed in early April, too late to affect the worst of the U-boat offensive which was forecast by the British Air and Naval Staffs in a memorandum of 8 March which warned 'The North Atlantic Convoys must now be considered *threatened*. We must be ready to deal with up to three convoys each being attacked by a pack of U-boats.' It continued:

> The numbers of U-boats now at sea have reduced very considerably the chances of evasive routeing. In the near future we must expect the majority of our convoys to be sighted and subsequently attacked . . . The scale of the attack will increase progressively as more and more U-boats are concentrated against our convoys unless we can make the U-boats pay for their successes a price which they cannot accept.

The Admiralty believed that 'a rate of exchange of about two ships lost from convoys for one U-boat sunk' would be acceptable to the Germans but it would be many weeks before the escorts got anywhere near this kill ratio.

Until the end of the first week in March 1943 the convoys had been successfully routed around the growing concentrations without coming up against any large pack attacks. Some 50 U-boats were now operating in the North Atlantic but fresh storm fronts had swept eastwards and the poor weather had hampered the German concentration. 'Special Intelligence' had also been instrumental in enabling the Tracking Room to establish a clear picture of the movements of Dönitz patrol lines, so that CINCWA in Liverpool and COMINCH in Washington could weave the convoys through.

On 3 March the Tracking Room received information from Special Intelligence that Dönitz had set up a new long patrol line north east of Newfoundland. Its northern wing was made up of the eight boats of the *Wildfang* Group which overlapped with the eleven boats of the *Burgraf* line. Together, this formidable 400-mile long dog-leg prepared to meet the slow eastbound SC 121 whose sailing plan had been passed to Dönitz by *B-Dienst*. The *Burgraf* line was also being approached on the other side by the slow westbound convoy ON 168, heading south from Greenland in deteriorating weather. Many of the ships were suffering badly from storm damage and only 41 out of the 52 vessels which had left Britain in well-disciplined columns were managing to keep in formation. Aware of the vulnerability of this convoy,

Shrinking the Air Gap:
Although the VLR Liberator Mk III's with their 800 mile patrol range were a key factor in the Battle, none operated into the Western side of the Air Gap until April 1943 and at the height of the March convoy battles only 23 were operational from bases in Northern Ireland. Aircrews (above) performed incredible feats of navigation and flying to attack U-boat packs (left) nearly a thousand miles from their bases.

CINCWA diverted it farther north, although some crews would have preferred to brave the U-boats rather than the appalling weather as seaman J. Lisle in HMS *Pimpernel* recalled:

> The weather steadily deteriorated. There was snow and ice and the temperature was down to 18 degrees F. There weren't many hours of daylight in these latitudes and the chance of meeting U-boats had gone for the time being, there was the new danger from icebergs.

Horton's tactics worked and although one large freighter began to break up in the heavy seas, ON 168 steered straight through a large gap in the *Wildfang* line, which had been caused by the earlier loss of U-529 until then unnoticed by U-boat Command.

The slow eastbound convoy SC 121 was not so lucky. On the forenoon of 6 March, escorted by Commander Heineman's A3 Escort Group, it reached the *Burgraf* patrol line. 'Heineman's Harriers' had only had a few hours in port to recover from the battle of ON 166 before they were sent out again and the ships were suffering from storm-damage to their Asdic, radar and vital HF/DF equipment. Shortly before noon, those escorts that still had their HF/DF sets in working order, picked up the ominous U-boat sighting signals to port and starboard. The lookouts on the nearest *Burgraf* U-boats had spotted the dim outline of the merchant ships in the driving blizzard and closed with their boats bucking and tossing in the churning seas. Dönitz ordered the closest boats of the *Westmark* group to split off and join the Wolf Pack. To make doubly sure of trapping the convoy, a second group, *Ostmark*, was established ahead of the convoy from the most northerly section of the Mid-Atlantic *Neuland* line.

Early on 7 March the *Westmark* pack struck the first blows, sinking the freighter *Egyptian* whose loss went almost unnoticed in the raging gale. Only the *Empire Impala* gallantly dropped behind to rescue survivors to be torpedoed and sunk shortly after daybreak.

As it headed eastwards on the morning of 8 March 1943, SC 121 ran into the *Ostmark* Group. Their first victim was the freighter *Guido* whose master had panicked and steamed on ahead of the convoy. Mountainous seas and the convoy defences newly reinforced by CINCWA halted German attempts to breakthrough that night, but the escort could do little to stop the pack dispatching four stragglers. After shadowing the convoy all day, the Pack began its concerted attacks again as soon as night fell and this time they succeeded in overwhelming the convoy's heavy defences.

Thirteen ships were sunk by the morning of 10 March in a German victory made more complete by the absence of any U-boat losses.

These were disturbing facts for the Allies. The *Westmark* and *Ostmark* packs were dogging SC 121 and Dönitz was concentrating the remaining easterly *Wildfang* and *Burgraf* boats into a new patrol line *Raubgraf* north of Newfoundland, ready to fall on the next eastbound convoys.

By now the Tracking Rooms on both sides of the Atlantic had a good idea of the size and disposition of the patrol lines south east of Greenland and COMINCH signalled the next two convoys, ON 169 and HX 228, course-

Hunt and Evasion: As the U-boat commanders patrolling east of Newfoundland planned to intercept the eastbound convoys (right) the Convoy and Routing section at COMINCH in Washington and the Eastern Sea Frontier H.Q. in New York (below) plotted the convoy tracks in order to route them around the Wolf Packs.

changes to clear the *Raubgraf* line. The ruse worked and U-boat Command lost HX 228 for three days until *B-Dienst* decyphered the signals giving the new route. Dönitz acted at once. The thirteen boats of the mid-Atlantic *Neuland* Group were ordered to sweep west to meet the sixty ships of HX 228 well protected by the experienced Group B3, led by Commander A. A. Tait DSO in the destroyer *Harvester*.

Suddenly, in the middle of this developing battle, the Allied Commanders were hit by an intelligence blackout. On 9 March, Admiral Edelsten, Assistant Chief of Naval Staff, hurriedly informed the First Sea Lord of the changed situation which could have disastrous implications for the Allies. 'The foreseen has come to pass. The Director of Naval Intelligence reported on 8 March that the Tracking Room will be "blinded" in regard to U-boat movements for some considerable period perhaps extending to months.'

This Allied difficulty was the direct result of a sudden move by Dönitz to ensure the impregnability of the U-boat Enigma. On 8 March he had ordered all U-boats in the Atlantic to activate the fourth rotor on their new Enigma *Schlüssel M* machines. At a stroke the *Triton* Code traffic was rendered several million times more difficult to unravel. Allied fears that it might take weeks or even months to decrypt the four-rotor Enigma were to prove premature, partly because the team at Bletchley Park had been warned of the new development, probably because hasty operators had prematurely activated their fourth rotor. Extra batteries of 'Bombs' had been hurriedly made available to click their way through the millions of additional permutations. In this way the delays which could have produced a complete intelligence blackout were soon reduced to a few days. Nevertheless, even this was sufficient to have a marked effect on the critical stage of the battle particularly for HX 228, because 'Special Intelligence' had failed to pick up the new dispositions of the *Neuland* Group in time to re-route the convoy.

Far out on the North Atlantic, the Wolf Pack closed in for the kill after HX 228 had steamed into the middle of its patrol line on 10 March. By a bitter irony the convoy had been covered in the morning by an American Support Group which included the escort carrier USS *Bogue*, whose aircraft had forced several U-boats down before the group had to turn for home to refuel. That night Kapitänleutnant Trojer in U-221 was the first to strike. Penetrating to the heart of the convoy under cover of a snow squall he torpedoed one freighter and at 2131 entered in his log:

> Fired two torpedoes at two large overlapping merchant ships. First torpedo hit. Ship disintegrated completely in flames and a vast cloud of smoke. Hundreds of steel plates flew like sheets of paper through the air. A great deal of ammunition exploded. Shortly afterwards scored another hit on a freighter, which also exploded. From bows to bridge the ship was under water. Heavy debris crashed against my periscope, which now became difficult to turn. The whole boat re-echoed with bangs and crashes.

Trojer dived to escape a counter-attack and then returned to torpedo a modern 5,000 ton freighter. He was so close that he had to go astern to avoid running into the exploding ship, reporting:

My periscope suddenly went completely black. I could hardly see a thing, while all the time heavy fragments of debris continued to shower down on us. The noise inside the boat was terrific. It felt as though we were being hit by a stream of shells. Heard clearly the noise of the sinking ship, and then all was quiet.

A lull in the battle lasted until shortly after one o'clock when the *Harvester*'s radar picked up a U-boat running in to make an attack. Depth-charges forced her to the surface and the *Harvester* opened up with everything that she could bring to bear. For some minutes the two conducted a violent minuet as the U-boat tried to circle inside the destroyer. Eventually Commander Tait succeeded in ramming his opponent, who was eventually finished off by the Free French corvette *Aconit*. But the *Harvester* had been severely damaged and, in the meantime, the U-boats penetrated the convoy again and sank two more ships before U-757 slammed a torpedo salvo into the Norwegian ammunition ship *Brant County*. Her spectacular end was logged by Convoy Commodore Dodd:

> The ship fired two white rockets, burst into flames, the fire was like an inferno and lit everything up like daylight. I could see the whole convoy and escorts ahead on both wings. She blew up at 0415 with a tremendous explosion throwing debris hundreds of feet into the air – the scene was quite indescribable.

The *Brant County* was followed by the destruction of another merchant ship and then in the daylight hours of 11 March, U-432 moved in on the crippled *Harvester* which was limping in the wake of the convoy packed with

An Eye for an Eye: HX 228 was attacked by a Wolf Pack on the night of 11 March 1943, but next morning the escorts hit back and the Free French corvette *Aconit* commanded by Lieutenant Jean Levasseur (below) destroyed U-432 (bottom) which had just torpedoed the destroyer HMS *Harvester* (left).

survivors. Her first torpedo disabled the destroyer and reduced her to a shambles, then according to one of the few survivors, Lieutenant Briggs, a second struck which

> sent the rear portion of the ship up and down on top of us and forced many of us underwater. On coming up I saw that the ship was broken in half . . . the fore and aft parts had become completely separated and the forepart for about fifty feet stuck straight out of the water and floated for some minutes. Eventually it sank, followed by what was left of the after part.

There were few survivors in the icy seas because the Free French corvette *Aconit*, racing to the rescue, had sighted U-432 and moved into the attack Forcing the U-boat to the surface the French ship raked her with gunfire, and then rammed her so that she immediately sank 'in a large patch of teutonic blood,' but she arrived too late to rescue more than a handful of *Harvester*'s survivors.

HX 228 was finally to lose four ships and the destroyer *Harvester* with her experienced commander and even though two U-boats were sunk, the Germans had successfully taken on a well-defended convoy. As they watched the increasing success of Dönitz's tactics of attrition, the Western Approaches Staff began to fear that the battle was swinging to the enemy. The tension rose at Derby House and Admiral Horton's operations room often became as stormy as the Atlantic. A member of his staff recalled Horton's bluff methods:

> Battles were generally fought at night now. After dinner he would arrive in the Plotting Room to watch the battle develop, to order reinforcements, to build plans for the next time. His words were always direct. 'Where is . . . ?' 'What is?' and sometimes 'Why not?' or 'Why the Hell not?' Then having grasped the situation, his decision would come in a flash.
>
> I remember one night when the battle was pretty serious. It had started later than usual and Sir Max had already turned in. He literally roared into the 'Plot' in rather worn and split pyjamas, hirsute fore and aft. Those present gave him plenty of sea room in anticipation of the coming storm. Then he settled down to work with us. He seemed to have an uncanny precision of what the enemy would do next, which came of course from his long experience of submarines.

Even before the battle of HX 228 had ended on 11 March with the arrival of the Liberator air patrols, Dönitz began setting up his patrol lines for the next major confrontation. The seven *Neuland boats* needing fuel, were ordered south to rendezvous with a Milch-cow and the rest were detailed to join up with the *Ostmark* Group to form the 17 boat-long *Sturmer* line which was directed to proceed westward in company with the overlapping eleven boats of the *Dränger* Group. This formidable force was designed to sweep a 600 mile-wide rake across the mid-Atlantic to trap any convoys not snared by the *Raubgraf* Group farther west.

Attrition
March–April

The Role of 'Huff-Duff': By 1943 surface escorts were equipped with radio direction finding equipment (HF/DF) which was used to pinpoint the position of U-boats when they transmitted sighting reports. For Escort Group commanders like Captain Donald Macintyre it played as important a part as radar in detecting the enemy:

'You had to have a good HF/DF operator – one who knew which wavelength to listen on because the U-boats changed it throughout the day according to atmospheric conditions. But if you could get that first sighting report and get an escort out to put that shadowing U-boat down, as likely as not you would get right through the German patrol line unharmed.

That first sighting signal was terribly important to the U-boats – and to us – it was a particular kind of a signal. We were familiar with it and it didn't have to be decoded but the HF/DF operator had to be expert enough to be able to tell whether it was a ground wave or a sky wave. The reflected sky wave might have been a U-boat reporting a convoy 500 miles away. The ground wave was not necessarily louder, but it had a different quality and this put the transmitting boat within 12-15 miles, near enough for a fast sloop or destroyer to get out along the bearing and catch him.'

The *Raubgraf* boats soon proved to be a weaker barrier than Dönitz expected when on 13 March, the westbound convoy ON 170 escorted by Captain Donald Macintyre's B2 Group cleverly passed through the patrol line, aided by the skilful use of HF/DF. After picking up a radio report from U-603 which had spotted one of Macintyre's corvettes HMS *Heather* covering the starboard wing, the seasoned escort commander used this ship as a decoy. The corvette was ordered to keep a steady speed to the south west drawing the Wolf Pack after her, whilst the convoy swung away on to a southerly course. This successful move revealed once again that the radio communications necessary for the U-boats to keep in contact with their HQ proved to be their Achilles heel.

Macintyre's evasion of the *Raubgraf* Group was taken as little more than a temporary setback by U-boat Command where Dönitz was preparing his dispositions to trap the far greater prize of HX 229, determined that his Wolf Packs would make a decisive killing. *B-Dienst* intelligence had revealed not only the convoy's sailing date, but also the complete schedule of its route across the Atlantic. Such detailed information was communicated to CINCWA by cable for security, only the barest minimum of information was sent on to the Admiralty Trade Division by coded radio signal. But on this occasion there had been a slip in the communications office at the Eastern Sea Frontier Command in New York and the convoy's plan had been radioed to the US Coastguard Patrol off Greenland. The damage had been compounded when the same source had transmitted a second similar signal by radio referring to a Casablanca-bound military supply convoy UGS 6 which had sailed from New York on 2 March 1943.

Yet in making their intelligence coup, the *B-Dienst* had failed to detect that the large HX 229 convoy had been split into two seperate parts. Because of the large number of vessels waiting to be convoyed across the Atlantic, COMINCH had directed that the 38 ships of HX 229 should leave New York on 8 March and the 37 vessels of HX 229 A should leave a day later. The two convoys were routed on different courses but even when *B-Dienst* picked up a totally different reference for HX 229 when it was at sea, U-boat Command still believed that there was only one convoy.

German hopes of a decisive killing were raised by their discovery that yet another convoy, SC 122, had cleared New York on 5 March and was also heading into the middle of their extensive patrol lines. On 12 March U-boat Command was momentarily confused when a message from COMINCH was intercepted directing HX 229 A north. The *Raubgraf* Group was ordered to be ready to intercept what was believed to be HX 229 but this directive was countermanded two days later, when a new signal was picked up, giving a totally different position for HX 229 and directing the convoy on to an easterly course, to avoid the *Raubgraf* line. Still unaware that there were two HX 229 convoys at sea, Dönitz regarded the first signal as an intelligence feint, and the *Raubgraf* boats were directed to close the new position where HX 229 and SC 122 were sailing just a few hundred miles apart, leaving a lucky HX 229 A to head north through waters now clear of the enemy.

Now the four day lag in 'Special Intelligence' began to play a crucial role in

Allied plans. When he issued his routing instructions COMINCH had assumed that the *Raubgraf* line was 400 miles north east of Newfoundland when in fact it was 250 miles farther south and already moving to intercept the two convoys. The Tracking Rooms were now depending on 'inspired guesses' about the position of the *Raubgraf* Pack as revealed by Commander Winn's summary for 15 March 1943: 'there is no Special Intelligence available for the period since 11 March and therefore it is not known with certainty how the U-boats are disposed.'

Winn had noted that a record number of 66 U-boats were believed to be in the North Atlantic and that six Type IX boats moving towards the USA had been given new orders 'but the area may be either between the Azores and the Antilles or in the Florida area.'

This smaller group code-named *Unverzagt* was, in fact, moving to intercept the American convoy UGS 6 supported by the *Wohlgemut* Group. The course of this convoy had been decyphered from the fatal intelligence leak in the message to the Greenland Coast Guard which had revealed the course of HX 229. An operation was launched against the American ships on 12 March but the U-boats achieved little. Forced to make submerged attacks by the efficient escort, the Germans could only account for three merchant ships in return for one of their number.

In the event, U-boat Command regarded the UGS 6 action as a side-show, compared with the bigger developments taking place a thousand miles to the north where the U-boats were gathering for the biggest convoy confrontation of the Atlantic war as the 88 merchant ships of convoy SC 122 and HX 229 closed the 21 strong *Raubgraf* Group. Three hundred and fifty miles ahead the 500 mile patrol line of 28 boats in the *Sturmer/Dranger* Groups were also advancing steadily westwards for a decisive showdown.

Atlantic Battleground: The dispositions of the U-boats and convoys (map) in the two days that culminated in the biggest convoy battle of the war. On the morning of 15 March, after HX 229 and SC 122 had passed unscathed through the *Raubgraf* patrol line . U-632's careful shadowing of the convoy allowed U-boat Command to order the *Raubgraf* boats to close in from astern. At the same time the *Sturmer* and *Dranger* lines were order to advance from ahead. By 17 March both HX 229 and SC 122 (88 merchantmen and 14 escorts) were locked in running battles with up to 50 U-boats from the combined Packs. During this time the American convoy UGS 6 was beating off attacks by 15 U-boats of the *Unversagt* and *Wohlgemut* Packs, South of the Azores.

MID-OCEAN BATTLE

The convoy defences were unevenly disposed to deal with the huge scale of this attack and SC 122 with nine escorts had the stronger defences because slow convoys were always in greater danger of attack. Even so, the most powerful escort had been assigned to HX 229 A which was by then slipping quietly away to the north, completely undetected. HX 229 was very different. It was in the hands of a hastily assembled 'scratch team'. The Royal Navy's B4 Escort Group had originally been given the job, but storm damage had reduced it to only three ships. To make matters worse, the senior escort officer, Commander Day, had found his destroyer *Highlander* needed docking for emergency repairs in St Johns and was unable to sail to catch up his group until 15 March, so that command of the escort was placed on the shoulders of Lieutenant Commander Luther in the destroyer *Volunteer*. The Group's remaining destroyer *Beverley* and two corvettes, *Anemone* and *Pennywort*, were reinforced by two old destroyers. 'The escort of this convoy was very inadequate' the CINCWA report later admitted, 'the task of the senior officer who was not the senior officer anyway was made more difficult by the absence of a rescue ship.'

Nevertheless, up to 15 March 1943 the two convoys had luck on their side and made exceptionally good progress, each passing undetected through the *Raubgraf* line. That night, Lieutenant Commander Luther radioed CINCWA for permission to take a more northerly course to shorten the passage home because of the reduction of the escort when the destroyer *Withington* had to turn back, short of fuel. Receiving no reply, Luther decided on his own initiative to alter course a few degrees to the north. It was an unfortunate decision, for, by a chance in a million, it brought the convoy across the path of a lone U-boat which was heading back to France with engine problems. Early on the morning of 16 March 1943 the convoy's masts were picked out by U-653's lookouts and she immediately signalled the sighting report: '*Beta, Beta. BD 1491 Geleitzug Kurs 70.*'

It gave the news of the convoys that U-boat Command had been anxiously anticipating for 24 hours. Standing in front of a large chart of the North Atlantic in their makeshift operations room in the Hotel am Steinplatz, Dönitz's staff surveyed the collection of pins making the U-boat patrol lines, and decided that eight of the nearest *Raubgraf* boats, together with two refuelling from the Milch-cow to the east were to move at full speed to intercept U-653's convoy which they wrongly believed to be SC 122. At the same time, eleven boats of the *Stürmer* Group were ordered to join the pack by the following morning and the remaining six boats were to take up a position to cut off any escape. This still left the *Dränger* Line to intercept the estimated course of a second convoy.

Early that afternoon, the first of the attacking boats homed in by U-653's signals arrived to shadow HX 229. It did not take the more experienced U-boat commanders long to find a weakness. Shortly before midnight, every ship in the convoy felt the sickening torpedo thud as a Norwegian freighter was hit and sank in a few minutes. The night was so bright that Snowflakes were hardly necessary to illuminate the scene as the escort tried an unsuccessful sweep. Two hours later, Kapitänleutnant Manseck in U-758 moved through the screen and fired four torpedoes in ten minutes into the columns of merchant ships. Three were hit and sank within minutes. There was little the overworked escorts could do, and by the fifth attack of the night, Commander Mayall the Convoy Commodore aboard MV *Abraham Lincoln* was so alarmed that he decided to act in order to save the convoy:

> I considered that the U-boats were either spread out on either side of our line of advance or were relaying along it. Something had to be done to shake them off. Waiting until I considered that they had dived at 0315 I ordered an emergency turn to port (by sound signal only) and at 0330 another emergency turn to port.' 'I consider these emergency turns had the desired effect of disorganising the U-boat plan. Anyway we were not attacked until 1105 on March 17th.'

Convoy under Siege: Snowflake rockets are fired (below) to illuminate the direction of a U-boat attack and the escorts carry out sweeps to prevent the U-boats closing in before firing their torpedoes (above, the U-boat's hydrophone operator times the torpedo's run and listens for an explosion indicating a hit).

As Mayall suspected, rescue operations and fruitless Asdic searches had reduced the convoy's defences to two escorts, allowing the U-boats to close in with disastrous results.

Luther's urgent signals that his convoy was under heavy attack alerted Admiral Horton to the fact that the weakly-escorted convoy was in considerable danger. The *Highlander*, accompanied by two corvettes, was now steaming for the convoy and there was a temptation to send temporary help from SC 122 then little more than a hundred and fifty miles away. Horton reluctantly decided that this was too risky, because it was highly probable that SC 122 would soon be caught up in the attack by the stream of U-boats converging on their prey. Instead, destroyers were ordered to sail from Reykjavik to join the convoy.

This painful decision was proved fully justified a few hours later when Kapitänleutnant Manfred Kinzel in U-288, of the *Stürmer* group, passed straight between the two escorts sweeping ahead of SC 122. At first, his sighting report in the early hours of 17 March threw U-boat Command into temporary confusion as they tried to resolve the identity of the convoys. This did not stop Kinzel exploiting his good fortune by firing all his torpedoes before withdrawing. Coming with no advance HF/DF warning the sudden ferocity of the attack had caught the escorts off guard. The white glow of the Snowflake soon revealed that two freighters were sinking, one was on fire and a fourth crippled and drifting astern after Kinzel's single-handed blitz.

Daylight on the morning of 17 March 1943 found both HX 229 and SC 122 surrounded by U-boats, determined to keep up an all day assault. Two stragglers were sunk from HX 229 and, with Dönitz signalling the *Stürmer* and *Dränger* boats to concentrate on SC 122, it looked as if St Patrick's Day 1943 would bring the U-boats an annihilating victory.

However, to the consternation of U-boat Command the action tilted firmly the other way. Suddenly the U-boat commanders assembling around SC 122 were astonished to find themselves having to crash-dive to escape air attack. Their suprise was even greater when they found that it was not a carrier plane swooping down on them in the Air Gap but a four-engined bomber carrying a lethal load of depth-charges. The VLR Liberator, which had taken off at midnight from its base 900 miles away in Castle Archdale, Northern Ireland, had been ordered to stretch its fuel reserves to the limit after urgent pleas from Horton to Coastal Command for air-cover over the threatened convoys. The sudden aggressive strikes of the Australian pilot, Flying Officer Cyril Burcher soon forced many of the *Sturmer* boats to submerge, including Kinzel's U-388 but the Liberator's patrol time over the convoys was short and soon the plane headed away east. Burcher's departure allowed Kinzel to return to the attack and sink another freighter, but the *Stürmer* pack's anticipation of an afternoon's happy hunting was ruined by the arrival of a second Liberator from 86 Squadron which forced the pack down again.

A hundred miles astern, the hard-pressed Luther and his overworked escorts had to battle on against the *Raubgraf* Pack without air cover that morning and two more ships were sunk, even though the convoy ranks had closed. Two stragglers were sent to the bottom in the afternoon by a U-boat

Aircraft to the Rescue: The arrival of the first Liberator patrols during the afternoon of 17 March rallied the hard-pressed escorts of HX 229. Successful depth charge attacks from the air (above, recorded by a Liberator during the battle) forced the U-boats under and for several crucial hours, the Pack lost contact.

circling astern. The situation was now looking black for Luther who was urgently signalling CINCWA for help as his escorts were 'performing a dual role of escorting and rescue work, there was little hope of saving more than a fraction of the convoy.'

At 2.30 that afternoon the spirits of everyone in HX 229 rallied at the sight of a Liberator which had managed to locate the convoy after a remarkable feat of navigation. The plane flew around the ships for four hours, the pilot risking his chances of a safe return, but his action forced the Pack to break off its operations although this was not at first apparent to Luther who, shortly before the aircraft's departure was flashed a message from the Liberator: '6 Hearses (U-boats) bearing 120 degrees. 25 miles. I go.' The horrified young escort commander misread this signal, believing that 6 U-boats were within 5 miles of his convoy. His view of HX 229's chances of surviving the approaching night were highly pessimistic,

> This shattering piece of information caused me very seriously to think. HMS *Mansfield*'s fuel condition precluded her being used for any high speed work and to send one escort back to deal with this pack would only defer their attack. I therefore decided to do nothing but await events and deal with them as best I could as they arose (I myself foresaw the worst and thought that we were in for a night very much worse than last) and only three escorts (one of them a lame duck) to fight the battle and do what we could for survivors.

At their Berlin Headquarters, Dönitz and his staff read the situation a different way, realising their hopes had been shattered when the U-boats radioed reports of the strong air cover encountered and of having to dive continuously to escape bombing attacks. Late that afternoon they were even more distrubed to find that the aircraft had forced the *Raubgraf* boats out of contact with HX 229.

Dönitz still hoped to be able to marshal his forces for an attack on the following night, particularly if the weather deteriorated and grounded the air patrols. But the packs were already weakening as some U-boats had to be withdrawn to refuel from the mid-Atlantic Milch-cows and others had to be sent north to establish a new *Seeteufel* patrol line to intercept a slow westbound convoy, ONS 1.

A resounding victory for the U-boats had been snatched from their grasp but Dönitz had achieved a spectacular blow against the two convoys in the three-day battle by sinking 22 ships on the North Atlantic main line. As Dönitz's staff retired that evening for their first full night's sleep in nearly four days, they could be well satisfied with the fact that losses for the first twenty days of March now totalled 97 ships of over 500,000 tons. In many people's minds in London as well as Berlin, the efficiency of the whole convoy system on which the Allied war effort so deeply depended was open to question.

'This is the greatest success ever achieved in a convoy battle' U-boat Command jubilantly proclaimed in a victory communiqué after its victories over HX 229 and SC 122. It went on to sing the praises of the U-boat commanders in sinking 22 ships which had been 'even more creditable because nearly half the U-boats involved scored at least one hit'.

In London at a meeting of the Anti-U-boat Committee on 22 March 1943, there were gloomy forthcomings that worse was to come and that Britain might be sliding to defeat at sea. The Admiralty was dismayed that two thirds of the total losses had been from heavily defended convoys. The grave situation was summed up in a report by Admiral Pound: 'there is insufficient shipping to allow us to develop the offensives against the enemy which have been decided on. Every ship sunk makes the situation worse.' The immediate prospects for reversing the upward trend of losses looked bleak:

We can no longer rely on evading the U-boat packs and hence we shall have to fight the convoys through them.
We cannot increase the number of escorts with the convoys *until the autumn*.
We are providing VLR aircraft for covering the convoys as rapidly as possible, but we shall not reach sufficient strength for effective counter attack *until mid summer*.

In the face of this pessimistic memorandum it was hardly surprising that the Admiralty was already alive to the frightening possibility that the convoy system might not be able to defend shipping against a sustained U-boat assault. Their official verdict was that 'the Germans never came so near to disrupting communications between the New World and the Old as in the first twenty days of March 1943'.

Some high-ranking naval staff officers were already thinking the unthinkable and wondering whether fewer losses would be risked by routing ships independently. The Commander-in-Chief of Western Approaches quickly replied that such suggestions would be putting the clock back, ignoring all the lessons of the First War and current experience. He pointed out that a closer examination of the facts indicated a different trend. The recent losses had been caused by a 'very inadequate escort' and 'the snowball effect of a convoy battle was here clearly illustrated with one misfortune piling on top of another'. He also emphasised that the decisive change in the battle brought about by the arrival of Coastal Command's VLR Liberators.

Aid from the sky:
Lieutenant-Commander John Luther's convoy HX 229 was saved from total annihilation by the intervention of the VLR Liberator squadrons (below, No. 120 squadron at Aldergrove, Northern Ireland) which flew well beyond their normal operational range of 800 miles to provide desperately needed air cover. One exhausted air crew arrived back having been airborne for 20 hours 30 minutes.

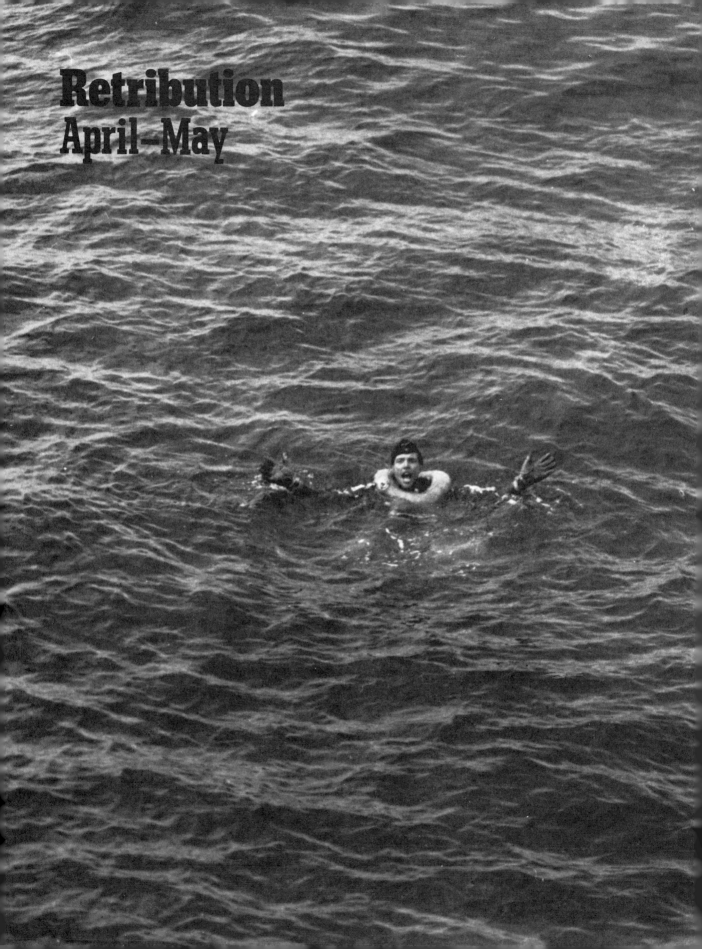

Retribution
April–May

All eyes were now fixed on the next wave of convoys, already ploughing across the Atlantic in the teeth of the equinoctial gales. They were already being stalked by the U-boats, aided by *B-Dienst* intercepts revealing the course of the westward-bound slow convoy ONS 1 and the two eastbound convoys SC 123 and HX 230. Anticipating a chance for another big attack, Dönitz had drawn up two new patrol lines, *Seewolf* of 17 U-boats and the more southerly *Seeteufel* Group of 15, to block the convoys' path. The merchantmen were duly sighted but the mountainous seas made it almost impossible for the U-boats to launch an attack. The Commander of U-260, Kapitänleutnant Purkhold, reported his difficulty in pursuing an 8,000 ton freighter in seas driven by hurricane-force gales:

> while trying to run before the storm at full speed the boat dived twice. By blowing tanks and putting my helm hard over and reducing speed I managed to hold her reasonably well on the surface. To remain on the bridge was impossible. Within half an hour the Captain and the watch were half drowned. Five tons of water poured into the boat in no time through the conning tower hatch, the voice pipe and the Diesel ventilating shaft.

As the weather moderated in the last days of March, the U-boats which, had fastened on to SC 123, discovered a strong defensive screen around the convoys, including the dumpy shape of the escort carrier USS *Bogue*, which managed to fly its Avengers and Wildcats to force the U-boats under. Only one ship was lost from these two convoys, and the overall shipping losses for March, to the relief of the Admiralty, were contained below 700,000 tons.

In April 1943 the tide began to turn, imperceptibly at first, but with gathering momentum. The number of U-boats at sea was as high as ever but the Admiralty monthly Anti-Submarine Report noticed with satisfaction the declining U-boat successes and observed that the tempo of the battle 'appears on recent experience to be waning'.

It was, however, a few weeks before the momentum of the Atlantic U-boat offensive began to show signs of declining. After their failure to intercept HX 230 U-boat Command managed to get sufficient boats refuelled from a Milch cow to form a 280-mile long patrol line midway between Greenland and Iceland to intercept the next fast convoy HX 231. The convoy, which was escorted by Commander Gretton's B7 Escort Group was spotted on 4 April and this gave time for the 15 boats of Group *Löwenherz* to concentrate into a Pack; in spite of the arrival of a Liberator that afternoon and an attempt to evade the patrol line by changing course to the north. Urged on by signals from Dönitz to put everything they had got into the attack, the Wolf Pack began a two day battle with the well-defended convoy. They managed to sink only two ships from it but were able to add to this by picking off four stragglers. In return, they lost U-635 to the escorts and U-632 to aircraft patrols before the Pack was called off.

The next week the patrol line managed to reform to intercept the westbound convoy ONS 176 and in a two-day operation revenged themselves on the escorts by sinking the destroyer HMS *Beverley* as well as four merchant ships. At the same time, another Pack managed to sink three ships from HX 232. Five days later the next fast convoy, HX 233 was successfully routed

Heineman's Triumph: A survivor from U-175 shouts for help after being sunk by Captain P. R. Heineman's Escort Group, led by the USCGC *Spencer*. Heineman had completed a successful depth charge attack (below) forcing the U-boat to the surface. The Germans raced for their guns but gave up the attempt to fight back after accurate gunfire from Heineman's two cutters and the merchant ships had reduced the U-boat's deck to a shambles (bottom, a survivor of the gun's crew sheltering behind the wrecked conning tower).

around the Wolf Packs after its experienced American led Escort Group had driven off the shadowing U-boat. The Harriers' USN Escort Unit A3, under the command of Captain P. R. Heineman in the coastguard cutter *Spencer* lived up to their reputation as the US Navy's No. 1 escort team by sinking U-175 as Kapitänleutnant Heydeman tried to carry out a submerged daylight attack on 17 April. Only one straggler was lost from this convoy and although it was becoming clear now to Dönitz that the U-boats were losing the momentum of their attacks, he was still determined to try and keep up the pressure by ordering a rapid turn-around of the operational boats at their French bases. By the end of April, U-boat Command placed high hopes on Group *Meise* which had been established across the bottleneck south of Greenland. The Pack did contact two convoys and a four day battle resulted around HX 234 and ONS 3 which began on 21 April. Seven ships were sunk but the Special Intelligence Summary reported that the Pack's operations had been 'remarkably feeble' and one of the *Meise*'s boats was sunk by a US aircraft flying cover for the convoys. Significantly, Commander Winn concluded that 'the U-boats engaged have made repeated and bitter complaints of the ubiquity and efficiency of the aircraft which were constantly with the convoy on 24 March'. U-boat Command had now directed its Commanders to try fighting back at the aircraft but such instructions, Winn dryly observed, were 'congenial only to the bolder type of commander whose absence from the HX 234 engagement was conspicuous.'

At the end of April, the statistics began to show a decisive swing against the U-boats. 313,000 tons of shipping had been lost, less than half the previous month's total. Most important, the biggest drop had been in the number of ships sunk in convoy. Even German propaganda broadcasts, the Admiralty monthly bulletin noted, were only claiming 'about half the March figure, or 425,000 tons. This may be due to a realisation that there are limits to the tonnage they can claim as sunk in the face of the obvious fact that supplies in vast quantities continue to arrive in North Africa.'

What German propaganda did not reveal was that April had also seen fourteen U-boats destroyed in the North Atlantic. Seven had been sunk by escorts and the same number by aircraft. The casualty rate being suffered by the U-boats making attacks on convoys had now risen to one destroyed for every three merchant ships, and the nerve of the U-boat commanders was plainly rattled by such dismal figures justifying Winn's comment.

> The outstanding impression felt on reading recent U-boat traffic is that the spirit of the crews which are at present out on operations in the North Atlantic is low and general morale is shaky.

Five powerful and free-ranging Support Groups were now available to back up the escort groups. Two of these, the US Navy's 5th and 6th Groups, included the escort carriers *Dasher* and *Bogue* and the Royal Navy's US-built escort carriers were also entering service after being delayed many months by extensive modifications insisted on by the Admiralty. The air cover provided by the growing numbers of land-based VLR Liberators had already made a significant contribution against the Wolf Packs that had previously been able to operate with impunity in the Air Gap.

The Defences Grow Stronger: With the successful completion of the Torch landings many surface escorts were released for duty on the North Atlantic by the spring of 1943. Horton was able to form five support groups, one of which included the escort carrier *Biter* (above), as well as anti-submarine sloops like the *Magpie* (below).

The improvement brought about by the steady build-up of the convoys' air defences was matched by a more streamlined organisation coming into operation between the Allied navies as a direct result of decisions taken by the Washington Convoy Conference in March. These would iron out the administrative chaos that had developed in convoy control in the North West Atlantic, where no fewer than five separate command structures had overlapped. Much to the surprise of the British and Canadians, Admiral King had endorsed their proposal made at the Washington Convoy Conference in March to divide the Atlantic theatre into two areas north and south of latitude 40°. A new Northwest Atlantic Command was set up at Halifax along the lines of Admiral Horton's Western Approaches Command. In deference to the Canadians, it was to be their entire responsibility and Rear Admiral Murray (RCN) was placed in control of an area which extended to the CHOP Line at 47 degrees west, where CINCWA took over. The Southern area below latitude 40 was to remain the responsibility of COMINCH in Washington.

Meanwhile the U-boats oceanwide campaign was kept up with sinkings from the Arctic to the Indian oceans but the decline in German fortunes was brutally confirmed in May 1943 by the battle of convoy ONS 5, a slow procession of 42 ships shepherded by Commander Peter Gretton's B7 Escort Group comprising the destroyer *Duncan*, a frigate and four corvettes. Ahead of the convoy, which had to contend with heavy seas, Dönitz had organised a formidable reception in the western Atlantic. The *Amsel* Group of 11 boats was patrolling off Newfoundland and to the north and east were the 17 boats of Group *Specht* and 14 of Group *Star*.

On 28 April 1943, a week after it had sailed, the convoy steamed at six knots into the danger zone. Radio signals picked up that day made Gretton aware that the first U-boats had made contact. 'Again that horrible sinking feeling appeared.' Soon the growing chatter of radio signals made it clear that the convoy was surrounded by 14 U-boats hungry for slaughter. The large Pack had been able to gather because the Iceland air patrols were severely hampered by bad weather and for long periods the convoy had been without air cover but Gretton's escorts resolutely drove off five attempted attacks and the Germans did not achieve their first success until after dawn on the 29 April, when the freighter *McKeesport* was torpedoed and sunk.

Meanwhile ONS 5's escorts were getting desperately low on fuel, having been unable to oil from an auxiliary tanker in the heavy seas. Gretton himself was obliged to hand over his command to Lieutenant Commander Sherbrooke in the frigate *Tay* in order to take two of his destroyers ahead to St Johns to refuel. He was soon followed by the *Vidette* but the arrival of the five destroyers of the 3rd Support Group strengthened the convoy's defences at a crucial time. On 4 May, frustrated at the dismal showing against SC 128, Dönitz decided to throw the full weight of all his Western Atlantic boats against ONS 5. Groups *Specht* and *Star* were massed into a powerful Group *Fink*, which was further bolstered by 12 more U-boats from the *Amsel* Group. Forty U-boats were now moving towards ONS 5, with Dönitz's exhortation: 'I am certain you will fight with everything you have got.

The besieged convoy's escort commanders were aware from the continuous U-boat radio chatter that they were up against a formidable pack and a vigorous and aggressive defence was mounted by running out along radar fixes to put down any U-boat that was closing in. By the early hours of 5 May 1943, the constant pressure of so many U-boats finally broke through the screen. In two hours, five ships succumbed to their torpedoes, but their radio reports revealed that the Germans also suffered badly.

> U-boat 31 reported considerable damage from depth charge attack . . . returning to port; U-boats 9 and 22 were also heavily depth-charged and attacked by gunfire . . . U-boat 7 was forced to submerge by a destroyer and U-boat 20, which had been badly damaged, was commencing to return to port via the supply boat . . . '

C-in-C Western Approaches, warned by Tracking Room reports of the growing menace to the convoy, ordered the 3rd Support Group to reinforce the convoy's defences. Royal Canadian Air Force Catalinas from Newfoundland managed to fly a number of uncomfortable sorties through the heavy turbulence at extreme range to keep the U-boats under. But the convoy's best defence proved to be the weather when a heavy storm raged for three days. This hampered the *Amsel* pack as well as the convoy, which could only make 20 miles a day. By the time the gale abated, Gretton was confronted with an escort commander's worst nightmare; the convoy had become scattered by the storm, thus opening up his defences, as the escorts hunted for stragglers.

Fortunately for Gretton, U-boat Command's attention was diverted by the chance to trap a bigger prize in the shape of the slow eastbound convoy SC 128, laden with war materials on the way to Britain. Groups *Specht* and *Star* had been ordered north to try to catch the convoy, but, to the exasperation of U-boat Command, it seemed to be extremely difficult to launch any kind of attack on the elusive formation. A petulant message went out from U-boat Command to the pack: 'Do not hold back . . . something can be done and must be achieved with 31 boats.'

All through the next day the *Fink* Pack kept up the pressure, picking off two stragglers and torpedoing two more ships in the convoy. Early in the forenoon U-boat Command ordered them to move ahead of the convoy to make submerged attacks and place themselves in a good position to smash their way in under cover of darkness. 'Immediately after the onset of night' Dönitz instructed, 'the drumroll must be timed to begin. Make haste, as there are forty of you there will be nothing of the convoy left.' *Fink* Group's commanders obeyed and pressed forward to the attack, but late in the afternoon the

Victory to the Escorts: In the six day running battle between the Wolf Packs and convoy ONS 5 the British B7 Escort Group led by Captain Peter Gretton assisted by the US Navy's 3rd Support Group beat off attacks by forty U-boats, sinking five for the loss of 12 merchant ships. It marked a decisive victory over the Wolf Packs and the end of their ascendancy over the escorts.

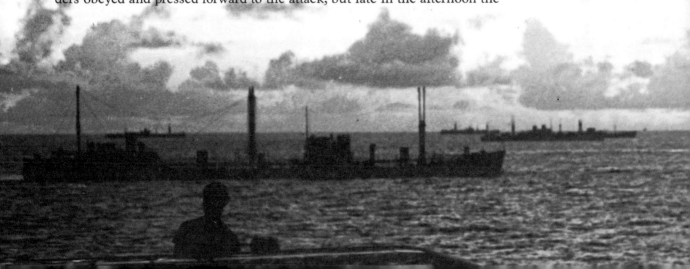

weather came to the aid of the convoy when it entered a fog bank. Although this hampered the air patrols, the radar-equipped escorts now had a distinct advantage. When the U-boats closed for what Dönitz confidently anticipated would be a decisive night's action, the tables were turned. Radar allowed the escorts to surprise the U-boats as they closed the convoy in poor visibility. No less than five U-boats, an eighth of the *Fink* Group, were wiped out in a matter of hours; only one succeeded in penetrating the defences to sink two freighters. The official report spelt out the scale of the victory, over the biggest Wolf Pack ever to attack a convoy.

> During the night of the 5th/6th 24 attacks were attempted on the convoy. All were repulsed and 5 U-boats were sunk. *Oribi* and *Sunflower* rammed one each, *Snowflake* destroyed one with depth charges, *Loosestrife* depth-charged one which surfaced and blew up and *Vidette* claimed a hit with a hedgehog.

A large number of U-boats had also been damaged. Next day U-boat Command ordered the attack to be broken off, but not before Dönitz had radioed a homily to the defeated commanders:

> This convoy battle has once again proved that conditions on a convoy attack are always most favourable at the beginning. He who exploits the moment of surprise on the first night and presses home the attack with all his power, he is the man who is successful.

The tally of attrition on ONS 5 made disconcerting news for U-boat Command. Twelve merchant ships had been sunk but five U-boats had been destroyed by the escorts. Two others had collided in the mass of boats manoeuvring round the convoys and foundered, making a loss of seven in all. The lessons were clear, there was a limit to the size of a Wolf Pack attack and, if the U-boats tackled a well-defended convoy, they could expect to suffer unacceptable losses.

Events were to prove that the triumph of ONS 5's escorts was not a freak. U-boats continued to be sunk at an average rate of one a day throughout May, so that by the end of the month the long Atlantic campaign had moved decisively and finally in the Allies favour. As the Admiralty put it:

> Historians of this war are likely to single out the months of April and May 1943 as the critical period during which strength began to ebb away from the German U-boat offensive . . . because for the first time U-boats failed to press home attacks on convoys when favourably situated to do so. There is ground for confident estimate that the enemy's peak effort is passed. Morale and efficiency are delicate and may wither rapidly if no longer nourished by rich success.

The Turning Point: At the end of April 1943 the offensive by more than a hundred U-boats in the Atlantic was losing its momentum as the convoy defences were strengthened by new free-ranging support groups, escort carriers and the long range Liberator patrols into the Air Gap. The Allied U-boat Tracking Rooms aided by rapid decyphering of the German Atlantic U-boat traffic allowed the convoys (above) to be routed around the Wolf pack patrol lines and new Allied codes introduced at the same time effectively blacked out the *B-Dienst* intelligence to U-boat Command. Dönitz appreciated that only the rapid construction of a new type of U-boat weapon could retrieve the situation.

16. Race Against Time

'We had lost the Battle of the Atlantic'
KARL DÖNITZ after calling off the
1943 offensive on the Atlantic Convoys
on 24 May.

Even though U-boat strength in the Atlantic rose to a peak of 120 in May the commanders were finding it increasingly difficult to locate and attack the well defended convoys. Not only were the Tracking Rooms and 'Special Intelligence' giving advance warning of the movements of the patrol groups, but U-boat Command was finding its own source of intelligence information drying up. Changes in the British cyphers had been introduced which cut off much of the *B-Dienst* information which Dönitz had used so successfully to deploy his patrol lines: 'This valuable assistance ceased . . . It was of course possible, granted a sufficiently large number of messages, to breakdown the code, but advantage could no longer be derived from this, as the enemy was now changing the code at shorter intervals than formerly so that the wearying labour of breaking it down had to be recommenced each time.'

It was a very black month for the attackers. Four days after their defeat on ONS 5, a 36 boat Pack sank only five ships from HX 237 and SC 129 and a week later, the 17 Strong *Donau* Group lost 6 boats in an action against SC 130 that failed to sink a single merchant ship. Dönitz felt this defeat particularly deeply because his own son went down with the U-954.

It seemed that the U-boats could do little against well co-ordinated and continuously improving air and sea defence as a new generation of weapons came into service. On 12 May 1943 the first of the airborne acoustic homing torpedoes (Fido) was dropped. These were designed to follow a submerging U-boat, by homing in on the noise of its propellers. Aircraft began to be fitted with rocket projectiles and the first of the operational MAD (magnetic anomaly detector) aircraft started flying off North Africa equipped with a detecting device that could pick up a submerged U-boat's magnetic field. The Anti-U-boat Warfare Committee also enthusiastically received reports that American helicopter development was going ahead. The first six MAC ships (merchant aircraft carriers) were also operating with the convoys and these, together with the Royal Navy's new escort carriers, were soon proving valuable adjuncts to the Support Groups. They were equipped with Swordfish aircraft which found a new lease of life on anti-submarine duties. The 'Stringbags' endurance, slow speed and ability to carry rockets as well as torpedoes, together with the new ASV III radar, made them first rate U-boat killers. Controlled by radio up to 80 miles away, they proved exceptionally good at breaking up Dönitz's patrol lines.

On 7 May, ONS 7 was the last convoy to lose a ship that month and only a quarter of a million tons of Allied Shipping were sunk, but Dönitz had lost a staggering 41 U-boats. At the end of the month the attrition being suffered by the U-boat arm reached such a point that Dönitz called off the assault on the convoys. The combination of centimetric radar and air patrols led him to conclude that, 'Wolf Pack operations against convoys in the North Atlantic, the main theatre of operations and at the same time the theatre in which air cover was strongest, were no longer possible'. Operations against the convoys could only be resumed if 'we succeeded in radically increasing the fighting power of the U-boats . . . We had lost the Battle of the Atlantic.'

On 24 May 1943 the U-boats were ordered to the area west of the Azores well away from the heavily defended Allied convoys in the North Atlantic.

Counting the Cost: Those U-boats still at sea at the end of May were ordered to proceed 'using the utmost caution' to the area south west of the Azores where Dönitz hoped they would escape the heavy concentration of air and sea escorts in the North Atlantic destroyed a phenomenal 41 boats in the month (right), aboard the destroyer *Hesperus*, a seaman paints up the record of victories). Losses were heavy among the U-boat crews of whom only a percentage might escape to be rescued (below) and the Admiralty was quick to note: 'There is ground for a confident estimate that the enemy's peak effort is passed. Morale and efficiency are delicate and may wither rapidly if no longer nourished by rich success'.

At the end of May Dönitz reported to the Berghof and explained to Hitler why he had pulled out of the Battle. The intensification of air patrols and the arrival of the escort carriers were contributory factors but Dönitz made it clear that, 'The determining factor is a new location device, evidently also used by surface vessels, by means of which planes are now in a position to locate submarines'. He frankly told the Führer that, with losses running at 30%, 'we must conserve our strength, otherwise we will play into the hands of the enemy'. Until the battle against the convoys could be renewed with new weapons Dönitz announced: 'I shall proceed to more distant areas in the hope that the planes there are not as yet fully equipped with modern location devices. I intend however, to resume attacks on convoys in the North Atlantic at the time of the new moon, provided that the U-boats have additional weapons at their disposal by that time.'

Dönitz then got the Führer's approval for top priority to be given to developing new equipment to enable the U-boats to continue their campaign. An effective detector for countering allied centimetric radar was essential if the U-boats were to stand any chance of survival and although the anti-aircraft defences of the submarines were to be increased, he appealed for the Luftwaffe to provide air cover over the Bay of Biscay. But the Commander in Chief of the Kriegsmarine could no longer be confident about the future of the war at sea, confessing, 'it is impossible to foretell to what extent U-boat warfare would again become effective', he assured the Führer of his conviction that it had to be carried on, 'even if great successes are no longer possible'.

The Führer was becoming painfully aware, in the aftermath of the humiliating surrender of Axis forces in North Africa on 7 May 1943, that the Allied offensive could be expected to move across the Mediterranean and that there would be an invasion of Europe within a year. He insisted:

> There can be no talk of a let up in U-boat warfare. The Atlantic is my first line of defence in the West, and even if I have to fight a defensive war there, that is preferable to waiting to defend myself on the coast of Europe. The enemy forces tied up by our U-boat warfare are tremendous, even though the actual losses inflicted by us are no longer great. I cannot afford to release these forces by discontinuing U-boat warfare.

It was the chance Dönitz had been waiting for. If there was to be no let-up in the U-boat war, then the Führer had no choice but to underwrite plans already agreed between Dönitz and Speer to raise production to 40 a month. Without demure Hitler signed the order. The U-boat war was still on.

In order to be certain that his commanders and crews would follow him into the next, bitter phase of the campaign, Dönitz summoned a conference of his flotilla commanders at the HQ of the Senior Officer Submarines West, where his decision to fight on was unanimously agreed.

A programme of improvements for the Type VII U-boats to counter the air menace was urgently put in hand. In February 1943 a British *H2S* 10-centimetre radar set, with its vital magnetron device intact, had been salvaged from the wreckage of an RAF bomber shot down over Rotterdam. This gave the scientists working for the Luftwaffe their first insight into the secrets of the new device. Immediately the large electronic firm of Telefunken was asked to produce a new search receiver code-named *Naxos*, but the company had difficulty in making the ultra-high-frequency crystal detectors necessary. When it was eventually installed the U-boat crews soon found it wanting. It was not till July that an effective and radiation-free receiver, the *Hagenuk*, was ready and the German scientists embarked on a simultaneous and wasteful search for Allied detectors using infra-red radiations.

The German confusion over electronic countermeasures which stemmed from conflicting scientific advice and disorganised research plagued the fighting services. Unlike Britain and the United States, where scientists like Blackett, (Admiralty), Waddington (RAF) and Morse (USN) worked closely with the fighting units constantly trying to improve operational weapons efficiency there was intense rivalry between competing scientific and industrial firms inside the Third Reich. It was not until the end of 1943 that Dönitz set up a Naval Scientific Operations Staff, presided over by the electronics expert Professor Kuepfmüeller who brought about immediate improvements in the *Naxos* radar by the addition of a directional aerial. Steps were also taken to adapt the set to receive the latest Allied 3 cm radar. A fully equipped test boat, U 406, was fitted out to probe Allied electronic systems but it was sunk in February 1944 before contributing any useful results.

Improved electronics was only one way of ensuring U-boat survival, particularly against the Anti-Submarine aircraft. Steps were also taken to give commanders the chance of fighting back on the surface. Quadruple 20 mm flak batteries were installed abaft the U-boat's conning tower, as well as a 37 mm rapid fire AA gun. *Flakspezialisten* were added to the complement and surgeons included in the crews to tend the casualties expected as a result of Allied strafing. But the only certain way for the U-boats to remain safe from air attack was to operate as much as possible underwater and work was pressed ahead on the *Schnorchel*; a long tube which could be raised like a third periscope to the surface so as to suck in air which would enable the boat to run at periscope-depth on its diesels. The first *Schnorchel* boats did not enter operational service until early 1944. They were unpopular, because the valve at the top of the mast could be closed temporarily by a wave and in seconds the diesel engines would reduce the pressure in the boat to a near vacuum, causing immense personal discomfort to the crew whose eyes bulged as they fought for breath. However, the device gave the boats added underwater capability and prolonged the operational usefulness of the conventional Type VII's and IX's until the end of the war.

THE 'WONDER-SUBMARINES'

All these developments were stop-gaps. They could not radically increase the fighting power of the conventional U-boats. Only the high performance of a new submarine could restore the initiative to the Germans, and high hopes were still placed on the Walter programme which had been started the previous autumn. The development of the small Type XVII and a larger Type XVIII for Atlantic operations was not making the expected progress.

The Super U-boats: In a series of crucial conferences in May 1943 Dönitz and his Chief of Staff (above) began to strengthen the ability of his conventional U-boats to fight back with improved anti-aircraft armament, the Schnorchel and the development of U-boats like the 300 ton Type XVII (right), and the larger ocean going Type XVIII. But teething troubles with the advanced machinery led to the large 1600 tons streamlined Walter hull being adapted to take diesel engines and a greatly increased number of batteries. This design (below) became the Type XXI which could achieve a submerged speed of 17 knots faster than most escorts.

They had streamlined hulls and employed the new Walter hydrogen peroxide turbine units to give a design speed of approximately 30 knots, but there proved to be too many engineering problems with the new propulsion plants. Only three Type XVII's were ever tested whilst the larger Type XVIII had to be dropped because of technical problems.

The difficulties with the Walter boats deeply disappointed Dönitz, but in the middle of 1943 the German naval constructors, Bröking and Schürer, proposed that the streamlined hull designed for the Walter boats could be used with a boosted conventional battery-powered propulsion unit to give a 19 knot underwater speed and a capability of remaining submerged for 60 hours or more. Design work on the new boats was set in motion at top speed in May 1943. Tank trials were rushed ahead in Hamburg and Vienna and a wooden mock-up constructed. In addition to a large 1,600 ton Type XXI, development also began on a smaller Type XXIII boat of 215 tons for use in coastal waters. Work was still continued on the Type XXVI Walter design in the hope that the engineering problems could be overcome.

The plans for the new boats offered Dönitz the heady prospect of regaining the initiative at sea. They would be safe from aircraft and would be able to outrun almost every escort at their submerged speed. In addition the Type XXI would be able to dive to a planned 1,000 feet, well beyond the range of the depth-charges, whilst the new hydraulic system meant that the torpedoes could be reloaded semi-automatically.

Coming up with the right decision was one task, but re-equipping the U-boat arm with the new boats was another. The whole programme seemed doomed when Naval High Command construction experts estimated that the new fleet would not be ready before 1946 if conventional construction methods were used. At once Dönitz used his new relationship with Hitler to exempt skilled shipyard workers from enlistment and also won an important increase in steel allocation for the Navy, which had been treated as a Cinderella service in the division of the Reich's industrial output. In April he went further, and sought Hitler's permission for a new naval construction programme requiring an extra 30,000 tons of steel a month. To carry out the new tasks, Dönitz came to an understanding with Albert Speer. The Armaments Minister got on well with Dönitz and welcomed his proposal that his Ministry should take over naval construction but Speer's work was made more difficult by the Führer himself, who frequently gave priority to several different projects at the same time. With Hitler, Speer claimed,

> 'one was always at a loss, because he was not stable enough in projecting things. When Dönitz was telling him "The U-boat needs top priority" he would agree . . . Then along came Guderian [Inspector General of Armour] who would say, "We are really at the end with our tanks, and if we haven't first priority we're finished". So he signed.'

Speer's full co-operation was essential if the new Type XXI and XXIII programme was to stand any chance of success and the project was placed in the hands of his appointee, Otto Merker, a production engineer, who had made his name manufacturing fire engines. When, in early July 1943, the first blueprints were ready for Dönitz' approval, Merker presented his master plan for constructing the 1,600 ton U-boats at the rate of 30 a month. Such a phenomenal rate could only be achieved by emulating the US Liberty ship programme and using standardised mass production and prefabrication techniques. Merker's programme therefore divided the Type XXI design into eight basic sections which would be constructed inland close to the steel foundries. These large hull units would then be shipped by waterway to the Section Yards, where engines, gears, shaftings, pipes, cables and auxiliary machinery would be installed. Finally they were to be moved by sea to the yards of Deschimag (Bremen), Blöhm and Voss (Hamburg) and Schichau (Danzig) where the boats would be finally assembled, tested and handed over. It was hoped that the first of the new boats would be ready in the amazingly short time of 4½ months, and the first were planned to be in service by the Spring of 1944.

Until the new 'wonder-submarine' became available Dönitz had to improve his present U-boat fleet's ability to survive, but RAF Coastal Command had gone over to the offensive. Under the dynamic leadership of its new Commander-in-Chief, Air Marshal Sir John Slessor, there was a massive concentration of air strikes in the Bay of Biscay against U-boats on passage from their bases. It was a blow against:

> the trunk of the Atlantic U-boat menace, the roots being in the Biscay ports and the branches spreading far and wide to the North Atlantic convoys, to the Caribbean, to the eastern seaboard of North America . . . The obvious course was to fell the tree by cutting through its trunk.

Although the Admiralty also asked for the French bases to be given a 'thorough bombing', the massive raids by RAF Bomber Command, backed up by the precision attacks of the US 8th Air Force, produced meagre results. In the summer of 1943 Dönitz sarcastically remarked:

> The Anglo Saxon attempt to strike down our U-boat arm is being undertaken with all the means at their disposal. You know that the towns of St Nazaire and Lorient have been rubbed out as main submarine bases. Not a dog is left in these towns. Nothing remains – but the U-boat shelters.

The Germans suffered only small dislocation in these heavy raids, in which the US 8th Air Force joined, and their main problem became shortage of labour willing to work in the target area. The raids hardly endeared the Allied cause to the French inhabitants and they were costly in terms of

The new men: The huge Type XXI programme was put into the hands of Armaments Minister, Albert Speer (above) with Dönitz on a visit to the Norwegian bases) who was introducing highly successful mass-production techniques to war industries. The new U-boats were the only hope of avoiding the devastating air power wielded by Coastal Command Chief Air Marshal Slessor (below) whose Bay offensive took a heavy toll of U-boats.

aircraft losses, with over 100 heavy bombers destroyed from January to May 1943. The U-boat pens, which were self-sufficient on power supplies, were not affected. With their U-boats safe under the thick reinforced-concrete of the Todt shelters, and the crews dispersed into camps and rest centres in the Brittany countryside, operations were carried on unaffected by Allied bombing.

THE BAY OFFENSIVE

The Coastal Command 'Bay Offensive' was a far more deadly threat and had been worked out with great precision by RAF Operational Research scientists, who knew that a submarine would have to surface for five hours to keep its batteries 80% charged. At that time it became vulnerable to air attack and statistics showed that it would be possible, given enough aircraft, for a U-boat crossing the Bay to be forced to dive every 30 minutes.

Dönitz was shaken by the severity of the new Bay Offensive when it opened in April 1943. Boldly he decided to accept the air challenge. In May, U-boat commanders were ordered to submerge by night and sail on the surface by day, ready to repel any enemy aircraft with their newly installed flak batteries, but these new tactics played straight into the hands of Coastal Command. As Slessor reported:

> The habit of fighting back may cost us a few more aircraft; but if persisted in (which is at least open to doubt), it will undoubtedly mean more U-boats killed. It is up to us to take the fullest advantage of the good opportunities offered before the buzz goes round the Bay ports that fighting back is an expensive and unprofitable pastime.

Slessor's judgment was right. In the first week of May there were no fewer than 72 U-boat sightings and 43 attacks. By the end of the week three U-boats had been destroyed; six were sunk by the end of the month.

In spite of more flak batteries the U-boat commanders were at a serious disadvantage in trying to fight off attacking aircraft and Coastal Command pilots became very proficient at sweeping in fine on a submarine's bow where the flak battery was installed behind the conning tower on the specially designed platform, referred to by the U-boat men as the *'Wintergarten'*. The joke was soon to turn sour as the gunners, unable to bring their weapons to bear in time, were slaughtered by cannon fire from the attacking planes. Some commanders managed to swing their boats hard by the stern as the attack developed so as to clear a field of fire, but it was extremely difficult to outmanoeuvre the Allied aircrews.

After these bloody encounters Dönitz tried sending out special Flak U-boats to attract and then outshoot the Coastal Command planes. The first of these boats, U-441, bristled with two 2 cm four-barrelled cannons and a 3.7 cm rapid fire AA gun. On 24 May she shot down a Sunderland but sustained damage herself. In the next month another Flak-boat, U-778, fought a pitched battle with carrier-borne planes. Her commander later reported another success:

> A new machine, also a Martlet, delivered a low-flying attack, firing as it approached

Aircraft v. U-boats: Employing operational research and analysis techniques Allied aircraft flew intensive patrol patterns over the routes used by the U-boats from their French bases into the Atlantic. A daylight attack (above) on a surfaced U-boat on May 1 1943.

287

from starboard. Enemy received a large number of hits, turned away hard aport when over my stern and dropped four bombs, which fell about 25 yards astern of us. Emitting thick black clouds of smoke the aircraft crashed in a shallow curve into the sea. Find that with gunfire I can compel bomber aircraft to keep 3000 to 4000 yards away.

But the aircraft usually came off best in these skirmishes. In July, the encounter ended up with U-441 so severely strafed by Allied aircraft that ten men were killed and thirteen were badly injured, including the captain, leaving the surgeon to take the battered boat home. After this incident Dönitz ordered his boats to sail in groups so that their combined flak batteries would present a murderous concentration of fire. Spectacular battles were now fought on the waters of the Bay with the U-boat's twisting and turning and blasting away against the Allied aircraft flying just above the waves – ready to drop their depth-charges from a height of only 50 feet.

In answer to the U-boats' new tactics Slessor organised group air operations and committed still more aircraft to the offensive. Two areas, designated *Musketry* and *Seaslug*, were regularly patrolled in order to block the main exits of the Bay. Patrols of seven aircraft were programmed to fly along these corridors, their radar covering the whole field, and once a contact had been made it was possible to concentrate the group on to the enemy.

The offensive proved spectacularly successful and by the first week of August it had accounted for 41 U-boats. Dönitz finally had to accept defeat and the Coastal Command Review for that month commented:

> . . . it was too good to last; the enemy is now running submerged by day – except where he has been forced under by night patrols – and we believe he is surfacing at night only for the minimum time necessary to put in an adequate charge.

Sightings and U-boat kills fell off rapidly as the Germans started using a new route along the Spanish coastline less accessible to the Allied aircraft. The Admiralty now called for 160 more planes to maintain the impetus of the offensive, but Air Marshal Portal, was not prepared to reallocate any of Bomber Command's squadrons engaged in the strategic air offensive against Germany. The British Chiefs of Staff once again had to turn to the Americans. General Arnold of the US Army Air Force was favourable to the British request, and eventually two squadrons of Liberators arrived in Cornwall but Admiral King was less co-operative and it was clear that nothing further would happen with the US Army-Navy conflict still to be resolved.

The struggle had come to a peak in May when King had requested General Arnold to transfer more squadrons of his aircraft to Newfoundland so as to strengthen operations in support of the North Atlantic convoys. Arnold reluctantly complied but ordered that the squadrons were only to engage in 'offensive' operations and not escort the convoys. This enfuriated King who claimed, justifiably, that he had been given operational control of all Anti-Submarine operations. The US Army fiercely resisted King's demands because they intended to build up an Anti-Submarine air arm comparable with the RAF's Coastal Command. At the end of June there were few signs of a compromise being reached between the warring service chiefs.

It was not until July 1943, after the matter had been taken up again by Roosevelt and Churchill, that a compromise agreement was reached between the US Army and Navy. A deal was struck to exchange Liberators; the Army took those Navy planes equipped for heavy bombing in return for their Anti-Submarine squadrons. By the time this deal had been hammered out the opportunity for striking Slessor's hoped-for decisive blow in the Bay of Biscay had been missed for lack of 72 extra planes. Nevertheless, operations continued and it proved to be a fruitful area for harassing and trapping U-boats which now looked upon the Bay as their own 'Black Pit'.

KILLING THE MILCH COWS

U-boat Command also faced a far more effective American Anti-Submarine effort, the principal agency for which was the Tenth Fleet, which had been set up under the overall command of Admiral King on 9 May 1943. The day-to-day direction of the Command was in the hands of Admiral Francis Low, King's Chief of Staff, who allocated Anti-Submarine forces and controlled special units such as escort carrier support groups and the important VLR Liberator squadrons. The organisation was backed up by a strong U-boat intelligence system based on the Tracking Room.

Faced with the collapse of his main campaign in the North Atlantic, Dönitz decided on 26 May 1943 to build up a strong concentration of U-boats in the mid-Atlantic beyond the reach of air cover, where he hoped that his boats could re-establish their record of success against the American North African supply convoys. When German agents in Spain reported the sailing of the United States-bound convoy GUS 7A, the powerful *Trutz* group of 17 U-boats concentrated for a pack attack on 4 June 1943, but good advance intelligence from the Tenth Fleet in Washington warned the escort carrier *Bogue*'s task group to take immediate action. The *Bogue*'s pilots, with their recent experience in the hard-fought battle in the North Atlantic, were soon meting out punishment to the *Trutz* Group. Her Wildcats and Avengers effectively disrupted the patrol line and sank one U-boat. For three weeks, an increasingly frustrated U-boat Command tried repeatedly to intercept the heavy convoy traffic, but the US carriers always seemed to be on the spot to break up the Pack before it had even sighted a victim. By the end of the month the Tenth Fleet had scored a telling tactical victory and the surviving boats were withdrawn after only one convoyed ship had been sunk at the cost of two U-boats destroyed – one of them the *Trutz* Group's Milch-cow. The secret of the American success was directly attributable to accurate information about the movements of the U-boats obtained from Special Intelligence.

Throughout the summer months the US Navy's Task Groups based on the escort carriers *Bogue*, *Core* and *Santee* ranged across the central Atlantic. Their primary role was to protect convoys, but they were allowed to operate independently against any reported concentration of U-boats within striking distance, as long as they could get back to the convoy before the concentration could reach it. In 98 days of operations they accounted for 16 U-boats in their hunter/killer role, with their particular priority being to find and sink the

Death from the sky: The air offensive in the Bay was a brilliant success (above, an attack by Sunderland T of 201 squadron). Dönitz's attempts to switch the U-boats to the mid-Atlantic was frustrated by the US Navy's new Anti-Submarine Command, the Tenth fleet under Rear Admiral Francis Low's (left) hunter-killer groups (Below, the USS *Bogue*).

7. IM OZEAN
Maschinenmaat: „Schon wieder einer, der nicht seefest wird! Weiss der Teufel, warum sie uns jetzt solche lächerliche Pimpfe schicken. Und mit so was sollen wir angreifen!"

8. EIN AMERIKANER GEKNACKT
Günther (zu einem Kameraden): „Arme Teufel! Schade, dass wir sie nicht aufnehmen können. Bis zur amerikanischen Küste sind es 700 Meilen."

9. VON EINEM AMERIKANISCHEN FERNAUFKLÄRER ENTDECKT
Flugzeugbeobachter: „Da ist der Jerrys' Funkspruch an die Atlantikpatrouille'"

10. WASSERBOMBEN!
Oberleutnant (Ing.): „E-Maschinen ausgefallen! Boot fällt." *Kommandant:* „Tauchretter anlegen! Anblasen!"

Milch cows which sustained operations in the central Atlantic.

The US Navy pressed for, and got, British agreement to give priority to smashing the Milch cows by using the Special Intelligence position reports to locate them. The operations were carried out in a variety of different locations, usually by aircraft so as not to arouse German suspicions. U-118 was the first to be destroyed – by the *Bogue*, to be followed by U-487, which was surprised on 13 July by one of the *Core*'s Wildcats. It dived and attacked the Milch-cow as the crew were sunning themselves on deck. Their fast reactions in manning the guns and shooting down the first attacker almost saved them but shortly afterwards, a flight of three more Avengers swooped down to bomb the U-boat to destruction. Three days later, an aircraft from the *Core* sank U-87 which was searching for the Milch-cow in order to refuel.

Before the end of July three more U-tankers had been located in transit through the Bay of Biscay. On 4 August the Royal Canadian Air Force sank another off Iceland, three days later the Tenth Fleet's escort carrier *Card* sank U-460 north of the Azores and her planes dispatched another eight weeks later. Dönitz's elaborate supply system had been decisively knocked out; the U-boat campaign in the mid-Atlantic was crippled.

In spite of these critical losses and remote chances of victory against the ever-strengthening Allied Anti-Submarine forces, the morale of the U-boat crews seemed to be holding up extremely well. The casualty rate was highest in the boats manned by inexperienced crews and those with exceptionally daring Ace Commanders, but by the summer of 1943 few Aces survived and the average U-boat crew did not last more than three patrols before their boat was sunk – a fact which Allied propaganda was quick to exploit. Thousands of copies of *The Life of a U-boat Man*, with factually correct but emotionally loaded details to bring home the high casualty rate, were dropped over the French bases but there was no evidence that they had any more serious effect than the bombs which bounced off the concrete bunkers.

The U-boat arm was never short of new recruits and indeed the service had acquired the glamour of an elite force. The average age of the crews had rapidly dropped to less than 19 years with the huge influx of new men as the force expanded. Officers were now in the early twenties and many commanders only twenty one, but there was a stiffening of the young crews with a number of older men, normally in the engineering and technical section. The crews' determination to fight on turned almost entirely on the character of the commanding officer and his ability to inspire confidence.

Life of a U-boat man: As Allied air power took an increasing toll of Dönitz's fleet, the shortening odds of the U-boat man's chances of survival were publicised in propaganda strips (above). Yet the German crews, conscious of their great dependence on each other, showed few signs of cracking. On some boats this was helped by the fanatical Nazism of some of the young seamen. On other boats there was less reverence for the Führer (below). As one disapproving officer noted, 'You have to take pains with the younger officers . . . you can't let them hang the picture of the Führer on the left side of the bulkhead in the officer's mess and on the right one of a girl from a box of candy bought in Paris. That shows bad taste.'

11. GERAMMT!
Durch die Wasserbomben der Atlantik-patrouille schwer beschädigt, muss das U-Boot auftauchen und wird von einem britischen Zerstörer gerammt. Der Druckkörper wird aufgerissen.

12. EINIGE WERDEN GERETTET . . .
Der Kommandant und ein paar Leute, die vom Turm über Bord gesprungen waren, werden von einem englischen Rettungsboot aufgenommen.

13. . . . ABER ANDERE NICHT
Günther und die anderen Neulinge sind in dem sinkenden U-Boot eingeschlossen. Das Wasser dringt durch Leck und Turmluk ein.

14. VIER MONATE DANACH — EIN TELEGRAMM
„Günther Hartmuth ist den Heldentod für Führer und Vaterland gestorben. B d L.”
Die deutsche Marineleitung hat die Nachricht vier Monate zurückgehalten.

By 1943 the Kriegsmarine was so determined that its new commanders should set the right example that they sent a famous U-boat Ace, Korvetten Kapitän Lüth, to lecture officers under training at Weimar on the right way to handle themselves. His lecture concentrated on the stark and unglamourous side of U-boat life not revealed by the recruiting posters:

> Life aboard is monotonous for long periods. For many long weeks one must be able to bear failures, and when depth charges are added life becomes a 'war of nerves' . . . Unlike the plane the submarine cannot go away, but has to remain motionless without being able to defend herself or shoot back. All that requires men of the stoutest heart. The morale of the crew depends on the following factors: (1) The discipline aboard. (2) Success. If a commander is successful his crew will love him, even if he is a numbskull. (3) A well-organised daily routine aboard. (4) The example and correct attitude of the officers. (5) Real spiritual leadership for the men, together with a genuine concern for their personal welfare.

Lüth was aware that it was necessary to appeal to 'a man's iron will power to maintain his health and to overcome minor difficulties'.

The Commander also kept a careful eye on the crew's sexual appetites and claimed that he never had to cope with any sexual problems in his crew, not even in a mission lasting seven and a half months. 'To be sure I have not permitted the men to hang pictures of nude girls on the bulkheads and over their bunks. If you are hungry you shouldn't paint bread on the wall.' Lüth concluded his lecture with a telling reminder, 'My efforts on board, are directed towards keeping up the crew's morale when things are not going well . . . You just have to have the guts to stick it out.'

As the summer of 1943 drew to an end Lüth hoped just as much as Dönitz that the fresh offensive planned for that autumn would bring badly needed successes. In August 1943 the U-boats had sunk only 4 ships, the lowest monthly total since the war began. In the three months since May less than 200,000 tons had been sunk.

ATTACK. FOLLOW UP. SINK

In the last days of August 1943 a succession of 22 U-boats headed out of the Biscay bases bound for the mid-Atlantic. Carrying the new *W.Anz* search receiver sensitive to the Allied ten centimetre radar and the *Aphrodite* radar decoy balloon and accompanied by a Milch-cow it was the best equipped

Death of a U-boat: Cameras of 86 and 120 squadrons' Liberators recorded the destruction of U643 and 419 (above). Aircraft 'T' reported, 'the U-boat exploded forward of the conning tower, sinking immediately by the bows . . . Survivors were thrown into the water.' Only a handful were rescued by surface escorts.

U-boat group to leave the French bases to date. Its mission was to rekindle the flagging German campaign in the North Atlantic. Six other boats were on their way from Germany and Norway to strengthen the fleet which was to combine into Group *Leuthen* and there was every reason for its commanders to feel confident of achieving a morale-boosting triumph. Each carried a new weapon, the *Zaunkönig* torpedo, which was designed to home on to the precise pitch of the sounds generated by an escort vessel's propellors. Group *Leuthen* had been left in no doubt about the significance of its mission, and had been signalled by Dönitz: The Führer is watching every phase of your struggle, Attack. Follow up. Sink.

By 18 September Group *Leuthen*'s long patrol line was strung out across the path of two approaching convoys, ONS 18 and ON 202, sailing just over 100 miles apart, and well protected by strong sea and air defences. The next day a VLR Liberator of the Royal Canadian Air Force No. 10 Squadron drew first blood when it sank U-341. That night the battle began in earnest. After months of uneventful convoy passages across the Atlantic the escorts were eager for the fray but they did not at first appreciate that they were the principal targets of the attack. This became apparent shortly before dawn on 20 September, when the frigate HMS *Lagan* had her stern blasted off and 29 of her crew killed, in the first successful hit with a *Zaunkönig*. Exploiting the dislocation, the U-boats were able to torpedo two Liberty ships.

At sunrise, the convoy gained some respite when Liberators arrived on schedule, and in mid-morning Kapitänleutnant Manfred Kinzel commanding U-338 was sunk by a 'Fido' homing torpedo which was dropped in the swirl as the U-boat submerged after a fight with one of the patrolling RAF bombers. A fountain of water signalled the certain destruction of the commander who had played a key role in the critical convoy battles of March.

Western Approaches Command was determined to avoid the mistakes of the earlier battle of HX 229 when it had failed to reinforce a weakened escort. With the threat of renewed attacks by a large Wolf Pack orders were given for ONS 18 and ON 202 to link together to form a concentration of 66 vessels protected by a powerful combined escort of 15 warships. This move did not deter the U-boats. Attacking under cover of darkness on the second night their *Zaunkönig* torpedoes sank the destroyer *St Croix* and later blew apart the corvette *Polyanthus*.

Next day, the escorts achieved their revenge when the destroyer *Keppel* rammed and sank U-229 which was stealing up on the convoy. The Pack stayed with the convoy and, on 23 September, the Germans evened the score when a *Zaunkönig* homed in on the frigate *Itchen* blowing her out of the water and leaving only 24 survivors. Under this pressure the defensive screen began to yield and the U-boats sank four merchantmen. Skirmishing continued for another day until the foggy weather cleared. Then as the sound of engines filled the sky the Convoy Commodore relaxed: 'It was very nice to come into the open air and find it filled with Liberators.'

Group *Leuthen*'s devastating success in the battle boosted the morale of the U-boat arm, as lavish claims were radioed to Dönitz by his triumphant commanders. Most exaggerated the German achievements, which had been

292

The Last Throw: U-boat Command placed high hopes on the new *Zaunkönig* acoustic torpedo (above) when Dönitz decided to renew the offensive on the North Atlantic in the autumn. After some early successes the new weapon was soon mastered by Allied countermeasures. By early October what an Admiralty Special Intelligence summary called, 'the last dying struggle of the caged tiger' was petering out six U-boats were sunk whilst attacking convoy SC 143.

limited to the destruction of three escorts and six merchantmen, in exchange for three of *Leuthen*'s U-boats. Their success was far removed from the victories of March and Dönitz's hope for further successes petered out when Special Intelligence allowed the next wave of convoys to be routed around the *Leuthen* patrol line. It was not until early October that a second chance occurred when Group *Schlieffen* found itself in striking distance of SC 143. This time there was no fog to interfere with the work of the Allied air escort, which scored spectacular results. In a running action four U-boats were destroyed from the air and another two by surface ships. This was unpalatable news for Dönitz, who was also soon to be dismayed to learn that the *Zaunkönig* breakthrough was short-lived. Its secrets had already been detected by the skilful work of American intelligence interrogators who had provoked a captured U-boat Chief Petty Officer into a thoughtless boast about the new weapon's remarkable capabilities. Armed with this information, American scientists rapidly devised the Foxer, a counter-measure in the form of a pair of noisemakers towed on a bar astern of an escort. This simple device decoyed the *Zaunkönig* and cheated it of its primary target. Further attacks on convoys led to heavy U-boat losses and in October the Admiralty's monthly review reported:

> A remarkably successful month . . . only three merchant ships and one escort vessel were sunk in the North Atlantic and this failure to make any impression upon our shipping or supplies in the month following the much heralded return to convoy operations must have had an extremely depressing effect on U-boat commanders and crews.

Operations in distant waters also failed to bring U-boat Command any comfort. There were only minor successes off the coast of Brazil and West Africa and in the Indian Ocean, where a small group of U-boats operated with the Japanese. Thousands of miles away in the bitterly cold Arctic, Germany's sailors needed every ounce of determination to carry on the fight against depressing odds. The Russian convoys had been halted as the Arctic days lengthened in March. Hitler's Navy suffered a heavy setback in September 1943, when the *Tirpitz* was temporarily knocked out of the sea war after a successful attack by the Royal Navy midget submarines. Worse was to follow, when the Russian convoys resumed in November they proved too well defended for the U-boat packs. Hitler gave orders for a heavy surface attack and the last undamaged German capital ship, the *Scharnhorst*, was sunk on 26 December 1943 by Admiral Bruce Fraser during an abortive attack on JW 55B.

The German surface fleet, which had caused so much anxiety to Britain earlier in the war, had now been virtually extinguished. Only the U-boats remained as a potent threat and by late 1943 Allied intelligence had become aware of the massive Type XXI and XXIII construction programme under way inside the Reich. Even if shipping losses continued to decline, as the U-boats were contained and forced off the Atlantic, the British and Americans knew that they could not relax their guard.

The days of the large-scale Wolf Pack attack might now be over, but the U-boat menace still preoccupied the Allied Naval commanders, not least in the waters around Britain. By early 1944 Dönitz had pulled his boats eastward to a line extending from the Faröes to Brest and in these waters the U-boats seemed to be attempting to repeat his successes of the early war years when they had sunk large numbers of ships as the convoys neared their home ports. In this congested area the U-boats were proving hard to locate, now that they were fitted with the new *Naxos-U* search receiver, and sightings had fallen off towards the end of 1943.

THE SCHNORCHEL THREAT

In February 1944, the U-boats became even more elusive as the first *Schnorchel* boats became ready to test the mettle of the Allied defences, especially in the waters around Britain, where the heavy sea and air patrols could be avoided by using the device to remain continually submerged. At first, the omens for the *Schnorchel*-boats were bad. U-264 was sunk by a British destroyer and the new system failed to win the popularity of the commanders and their crews. In one way, U-boat men were relieved to be given protection against air attack, but this new immunity from air recconnaissance had to be paid for in terms of personal comfort. But, although radar could not at first pick up the *Schnorchel* masthead, its foaming wake could be spotted by any sharp-eyed observer, so that it only became safe at night; in the daylight hours the crews had to lie still and silent on their bunks to conserve oxygen until the breathing tube could be floated to the surface again. Apart from these effects on morale, the Schnorchel also had the severe disadvantage of cutting down the U-boat's mobility, since it could only proceed slowly under water while 'breathing'.

The inability of Allied air patrols to detect the *Schnorchel*-equipped U-boats now that they stayed submerged for a large part of their operational

The 'Snort': In mid 1943 work was rushed ahead on the *Schnorchel* ('Snort' to Allied seamen), a breathing tube which enabled the U-boats to use their diesel engines whilst submerged and to replenish their air supplies. Although the Germans had to accept the slower underwater speeds instead of operating on the surface, the *Schnorchel* provided some immunity from air attack and the number of Coastal Command sightings fell, even after the introduction of the new high definition 3 cm radar in 1944. With the conventional boats staying under for most of their war missions the initiative returned to the surface escorts, equipped with Hedghog and the new Squid anti-submarine weapons (below) HMS *Starling* of Captain Walker's highly successful 2nd Escort Group in action with conventional depth charges in British waters.

missions, led to a concentration of Allied escort forces in British waters, which immediately began to achieve results. In February 1944, Captain Walker's 2nd Escort Group sank six U-boats on a 27-day patrol with every contact hunted to destruction. Each submarine took an average of four hours and 106 depth-charges to be destroyed in methodical and patient attacks, but Walker's Group did not escape unscathed; the *Woodpecker* was sunk by an acoustic torpedo, although the *Spey* more than evened the account by sinking two U-boats in two days.

Dönitz' new tactics of concentrating in British waters played into the hands of the Escort Groups, which had been freed from the requirement to race to the aid of threatened convoys in mid-ocean. Time could now be devoted to killing the enemy, once they had been located, and operational research scientists supplied the necessary mathematical attack plans which ensured that any U-boat would face inevitable destruction once located. Anti-Submarine hunts now became much longer; one lasted for over 30 hours whilst the longest of the war took 38 hours.

Once a submarine was located, its destruction became far more certain because of the growing armoury of anti-submarine weapons. The Squid, a three-barrelled mortar which hurled its bomb-shaped projectiles ahead of the attacking craft, had made its appearance. It exploited the growing refinements in detection technology, the weapon being targetted automatically by an Asdic depth predictor. A new American Anti-Submarine system was also put into operation in early 1944 when the Magnetic Anomaly Detector (MAD) entered service in the Straits of Gibraltar. It functioned by recording the change in the magnetic field as an aircraft flew over a submerged U-boat. Specially equipped Catalinas carrying the MAD gear, appropriately called 'Madcats', attacked any contact with rocket-propelled retro-bombs. Two U-boats attempting to pass through the Straits of Gibraltar were sunk by this system which was used in conjunction with surface escorts.

A further major advance in enabling aircraft to detect submerged submarines was introduced with the sonar buoy, which could be dropped from the air to monitor underwater activity, transmitting its information to a plane flying overhead. This method was used in the successful campaign waged by the US Navy escort carrier groups in the central Atlantic and off the Cape Verde Islands in March 1944. Already the Germans were suffering from increased air patrols as a result of Portugal's agreement to allow Britain to establish an air strip on the Azores at the end of 1943. By early 1944, the Americans were being allowed to extend these facilities and Dr Salazar, Portugal's ruler, gave permission for US Navy patrols to be flown from the islands in July, although the aircraft were to carry both British and American insignia to satisfy diplomatic niceties.

With the tide flowing inexorably against him, Dönitz's main objective in 1944 was to keep the U-boat campaign going long enough for the new submarines to be given a chance to enter service and make a decisive impact on the war. Work was still progressing on the revolutionary Walter boats, the 300 ton Type XVII and the 740 ton Type XXVI. With its ingolin powered engines the smaller boat was expected to reach an underwater speed of 20 knots whilst the bigger Type XXVI was planned to achieve 24 knots. This phenomenal performance, together with its capability to launch ten torpedoes at a target, led Allied intelligence to conclude that an improved Type XXVI was 'the most advanced type of submarine that can be foreseen'. Fortunately for the British and Americans, the temperamental closed cycle Walter engine was still unproven and causing severe teething problems and the difficulties of handling the highly corrosive hydrogen peroxide fuel delayed and dogged the whole project.

For this reason, Dönitz had concentrated the main effort on the Types XXI and XXIII, with Speer's Armaments Ministry committing a large slice of Germany's scarce industrial war resources to the programme. In July 1943 a design centre was set up in the Harz mountains far from the Allied air raids, and over 600 engineers, draughtsmen and construction experts had been sent to work there. Their progress was slow, partly because there were so many alterations and modifications made necessary because the submarines were being produced straight from the drawing board. There was tension and ill co-ordination between the Blankenberg centre and the main assembly yards, which were dominated by traditional naval contructors.

The objective of the project's director, Otto Merker, was to hold firmly to a target of 4½ months for the production of each Type XXI, but this met with bitter criticism from the ship assembly yards who complained that 'building was too much on top of designing'. Deschimag and Blöhm and Voss claimed that 'their reputations would be ruined if they adhered to the drawings supplied'. They tried hard to adjust themselves to the urgent time schedules of mass prefabrication, but complained bitterly at the quality of work turned out by the steel yards and shoddy workmanship.

Labour shortages also affected the programme and skilled workers in the 40,000 strong work force were diverted to the manufacture of the *Schnorchel*, affecting work on the new U-boats. As a result of these problems, the overall number of Type XXI's on order was cut to a total of 195. In spite of all the difficulties, however, the first Type XXI was launched in April 1944 at the Deschimag yard in Bremen. Unfortunately it turned out to be somewhat different in performance from what the designers had intended. The maximum submerged speed was now only 16.4 knots instead of 18 knots and the Blankenberg centre admitted that the submarine's diving performance was 'a great disappointment'. As one engineer recalled:

The staff hoped for 300 metres. After a lot of trouble they obtained 160 metres, and eventually 200 metres. The torpedo hatch was too weak...

Deschimag delivered the first Type XXI to the Navy in June 1944 and output began to speed up as three more submarines followed during the next month, and seven were handed over in August. As the tempo quickened, the German constructors began to be confronted with the frustrations arising from the effect of Allied strategic bombing. High-flying reconnaissance planes had photographed the construction of a Type XXI at the Schichau Yard in Danzig in the spring of 1944, and bombers were soon targeted on to the key installations. According to Merker, 'After the Spring of 1944 a great deal of rebuilding of facilities had to be done, and there were many stoppages of 3-4 weeks at various yards.'

Indirect attacks also had a serious effect. The big raids on Berlin, Frankfurt and Vienna affected the output of electric motors whilst diesel engine production was halted for four weeks, following damage to the M.A.N. plant at Augsburg. In Merker's estimation, 'At least 150 Type XXI submarines were not built because of air attacks'. The only consoling factor in Dönitz's mind was that his strategy of tying down Allied naval resources was working:

> The number of enemy aircraft and escort vessels, U-boat killer groups and aircraft carriers allotted to anti-U-boat forces, far from decreasing has increased. For the submariners the task of carrying on the fight solely for the purpose of tying down enemy forces is a particularly hard one.

RECKLESS TACTICS

Apart from this important role of absorbing the strength of the Allied navies in early 1944, U-boat Command resisted the invasion of Fortress Europe. In June, steps had been taken to restrict operations against shipping in the Atlantic by non-*Schnorchel* submarines and a formidable concentration of 49 U-boats, designated the *Landwirt* Group, was held ready in the Biscay ports to repel the Second Front. It would be supported by the 22 submarines of the *Mittel* Group stationed in Norway.

On June 6th thousands of Allied ships and landing craft poured across the Channel. Dönitz did not hesitate to send his forces to sea, with exhortations to use every means to stop the invasion. In a special command he declared:

> Every man and weapon destroyed before reaching the beaches lessens the enemy's chances of ultimate success. Every boat that inflicts losses on the enemy while he is landing has fulfilled its primary function even though it perishes in so doing.

The odds were heavily weighted against the U-boats once they moved out of their shelters, and chances of survival, particularly of the non-*Schnorchel* boats, were extremely slender in the face of the vast precautions taken by the Allies to seal off the entrance to the English Channel and the Irish Sea. No fewer than 350 aircraft were deployed to patrol 20,000 square miles of sea, so that a surfaced U-boat could expect to see an enemy aircraft once every 30 minutes. Six submarines were sunk in the first days of the invasion and those ordered south from their Norwegian bases suffered little better, so that Allied naval intelligence disdainfully described the reaction of U-boat Command to the invasion as 'prompt, energetic, but remarkably confused'.

The escort forces were, nevertheless, warned to be prepared for 'reckless tactics' as the enemy tried to penetrate the invasion area, teeming with shipping. Three submarines managed the 'heroic achievement' of reaching St Peter Port in the Channel Islands, by which time their crews were suffering badly from accummulating carbon dioxide poisoning. Only one U-boat succeeded in penetrating the invasion area nine days after D-Day, but she was soon driven off by the overwhelming escort forces after sending a tank-landing ship to the bottom. This was the sum total of the Herculean efforts of

U-Boat Assembly Line: Completely novel construction techniques were adopted by Otto Merker, Speer's production expert for the Type XXI and XXIII U-boat programme. The design was built in 8 large sections in factories all over Germany and then shipped to the U-boat yards for final assembly. Merker hoped to build a complete Type XXI in 25 weeks and a total of 33 a month were to be turned out in the three main yards of Schichau (Danzig) Blohm and Voss (Hamburg) and Deschimag (Bremen).

MURMANSK

REYKJAVIK

ST. JOHNS

HALIFAX

NEW YORK

AZORES

GIBRALTAR

PORT OF
SPAIN

SIERRA
LEONE

NATAL

ASCENSION I.

•   ALLIED AND NEUTRAL MERCHANT SHIPS SUNK
○   U-BOATS SUNK
████ CONVOY ROUTES
⌒   ALLIED AIR COVER ZONES
▨   AXIS AND AXIS OCCUPIED TERRITORY,
    31 MAY 1944
    7 MAY 1945

MERCATOR PROJECTION

ALLIED SHIPPING LOSSES 1ST JUNE
1943–8TH MAY 1945

Smashing the Transport System: After D-Day the Germans concentrated their U-boats in British waters, but the Allies were far more concerned about the long-term threat of the Type XXI. By August 1944, eight of the new boats were handed over to the German Navy to begin retraining crews and 80 had been delivered by the end of 1944, but problems and intensive aerial mining of the Baltic training waters delayed the entry of the new boats into service. At the same time heavy Allied raids were mounted to disrupt production. German hopes that their canals would provide a bomb-proof transport system proved misplaced. (Above, the empty Dortmund Ems-Canal pockmarked by bomb craters). Although some 107 prefabricated sections had passed along the Mitteland Canal in September 1944, this fell to just 17 by December of that year.

U-boat Command to act as a first line of defence in the West, and the submarines were ordered to withdraw to their shelters, leaving Allied Intelligence to comment: 'U-boat strategy is in the doldrums and no great confidence is felt in the Channel operation.'

The Germans were not allowed to remain in the comparative security of their reinforced pens for long. Just two months after the D-Day landing the divisions of General Patton were racing through Brittany with Brest and Lorient as their main objectives. U-boat Command hastened its evacuation plans, despatching its Atlantic submarines, heavily laden with personnel and equipment, around the North of Scotland to their Norwegian bases. Most of them successfully evaded Coastal Command's heavy air offensive.

But the Russian advance in the east worried Dönitz far more than the forced retreat from the Biscay bases, because the Baltic training areas and Type XXI construction yards at Danzig were essential for U-boat Command's war plans. He urged Hitler to maintain the strongest resistance against the Red Army in the North even at the expense of depriving other parts of the Front of much needed men and supplies, whilst Norwegian bases began to be developed as alternative operational centres for the U-boats. The importance of the Baltic was also clear to the Western Allies who aimed to disrupt German operations by an extensive campaign with sophisticated magnetic mines which would make naval training extremely hazardous. When these operations began in late 1944, there were immediate dividends for the RAF in the destruction of one Type XXI.

As the Baltic became increasingly untenable, the Allies maintained a careful watch on the waters around Norway, where they suspected that Dönitz planned to create a substantial force ready for a last ditch stand. Repair facilities and U-boat shelters were under construction at Bergen, and a steady stream of U-boats sailed for Norwegian waters. Their attacks were effectively contained by very powerful Allied escort forces, with the result that not a single merchant ship was sunk of the 159 that sailed for Russia in the latter half of the year.

Meanwhile, there was an increasing German concentration on British coastal waters and the Special Intelligence Summary warned:

Very stringent instructions have been issued to commanding officers to press forward into focal areas where shipping is certain to be found and to steel themselves for the inevitable encounters with A/S forces.

Dönitz threw all the strength of his personality behind a new effort to sink more ships in British waters, proclaiming that: 'The resumption of U-boat warfare must and will be Germany's main aim in the war against the Western powers and all engaged in naval and arms production will work for this with fanatical energy.' The Admiralty were expecting an operational U-boat fleet of 185 submarines to be pitted against them in December 1944, of which 15 would be the new Type XXI and 10 the new Type XXIII's but, rather baffled, the Special Intelligence Summary reported a few weeks later, 'the striking disproportion between the meagreness of the force so far deployed and the magnitude of the fleet of boats which . . . must from any prudent point of view be considered in a state of operational readiness.

The Allied navies would, in fact, have experienced the full impact of the new U-boats, but for the steady bombing of the Reich's communication and production network. Much of the RAF's attention had been concentrated on the waterways along which the large prefabricated submarine sections were transported, and in September 1944 the aqueduct of the Dortmund Ems Canal was left in ruins, leaving barges high and dry for a six-mile stretch. The Mitteland Canal received the same treatment and the transport situation in general was catastrophically bad.

The pace of Type XXI development could only be surmised by Allied intelligence at this time because a blackout had descended on U-boat communications, mainly due to the fact that the submarines spent so much of their time submerged. For once the Tracking Room found it difficult to glean the information it needed. In addition the Germans had changed their cyphering system, introducing a substantial 'element of hypothesis into the picture presented by the U-boat plot.'

Such minor setbacks could do little to reverse the tide or enable the Germans to strike back at the Atlantic lifelines. Of the merchant ships convoyed across the Atlantic in the last three months of 1944, only 14 were sunk, in return for the destruction of 55 U-boats. Conscious of these failures Dönitz used his submarines in support of the general land campaign, which was being bitterly fought in Europe. A number of U-boats were placed far out in the Atlantic to report on the weather. This information was of great assistance during Von Runstedt's Ardennes Offensive in the middle of December. In a more spectacular way, at the end of 1944, a fleet of 'small battle units' was launched against Allied shipping entering the Scheldt. These midget submarines, like the 16-ton *Seehund*, and the 6½ ton *Biber*, supported E-boat flotillas in a last-ditch attempt to cut the Allied supply line.

The Admiralty still feared that events might be swinging back in the U-boats' favour and the Secret Intelligence Summary for late January 1945 dispelled any illusions that the menace had been finally mastered,

> An early intensification of the U-boat war is apparently intended, for it was stated in a Naval Command Situations Report of 26th January that Hitler had ordered the U-boat war to be strengthened by every means . . . the view was expressed that U-boats could exert a decisive influence on the war against the Anglo Saxons particularly if successes in sinking increased with the employment of the new type boats.

The First Sea Lord, Admiral of the Fleet Sir Andrew Cunningham, was aware of the new threat which could manifest itself at any time in the next few months. Would the armies advancing from east and west cause the Reich to collapse before the new U-boats were unleashed? Should they appear in large numbers, they would reinforce the *Schnorchel* fleet of some fifty boats which was already causing serious problems. With such considerations in mind, the First Sea Lord wrote in early 1945:

> We are having a difficult time with the U-boats. There is no doubt that the schnorchel has given them a greater advantage than we first reckoned on . . . The scientists have not yet caught up and the air are about 90% out of business.

The Fleet that Never Sailed: When the British entered Hamburg in May 1945 they were shaken by the huge size of the Type XXI programme. The new boats were to be equipped with anti-radar coated *Schnorchel* heads, radar search receivers, highly sensitive hydrophones able to pick up a ship at 50 miles and new acoustic torpedoes. The tubes could be hydraulically reloaded in ten minutes able to be fired from a depth of 150 feet. In addition to the fleet on the stocks (above) over 100 Type XXI's were ready for operations by May 1944, but only U-2511 commanded by Kapitän Adalbert Schnee sailed on a war mission.

THE NORWEGIAN REDOUBT

Early in 1945 steps were taken by the Allies to build up the escort forces in British waters to unprecedented levels. 300 smaller ships were held up from sailing for the Pacific, and no less than 37 Escort Groups were operating around the British Isles, using 426 warships, mostly frigates. Allied intelligence officers were now becoming apprehensive that the Germans planned to make a last ditch stand in Norway. Training flotillas were being hastily moved west from Danzig and other units were being hurriedly equipped with the *Schnorchel* and made ready for battle, even though many of the U-boats were obsolete. Unlike the other Nazi leaders, Dönitz showed no interest in a Bavarian redoubt, and he began to assume responsibility for much of the administration of Northern Germany as the Reich fell apart.

If Dönitz, who still inspired considerable loyalty in his U-boat crews, was to continue the war in the hope that events would miraculously turn in his favour, he was likely to make his stand in Norway. The Allied Intelligence Staff tried to keep a close eye on the growing number of submarines transferred to the north. They were unaware that the first Type XXIII had gone into action from Norway at the end of January, when Oberleutnant Hass left Bergen in U-2324. On 18th February, he sank a ship off the British coast but his two torpedoes had been expended. Other Type XXIII's were also coming into service and none had been seriously bothered by Allied Anti-Submarine measures.

In March 1945 28 U-boats sailed for Norway as conditions in the Baltic became almost untenable. In spite of the colossal difficulties, the U-boat Arm showed no sign of cracking. In April Admiralty Intelligence reported:

> It is evident that delays of accumulating magnitude are being experienced by boats on passage in the Baltic and that the growing congestion in ports and training areas is developing gradually into a stifling condition of frustration; yet for the time being a still immense effort and apparently virile enthusiasm is being directed towards the mounting of a major U-boat offensive. The performance continues to fall far short of the intention. It would be premature to assume any relaxation of morale; U-boats actually on operations as contrasted with base staffs and training flotillas appear on the whole still to be determined and courageous. There may be a fair proportion of fanatical Nazis among the officers and it is probable that some may prefer to sacrifice themselves in a desperate attack rather than survive to suffer the defeat that is now generally accepted even in U-boat circles as inevitable.

In the last five weeks of the war the exodus towards Norway became massive. Allied air power descended furiously on the groups of U-boats sailing north from Kiel and the Baltic. Air strikes by Coastal Command, as well as by rocket-firing Typhoons of the Second Tactical Air Force which had moved within range of the U-boat bases, took a heavy toll.

At last, in April 1945, U-2511, the first Type XXI, put to sea for a sortie into the Atlantic. Commanded by one of Dönitz's staff officers, Kapitän Adalbert Schnee, she soon demonstrated the phenomenal improvement in U-boat potential which the new Type represented. When Schnee was picked up on a corvette's Asdic in the North Sea, the submerged submarine raced away from the enemy at sixteen knots, a speed he was able to maintain for over an hour, leaving a fading Asdic echo on the baffled corvette captain's screen.

Setting course for Panama, where he planned to make a series of devastating attacks, Schnee was already well on passage when the surrender signal arrived at 3.14 on May 4th 1945, ordering all Commanders to return to base. It was a painful moment, for Schnee in particular, who, like many Commanders, discussed with his officers what they should do. Proposals to sail the submarine to Argentina where it could be sold, were laughed out of court, and any ideas of a revenge attack dismissed. U-2511 would return to base. It was not an easy journey home, calling for all of Schnee's self-restraint when the unmistakeable shape of a heavy cruiser was sighted through U-2511's periscope. At first indeed it was too much for the German commander. He decided to attack. Effortlessly the submarine slipped through the defensive screen, without any signs of detection. Watching the big ship sitting in the middle of the periscope sights, Schnee prepared to release a deadly salvo of torpedoes, but at the last moment changed his mind. The torpedoes were never fired and the U-2511 turned for home.

SURRENDER

According to Admiralty instructions the 43 U-boats at sea were now all ordered to surface, report their positions and then proceed to designated ports, flying a black surrender flag. None of them complied at first, but then, one by one, they slowly began to surrender. As they did so the Submarine Tracking Room kept a careful check on their positions and numbers, to ensure that none slipped away to a secret hideout, or made a last ditch attack. The U-boats headed for different ports, 23 arriving in Britain, three going to the United States and four to Canada. Others set course for Norway or Kiel, and one scuttled herself off Oporto, the Commander being severely punished by the British for doing so. Only two, U-530 and U-977, were unaccounted for until they arrived in Argentina weeks after the end of hostilities.

Dönitz had kept control of the difficult situation and issued a moving signal to his U-boat men shortly after the surrender directive:

> My U-boat men! Six years of war lie behind us. You have fought like lions. An overwhelming material superiority had driven us into a tight corner from which it is no longer possible to continue the war. Unbeaten and unblemished you lay down your arms after a heroic fight without parallel.

Dönitz's strong personality, untainted by the worst excesses of National Socialism, had brought him to the highest position in Germany. As the Reich crumbled and feuds had broken out in the Nazi hierarchy, Dönitz had been shaken to find himself named by the Führer as his successor. The next afternoon he was informed of Hitler's death and appointed President of the Reich. In the last few days before total collapse, Dönitz could do little more than evacuate as many people as possible from the path of the advancing Russians in the Baltic, and try to establish a foundation for an understanding

302

Final Surrender: On May 4 1945 Dönitz followed his cease-fire order to all U-boats with the message, to their crews, 'Unbeaten and unblemished you lay down your arms after a heroic fight without parallel.' Of the 43 boats at sea, 23 made for British ports flying the black surrender flag. Others went to the United States, Norway or their home bases and one reached South America. The crews felt their defeat bitterly (below), the crestfallen men of a U-boat arriving back at Wilhelmshaven) and over 200 boats were scuttled in defiance of Dönitz's orders. Most of the 400 strong surviving U-boat fleet would find its final resting place on the bottom of the Atlantic, after the Allies decided to scuttle them off the west coast of Ireland.

with the West. In pursuing this policy he felt bound not to implement the secret scheme *Regenbogen* (Rainbow), which directed that all U-boats should be scuttled. For once, many of Dönitz's commanders refused to follow him. In defiance of his wishes, 200 U-boats of all kinds were sent to the bottom by their crews before the capitulation of Germany came into effect on the morning of May 5th 1945. The new Reich's President still held together the vestiges of a government in Flensburg, perhaps hoping to fill the vacuum, but on 23 May 1945 Admiral Dönitz was arrested by the Allied Control Commission and later found himself alongside the other Nazi leaders to be tried at Nuremberg.

The Atlantic war was over. It had been costly to the Allies. No fewer than 2,603 merchant ships had been sunk, totalling over 13½ million tons, as well as 175 Allied naval vessels. On the German side, of the 1,162 U-boats built 784 were lost. The majority fell victim to aircraft in the later years of the war, but the escorts also came into their own in hunting the Schnorchel boats. The losses of the U-boat Arm were terrible indeed. Of 40,900 men recruited, 28,000 lost their lives, and 5,000 were taken prisoner. On the Allied side 30,248 merchant seamen died, as well as thousands of men from the Royal Navy and RAF.

It was the one campaign of the Second World War that lasted from the first day to the last.

German U-boat Operations 1939–1945

Year	Quarter	Total Fleet	Daily Average Numbers		Atlantic Theatre		
			Operational in Atlantic	Engaged in Atlantic	Sunk	New U-boats Commissioned	Ships Sunk by U-boats
1939	Sept–Dec	57	12	5	9	2	105
1940	Jan–Mar	51	11	5	6	4	80
	Apr–Jun	49	10	7	8	9	75
	Jul–Sep	56	10	8	5	15	150
	Oct–Dec	75	11	9	3	26	130
1941	Jan–Mar	102	20	12	5	31	100
	Apr–Jun	136	25	15	7	53	150
	Jul–Sep	182	30	17	6	70	90
	Oct–Dec	233	35	16	17	70	70
1942	Jan–Mar	272	45	13	11	49	225
	Apr–Jun	315	60	15	10	58	240
	Jul–Sep	352	95	25	32	61	290
	Oct–Dec	382	100	40	34	70	260
1943	Jan–Mar	418	110	50	40	70	200
	Apr–Jun	424	90	40	73	69	120
	Jul–Sep	408	60	20	71	68	75
	Oct–Dec	425	70	25	53	83	40
1944	Jan–Mar	445	65	30	60	62	45
	Apr–Jun	437	50	20	68	53	20
	Jul–Sep	396	40	15	79	50	35
	Oct–Dec	398	35	20	32	67	17
1945	Jan–May	349	45	20	153	93	55
					Total 782	Total 1,133	

Source: Official History; *War at Sea* Vol. 1–3. Courtesy H.M. Stationery Office

Casualties to Personnel of British Merchant Ships 1939–1945

Period	Number of Ships Lost		Total Crew (including D.E.M.S.) in Ships Lost		No. of Crew Lost (including D.E.M.S.) in Ships Lost		Percentage of Crew Lost in Ships Lost	
	by U-boat	by all enemy causes	by U-boat	by all enemy causes	by U-boat	by all enemy causes	by U-boat	by all enemy causes
3 Sept–31 Dec, 1939	50	95	2,361	3,857	260	495	11	13
1940	225	511	11,285	22,923	3,375	5,622	30	25
1941	288	568	14,426	25,345	5,632	7,838	39	31
1942	452	590	28,259	36,200	8,413	9,736	30	27
1943	203	266	13,104	17,412	3,826	4,606	29	26
1944	67	102	4,440	5,931	1,163	1,512	26	25
1st Jan–8th May, 1945	30	45	1,446	2,081	229	323	16	16
Total	1,315	2,177	75,321	113,749	22,898	30,132	30	26

Source: Admiralty Trade Division Records

The Lease-Lend Food Supply List for August–November 1941 (Long tons)

Commodity	August	September	October	November
Beans	16,000	15,000	10,000	15,000
Lard	30,750	13,000	18,000	18,000
Glucose	380	350	300	350
Starch	14,600	9,000	12,000	9,000
Casings	405	300	200	200
Canned Meat	7,143	9,000	14,000	14,000
Canned Fish	1,100	16,000	28,000	28,000
Cheese	4,000	6,000	6,000	6,000
Evaporated Milk	15,625	18,000	40,000	40,000
Milk Powder	707	2,000	4,000	4,000
Milk Products	—	2,000	3,000	3,000
Raisins	2,500	4,000	15,000	20,000
Prunes	15,000	15,000	15,000	15,000
Dried Pears	4,000	—	3,000	—
Dried Apricots	—	—	4,000	5,000
Dried Peaches	—	—	2,000	10,000
Dried Apple Rings	—	10,000	10,000	—
Fruit Pulp	2,500	4,000	5,000	5,000
Pectin and Pomace	148	40	40	40
Tinned Tomatoes	5,000	5,000	5,000	5,000
Soya Beans and Flour	3,000	3,000	3,000	3,000
Pork and beans	—	10,000	10,000	—
Slab Chocolate	5,000	5,000	5,000	5,000
Canned Fruit	50,000	50,000	—	—
Oranges	40,000	40,000	—	—
Rice	25,000	25,000	25,000	25,000
TOTAL	242,858	261,690	237,540	230,590

Source: Ministry of Food Records

Gains by New Construction and Losses of Merchant Ships of 1,600 gross tons and over 1939–1945
(Thousand gross tons)

Year	Losses	New Construction			Net Change
		British Empire	U.S.A.	Total	
1939 (4 months)	810	231	101	332	(−) 478
1940	4,407	780	439	1,219	(−) 3,188
1941	4,398	1,169	815	1,984	(−) 2,414
1942	8,245	1,843	5,339	7,182	(−) 1,063
1943	3,611	2,201	12,384	14,585	(+) 10,974
1944	1,422	1,710	11,639	13,349	(+) 11,927
1945 (4 months)	458	283	3,551	3,834	(+) 3,376
Total	23,351	8,217	34,268	42,485	(+) 19,134

Source: Admiralty Trade Division Records

British Allied and Neutral Merchant Ship Losses 1939–1945 (in tons)

	Worldwide Axis Operations						Atlantic Theatre	
Month	U-boats	Aircraft	Mines	Surface Warships and Raiders	Unknown causes	TOTAL	All causes	of total
1939								
Sep	153,879	—	29,537	5,051	6,378	194,845	194,845	100
Oct	134,807	—	29,490	32,058	—	196,355	196,355	100
Nov	51,589	—	120,958	1,722	—	174,269	173,563	99.6
Dec	80,881	2,949	82,712	22,506	875	189,923	189,923	100
Total	421,156	2,949	262,697	61,337	7,253	755,392	754,686	99.9
1940								
Jan	111,263	23,693	77,116	—	2,434	214,506	214,506	100
Feb	169,566	853	54,740	1,761	—	226,920	226,920	100
Mar	62,781	8,694	35,501	—	33	107,009	107,009	100
Apr	32,467	13,409	19,799	5,358	87,185	158,218	158,218	100
May	55,580	158,348	47,716	6,893	19,924	288,461	285,893	99.1
Jun	284,113	105,193	86,087	61,587	48,527	585,496	317,421	54.2
Jul	195,825	70,193	33,598	80,796	4,501	386,913	365,074	94.6
Aug	267,618	53,283	11,433	63,350	1,545	397,229	353,004	88.9
Sep	295,335	56,328	8,269	96,288	8,352	448,621	403,504	89.9
Oct	352,407	8,752	32,548	32,134	17,144	442,985	418,264	94.4
Nov	146,613	66,438	46,762	123,671	2,231	385,715	294,054	76.2
Dec	212,590	14,890	54,331	55,728	12,029	349,568	322,612	92.3
Total	2,186,158	580,074	509,889	511,615	203,905	3,991,641	3,654,511	91.6
1941								
Jan	126,783	78,597	17,107	80,796	532	320,240	309,762	96.7
Feb	196,783	89,305	16,507	89,096	11,702	403,393	368,759	91.4
Mar	243,020	113,314	23,585	138,906	10,881	529,706	517,551	97.7
Apr	249,375	323,454	24,888	91,579	42,245	687,901	381,389	55.4
May	325,492	146,302	23,194	15,002	1,052	511,042	436,544	85.42
Jun	310,143	61,414	15,326	17,759	27,383	432,025	415,255	96.1
Jul	94,209	9,275	8,583	5,792	3,116	120,975	113,078	93.5
Aug	80,310	23,863	1,400	24,897	230	130,699	103,452	79.2
Sep	202,820	40,812	14,948	22,910	4,452	285,942	254,851	89.1
Oct	156,554	35,222	19,737	3,305	3,471	218,289	195,886	89.7
Nov	62,196	23,051	1,714	17,715		104,640	85,500	81.7
Dec	124,070	72,850	63,853	6,661	316,272	583,706	113,802	19.5
Total	2,171,070	1,017,422	230,842	487,204	421,336	4,328,558	3,295,909	76.1
1942								
Jan	327,357	57,086	10,079	3,275	22,110	419,907	296,136	70.53
Feb	476,451	133,746	7,242	—	62,193	679,632	440,889	64.9
Mar	537,980	55,706	16,862	25,614	198,002	834,164	562,336	67.4
Apr	431,664	82,924	15,002	131,188	1,679	674,457	493,810	73.2
May	607,247	59,041	18,795	19,363	631	705,050	644,827	91.5
Jun	700,235	54,769	19,936	48,474	10,782	834,196	652,487	78.22
Jul	476,065	74,313	8,905	54,358	4,472	618,413	533,494	86.3
Aug	544,410	60,532	—	50,516	5,675	661,133	543,920	82.3

	Worldwide Axis Operations						Atlantic Theatre	
Month	U-boats	Aircraft	Mines	Surface Warships and Raiders	Unknown causes	TOTAL	All causes	of total
1942 cont								
Sep	485,413	57,526	—	24,388	—	567,327	533,274	94.0
Oct	619,417	5,683	5,157	7,576	—	637,833	560,590	87.9
Nov	729,160	53,868	992	19,178	4,556	807,754	573,732	71.0
Dec	330,816	4,853	1,618	12,312	1,532	348,902	314,745	90.2
Total	6,266,215	700,020	104,588	396,242	323,632	7,790,697	6,150,340	79.0
1943								
Jan	203,128	25,503	18,745	7,040	6,943	261,359	204,626	78.3
Feb	359,328	75	34,153	4,858	4,648	403,062	315,206	78.2
Mar	627,377	65,128	884	1,742	—	693,389	538,695	77.7
Apr	327,943	3,034	11,961	1,742		344,680	252,533	73.3
May	264,853	20,942	1,568		12,066	299,428	205,598	68.7
Jun	97,753	6,083	4,334	17,655		123,825	30,115	24.3
Jul	252,145	106,005	72	7,176		365,398	187,877	51.4
Aug	86,579	14,133	19		19,070	119,801	255,573	78.2
Sep	118,841	22,905	4,396	9,977	300	156,419	54,545	34.9
Oct	97,407	22,680	19,774			139,861	61,085	43.7
Nov	66,585	62,452	6,666	8,538	150	144,391	40,686	28.2
Dec	86,967	75,471	6,086	—	—	168,524	53,871	40.0
Total	804,277	309,729	41,347	43,345	19,520	1,218,219	453,752	37.2
1944								
Jan	92,278	24,237	7,176	6,420	524	130,635	43,009	32.9
Feb	92,923	21,616		2,085	231	116,855	16,628	14.2
Mar	142,944	—	7,176	7,840		157,960	41,562	26.3
Apr	62,149	19,755			468	82,372	48,231	58.6
May	24,424	2,873				27,297	17,277	63.3
Jun	57,875	9,008	24,654	1,812	10,735	104,084	82,728	79.5
Jul	63,351		8,114	7,219	72	78,756	48,580	61.7
Aug	98,729		7,194	7,176	5,205	118,304	60,519	51.2
Sep	43,368		1,437			44,805	37,698	84.1
Oct	7,176		4,492			11,668	1,722	14.8
Nov	29,592	7,247		1,141		37,980	16,708	44.0
Dec	58,518	35,920	35,612		4,863	134,913	91,097	67.5
Total	358,609	52,175	81,503	17,348	20,875	530,510	339,052	63.9
1945								
Jan	56,988	7,176	16,368	2,365	—	82,897	75,722	91.3
Feb	65,233	7,177	18,076	3,889	941	95,316	88,130	92.5
Mar	65,077	—	36,064	3,968	6,095	111,204	111,204	100
Apr	72,957	22,822	8,733	—	—	104,512	81,690	76.2
May	10,022	7,176	—	—	—	17,198	10,022	58.3
Jun	11,439	—	7,176	—	—	18,615	0	0
Jul	—	—	7,210	—	27	7,237	39	0.5
Aug	—	—	36	—	—	36	36	100
Total	281,716	44,351	93,663	10,222	7,063	437,015	366,852	83.9

Source: Official History; *War at Sea* Vol. 1–3. Courtesy H.M. Stationery Office

Convoy Tactics

A convoy was a very vulnerable target since it covered a large area of sea – depending on the number of ships. A 45 ship convoy (below **1**) made up of 9 columns, disposed at a safe distance of about half a mile and four miles long, would spread itself over more than 20 square miles. The innermost columns would consist of tankers and ammunition ships and leading the centre column would be the merchant ship carrying the Convoy Commodore. Following up astern – if the convoy was fortunate – would be a specially equipped Rescue Ship.

The Defenders

To protect the convoy's perimeter (above 18 miles), was a major task for the escort vessels which would be under the command of a Senior Escort Officer – operating by UHF radio link. The escorts would be disposed in a close screen around the convoy some 3-4 miles distant so that ideally each ship's radar and visual range overlapped. Some 5-9 miles ahead of the convoy, dependent on weather and visibility, an advance screen would be sweeping the route with radar and Asdic.

The Attackers

The favoured method of the Wolf-Packs was a combined surface attack by night from a position ahead, but daylight attacks usually took place submerged when the U-boat would use its high surface speed to get well ahead of the convoy and then close at periscope depth. Periscope techniques were laid down in Dönitz's "Handbook for U-boat Captains". The 1942 edition stipulated . . . 'depending on visibility, the slender part of the *periscope may be kept extended down to a distance of 4,000 to 5,000 metres.* At a shorter distance than this, the periscope should only be used at brief intervals and only a few centimetres of it should be shown, as far as possible keeping it never more than just awash, but taking frequent looks and proceeding at slow speed.' The U-boat commander would conduct his attack from the command post in the lower part of the conning tower (**2**) and he was urged to '*Keep a good hold on your nerves*' so that he could get very close to the convoy.

At ranges above 1000 metres the U-boat *Handbook* suggested firing 'Browning shots' from a shallow angle ahead. These consisted of a fan (*Fächer*) of torpedoes, one of which would have "a strong chance of hitting for certain". As the commander closed his target, the Executive Officer would calculate the angle, course and other details for the attack on a special computer, the *Vorhaltrechner*, which fed information automatically into the torpedoes. After he had lined up the target squarely in his cross wires, the Commander pressed a firing button, shouting at the same time 'Los!' as the torpedoes left their tubes, and steered themselves on to their set course. In practice, commanders kept the angle of attack to a minimum to ensure greater accuracy.

In a surface attack, the Executive Officer took control of the weapons as the Commander directed the boat. The same mechanism was used, with sighting made through binoculars on the bridge (**3**). Such attacks were the preferred method of operation since, '*When surfaced the commanding officer of a U-boat remains master of the situation.*

Submerged the U-boat becomes blind and slow.' Surface attacks were only carried out at night because the U-boats were hard to see due to their 'low slender silhouette which disappears almost entirely into the water except for the conning tower . . .' Commanders were instructed to close from the windward to reduce the bow wave which was easily seen in a calm sea and also because this side of the convoy offered 'the worse observation conditions for the enemy, especially with wind and rain'. Commanders were also instructed *'in no case, when attacking by night is it permissible to overestimate the enemy's hydrophone listening and allow this consideration to hinder making a decisive attack at close range.* Conditions are less favourable for locating a surfaced U-boat than a submerged one owing to the waves. Before submerging or going deep alter course radically. Remember that the first and most dangerous depth-charges will be dropped in a pattern at the diving point and in the direction of the supposed withdrawal . . . Thoroughly exploit every opportunity to attack a group of enemy ships, using all your torpedoes. Immediately after attacking the first target, attacking a second and a third. The confusion resulting from the first explosion at night will make this easier.'

Counter-Attack

A well trained escort Group did not become as confused as Dönitz predicted. If the U-boat did get close enough to launch its torpedoes undetected in a night attack, the explosion would trigger off a pre-arranged sequence of countermeasures known as 'Raspberries', 'Artichokes' and 'Buttercups'. On the appropriate signal from the Senior Escort Officer, the escorts nearest the attacker would fire 'Snowflake' illuminant rockets and carry out sweeps to drive the U-boat under so that it became vulnerable to Asdic before it could use its high surface speed to escape. The sweeps and subsequent Asdic hunts would be carried out until the U-boat was destroyed or forced well astern of the convoy. But countermeasures had to be judged according to the scale of the attack, since vulnerable gaps could be left in the defences which other U-boats would be able to exploit and the Escort Commander had to remember that his first duty was the 'safe and timely arrival of the convoy'.

The Asdic Hunt

A submerged U-boat was 'blind and slow' and vulnerable to depth-charges. These dustbin-sized underwater bombs (below **4**, a Mark VII filled with Torpex explosive) were triggered by a depth sensitive firing pistol and would be lethal if they exploded within 20 feet of a U-boat. Dropping a pattern of depth-charges this close to a U-boat several hundred feet below the surface was a task that called for great skill on the part of the Escort Commander and his Asdic Operator who controlled the transmitter on the hull and swept underwater with a beam of sound pulses (below **5**) to trap the U-boat (**5A**). His ears had to be highly attuned to changes in the Doppler effect of the continuous pinging echoes which would indicate whether the U-boat was turning towards or away from the escort in order to escape (**5B**). As the Asdic cone widened, its accuracy diminished and, in normal conditions, its maximum

effective range was about 2,500 yards. So the deeper the U-boat dived (**5C**) the better its chances of escape and experienced U-boat commanders knew how to exploit the different temperature and salinity layers in the ocean as cover.

If the U-boat could be held by Asdic long enough, the escort attempted an attack run to drop its depth-charges directly over the target but contact became increasingly critical as the range shortened and the cone narrowed until at 300 yards, it would be lost completely so that the pattern had to be released 'blind' over the U-boat's estimated position. The pattern of up to 14 charges would be released from traps in the stern and hurled from explosively fired Mark IV throwers (right **6**)). The moment of release would be determined by an automatic clockwork timing device, but the depth set on the firing pistols had to be estimated in the final minutes of the hunt.

The chances of a successful kill were considerably increased if the hunt was conducted by two escorts; one would maintain Asdic contact and pass the range and bearing to the second ship which made the attack-run. After 1942, to overcome the loss of contact in a single escort hunt, an increasing number of ships were fitted with the *Hedgehog* (previous page, 7). This was a mortar of 24 bombs (above 7) filled with 32lbs of Torpex and fired ahead of the ship as the U-boat was held in the Asdic beam. They were armed as they passed down through the water and exploded on contact. However the *Hedgehog*'s disadvantage – shared with the similar small US Navy *Mousetrap* was that it required a very meticulous attack approach and even a near miss did not result in the underwater explosion that shook up a U-boat crew and gave the escort's complement a sense of achievement.

It was not until the *Squid* began to be introduced in late 1943 that the escorts were given a truly efficient means of destroying submerged U-boats. This three-barrelled mortar (below 8) which hurled 100lb depth charges ahead or abeam with their firing pistols set automatically during the final seconds of the attack run, was operated in conjunction with the *Type 147B* Asdic transmitter that projected a narrow and very manouvrable beam (below 9) providing an accurate depth-ranging system. It complemented the *Type 144 Q* beam Asdic which came into service during the summer of 1943 and consisted of a wide fan shaped beam (white) integrated with a narrow vertical beam operating on a higher frequency of sound pulses to allow contact to be kept with the deep diving U-boats.

Main Beam

147 B Beam

E Attachment Beam

KEY TO QUARTERLY SCORE CHARTS

Atlantic

World

Nº of U-boats Sunk

Total Tonnage Built 100,000 Tons

Total Tonnage Lost 100,000 Tons

Nº of U-boats Operational

Nº Ships Sunk over 1600 Tons

Acknowledgements

In the space of a single volume we must first acknowledge that it would have been impossible to do full justice to every aspect of the colossal struggle known as the Battle of the Atlantic. What we have set out are the main political and military developments based on information drawn from the recently released official records, authoritative publications, personal memoirs and contemporary sources. This perspective has been set against the eyewitness accounts, personal recollection and contemporary reports of a wide cross section of people involved at different levels on both sides of the battle.

On the German 'side of the hill' we are particularly indebted to Grossadmiral Karl Dönitz for receiving us to discuss the campaign he directed and to Albert Speer for an insight into the effects of the U-boat war on Hitler's thinking and the huge Type XXI programme. The mainstay of our research effort in Germany was Professor Jürgen Rohwer of the Bibliotek für Zeitgeschichte, Stuttgart, the leading authority on the U-boat war, who not only encouraged us but unlocked many doors and provided much valuable material. Amongst the many former officers of the Kriegsmarine contacted, we especially wish to thank Kapitän Hans Meckel for his account of the operations of Dönitz's headquarters and his fellow officers Kurt Diggins, Otto Kretschmer, Werner Schuenemann, Adalbert Schnee, Reinhard Suhren, Otto Schuhart, Herbert Schulze, Bode Thielo and Otto Westphalen who, together with Jochen Ahme of the *Verband Deutscher U-bootfahrer,* provided first-hand information about U-boat operations.

First amongst the many distinguished Allied senior officers we have consulted we should like to express our gratitude to Vice-Admiral B. B. Schofield, the distinguished naval historian who was Director of Admiralty Trade Division during the most critical years of the Battle of the Atlantic. Marshal of the Royal Air Force Sir John Slessor was able to give a valuable insight into the more turbulent aspects of the Anglo-American 'special relationship' and we are most grateful to him and to Air Vice-Marshal Sir Edward Chilton for allowing access to their material. Captain Haslam of the Air Historical Branch also gave an insight into the role maritime airpower played in the defeat of the U-boats. For providing the inside story of the intelligence war we must thank Vice-Admiral Sir Norman Denning and Patrick Beesly – Commander Winn's assistant in the Operational Intelligence Centre's Tracking Room, who, although about to publish his own very revealing account 'Very Special Intelligence' unhesitatingly gave us access to his new material. Vice-Admiral Sir Peter Gretton and Captain Donald Macintyre generously gave us the benefit of their unrivalled sea-going experience as Britain's most distinguished convoy escort commanders and no account of the Battle would be complete without the contributions we have received from many merchant seamen and former naval officers including: J. Atkinson, H. A. Beaumont, K. Bates, J. Burns, G. J. Carr, Capt. R. V. E. Case, Capt. J. H. Drew, J. Harrison, W. Hughes, R. J. Hunter, W. D. Jeffries, C. Johnstone, J. Kewin, E. F. Lawlor, J. Lee, J. Lisle, J. Marshall, J. Magill, P. Malmsteen, C. Moss, A. McKellar, J. Newall, J. Oakley, J. Perry, U. Peters, D. Roberts, G. Welsh, M. Wilburn, D. H. Willett.

In the United States we have been fortunate in receiving the assistance of Admiral Gene La Rocque, Colonel William Corson, Dr. D. C. Allard, Head of the US Navy Operational Archives, his assistant Mrs Lloyd, and J. Trimble of the US National Archives. We should also like to thank Dr C. J. Kitchen, Mrs B. Shenton and J. Millen of the British Public Records office, Dr Haupt of the Bundesarchiv and the staff of the British Museum Library, Royal United Service Institute Library, the Naval Historical Library, the London Library and the German Historical Institute for all their assistance and forbearance.

Assembling the considerable body of information and pictures for this project would have been impossible without the help of those who contributed to our team of researchers – Diana Hamilton and Mary Herne in New York; Jonathan Moore in London and H. J. Ketzer and H. R. Zellweger in Germany. Dilys Hubbard and Ursula Kelf put a great deal of effort into typing through the many drafts. The dramatically effective design is the product of many hours of work by Colin Reed and we should also like to acknowledge the assistance of Ron Clark and Patrick Yapp. The outstanding cartography is by Richard Natkiel and the clear technical illustrations drawn by Pierre Tilley.

Finally our thanks are extended to our editors – Philip Ziegler of Collins and James O'Shea Wade of Wade/Dial Press for their inexhaustible confidence and patience. Their interest together with the devotion of Jackie Baldick, and the encouragement of Rear Admiral Morgan Giles has made this project possible.

Bibliography and Sources

In writing this comprehensive account of the 'Battle of the Atlantic' the authors have drawn upon a wide range of published and unpublished source material in Britain, Germany and the United States.

GENERAL HISTORY

Published Sources

History of the Second World War, Her Majesty's Stationery Office, London.
Grand Strategy
    Vol. I (To 1939), N. H. Gibbs.
    Vol. II (Sept 1939–June 1941), J. R. M. Butler.
    Vol. III (June 1941–Aug 1942), J. M. A. Gwyer and J. R. M. Butler.
    Vol. IV (Aug 1942–Aug 1943), Michael Howard.
    Vol. V (Aug 1943–Sept 1944), John Ehrman.
    Vol. VI (Oct 1944–Aug 1945), John Ehrman.
The War at Sea. 3 Vols. S. W. Roskill.
The Strategic Air Offensive against Germany, Noble Frankland and Charles Webster.
Behrens, C. B. A. *Merchant Shipping and the Demands of War.*
Duncan Hall, H. *North American Supply,* London 1955.
Hammond R. J. *Food,* London 1951.
U.S. Naval Operations in World War II, S. E. Morison, Boston.
    Vol. I, The Battle of the Atlantic (Sept 1939–May 1943), 1947.
    Vol. II, The Atlantic Battle Won (May 1943–May 1945), 1956.
U.S. Army in World War II. Office of Chief of Military History, Wash., 1964.
    Guarding the United States and its Outposts, Conn. Stetson and Fairchild, Byron.
    The Framework of Hemisphere Defense, Conn, Stetson, and Fairchild, Byron, 1960.
    Chief of Staff. Prewar Plans and Preparations, Mark S. Watson, 1950.
U.S. Army Forces in World War II, Craven, Wesley, F. and Cate, James, L., Chicago, 1948.
The Naval Service of Canada, Official History.
The Second World War, Winston S. Churchill, London 1948–53.

POLITICAL and ECONOMIC

Published Sources

Bethell, Nicholas. *The War Hitler Won,* London 1972.
Connery, Robert H. *The Navy and Industrial Mobilisation in World War II, 1951.*
Blum, John Morton. *Roosevelt and Morgenthau,* Boston 1970.
Briggs, Susan. *Keep Smiling Through The Home Front 1939–45,* London, 1975.
Bullock, Alan. *Hitler. A Study in Tyranny,* London 1952. *The Life and Times of Ernest Bevin,* London 1967.
Burns, James McGregor. *Roosevelt. Soldier of Freedom,* New York 1970.
Calder, Angus. *The People's War,* London 1968.
Chadwick, Mark Lincoln. *The Hawks of World II,* N. Carolina 1968.
Cole, Wayne S. *America First – The Battle Against Intervention,* Madison 1953.

Compton, James V. *The Swastika and The Eagle,* Boston 1967.
Duffer, Horst. *Weimar, Hitler und die Marine,* Düsseldorf 1973.
Fest, Joachim. *Hitler,* Berlin 1974.
Gilbert, Martin. *Winston S. Churchill,* Vol. V, London 1977.
Feis, Herbert. *The Road to Pearl Harbour,* Princeton 1950. *Churchill, Roosevelt and Stalin,* Princeton 1957.
Goodhart, Philip. *Fifty Ships that Saved the World,* London 1965.
Harriman, Averell, and Abel, Elie. *Special Envoy,* New York 1976.
Hillgrüber, Andreas. *Hitlers Strategie-Politik und Kriegführung 1940–41,* Frankfurt 1965.
Hull, Cordell. *Memoirs,* 2 Vols. New York 1948.
Ickes, Harold. *The Secret Diary of Harold Ickes,* New York 1953–4.
Loewenheim, Francis L. Langley, Harold, Jonas, Manfred. *Roosevelt and Churchill: their Secret Wartime Correspondence,* New York 1975.
Lash, Joseph P. *Roosevelt and Churchill,* New York 1977.
Langer, William and Gleason S. Everett. *The Challenge to Isolation,* New York, 1952. *The Undeclared War,* New York 1953.
Marder, Arthur. *From the Dardanelles to Oran,* London 1974.
Land, Emory S. *Winning the War with Ships,* New York 1958.
Parkinson, Roger. *Blood, Tears, Toil and Sweat,* London 1973.
Roosevelt, Elliot. *Ed. FDR. His Personal Letters,* New York 1950.
Rosenman, Samuel I. *Ed. The Public Papers and Addresses of Franklin D. Roosevelt.* 13 Vols, New York 1938–51.
Sherwood, Robert E. *The White House Papers.* 2 Vols, New York 1948.
Shirer, William. *The Rise and Fall of the Third Reich,* New York 1959. *Berlin Diary,* 1970.
Speer, Albert. *Inside the Third Reich,* London 1970.
Stimson, Henry L. and Bundy, McGeorge. *On Active Service in Peace and War,* New York 1948.
Trevor Roper H. R. *Hitler's War Directives,* London 1964.
Kimball, William F. *The Most Unsordid Act Lend-Lease 1941–43,* Baltimore 1969.
King, Ernest J. and Walter Whitehall. *Fleet Admiral King,* New York 1952.
Koskoff, David E. *Joseph P. Kennedy. A Life and Times,* New Jersey 1974.
Morton, H. V. *Atlantic Meeting,* London 1943.

Unpublished Sources

The main information on the overall direction of the campaign, its role in Anglo-American strategy, the progress of North American supply and the siege of Britain has been drawn from the official British archives in the Public Record Office, London. The principal sources have been as follows:
Cabinet Minutes – case reference CAB 65.
Cabinet Memoranda – CAB 66.
Minutes and Reports of Defence Committee – CAB 68, 69.
Chiefs of Staff Committee Minutes – CAB 79, 80.
War Cabinet Ministerial Committee on Food Policy – CAB 74.
Battle of the Atlantic Committee, Minutes and Memoranda – CAB 86.
Anti U-Boat Warfare Committee – CAB 86.
Lend Lease and Relations with the Roosevelt Administration – CAB 115.

Prime Minister's Correspondence – Prem 1.
Ministry of Agriculture and Food Permanent Record of Operations (1939–1954) – MAF 75.
British Food Mission to Washington – MAF 97.
US National Archives, Washington D.C.
Records and Hearings of the War Production Administration.
The US Maritime and War Shipping Administration.
The Food Lend Lease Administrator.

THE CAMPAIGN

Published Sources

Abbazia, Patrick. *Mr Roosevelt's Navy*, Annapolis 1975.
Bekker, Cajus. *Hitler's Naval War*, Hamburg 1971.
Beesly, Patrick. *Very Special Intelligence*, London 1977.
Betzler, Cmdr. *War in the Southern Oceans*, London 1961.
Boeckheim, Gunter. *U-Boote*, London 1975. *Atlantic U-Boote*, Berlin 1977.
Broome, J. *Convoy is to Scatter*, London 1970.
Bunker, J. Gorley. *Liberty Ship*, Annapolis 1972. *U-Boat Hunters*, London 1976.
Chalmers, W. S. *Max Horton and Western Approaches*, London 1951.
Creighton, Admiral K. *Convoy Commodore*, London 1953.
Dönitz, Karl. *Die U-Bootswaffe*, Berlin 1939. *Memoirs*, Bonn 1958.
Elliott, Peter. *Allied Escort Vessels of World War II*, London 1977.
Easton, Alan. *Enemy Submarine: The Story of Gunther Prien*, London 1954.
Farago, Ladislas. *The Tenth Fleet*, New York 1962.
Frank, Wolfgang. *The Sea Wolves*, New York 1955. *Enemy Submarine – U-47*, London 1954.
Giese, Fritz E. *Die Deutsche Marine*, Frankfurt 1956.
Gilbert, Felix. *Hitler Directs His War*, New York 1950.
Gretton, Sir Peter. *Convoy Escort Commander*, London 1964.
Herlin, Hans. *Verdammter Atlantik*, Hamburg 1959.
Herzog, Bodo. *Schlachtschiff Bismarck*, Frankfurt 1975. *U-Boote im Einsatz*, Frankfurt 1974.
Kahn, David. *The Code-breakers*, London 1970.
Kennedy, Ludovic. *Pursuit: The Chase and Sinking of the Bismarck*, London 1974.
Macintyre, Donald. *The Battle of the Atlantic*, London 1961. *U-Boat Killer*, London 1956.
Martiensssen, Anthony. *Hitler and His Admirals*, New York 1956.
Middlebrook, Martin. *Convoy*, London 1976.
Von der Porten, Edward. *The German Navy in World War II*, London 1970.
Peillard, Leonce. *La Bataille de l'Atlantique*, Paris 1974. *U-Boats to the Rescue*, London 1970.
Price, Alfred. *Weapons of Darkness*, London 1971. *Aircraft versus Submarines*, London 1973.
Raeder, Erich. *The Struggle for the Sea*, London 1959.
Rayner, D. A. *Escort: The Battle of the Atlantic*, London 1953.
Robertson, Terence. *The Golden Horseshoe*, New York 1956. *Walker R.N.*, London 1957.
Roskill, S. W. *A Merchant Fleet at War*, London 1962. *The Secret Capture*, London 1959.
Rohwer, Jurgen. *Die U-Boot Erfolge der Aschenmächte 1939–45*, Munich 1968. *Geleitzugschlachten in März 1943*, Munich 1975.
Rüge, Friedrich. *Der Seekrieg*, Annapolis 1957.
Schaeffer, Heinz. *U-Boat 997*, New York 1952.
Schull, Joseph. *The Far Distant Ships: An Official Account of Canadian Naval Operations in World War II*. Ottawa 1961.
Schmidt, Paul. *Hitler's Interpreter*.

Schofield, B. B. *British Sea Power*, London 1968. *Russian Convoys*, London 1960. *The Rescue Ships*, London 1968.
Slessor, Sir John. *The Central Blue*, London 1956.
Stevenson, William. *A Man Called Intrepid*, London 1976.
Waddington, Prof. C. H. *Operational Research*.
Warlimont, Walter. *Inside Hitler's Headquarters*, London 1964.
Watts, Anthony J. *The Hunters and the Hunted*, London 1976.
Wegener, Wolfgang. *Die Steestrategie des Weltkrieges*, Berlin 1929.
Winterbotham, F. W. *The Ultra Secret*, London 1974.
Woodward, David. *The Tirpitz and the Battle for the North Atlantic*, New York 1953.
Warren, Austin. *Red Duster at War*, London 1941. *Merchantmen at War*, London 1943.
Winter, Capt. J., U.S.C.G. *Bloody Winter*, New York 1967.

Unpublished Sources

The authors have conducted research in both the British and American archives, a great deal of German material is also contained in Washington and London. The principal unpublished sources in Britain are contained in the files of the Public Record Office classification *ADM 199*. The following are among the main references used by the authors:

ADM 199

1–7	*Convoy system introduction. Orders to Commodores, sailing regulations.*
47–63	*Convoy Reports, including HX and SC convoys.*
121–24	*Anti-U-Boat Operations, 1940–41.*
226–230	*U-Boat attacks on Merchant ships, 1943.*
241	*Anti-U-Boat Warfare Policy.*
240	*Bombing of the Biscay Bases, 1942–44.*
423	*Western Approaches Command War Diary.*
463	*Royal Canadian Navy Monthly Review*, Jan 1943–Aug 1945.
575–78	*HX and ON Convoy Reports.*
691	*Proceedings of the Bailey Committee on Anglo American Naval Co-Operation, 1940–46.*
875–887	*Azores Facilities.*
1123–35	*Anti-U-Boat Warfare Reports.*
3057–63	*Monthly Anti-Submarine Reports.*
1406	*Anti-U-Boat Operations in the Bay of Biscay.*
1408	*US Escort Carrier Operations.*
2073–194	*Admiralty Trade Division Reports.*

Führer Naval Conferences

In addition to the material contained on the Admiralty files *RAF Coastal Command* records are filed under *AIR 15* at the Public Record Office. These contain valuable accounts of the Bay Offensive and of anti-submarine policy before and during the War.

Restricted Official Naval Staff History

The Defeat of the Enemy Attack on Merchant Shipping.

US National Archives. Naval Records. Washington D.C.

Records of C in C US Fleet.
Report 51. US Navy Operations Evaluation Group.
Interrogation and Essay by Karl Dönitz.
Report on German Naval High Command by Admiral Assmann.
Training Lecture to new U-boat Commanders by Kapitänleutnant Lüth, 1943.
The German Secret Supply Service.
Selected Micro Film Records of German Naval Archives.

Index

313

Action Atlantic: A Photographic Essay

FLOTSAM OF BATTLE: Wreckage from a cargo of eggs (below). The U-boats came so close to winning the tonnage war that the Germans began dropping propaganda pamphlets (inset right) over Britain. The Ministry of Food campaigned (inset left) to cut imports by a third.

Photographs from Bundesarchiv, Imperial War Museum, U.S. National Archives, and Nautic Visual Services.

MINISTRY **MF** OF FOOD

THE WEEK'S

FOOD FACTS № 8

Remember to pin up this useful advertisement in your kitchen

Do without that second helping, that extra snack, unless you really need them. Turn today's scraps into tomorrow's soups and savouries. *Our waste is Hitler's weapon.*

Save food! Save money! Save cargo space for munitions!

Remember to turn on the wireless at 8.15 every morning. You'll hear many useful household hints.

The Battle of the Atlantic is being lost!

The reasons why:

1. German U-boats, German bombers and the German fleet sink and seriously damage between them every month a total of 700 000 to 1 million tons of British and allied shipping.

2. All attempts at finding a satisfactory means of defence against the German U-boats or the German bombers have failed disastrously.

3. Even President Roosevelt has openly stated that for every five ships sunk by Germany, Britain and America between them can only build two new ones. All attempts to launch a larger shipbuilding programme in America have failed.

4. Britain is no longer in a position to secure her avenues of supply. The population of Britain has to do with about half the ration that the population of Germany gets. Britain, herself, can only support 40% of her population from her own resources in spite of the attempts made to increase the amount of land under cultivation. If the war is continued until 1942, 60% of the population of Britain will starve!

All this means that starvation in Britain is not to be staved off. At the most it can be postponed, but whether starvation comes this year or at the beginning of next doesn't make a ha'porth of difference. Britain must starve because she is being cut off from her supplies.

Britain's losing the Battle of the Atlantic means

Britain's losing the war!

"U-BOATS ARE THE WOLVES OF THE OCEAN. ATTACK! REND! DESTROY! SINK!" So the architect of the Atlantic U-boat war, Admiral Karl Dönitz (right), summed up the objective for his men at the start of the war. Drawing on his own experiences as a U-boat commander in the First World War, Dönitz devised and drilled his fifty-strong force in the "Rudel-taktik"—coordinated attacks by groups of boats—to overwhelm the defences of an escorted convoy. The "Wolf Packs" soon proved brilliantly successful, justifying Dönitz's pre-war predictions that they would be a decisive factor in the war at sea. Fortunately it was two years before Hitler appreciated their potential. Deprived of steel and production facilities, it was to be early 1943 before Germany had built up the fleet to 300 U-boats that had been predicted as necessary for final victory. It was too late. By this time Allied counter-measure and escort numbers had built up to meet the assault.

Yet such was the dedication and loyalty inspired by Dönitz's leadership that the U-boat men considered themselves "personally hired," so their morale never broke and held when the campaign began to go against them. For two more years they continued to sail on patrols, facing the knowledge that often one out of every three boats would not return.

1. Prewar recruiting posters reveal the U-boat arm's elite status
2. Kapitänleutnant Lehmann-Willenbrock of U-96
3. Kapitänleutnant Loeser of U-373 snatching a cigarette break as the rest of his watch keeps a sharp lookout
4. The badge worn by all U-boatmen who completed patrols in the Atlantic
5. The hydrophone operator was the "ears" of a U-boat
6. Kapitänleutnant Hardegen on the conning tower of U-123
7. Kapitänleutnant Topp taking U-552 out on patrol
8. U-67's edelweiss insignia and her captain Müller-Stockheim

Freiwillig zur

KRIEGSMARINE

TYPE VIIc U-BOAT: The "standard" U-boat which comprised the bulk of the German underwater fleet for most of the war was highly manouvreable and able to dive in less than thirty seconds. The success of the Wolf Pack's tactics depended on its low profile, enabling it to take advantage of its 17-knot surface speed to operate as a submersible torpedo boat and penetrate the convoys undetected at night. Its drawback was its low underwater speed and limited range submerged. By 1942 increasing numbers of radar-equipped Allied escorts and aircraft were breaking up the packs and Dönitz was already planning to replace them with a new generation of "super" U-boats. The type XXI were developed to have an underwater speed fast enough to outrun the escorts and a crash programme of construction was instituted in the summer of 1943. But in spite of a massive industrial effort, none of the "super" U-boats saw operational service in time to affect the course of the war.

Length 220 feet, breadth 20 feet, draught 15¾ feet.
Surface Displacement 769 tons.
Maximum Speed: surfaced 17 nots, submerged 7.6 knots.
Endurance: surfaced 6,500 miles, submerged 80 miles.
Armament: 5 × 21 in torpedo tubes, 14 torpedoes.
1 × 88 mm gun, 1 × 20 mm machine gun. (In 1943 this became
1 ×-37 mm Flak, 2 twin 20 mm Flak machine guns.)

"ATTACK AND KEEP ON ATTACKING. Do not let yourself be shaken off; if the boat is temporarily forced to dive, follow up in the general direction of the convoy. Try to get in touch again and once more ATTACK!" Through a series of similar operational orders Dönitz stressed the aggressiveness he expected of his hand-picked commanders. Many like Kapitän-leutenant Reinhard Sühren of U-564 (top right) painted personal good luck symbols on their conning towers. The low silhouettes and open conning towers of the German boats (below, U-86) were good platforms for their captains to direct night surface attacks. They contrasted with the high, enclosed bridges of the Italian "Atlantic Flotilla" boats (below right) and their poor performance confirmed Dönitz's view that his ebullient allies were unsuited to the Wolf Pack operations.

"DO NOT RESCUE PEOPLE or take them with you. Do not trouble about the steamers' boats. Weather conditions and distance from land are immaterial. Think only of your own boat and endeavour to achieve the best success as soon as possible! WE MUST BE HARD IN THIS WAR." Dönitz's order of 1940 marked the end of German observance of the Prize Laws and the commencement of unrestricted submarine warfare. Yet even as the Battle entered its ruthless phase, U-boat commanders frequently surfaced, when circumstances permitted, to give their victims' crews a chance to take to their boats or transfer food, cigarettes, and charts. But in the bitter convoy battles on the main north Atlantic lifeline, there was little opportunity for either side to observe such civilised niceties.

TIN-CAN LIFE: The strains of several months' patrol in the confined spaces of a U-boat sapped the efficiency of even the most hardened crews. The grinding monotony of most days might be punctuated by brief spells of intense action. Then some men might succumb to what the Germans called "Blech-koller"—tin-can neurosis—which could be brought on when a boat was unlucky enough to be hammered by depth charging. Commanders took every opportunity to encourage activities from card game tournaments to shark fishing to vary the daily routine. For those U-boats out on patrol at Christmas, improvising a celebration stretched the ingenuities of crews determined to bring a festive air to their cramped quarters.

"Apart from watches there is endless work—sometimes ten to twelve hours a day—caring for the torpedoes, those little technical marvels, tending the engines, keeping the boat clean and in good trim. Still there are hours of leisure that one cannot sleep away. The important thing is to keep the men intellectually interested. Of course we arrange chess and 'skat' tournaments as well and a painting competition. We even had singing contests before the microphone over all the loudspeakers. . . . Good books are particularly valuable and the longer the cruise the more often men came for something to read. Something from Germany's past, for instance. How the Reich developed from the community of German peoples."
Broadcast by Kapitänleutnant Lüth

THE HUNTER'S RETURN: It was part of Dönitz's policy to ensure that his returning U-boats were always greeted by an enthusiastic dockside reception. Above: Kapitänleutenant Hardegen arrives at Lorient in March 1942 after opening the Blitz on the U.S. East coast shipping lanes. German personnel and nurses from the hospitals in the French Biscay ports were given time off to take part in the welcoming committees. The top Ace commanders and their crews would be given film-star treatment, broadcasting and touring the Reich with receptions and skiing holidays. For most crews their three to four weeks ashore after a patrol was divided between home leave in Germany and spells in the special "U-boat Rest Camps" (bottom right) or just snatching a break during harbour duty (top right).

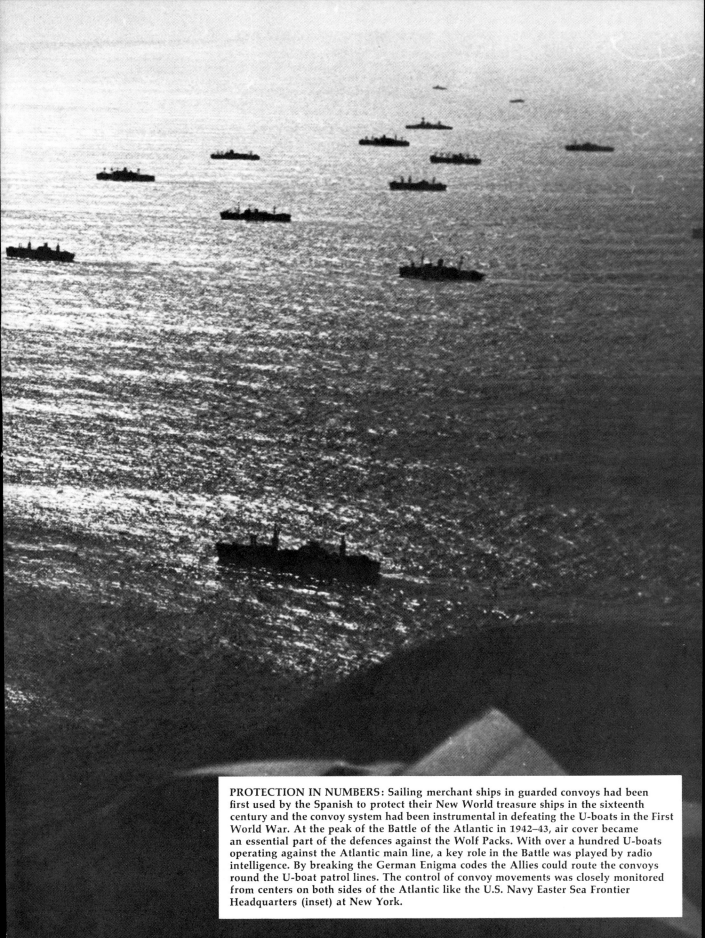

PROTECTION IN NUMBERS: Sailing merchant ships in guarded convoys had been first used by the Spanish to protect their New World treasure ships in the sixteenth century and the convoy system had been instrumental in defeating the U-boats in the First World War. At the peak of the Battle of the Atlantic in 1942–43, air cover became an essential part of the defences against the Wolf Packs. With over a hundred U-boats operating against the Atlantic main line, a key role in the Battle was played by radio intelligence. By breaking the German Enigma codes the Allies could route the convoys round the U-boat patrol lines. The control of convoy movements was closely monitored from centers on both sides of the Atlantic like the U.S. Navy Easter Sea Frontier Headquarters (inset) at New York.

DANGEROUS WATERS: The approach of sunset in mid-Atlantic (an eastbound convoy seen from the quarterdeck of a U.S. destroyer) was an ominous time. If radio chatter had been picked up from a gathering U-boat pack, darkness would bring the certainty of attack. For seamen on and off watch (right) on Navy and merchant ships alike there was the constant knowledge and expectation of the sudden crunch of a torpedo explosion that might pitch them into the cold Atlantic waters—they referred to it as "The Hammer".

AN UNHOLY ALLIANCE: Dönitz's deployment of a hundred U-boats early in 1943 coincided with the worst series of storms to sweep across the north Atlantic in fifty years. Blizzards and hurricane-force gales raised 60-foot seas that smashed many merchant ships as effectively as the German torpedoes. Even the U-boats frequently were forced to submerge to escape the terrible weather, but there was no let up for the convoys. Here the U.S. Coast Guard cutter <u>Ingham</u> struggles into the teeth of a gale to keep the columns of merchantmen from straggling and falling prey to the waiting U-boats.

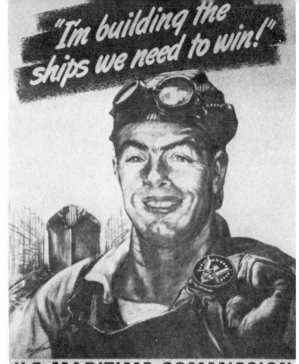

"I'm building the ships we need to win!"

U.S. MARITIME COMMISSION

THE BATTLE ON THE SLIPWAYS: On both sides of the Atlantic the race to build merchant ships faster than the U-boats could sink them went on around the clock. Work on Liberty ships (below) in a U.S. West coast yard continued by floodlights and by using mass production techniques and encouraged by posters (right) and large bonus payments, the output of the yards reached record levels. In both the United States and Britain women played a significant role in winning the tonnage war. Fifty-year-old Mrs. Agnes Smith (far right), mother of ten who had worked in an engineering shop to defeat the U-boats in the First War, "did her bit" again as a foreman in a Tyneside shipyard whilst her husband worked in a neighbouring one as a fitter's helper.

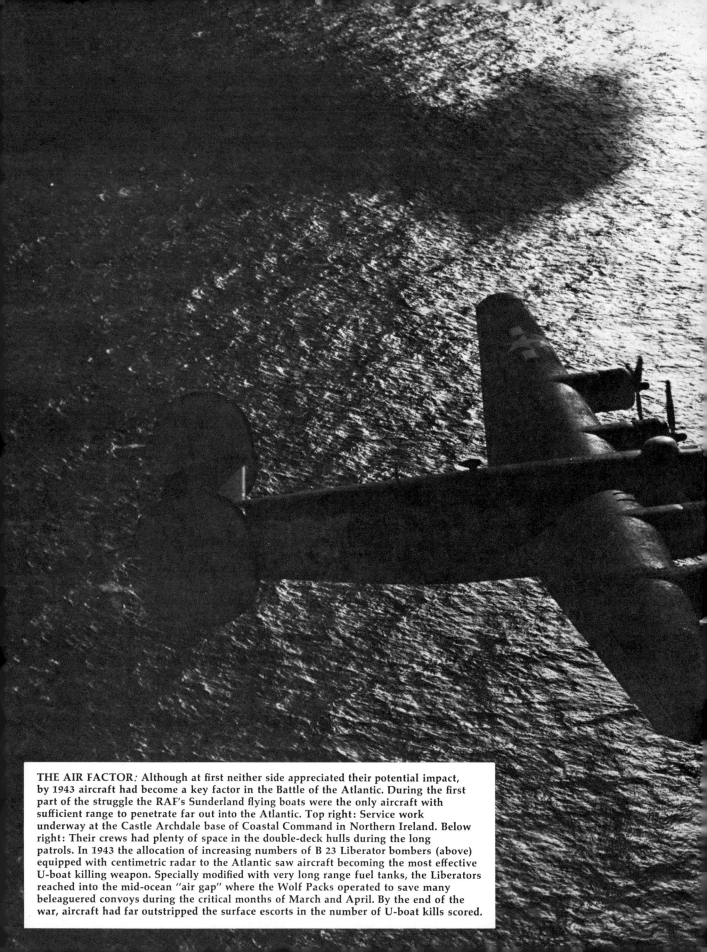

THE AIR FACTOR: Although at first neither side appreciated their potential impact, by 1943 aircraft had become a key factor in the Battle of the Atlantic. During the first part of the struggle the RAF's Sunderland flying boats were the only aircraft with sufficient range to penetrate far out into the Atlantic. Top right: Service work underway at the Castle Archdale base of Coastal Command in Northern Ireland. Below right: Their crews had plenty of space in the double-deck hulls during the long patrols. In 1943 the allocation of increasing numbers of B 23 Liberator bombers (above) equipped with centimetric radar to the Atlantic saw aircraft becoming the most effective U-boat killing weapon. Specially modified with very long range fuel tanks, the Liberators reached into the mid-ocean "air gap" where the Wolf Packs operated to save many beleaguered convoys during the critical months of March and April. By the end of the war, aircraft had far outstripped the surface escorts in the number of U-boat kills scored.

VICTORY TO THE ESCORTS: By the end of April 1943 the tide of battle was clearly turning in the Allies' favour as the increasing numbers and efficiency of air and sea escorts saw a dramatic fall in shipping losses and a dramatic rise in U-boat casualties. One of the boats, whose end marked this turning point, was U-175 which was forced to the surface by accurate depth charging whilst making an attack on convoy HX 133 on 17 April. Below: U-175 after being shelled from the U.S. Coast Guard cutter Spencer shortly before sinking.

PRIZE CAPTURE: On 4 June 1944, off the West African coast, a U.S. task force commanded by Captain Daniel V. Gallery brought U-505 to the surface after depth charging by the destroyer <u>Chatelain</u>. Under heavy fire from the task force and the escort carrier <u>Guadalcanal's</u> aircraft, the panic-stricken crew abandoned ship, neglecting to set off their scuttling charges. Above: Boats from the U.S. destroyer Pillsbury reached U-505 to effect a remarkable capture and the U-boat was towed to Bermuda intact. Today the prize survives as an exhibit in Chicago.

THE FACE OF DEFEAT: The terror shown by a survivor from a U-boat sunk by the Canadian frigate <u>Swansea</u> in late 1944 is testimony to the ordeal faced by the German U-boat crews during the final years of the war. Against overwhelming odds Dönitz's men grimly continued their campaign to the bitter end in spite of casualty rates of over 30 per cent.

Scharnhorst sunk,
26 Dec 1943

from
1941

Arctic Circle

REYKJAVIK

TRONDHEIM?

MURMANSK

ARCHANGEL

Supplies to Russia

MOSCOW

KIEL
WILHELMSHAVEN

LIVERPOOL

Battle of the Atlantic
(Peak 1941-43)

QUEBEC
MONTREAL
HALIFAX
ST. JOHNS

Bismarck sunk,
27 May 1941

LORIENT

NEW YORK

1942

AZORES

1943-44

GIBRALTAR   MALTA

Mediterranean
partially closed
1940-43

HAIFA

ALEXANDRIA

SUEZ

Supplies
to Russia

BAN
SHA

1942

German Mid-Atlantic
refuelling zone

CAPE VERDE
IS

Airborne supplies
to Middle East

PANAMA

PORT OF SPAIN

1942

DAKAR

TAKORADI   LAGOS

Equator

1942

1941

NATAL

ASCENSION I

RIO DE JANEIRO

1939-40

1939-44

1939-44

LOURENÇO
MARQUES

MONTEVIDEO

Battle of the River Plate,
13 Dec 1939

Graf Spee sunk,
13 Dec 1939

CAPETOWN

1939-44